THE CLASSICAL LEGACY IN RENAISSANCE POETRY

LONGMAN MEDIEVAL AND RENAISSANCE LIBRARY

General editors:
CHARLOTTE BREWER, Hertford College, Oxford
N. H. KEEBLE, University of Stirling

Published titles:

Piers Plowman: An Introduction to the B-Text
James Simpson

Shakespeare's Mouldy Tales: Recurrent Plot Motifs in Shakespearian Drama
Leah Scragg

Robin Sowerby

THE CLASSICAL LEGACY
IN RENAISSANCE POETRY

LONGMAN
LONDON AND NEW YORK

Longman Group UK Limited,
Longman House, Burnt Mill,
Harlow, Essex CM20 2JE, England
and Associated Companies throughout the world.
Published in the United States of America
by Longman Publishing, New York

First published 1994

ISBN 0 582 055482 PPR
ISBN 0 582 055490 CSD

British Library Cataloguing-in-Publication Data

A catalogue record for this book is
available from the British Library

Library of Congress Cataloging in Publication Data

Sowerby, Robin.
   The classical legacy in Renaissance poetry / Robin Sowerby.
      p.   cm. — (Longman medieval and Renaissance library)
   Includes bibliographical references (p.) and index.
   ISBN 0–582–05549–0. — ISBN 0–582–05548–2 (pbk.)
      1. English poetry—Early modern, 1500–1700—History and criticism.
   2. Classical poetry—Appreciation—England—History.   3. English
   poetry—Classical influences.   4. Renaissance—England.
   5. Classical poetry—Translations into English—History and
   criticism.   6. Classicism—England.   I. Title.   II. Series.
   PR535.C67S65   1994
   821'.309142—dc20   93—34667
                                                                     CIP

Set in 10/12 Bembo by 8
Produced by Longman Singapore Publishers (Pte) Ltd.
Printed in Singapore

To Alison
sine qua non

Contents

descriptas servare vices operumque colores
cur ego si nequeo ignoroque poeta salutor?
cur nescire pudens prave quam discere malo?

Why if I cannot keep to and do not understand the different types and
styles of poetic forms as laid down am I hailed as a poet? Why do I prefer
in false modesty not to know than to learn?

publica materies privati iuris erit, si
non circa vilem patulumque moraberis orbem,
nec verbo verbum curabis reddere fidus
interpres, nec desilies imitator in artum,
unde pedem proferre pudor vetet aut operis lex.

Material in the public domain will become subject to your private rights if yo
do not linger along the broad and common track and are not concerned to
render word for word as a faithful translator and do not in imitating plump f
narrow method where timidity or the rules of the genre impede your progres

          vos exemplaria Graeca
nocturna versate manu, versate diurna.

For yourselves, handle your Greek models by day, handle them by night.

nil intemptatum nostri liquere poetae,
nec minimum meruere decus vestigia Graeca
ausi deserere et celebrare domestica facta,
vel qui praetextas vel qui docuere togatas.
nec virtute foret clarisque potentius armis
quam lingua Latium, si non offenderet unum
quemque poetarum limae labor et mora.

Our poets have left nothing unattempted nor have they deserved least praise
when they have dared to leave the paths of the Greeks and to celebrate deeds ;
home, whether they have presented native tragedies or comedies. Nor would
Latium be more pre-eminent in valour or military prowess than in literature i
the labour of the file and the time it takes were not irksome to her poets one
and all.

          (Horace, *Art of Poetry*, 86–8; 131–5; 268–9; 285–91)

Introduction

In his fine tribute to the bard, Ben Jonson remarks upon Shakespeare's 'small Latin and less Greek'.[1] Small his scholarship may have been by Jonson's more learned standards, but the description of its extent filled two weighty volumes by the American scholar T.W. Baldwin,[2] who sought, not in vain, to prove that Shakespeare was well served by his grammar-school education at Stratford. What his alert mind absorbed at school must have been supplemented by his extra-mural education in the theatre for acquaintance with the classical world came naturally within the general ambience of Renaissance culture. This no longer being the case, modern audiences even in academic quarters sometimes find Shakespeare's relatively modest learning a formidable accomplishment that is a barrier to appreciation of his plays. The cause is not far to seek.

With the continuing decline of classical studies as a school subject and the growing tendency amongst teachers of English to choose modern authors for study in schools, it is increasingly the case that when students of English are finally faced with earlier literature sometimes quite late in their careers since syllabuses in higher education now also tend to push to the margins what had previously been the central core of a degree in the humanities, they are seriously handicapped by unfamiliarity with the classical tradition underpinning so much of our culture in the Renaissance

1. 'To the Memory of My Beloved, the Author Mr William Shakespeare: And What He Hath Left Us', 31 in Parfitt, G. (ed.) (1975) *Ben Jonson: The Complete English Poems*, Penguin, p. 264. All quotations from Jonson's poems are from this edition unless otherwise stated.
2. Baldwin, T.W. (1944) *William Shakspere's Smalle Latine and Lesse Greeke*, 2 vols, University of Illinois Press, Urbana.

and beyond. This book, which is a modest attempt to describe and illustrate the main lines of classical influence flowing through the Renaissance, has been written primarily with the needs of such readers in mind, though it is hoped that it might also be of interest to readers who have some Latin and Greek, since it seeks to define not only the classical legacy as it came down to the Renaissance but also some of the ways in which that legacy has been received in translation, transformed by imitation and put to creative uses by modern poets working under classical influence.

The arrangement by genre besides being an orderly and clear way of containing the great variety of the classical tradition is also a reflection of the legacy itself as transmitted from antiquity and received in kind in the Renaissance. Within each chapter the sequence is broadly chronological, beginning with the Greeks, though much more emphasis is placed on the more familiar Latin texts by which the ancient legacy was chiefly mediated to the modern world. More space has been given to Seneca, for example, than to the individual Greek tragedians, because it was the Romans rather than the Greeks who influenced the Renaissance. The general organisation of the book and its particular emphases are designed to reflect and illuminate the actual historical processes of transmission and reception.

The opening chapters introduce broader and more fundamental aspects of the classical tradition concerning the dominating influence of Latin and the difficulty of Greek, the reception of classical texts in a prevailing Christian culture, the theory and practice of literary imitation, and the rules of art. On epic, limitation of space precludes treatment of related works such as Milton's *Paradise Lost*, but Homer and Virgil are represented in the translations of Chapman and Dryden, which are set in the context of Renaissance debate about their originals. Wherever possible throughout the book Renaissance translations are used and Renaissance perspectives on the classics are presented through these translations and through the verdicts and discussion of the classics by Renaissance poets, critics and commentators themselves. In the chapter on drama, Seneca is characterised in comparison with the Greeks and represented in the Tudor translation. Representative plays are then used to characterise the kinds and varieties of ancient comedy to which Jonson's comic theory and practice are related. It is particularly in this chapter on drama that influential features of the ancient critical tradition usually labelled Aristotelian are exemplified and discussed during analysis of plays which were seen to embody 'the rules' and from which these rules were drawn.

In subsequent chapters devoted to smaller-scale genres, after due delineation of the classical heritage in each case there is more scope for discussion of imitations and related poems such as Spenser's *Shepherd's Calendar*, Marlowe's *Hero and Leander*, Shakespeare's *Venus and Adonis*, Hall's *Virgidemiae*, Milton's *Lycidas*, Marvell's 'Horatian Ode', Cowley's *Pindaric Odes* and Oldham's imitations of Horace and Juvenal. In illustrating the classical legacy it is occasionally the case that the use of a particular translation breaks the chronological sequence. For example, in the chapter on pastoral, Dryden's translation is used in the foundation section on Virgil before the treatment of vernacular pastoral in Spenser and Milton. Dryden's is a better translation that better represents the original than earlier versions that might have been used. It is one of the intentions of the book to show the classical heritage at representative moments in its best light, and so to introduce the most creative responses to it, whether in formal translation, imitation or adaptation.

Although the organisation and emphases for the most part reflect the actualities and processes of transmission whereby new life is perpetually being given to old forms which are themselves transformed in the process, the very breadth of the material covered – each chapter (indeed each section within chapters) has been the subject of numerous full-length studies – has necessitated some telescoping of literary history. Any survey of classical influence will conclude that the streams flowing from the springs of Helicon did not remain pure for long. Quite apart from what happened to them at Rome, they went underground in the Dark Ages to re-emerge muddied with strange foreign infusions as they made their chaotic descent to the modern world which was to see their renaissance with greater clarity. Many classical authors had an after-life in the Middle Ages which influenced their reception in the Renaissance. Reference is made, for example, to allegorical interpretation of classical epic and classical myth, but it has not been possible to explore the medieval background in any depth. There is, too, in every genre, a considerable body of Renaissance literature in Latin, some of which became celebrated in its own right and influenced vernacular practice. It has not been possible to consider this as a general phenomenon, though there is a representative section on the neo-Latin pastorals of Petrarch and Mantuan. Furthermore, as far as English literature is concerned, its Renaissance followed those of France and Italy. At least two of Wyatt's Horatian satires are versions of Italian originals. Surrey may have been influenced in his choice of blank verse for the translation of Virgil by Italian predecessors. Jonson's knowledge of Pindar may have come chiefly by way of the odes of Ronsard. The medieval inheritance, neo-Latin, and earlier vernacular attempts all complicate the history of classical influence upon English literature, some of the subtleties and intricacies of which necessarily have to be elided in a general account.

The Renaissance is marked by a desire on the part of the early humanists and their successors – those who consciously sought a revival specifically of classical Latin – to go back to first principles and original sources. This led indirectly to the Reformation in religion and to a comparable renewal in vernacular culture. A classical revival, however, can never be pure; influence if it is to express itself creatively will result in transformation as impulses from the past combine with present consciousness to create something new. It is worth stating this obvious point positively to set against a recent account that has itself been influential:

> Poetic Influence – when it involves two strong authentic poets – always proceeds by a misreading of the prior poet, an act of creative correction that is actually and necessarily a misinterpretation. The history of fruitful poetic influence, which is to say the main tradition of Western poetry since the Renaissance, is a history of anxiety and self-saving caricature, of distortion, of perverse wilful revisionism without which modern poetry as such could not exist.
>
> (*The Anxiety of Influence*)[3]

Harold Bloom has his own argument about modern poets and their relation to powerful precursors, but in so far as he extends it to have general application, it becomes itself a perverse distortion that no Renaissance poet would have recognised as a valid account of the creative process of cultural renewal in which he was involved. The doctrine of literary imitation in ancient Rome and

3. Bloom, H. (1973) *The Anxiety of Influence: A Theory of Poetry*, Oxford University Press, New York, p. 30.

the Renaissance which is the subject of the quotations from Horace that form the epigraph to this book, and that are further discussed in the epilogue to it, certainly requires wilful revisionism on the part of the imitating poet. It requires in fact critical judgement and discrimination and involves humanist choice about the value of what comes down from the past and the ways in which it may be fruitfully used in the present. Of course much more is involved in the creative process – is it naive to talk of poetic inspiration? – but it is a part of the classical tradition coming from Aristotle and Horace that the poet is a free agent who can train himself in his art and can consciously make critical choices about it. If literary influence is to be accounted for in psychological terms, then it has to be allowed that much more than anxiety can be involved in the dialogue between past poets and present practitioners, particularly when they are working in different languages and cultures. A Renaissance vernacular poet secure in his own language might feel an easier freedom in relation to the classical tradition than a modern poet facing his immediate predecessors writing in the same language. In fact for Renaissance poets the classical tradition provided challenging sources of inspiration upon which they drew to raise and improve the standards of vernacular culture.

In illustration of the classical legacy, little Greek has been quoted, but it would have been a betrayal not to have included some Latin. Celebrated and influential passages in easier texts are cited with literal versions. Unless otherwise indicated in the notes, these have been provided by the present writer. The Latin is quoted in the standardised modern form used in the series of Oxford Classical Texts, though the Renaissance vulgate of any classical text will differ in many places. Only where such differences are germane to the discussion at hand is mention made of them. References to classical texts have long been standardised and may be located in any modern edition of the author concerned. Classical names are given in the form in which they are most familiar in English. The titles of classical works are usually translated except in cases where more than one translation exists where the original is retained to avoid confusion. The Plautine play which takes its title from its main character, the swaggering or boastful soldier, is referred to in its Latin title, the *Miles Gloriosus*.

After some hesitation it was decided to modernise spelling, punctuation and orthography of all English texts except where convention dictates otherwise, as in the case of Spenser, and in one specific instance where the old spelling 'satyr' has been retained for reasons that will become clear in the chapter on the genre. As a consequence, earlier texts like the Tudor Seneca or Golding's Ovid look less alien than they otherwise might appear in comparison with, say, a modernised text of Shakespeare, except that the occasional obsolete word or archaic formation will necessarily stand out even more in a modernised text. It is hoped that occasional oddities within a generally consistent pattern will not be burdensome or offensive to readers.

Chapter 1

Epic

Be Homer's works your study and delight,
Read them by day, and meditate by night;
Thence form your judgement, thence your maxims bring,
    And trace the Muses upward to their spring;
    Still with itself compared, his text peruse;
    And let your comment be the Mantuan muse.
           (Pope, *An Essay on Criticism*, 124–9)

        vos exemplaria Graeca
nocturna versate diu, versate diurna.
    (Horace, *The Art of Poetry*, 268–9)

Take you the Greek examples, for your light
In hand, and turn them over, day and night.
    (Jonson, *The Art of Poetry*, 397–8)

Writing at the end of our period in 1709, Pope's injunction to the aspiring critic echoes that of his classical mentor Horace to the aspiring poet; both assert the fundamental primacy of the Greek tradition for the formation of the artistic judgement necessary alike for the critic and the poet. While Horace refers generally to the Greek classics, Pope, expressing the admiration of the Renaissance humanists for epic as the highest genre (to the extent that they contradicted Aristotle for whom tragedy is pre-eminent),[1] may seem to be limiting the Horatian precept though the clarification that makes Homer the *fons et origo* of the classical tradition as the exemplary embodiment of the rules of art – the maxims to be derived are of course critical not moral – also makes

---

1. *Poetics* XXVIff.

him the supreme poetic archetype. The intelligent reader following the principle of the Alexandrian critic Aristarchus, *homeron ex
homerou saphenizein*[2] ('to make Homer clear with reference to
Homer himself'), need only immerse himself in the poetry;
nevertheless, in a Renaissance perspective going beyond the
Roman Horace, Pope enjoins that Homer be read in conjunction
with the Mantuan muse, the poetry of Virgil, which in his epic
poem the *Aeneid* imitating the *Iliad* and the *Odyssey* is the most
illuminating tribute to Homer's artistry.

The primary status accorded to the heroic poem in the generic
hierarchy is equally apparent in the early Renaissance, evident in
all the Elizabethan rhetorical handbooks and in such treatises as
Sidney's *Defence of Poesy*[3] but no early poet or critic writes with
Pope's assurance or confidence about Homer, with the exception
of Chapman who translated him, and it was only during the
experience of translation that Chapman came to know his own
mind about Homer, for it cannot be said that the Greek poet was
a familiar entity in the culture of sixteenth-century England.

In the Latin West, many of the Roman classics had had an after-
life in the Middle Ages and came to have a firm place in the
educational system of the early grammar schools (one of the
primary functions of which was to teach pupils to write and speak
Latin) but knowledge of Greek was lost in the Middle Ages, and
Greek, which never came to have the importance of Latin, had a
subordinate and an insecure position in the schools.[4] Even in the
learned world of international scholarship attention to Homer was
fitful. While there are many editions of Virgil's works and
commentaries upon them pitched at various levels for scholar and
schoolboy, among the small number of editions of Homer in the
period between the first printed edition of 1488 and the end of the
seventeenth century is only one full-length commentary which
did not appear till 1583.[5]

2. The phrase contains one of the earliest articulations of the principle of
    historical criticism: 'to explain Homer by his own usage'.
3. See Smith, G.G. (ed.) (1904) *Elizabethan Critical Essays* (2 vols), Oxford
    University Press.
4. See Clarke, M.L. (1959) *Classical Education in Britain 1500–1900*, Cambridge
    University Press, and Baldwin, T.W. (1944) *William Shakspere's Small Latine
    and Lesse Greeke*, 2 vols, University of Illinois Press, Urbana.
5. Spondanus, J. (ed.) (1583) *Homeri quae extant omnia . . . cum versione . . .
    Perpetuis in Iliada simul et Odysseam J Spondani . . . Commentariis* Basle.

It is something of an irony that the epic tradition flowing from Homer had virtually lost contact with its originator, so that in his revival in the Latin culture of Christendom, the *Iliad* in particular proved to be an alien text. The gulf between the English Renaissance and the Greek may be suggested by the account given by Spenser of the scope of *The Faerie Queene* in his letter to Raleigh of 1589:

> The general end therefore of all the book is to fashion a gentleman or noble person in virtuous or gentle discipline . . .. In which I have followed all the antique poets historical, first Homer who in the persons of Agamemnon and Ulysses hath ensampled a good governor and a virtuous man, the one in his Ilias, the other in his Odysseis; then Virgil, whose like intention was to do in the person of Aeneas.[6]

Spenser's chivalric intention follows the romance tradition and expresses what was generally held to be the highest function of the epic form. The *Odyssey* with its wise hero guided by Athene, goddess of wisdom, and the *Aeneid* with a hero whose chief virtue is *pietas*, came to the Renaissance with well-established allegorical interpretations and could easily be accommodated to Renaissance norms.[7] But there is no comparable allegorical reading for the *Iliad*: the poem hardly fits Renaissance expectations, so that it is not surprising that Spenser makes no mention of Achilles but tries instead to find his ideal figure in Agamemnon. Yet it takes a considerable stretch of the imagination to find in Agamemnon a 'good governor'. On the contrary, it is basic to the simple design of Homer's plot that Agamemnon is a bad governor. It is his folly that precipitates the quarrel with Achilles which has such ruinous consequences for the Greeks. As if to underline the weakness of leadership in the Greek camp, there follows in Book II Agamemnon's disastrous trial of the army which almost results in the abandonment of the siege. The situation is only retrieved by good government on the part of Odysseus. Spenser's remark does not suggest that the *Iliad* was very familiar to himself or his readers.

6. The letter usually accompanies the text of the poem, as in Hamilton, A.C. (ed.) (1977) *The Faerie Queene*, Longman, p. 737.
7. Allen, D.C. (1970) *Mysteriously Meant: The Rediscovery of Pagan Symbolism and Allegorical Interpretation in the Renaissance*, Johns Hopkins Press, Baltimore and London.

Sidney's comments in his *Defence of Poesy* are no more reassuring. Sidney expatiates at considerable length on the exemplary character of Virgil's Aeneas, making direct reference to incidents of the epic as he does so. On Homer, he uses the hearsay testimony of Plutarch writing about Alexander the Great: 'the chief thing he ever was heard to wish for was that Homer had been alive. He well found he received more bravery of mind by the pattern of Achilles than by hearing the definition of fortitude'.[8]

Of the ancient testimonies to Homer's merits, none was more famous or oft-repeated in the Renaissance than this (there is a more spirited version of it in Chapman's dedication to Essex in 1598). The story that Alexander had carried with him on his conquests a copy of the *Iliad* prepared by his tutor Aristotle, calling it *tēs polemikēs aretēs ephodion* ('a portable treasury of all military knowledge and virtue'),[9] and that at the tomb of Achilles he had pronounced the Greek hero fortunate in having such a herald of his fame, satisfied every Renaissance requirement relating to a heroic poem. If not an epic of achievement in itself, like the *Aeneid* and the *Odyssey*, the *Iliad* had provided the inspiration for universal empire. Moreover, Alexander was no barbarian like Tamburlaine but a pupil of the great philosopher who had spread Greek civilisation throughout the East, a philosopher-conqueror if not a philosopher-king. As Augustus might be seen to lie behind Aeneas, so Alexander lay ahead of Achilles. The *Iliad* was vindicated, for it could be seen to comply with the function of epic, as it is described by Spenser, the laudatory presentation of exemplary patterns of excellence for future imitation.

Though the anecdote seemed to offer a grand illustration of the inspiring and commemorative function of epic, in reality it was no more than a fig-leaf to cover Homer's nakedness. The fortitude of the Homeric Achilles is not in doubt, but clearly the despoiler of Hector's corpse is not an ideal figure in the poem in which he first features. In subsequent literature he is often almost vicious; in Virgil's *Aeneid*, for example, as the killer of the young Troilus

---

8. Duncan-Jones, K. (ed.) (1989) *Sir Philip Sidney*, Oxford University Press, p. 283. All quotations from 'The Defence of Poesy' are from this edition. For the source of the anecdote see next note.
9. Plutarch, 'Life of Alexander', VIII, 2.

(not mentioned in Homer) he is *saevus* and *ferus*, savage and wild. We may recall here the well-known characterisation of him in Horace:

impiger, iracundus, inexorabilis, acer,
iura neget sibi nota, nihil non arroget armis.
(*The Art of Poetry*, 121–2)

(Indefatigable, irascible, inexorable, violent, let him deny knowledge of any laws, let him always make appeal to the sword.)

As for the *Iliad* in general, Horace has this to say:

quidquid delirant reges, plectuntur Achivi.
seditione, dolis, scelere atque libidine et ira
Iliacos intra muros peccatur et extra.
(*Epistle* I, 2, 14–16)

(In whatever way the kings go mad, the Greeks reap the consequences. With sedition, trickery, crime, lust, and anger, there is iniquity within and without the walls of Troy.)

This must have sounded in the Renaissance like the argument of the devil's own epic. That the *Iliad* should be grounded in a passion, the anger of Achilles which Homer himself in the poem's proposition calls *oulomenen* (mad and pernicious), went radically against the grain of expectation and desire.

Homer's *Iliad* and Chapman's translation

Nevertheless, English eyes were opened to the character and merits of the Greek by the Homeric translations of Chapman. He informs his readers that his own eyes were only fully opened in the course of translating the last twelve books in 1611 when 'the first free light of my author entered and emboldened me'.[10] His translation was undertaken in three distinct stages. In 1598 he published *Seven Books of the Iliads* with a dedication 'To the most honoured now living instance of the Achillean virtues eternized by

10. Nicoll, A. (ed.) (1957) *Chapman's Homer* (2 vols), Routledge & Kegan Paul, vol. 1, p. 90.

divine Homer, the Earl of Essex.' In 1608 he made some minor revisions to the books already translated (I, II, VII–XI) and added the intervening books to produce *Homer . . . in Twelve Books*. In 1611 he translated the second half of the poem and retranslated the first two books (except for the catalogue of forces at the end of the second book).

In the 1598 preface, he solicits the attention of the noble earl by stressing not only the moral excellence of the work but also its contemporary interest. His emphasis upon 'ancient stratagems and disciplines of war' and 'the horror of arms endlessly thundering'[11] is not merely to be accounted for by the character and status of the addressee, for Chapman, who had been a soldier himself, responded energetically to the fighting spirit of the original from the beginning. And the *Iliad* is a poem in which the *arete* or worth of its aristocratic heroes is proved on the battlefield. In this there is no distinction between Greeks and Trojans. Remarkably the enemy is not envisaged as racially or culturally inferior. Achilles and Hector are supreme heroes because they are the best warriors. Their creed is suggested in the advice reportedly given by Peleus to his son Achilles as he set out for war *aein aristeuein kai hypeirochon emmenai allōn* (XI, 784) 'always excel and keep pre-eminent above the rest'. The fullest analysis of the impulse that motivates the resolve of the hero occurs in the great speech of Sarpedon to Glaucus 'never equalled' in Chapman's words in a marginal note,[12] 'by any (in this kind) of all that have written':

> Glaucus, say why are we honoured more
> Than other men of Lycia in place – with greater store
> Of meats and cups, with goodlier roofs, delightsome gardens, walks,
> More lands and better, so much wealth that court and country talks
> Of us and our possessions and every way we go
> Gaze on us as we were their gods? This where we dwell is so:
> The shores of Xanthus ring of this: and shall not we exceed
> As much in merit as in noise? Come, be we great in deed
> As well as look, shine not in gold but in the flames of fight,
> That so our neat-armed Lycians may say: 'See, these are right
> Our kings, our rulers: these deserve to eat and drink the best;

11. Nicoll, A. (1957) vol. 1, p. 506. The 1598 prefatory material and the 1598 translations of books 1 and 2 are included after the full 1611 version here.
12. Nicoll, A. (1957) vol. 1, p. 247.

These govern not ingloriously; these thus exceed the rest,
Do more than they command to do.' O friend, if keeping back
Would keep back age from us, and death, and that we might not wrack
In this life's human sea at all, but that deferring now
We shunned death ever – nor would I half this vain valour show,
Nor glorify a folly so, to wish thee to advance:
But, since we must go though not here, and that, besides the chance
Proposed now, there are infinite fates of other sort in death
Which (neither to be fled nor 'scaped) a man must sink beneath –
Come, try we if this sort be ours and either render thus
Glory to others or make them resign the like to us.

(XII, 311–32, translating 310–25)

But the *Iliad* is only incidentally a celebration of the heroic warrior code, what might be called, in Chapman's phrase, the Achillean virtues. Homer announces his subject in his proposition and invocation to the muse at the opening:

Achilles' baneful wrath resound, O goddess, that imposed
Infinite sorrows on the Greeks, and many brave souls loosed
From breasts heroic – sent them far, to that invisible cave
That no light comforts; and their limbs to dogs and vultures gave.
To all which Jove's will gave effect; from whom first strife begun
Betwixt Atrides, king of men, and Thetis' godlike son.

In the ninth year of the siege of Troy, the god Apollo is angry because Agamemnon, the son of Atreus (Atrides), will not restore for ransom the daughter of one of his priests captured before the siege of Troy whom the Greek leader had taken as his prize in the general allotment of spoils. The god has sent a plague to infest the Greek camp. In a council called by Achilles, son of the goddess Thetis, to determine a course of action, the Greek leader quarrels with their best fighter. Agamemnon agrees to give up his prize but says that he will make up his loss by depriving Achilles of his spoils of war, the slave girl Briseis. Feeling slighted and dishonoured Achilles angrily withdraws from the fighting. Agamemnon then sends heralds to Achilles' camp to take away Briseis. Achilles denounces Agamemnon, but bids his comrade-in-arms Patroclus give her up. At this point in his translation of 1598 Chapman offers a remarkable embellishment of Homer:

This said, Patroclus well allowed the patience of his friend,
Brought Briseis forth, and to her guides her comforts did commend

With utmost kindness, which his friend could not for anguish use.
She wept and looked upon her love; he sighed and did refuse.
O how his wisdom with his power did mightily contend –
His love encouraging his power and spirit, that durst descend
As far as Hercules for her, yet wisdom all subdued
Wherein a high exploit he showed, and sacred fortitude.

(357–64)

Here we have the patience of Achilles, kindness to Briseis on the part of Patroclus, love not only of Achilles for Briseis but of Briseis for him, and an almighty struggle in which the wisdom of Achilles triumphs over his power and spirit. In the struggle both the chivalric (love and kindness) and the Homeric (spirited physical daring) finally yield to the Stoic: patience and sacred fortitude. These values in this order constitute the Achillean virtues of 1598.

The original is much simpler:

Ὣς φάτο, Πάτροκλος δὲ φίλῳ ἐπεπείθεθ᾽ ἑταίρῳ,
ἐκ δ᾽ ἄγαγε κλισίης Βρισηΐδα καλλιπάρῃον,
δῶκε δ᾽ ἄγειν· τὼ δ᾽ αὖτις ἴτην παρὰ νῆας Ἀχαιῶν·
ἡ δ᾽ ἀέκουσ᾽ ἅμα τοῖσι γυνὴ κίεν· αὐτὰρ Ἀχιλλεὺς
δακρύσας ἑτάρων ἄφαρ ἕζετο νόσφι λιασθείς,

(I, 345–49)[13]

(Patroclus obeyed his friend and brought Briseis of the lovely cheeks out of the hut and gave her up for them to take; they went again along by the ships of the Achaeans; the woman went with them unwillingly; but Achilles in tears sat apart from his friends in withdrawal.)

In the Greek, Briseis is simply Achilles' prize, his *geras*, his spoil of war; he would have felt an equal insult to his honour if it had been a horse or a shield that Agamemnon had proposed to take. This archaic code of honour in which the slave-girl is merely a material possession, a pawn in a game of power, did not transfer naturally into the Elizabethan world. Our gallant translator complicates the issue by making Achilles feel love for Briseis. This is not altogether unHomeric since later on Achilles does say

13. Allen, T.W. (ed.) (1931) *Homeri Ilias*, Oxford University Press.

that he loved the girl (IX, 343). However, the introduction of a romantic element in this opening scene creates a problem. To give up the fair lady without a fight ill becomes a romantic hero, so that Achilles has to be made the embodiment of a virtue that transcends the passions. The parting with Briseis becomes a labour requiring the fortitude of Hercules when he descended into Hades to capture Cerberus. Hercules, unlike Achilles, was a real hero of the Renaissance. His choice at the crossroads where the ways of pleasure and of virtue met was a famous *topos*. Hercules, of course, chose virtue and laboured valiantly for the rest of his life as a consequence. The choice of Achilles for a short life of the greatest fame in preference to a long life of obscurity (IX, 410–16) – a starker version of the choice of life implicit in the attitudes articulated by Sarpedon – was neither so well known nor so morally appealing. In making Achilles a moral man in terms that were appreciated in his times, Chapman developed a hint that he took from the moralising Renaissance commentary in which this moment is regarded as a fine *exemplum patientiae*, 'an example of patience'.[14]

The passage was subject to a radical revision in the version of 1611:

> Patroclus did the rite
> His friend commanded and brought forth Briseis from her tent,
> Gave her the heralds, and away to th' Achive ships they went.
> She sad, and scarce for grief could go. Her love all friends forsook
> And wept for anger.
>
> (348–52)

The romantic element has not quite gone, for Briseis loves Achilles, but Achilles weeps for anger: he is no longer the Stoic of 1598.

Comparing the two poems in his *Poetics* Aristotle remarks on a fundamental difference between the *Iliad* which has a simple plot and is *pathetikon*, that is based on emotion and turning on calamity, and the *Odyssey* which has a complex plot and is *ethike*, that is turning on character (XXIV, 3). Chapman's revision of 1611 moves away from the moralising ethical tendency of 1598. In translating the second half of the poem he came up against the

14.   Spondanus, J. (1583) p. 17, note f.

consequences of Achilles' anger and its fully baneful character, in short with Achillean vices as well as Achillean virtues, for in his extremity and excess it becomes apparent that Achilles cannot be assimilated to any Stoic or Christian ideal. The 1611 revision embodies the fruits of his later recognition that the *Iliad* is, in Aristotle's word, *pathetikon*.

In the second half 'driving through his thirteenth and last books', Chapman tells us,[15] 'I drew the main depth and saw the round coming of this silver bow of our Phoebus, the clear scope and contexture of his work, the full and most beautiful figures of his persons.' He newly appreciated the artistic design of the poem. It may seem surprising that the surviving Greek tradition, while offering valuable critical insights on Homer's spirit and style in the writing of Longinus and Dionysius of Halicarnassus,[16] has little by way of helpful general comment on the 'scope and contexture' of the *Iliad*. Perhaps because of the basic unfamiliarity with all things Greek, and because of the strong assumption inherited from the chivalric tradition that an epic celebrated an exemplary heroic ideal, little if anything was made in the Renaissance of the hint from Aristotle that the *Iliad* involves *pathos*, or of the general but unspecified tradition that Homer was the father of tragedy. Chapman seems only to have discovered for himself the full significance of Homer's handling of the wrath of Achilles (which gives rise to what he calls in his later preface to the *Odyssey* 'predominant perturbation'[17] in the poem) in the close imaginative engagement of 1611. Indeed it is entirely possible that in 1598 he had not read the second half.

The plot of the *Iliad* in addition to *pathos* has other elements identified by Aristotle in his analysis of the best sort of tragedy, that is, error (*hamartia*) reversal (*peripeteia*) and recognition (*anagnoresis*).[18]

The initial error occurs in the opening quarrel, and here Agamemnon is chiefly to blame. In Achilles' eyes the Greek leader is abusing his power and is guilty of *hubris*, arrogant behaviour that offends the gods (I, 203). Agamemnon is rebuked for bad

15.   Nicoll, A. (1957) vol. 1, p. 43.
16.   Longinus, *On the Sublime* IX; Dionysius of Halicarnassus, *On Literary Composition* III.
17.   Nicoll, A. (1957) vol. 2, p. 4.
18.   *Poetics* X, XIII.

judgement and stupidity by Thersites (II, 225–42), Odysseus (IV, 349–55) Diomedes (IX, 32–49) and Nestor (IX, 96–113). He admits his own folly (*ate*, delusion or recklessness) privately before the Greek elders (IX, 115–16) and publicly before the army (XIX, 72–144). After the quarrel, Achilles asks his goddess mother to persuade Zeus to grant the Trojans success, so that the Greeks will be forced to recognise his worth. Zeus agrees, and the Trojans advance from the city to camp upon the plain. Faced with this threat, the Greeks petition Achilles (Book IX). Agamemnon now offers generous gifts of compensation going beyond what was required by good form alone. But the insult to his honour is felt so deeply that Achilles remains obdurate requiring nothing less than the complete humiliation of Agamemnon. In the eyes of the other characters Achilles is seen to be acting as if he were a law unto himself; he is compounding the error of Agamemnon by his own stubbornness and pride.

The response of Achilles to Agamemnon's insult is dispropor-tionate to the offence but it has its origins in something pure and noble. All the heroes share his heroic aspiration for glory, but in none of them is it to be found in so intense a form. He is not greatly interested in the Greek cause; he does not feel he has been wronged by the Trojans (I, 152–60) and he is not fighting for hearth and home like the great patriot Hector. Achilles is bent upon heroic achievement for its own sake not for what it brings with it in the way of material possessions, social position, a just revenge or the defence of loved ones. He fights simply and solely for glory. This purity of motive and aspiration is reflected in the choice he makes in remaining at Troy, preferring a short life with glory to a long life without fame (IX, 410–16). Ironically we hear of this choice which reveals the full magnanimity of Achilles just at the moment when in his anger he is threatening to throw it away by going home, so that our idea of Achilles' greatness is inextricably bound up with the anger that threatens its overthrow and ruin. Nevertheless, we can see here the purity of his motives and can appreciate his absolute sense of his own worth and of the honour due to him because of it. Any diminution of this honour diminishes the whole man for honour is indivisible, and renders his choice of life null and void. There is honourable truth in this feeling, and Achilles honours this single truth so absolutely that he is blind to all other truths, so that his purity proves to be the ruin not only of many others but of himself too. His exceptional sense of personal honour springing from his single-minded and untainted aspiration to glory is at once the source of his greatness and his great error. This paradox lies at the heart of Homer's tragic vision.

In Book XVI, the pivot of the main action, comes the reversal that results in unforeseen and calamitous consequences. The Trojans have had further success and even Patroclus remarks to the stubborn Achilles that while doctors are treating the leading Greeks, he alone is untreatable (21–35). When Achilles relents to the point of allowing Patroclus to fight in his place wearing his armour, there are the first signs of recognition of his error, and he admits that a man cannot be angry forever (60–1). The concern for his honour is still over-riding; Patroclus must only save the ships now threatened by the Trojans; he must not fight on to Troy or he will diminish the honour of Achilles (80–90). But there is magnanimity as well as irony in his final wish that both he and Patroclus may survive to take Troy together (97–100). Neither lives to do so.

The calamitous death of Patroclus, whom he loves more than his own life (XVIII, 81–2), at the hands of Hector, becomes the calamity of Achilles. When the news reaches him, in conversation with Thetis he fully recognises his own error and folly. The gods have done much for him but there is no pleasure in achievement any more. He is ready for death, regrets his special destiny as the son of a goddess and recognises the insidious effects of anger that can darken the wisest mind, is sweeter than honey and spreads like smoke. But the quarrel with Agamemnon must be put behind him, and he yields to necessity accepting the fate which Thetis has revealed to him. He resolves to seek glory and the death of Hector (XVIII, 79–126)

In the ensuing combat, Achilles, whose purity of motive is now tainted by the desire for revenge into which his anger has been newly channelled, is resolute for death. His encounter with Aeneas (Book XX) has none of the chivalry that characterised the duels of Paris and Menelaus (Book III), Glaucus and Diomedes (Book VI) or Hector and Ajax (Book VII) in the earlier part of the poem. When the pitiful Tros faces the terrible Achilles, Homer makes a rare intervention of his own to tell us of the remorseless character of his hero. In his translation, Chapman, no longer straining against the grain of the original, does not alter what he finds but renders Homer's judgement with emphatic clarity:

> Then Tros, Alastor's son, made in, and sought to scape their chance
> With free submission. Down he fell, and prayed about his knees
> He would not kill him, but take ruth, as one that Destinies
> Made to that purpose, being a man born in the self same year
> That he himself was. O poor fool, to sue to him to bear
> A ruthful mind; he well might know he could not fashion him
> In ruth's soft mould; he had no spirit to brook that interim
> In his hot fury, he was none of these remorseful men,
> Gentle and affable, but fierce at all times, and mad then.
>
> (XX, 406–14, translating 463–8)

As if to clarify his new conception of Achilles and the scope of the poem, Chapman adds 'Forth flew the prince of tragedies' (420). Soon after this, in the encounter with Scamander, the translator is equally direct in rendering the mad fury of Achilles:

> Twelve fair young princes then
> He choosed of all to take alive, to have them freshly slain
> On that most solemn day of wreak resolved on for his friend.
> These led he trembling forth the flood, as fearful of their end
> As any hind calves: all their hands he pinioned behind
> With their own girdles worn upon their rich weeds, and resigned
> Their persons to his Myrmidons to bear to fleet – and he
> Plunged in the stream again to take more work of tragedy.
>
> (XXI, 27–34, translating 27–33)

The darkening moral tone of the poem is apparent in the many images of corpses exposed to dogs and carrion birds.

In the final encounter, Chapman rises to the challenge of Homer's Greek in his evocation of the fearsome Martial energy of Achilles:

> and now Achilles comes; now near
> His Mars-like presence terribly came brandishing his spear.
> His right arm shook it; his bright arms like day came glittering on,
> Like fire-light, or the light of heaven shot from the rising sun.
> This sight outwrought discourse; cold fear shook Hector from his stand.
> No more stay now; all ports were left; he fled in fear the hand
> Of that fear-master, who, hawk-like, air's swiftest passenger,
> That holds a timorous dove in chase, and with command doth bear
> His fiery onset; the dove hastes; the hawk comes whizzing on;

> This way and that he turns and winds and cuffs the pigeon,
> And till he truss it his great spirit lays hot charge on his wing:
> So urged Achilles Hector's flight.
>
> (XXII, 115–26, translating 131–43)

When he finally stands his ground, the chivalrous Hector proposes a compact whereby the victor does no more than take the spoils of the loser, restoring his body for burial (XXII, 254–9). These are the conditions that had been agreed upon in the earlier combat with Ajax (VII, 76–86). Achilles will have none of it:

> Hector, thou only pestilence in all mortality
> To my sere spirits, never set the point 'twixt thee and me
> Any conditions; but as far as men and lions fly
> All terms of covenant, lambs and wolves, in so far opposite state
> (Impossible for love t'atone) stand we, till our souls satiate
> The god of soldiers. Do not dream that our disjunction can
> Endure condition. Therefore now all worth that fits a man
> Call to thee, all particular parts that fit a soldier;
> And they all this include (besides the skill and spirit of war)
> Hunger for slaughter, and a hate that eats thy heart to eat
> Thy foe's heart. This stirs, this supplies in death the killing heat;
> And all this needst thou. No more flight. Pallas Athenia
> Will quickly cast thee to my lance. Now, now together draw
> All griefs for vengeance, both in me and all my friends late dead
> That bled thee, raging with thy lance.
>
> (XXII, 224–38 translating 261–72)

The definition here of what it takes to be a soldier – all Chapman's filling out of Homer – is quite incompatible with his earlier ideal of Stoic fortitude. With his dying breath Hector again begs for mercy for his corpse. Achilles again refuses in fury:

> 'Dog', he replied, 'urge not my ruth by parents, soul, nor knees.
> I would to God that any rage would let me eat thee raw,
> Sliced into pieces, so beyond the right of any law
> I taste thy merits. And believe it flies the force of man
> To rescue thy head from the dogs. Give all the gold they can,
> If ten or twenty times so much as friends would rate thy price
> Were tendered here, with vows of more, to buy the cruelties
> I here have vowed, and, after that, thy father with his gold
> Would free thy self – all that should fail to let thy mother hold
> Solemnities of death with thee and do thee such a grace
> To mourn thy whole corpse on a bed – which piecemeal I'll deface

With fowls and dogs.' He (dying) said: 'I (knowing thee well) foresaw
  Thy now tried tyranny, nor hoped for any other law,
  Of nature, or of nations: and that fear forced much more
  Than death my flight, which never touched at Hector's foot before.
  A soul of iron informs thee. Mark, what vengeance th' equal fates
  Will give me of thee for this rage, when in the Scaean gates
  Phoebus and Paris meet with thee.'
                              (XXII, 296–313, translating 345–60)

Hector's judgement that Achilles is beyond the pale is Chapman's
addition. Homer says simply that Achilles has a heart of iron. He
then fastens Hector's body to his chariot and drags him away. For
several days at dawn he hauls Hector's corpse three times around
the funeral mound of Patroclus. As she had said farewell to
Hector, Andromache recalled how Achilles had chivalrously
reverenced the bodies of her family killed at Thebe (VI, 414–28).
How far below his previous magnanimity has he now fallen: so
far that his behaviour becomes offensive to the gods, who put a
stop to it.

In the final book comes the second and fullest recognition
scene in the meeting with Priam who comes by night to the tent
of Achilles to ransom his son's corpse. Here Achilles is restored to
humanity by the pleas of Priam who reminds him of his own aged
father, Peleus. In his gentle treatment of Priam there is true
magnanimity:

          Poor man, thy mind is scared
  With much affliction. How durst thy person thus alone
  Venture on his sight that hath slain so many a worthy son
  And so dear to thee? Thy old heart is made of iron. Sit
  And settle we our woes, though huge, for nothing profits it.
  Cold mourning wastes but our lives' heats. The gods have destinate
  That wretched mortals must live sad. 'Tis the immortal state
  Of Deity that lives secure. Two tuns of gifts there lie
  In Jove's gate, one of good, one ill, that our mortality
  Maintain, spoil, order; which when Jove doth mix to any man,
  One while he frolicks, one while mourns. If of his mournful can
  A man drinks only, only wrongs he doth expose him to.
  Sad hunger in th' abundant earth doth toss him to and fro,
  Respected nor of gods nor men. The mixed cup Peleus drank;
  Even from his birth heaven blest his life; he lived not that could thank
  The gods for such rare benefits as set forth his estate.
  He reigned among his Myrmidons most rich, most fortunate,

And (though a mortal) had his bed decked with a deathless dame.
And yet withall this good, one ill god mixed, that takes all name
From all that goodness – his name now (whose preservation here
Men count the crown of their most good) not blest with power to bear
One blossom but my self, and I shaken as soon as blown.
Nor shall I live to cheer his age and give nutrition
To him that nourished me. Far off my rest is set in Troy,
To leave thee restless and thy seed. Thy self, that did enjoy
(As we have heard) a happy life – what Lesbos doth contain
(In times past being a blest man's seat) what the measured main
Of Hellespontus, Phrygia, holds, are all said to adorn
Thy empire, wealth and sons enough – but, when the gods did turn
Thy blest state to partake with bane, war and the bloods of men
Circled thy city, never clear. Sit down and suffer then.
Mourn not inevitable things; thy tears can spring no deeds
To help thee, nor recall thy son; impatience even breeds
Ill upon ill, makes worst things worse. And therefore sit.

(XXIV, 463–96, translating 518–51)

In his acceptance and resolution here, so dearly won, we find the noble simplicity and quiet grandeur that have sometimes been regarded as the hallmarks of the classic spirit. How vulnerable and fragile this is before the onset of passion is wonderfully clear in the momentary anger that flares up in Achilles when Priam is impatient to see Hector. But Achilles collects himself, and urges Priam to share a meal. The taking of food symbolises the practical acceptance of continuing life and the recognition that even the passion of grief must yield to necessity. Amid the ruins of human hope and in the knowledge of imminent death, Achilles for the first time sees life steadily and sees it whole.

In its pristine form we may conjecture that the myth of Achilles is first and foremost one which expresses what it takes to be a supreme hero. Zeus allows Thetis to produce a child who will excel all heroes (XVIII, 436–7). But Destiny has given Achilles a choice; an early death is the price if he chooses the heroic life (IX, 410–16). Achilles consciously makes the choice in full knowledge of its ultimate cost. The Homeric Achilles is, of course, supremely heroic, but Homer has developed the tragic possibilities latent in the myth. The heroic choice is taken for granted and is of secondary significance. The centre of Homer's action is the defeat of heroic expectation through folly and passion. Achilles is not a hero in control of his own destiny but the victim of the arbitrary power of another man's folly and the imperious demands of his own nature. What happens to him in the poem is determined not by any external decree of the gods but by his own absolute sense of his personal honour. The climax of the poem is not the full-hearted celebration of heroic achievement but an act in which the glory of the hero is clearly tarnished. The knowledge in which the greater humanity of the hero is revealed is not the confident knowledge of what his own heroic choice has cost him, but a bitter recognition of his own error and then acceptance of necessary suffering as the universal condition. The original heroic myth of Achilles has become a vehicle through which Homer expresses a tragic vision revealing a deeper humanity beyond the heroism of the hero.

Homer and Aristotle: the form of the Homeric poems

What then are the critical maxims to be derived from Homer? They are many and various, but the grandest and simplest concerns the artistic unity and concentration famously prescribed by Aristotle on the authority of Homer in his *Poetics*:

> A plot does not have unity, as some people think, simply because it deals with a single hero. Many and indeed innumerable things happen to an individual, some of which do not go to make up any unity, and similarly an individual is concerned in many actions which do not combine into a single piece of action. . . . But Homer, supreme also in all other respects, was apparently well aware of this truth either by instinct (*physis*) or from knowledge of his art (*techne*). . . . in that even with the Trojan war, which has a beginning and an end, he did not endeavour to dramatize it as a whole, since it would have been either too long to be taken in all at once or, if he had moderated the length, he would have complicated it by the variety of incident. As it is, he takes one part of the story only and uses many incidents from other parts such as the Catalogue of Ships and other episodes with which he diversifies his poetry.[19]

(VIII, XXIII)

19. Fyfe, W.H. (translator) (1927) *Aristotle: The Poetics*; *'Longinus': On the Sublime*; *Demetrius*; *On Style*, Loeb Classical Library, Heinemann, London, Harvard University Press, Cambridge, Mass. Subsequent quotations from the *Poetics* are in this translation.

In concentrating the main action of the *Iliad* upon the anger of
Achilles, Homer does not waste time in telling us about inessential
aspects of Achilles' life and character that do not have a bearing
upon his anger, nor does he obscure his main theme by telling the
tale of Troy from the beginning. He begins in the middle of
things *in medias res*: the phrase is from Horace (*The Art of Poetry*,
148) praising Homer in Aristotelian terms. He selects only those
particulars that relate to his central theme which has a clear
beginning in the quarrel scene, a middle in all the consequences
that flow from it and an end in the resolution of the anger. The
clear chain of cause and effect in the main action has all the
requirements of the classically well-made plot that Aristotle made
famous in the *Poetics*. Of course this plot is diversified, enriched
and extended by many episodes, but they do not take us to places
far away from the plain of Troy or extend the temporal
framework within which the main action takes place. In the final
analysis, they are subordinate to the main action of the irreducible
plot. It is this remarkable artistic cohesion and control that
distinguishes Homer from other oral poets with whom in recent
times it has been fashionable to compare him.

From the concentration and unity of a clear and simple design
stems the universality for which Greek art has always been
famous. For the main plot of the *Iliad* gives us a pattern of
behaviour that in its causes and effects represents a probable if not
inevitable sequence. Underneath all that is particular and individual,
the anger is typical in its causes and consequences, and it is
Homer's method or art that enables us to see this. Homer the
artist has therefore accomplished in his poetry all that Aristotle the
philosopher and critic held to be the end of art; he has imposed
form and order on the undifferentiated matter and random chaos
of life, thus enabling us to see through the particular to the
universal. This imposition of form is not therefore simply an
aesthetic matter. It is the means whereby the poet clarifies and
communicates moral truth about the human world he is
representing in his poem.

Although Aristotle makes distinctions between the *Iliad* and the
Odyssey finding the latter to be more complex by virtue of its
many recognition scenes brought about by Odysseus' disguise as a
beggar in his own house[20] – the secondary plot featuring the

20. *Poetics* XXIV 3.

journey of Telemachus in quest of his father and his return home,
and the use of retrospective narrative in the account of the hero's
adventures to the Phaeacians are further Odyssean complexities –
the essential truth about the structure of the two poems is the
same:

> For in writing an *Odyssey* he did not put in all that ever happened to
> Odysseus, his being wounded on Parnassus, for instance, or his
> feigned madness when the host was gathered (these being events
> neither of which necessarily or probably led to the other), but he
> constructed his *Odyssey* round a single action in our sense of the
> phrase. . . . Now in drama the episodes are short, but it is by them
> that the epic gains its length. The *story* (*logos*) of the *Odyssey* is quite
> short. A man is for many years away from home and his footsteps are
> dogged by Poseidon and he is all alone. Moreover, affairs at home are
> in such a state that his estate is being wasted by suitors and a plot laid
> against his son, but after being storm-tossed he arrives himself, reveals
> who he is, and attacks them, with the result that he is saved and
> destroys his enemies. That is the essence, the rest is episodes.
>
> (*Poetics* VIII and XVII)

Here may be suggested the shaping influence of Homer on
subsequent Greek art reflected in Aristotle's aesthetic analysis
which, both directly and indirectly, has been powerfully influential in the European mainstream.

The *Odyssey*

In some respects the *Odyssey* might be considered to be more
easily accommodated to Renaissance expectations and taste, for its
hero can be readily assimilated to the ideal Christian outlook.
Indeed like Hercules, Ulysses who is most often referred to in this
his Roman name, is truly a hero of the Renaissance to the extent
that in Jonson's *Volpone*, Sir Politic, the Englishman abroad and
would-be Machiavellian plotter, can scoff at the humanist
commonplace:

> That idle antique stale grey-headed project
> Of knowing men's minds and manners, with Ulysses.
>
> (II, i, 9–10)

For the Homeric Odysseus, unlike his companions, is wise, intelligent and a man of the world, as Chapman emphasises:

> The cities of a world of nations,
> With all their manners, minds and fashions,
> He saw and knew; at sea felt many woes,
> Much care sustained, to save from overthrows
> Himself and friends in their retreat for home.
> But so their fates he could not overcome
> Though much he thirsted it. O men unwise,
> They perished by their own impieties.
>
> (I, 5–12)[21]

The strongly moralised reading of the Odyssey is quite traditional:

> Again, what virtue and wisdom can do, he has proposed Ulysses as an example for our instruction, he who tamed Troy and looked with discerning eyes upon the cities and manners of many men as he was planning a return for himself and his comrades; many difficulties he endured but could never be overborne by the waves of adversity. You know the Sirens' songs and the potions of Circe – if he had stupidly and greedily drunk these along with his companions he would have become the base and senseless slave of a harlot, he would have lived the life of a filthy dog or a sow that wallows in the mire. We are but ciphers, born merely to feed on the fruits of the earth, like the feckless suitors of Penelope . . . .
>
> (Horace, Epistle I, 2, 17–28)

More than the Iliad, the Odyssey lends itself to the allegorical interpretations with which all the great works came down from antiquity to the Renaissance. According to the traditional interpretation of the allegorisers,[22] Odysseus, because of his wisdom, is able to enjoy pleasure but does not become a slave to it; he masters Circe, makes her his friend and sleeps with her without danger to himself. The episode becomes a lesson in temperance rather than abstinence. The Lotus-eaters and the Sirens represent different forms of the seductive temptation to hedonism and irresponsibility. In the Cyclops we see basic human savagery, the state of nature in which the individual will is not controlled and civilised by the social bond. In the main action the defeat of the greedy suitors, who are all excess and appetite, is

21. Nicoll, A. (1957) vol. 2, p. 12.
22. Allen, D.C. (1970) Mysteriously Meant.

accomplished by the man of control who uses his intelligence. In his own translation Chapman, it has been convincingly argued,[23] developed his own version of the allegorical tradition whereby Odysseus triumphed over his external foes (the suitors of Penelope who are laying waste to his resources and plot the death of his son) not merely through his superior intelligence but by virtue of his own self-conquest. According to Chapman, the decision that Odysseus makes at the start of the poem to leave the island of Calypso, where he had been staying at the nymph's insistence for seven years, marks the beginning of the regeneration of the hero which is completed among the Phaeacians, upon whose island he is shipwrecked and where he confesses past weaknesses (his 'wanderings') in the course of his after-dinner narrative, rededicating himself to the domestic virtues represented by their queen Arete. Having left Circe and Calypso, the obeisance before Arete marks Odysseus' return to the moral life, so that he is now made worthy of the faithful Penelope, whose constant virtue is celebrated throughout the poem and directly contrasted to the inconstancy of Helen, the wife of Menelaus, who yielded to the visiting stranger Paris, thus occasioning the Trojan War; and of Clytemnestra, who took Aegisthus to bed and murdered her husband Agamemnon on his return from Troy.

Though the moral content of the *Odyssey* was easier to assimilate to a Christian outlook than that of the *Iliad*, the poem laboured under the disadvantage that in leaving Troy its hero could be said to have left behind him the heroic world. The wanderings of an adventurer thirsting for knowledge and experience captured the imagination of Dante and men of the Renaissance: Ulysses, in the *Inferno*, enjoins his men:

> Considerate la vostra semenza:
> Fatti non foste a viver come bruti
> Ma per seguir virtute e conoscenza
> (*Canto* XXVI, 118–20)[24]

(Consider your destiny: you were not made to live like brutes but to follow virtue and knowledge.)

23. Lord, G. de F. (1956) *Homeric Renaissance: The Odyssey of George Chapman*, Chatto & Windus, Ch. 3, 'Dynamic Allegory in Chapman's *Odyssey*'.
24. For further discussion see Stanford, W.B. (1963) *The Ulysses Theme: Studies in the Adaptability of a Traditional Hero*, Basil Blackwell.

But the thirst for knowledge and the acquisition of wisdom are not quite Homer's subject. In contrast, the motivating force that dominates the Homeric Odysseus from the moment we see him grieving for Ithaca on the island of Calypso is *nostalgia*, most obviously the painful longing for the return to hearth and home but also secondarily for the heightened existence made possible when conditions for the heroic life obtain at Troy. The whole movement of the poem is in fact away from the heroic to the domestic, from the great patriotic adventure that had ostensibly united the Greek warriors to the domestic concerns of one of their number. At the opening of the poem Odysseus is the destroyer of Troy; at the close, after the slaying of the suitors, he is merely the master of his own house. From antiquity may be recalled here the famous judgement given in the Greek treatise *On the Sublime*, emanating from the first century AD and attributed to the rhetorician Longinus that the *Odyssey* lacked the heroic vigour of the *Iliad*:

> The *Odyssey* is an instance, how natural it is to a great genius, when it begins to grow old and decline, to delight itself in narrations and fables. For, that Homer composed the *Odyssey* after the *Iliad*, many proofs may be given . . . .. From hence in my judgement it proceeds, that as the *Iliad* was written while his spirit was in its greatest vigour, the whole structure of that work is dramatic and full of action; whereas the greater part of the *Odyssey* is employed in narration, which is the taste of old age; so that in this latter piece we may compare him to the setting sun, which has still the same greatness but not the same ardour or force. He speaks not in the same strain; we see no more that *sublime* of the *Iliad* which marches on with a constant pace, without ever being stopped or retarded: there appears no more that hurry and that strong tide of motions and passions, pouring one after another: there is no more the same fury, or the same volubility of diction, so suitable to action, and all along drawing in such innumerable images of nature. But Homer, like the ocean, is always great, even when he ebbs and retires; even when he is lowest and loses himself most in narrations and incredible fictions; as instances of this we cannot forget the descriptions of tempests, the adventures of Ulysses with the Cyclops, and many others. But though all this be age, it is the age of Homer – and it may be said for the credit of these fictions, that they are beautiful dreams, or if you will, the dreams of Jupiter himself. I spoke of the *Odyssey* only to show, that the greatest poets when their genius wants strength and

warmth for the pathetic, for the most part employ themselves in painting the manners. This Homer has done, in characterising the suitors, and describing their way of life; which is properly a branch of comedy, whose peculiar business is to represent the manners of men.

(IX, 11–15)[25]

Praise of Homer in terms that suggest real appreciation of the poems is rarer than might be supposed. The truth is that easy familiarity with the Greek language in the early Renaissance was rare and that the Greek poet was an alien spirit in the Latin-based culture of Christendom.

The *Aeneid*

There can be no doubt, however, about the genuine admiration accorded to Virgil. Sidney, for example, has little to say about Homer but is eloquent in his advocacy of Virgil:

Only let Aeneas be worn in the tablet of your memory, how he governeth himself in the ruin of his country; in the preserving his old father, and carrying away his religious ceremonies; in obeying God's commandment to leave Dido, though not only all passionate kindness, but even the human consideration of virtuous gratefulness, would have craved other of him; how in storms, how in sports, how in war, how in peace, how a fugitive, how victorious, how besieged and how besieging, how to strangers, how to allies, how to enemies, how to his own; lastly, how in his inward self, and how in his outward government – and I think, in a mind not prejudiced with a prejudicating humour, he will be found in excellency fruitful, yea even as Horace saith,

melius Chrysippo et Crantore

(*Epistle* I, 2, 4)

'better than the old philosophers Chrysippus and Cantor'[26]

Jonson, too, in dismissing the heroes of romance in favour of those of classical epic is more specific and more eloquent in his admiration for Virgil's hero:

25. In the version of Pope cited in the 'Postscript' to his translation of the *Odyssey* of 1726, see Butt, J. (gen. ed.) et al. (1939–69) *The Twickenham Edition of the Poems of Alexander Pope*, 11 vols, Methuen, vol. 10, p. 382.
26. 'The Defence of Poesy', 802 in Duncan-Jones, K. (1989) p. 231.

Did you o'er know, or hear of the lord Beaufort,
Who serv'd so bravely in France? I was his page,
And ere he died, his friend: I follow'd him,
First, in the wars, and, in the times of peace,
I waited on his studies; which were right.
He had no Arthurs, nor no Rosicleers,
No knights o' the sun, nor Amadis de Gauls,
Primalions, Pantagruels, public nothings;
Abortives of the fabulous dark cloister,
Sent out to poison courts and infest manners;
But great Achilles, Agamemnon's acts,
Sage Nestor's counsels, and Ulysses' sleights,
Tydides' fortitude, as Homer wrought them
In his immortal phant'sy, for examples
Of the heroic virtue. Or, as Virgil,
That master of the epic poem, limn'd
Pious Æneas, his religious prince,
Bearing his aged parent on his shoulders,
Rapt from the flames of Troy, with his young son:
And these he brought to practice, and to use.

(*The New Inn* I, vi, 119–38)[27]

'Pious Aeneas his religious prince' who dutifully subdues his own
will to the higher purposes of the divine seemed a surer pattern of
virtue than the egotistical Achilles, overborne by the excesses of
anger, or the wily and materialistic Odysseus who triumphs
through deception and disguise. Jonson again used Aeneas as a
touchstone for virtue in his fine epigram 'To William Roe':

Roe (and my joy to name) thou'rt now to go
  Countries and climes, manners and men to know,
To extract and choose the best of all these known,
  And those to turn to blood and make thine own.
May winds as soft as breath of kissing friends
  Attend thee hence; and there may all thy ends,
As the beginnings here, prove purely sweet,
  And perfect in a circle always meet.
So when we, blest with thy return, shall see
  Thyself, with thy first thoughts, brought home by thee,

27. Cited in the section 'Classicism and Imitation' in Martindale, J. (ed.) (1985)
    English Humanism: Wyatt to Cowley, Croom Helm, pp. 132–3; line numbers
    in references to Jonson's plays are taken from Herford, C.H., Simpson, P.
    (eds) (1925–52) *Ben Jonson*, 11 vols, Oxford University Press.

We each to other may this voice inspire:
  This is that good Aeneas, passed through fire,
Through seas, storms, tempests; and embarked for hell,
  Came back untouched. This man hath travailed well.[28]

The flames through which Aeneas passed as he escaped from
Troy, the storm that wrecked him at Carthage where he
encounters Dido, and the journey to Hades undertaken to visit his
father, where his destiny is finally clarified, are trials all stoically
endured. In the medieval allegories of the poem,[29] the journey
and travail of Aeneas are seen to represent man's earthly
pilgrimage through this vale of tears, while the hero's piety shows
what is necessary if the heavenly city (Rome) is finally to be
gained after death. For the Italian humanists of the Renaissance as
they rediscovered all around them the beauty and lost grandeur of
the remains of ancient Rome, the *Aeneid* was restored to its
position as the seminal work of art that gave expression and
meaning to the grandeur and majesty of Roman civilisation at its
peak. For Virgil proposes as his subject a hero whose concern is
not like Achilles, with his own honour, and whose task is not
merely to restore order to his own house on an obscure island, as
Odysseus had done, but one who labours till he founds a city *dum
conderet urbem* (1, 5) which is to be the parent city of Rome itself:

Arms and the man I sing, who, forced by fate,
And haughty Juno's unrelenting hate,
Expelled and exiled, left the Trojan shore.
Long labours, both by sea and land, he bore
And in the doubtful war, before he won
The Latian realm, and built the destined town;
His banished gods restored to rites divine,
And settled sure succession in his line,
From whence the race of Alban fathers come,
And the long glories of majestic Rome.
                (Dryden, *Aeneis* 1, 1–10)[30]

28. No. 128, Parfitt, G. (1975) p. 84, who prints 'travelled' in the final line;
'travailed' is printed in Donaldson, I. (ed.) (1975) *Ben Jonson: Poems*, Oxford
University Press.
29. Allen, D.C. (1970) *Mysteriously Meant*.
30. Dryden's *Aeneid* constitutes the third volume of Kinsley, J. (ed.) (1958) *The
Poems of John Dryden*, 4 vols, Oxford University Press. For comment see
Hopkins, D. (1986) *John Dryden*, Cambridge University Press, pp. 157–67.

The labour which is to be initiated through Aeneas is difficult and momentous:

tantae molis erat Romanam condere gentem.

(33)

Such time such toil required the Roman name,
Such length of labour for so vast a frame.

(48–9)

When Aeneas is shipwrecked on the coast of Carthage, his mother, the goddess Venus, appeals to Jupiter, who assures her of his fated role:

Know, I have searched the mystic books of fate:
Thy son, (nor is the appointed season far)
In Italy shall wage successful war,
Shall tame fierce nations in the bloody field,
And sov'reign laws impose and cities build,
Till, after ev'ry foe subdued, the sun
Thrice through the signs his annual race shall run:
This is the time prefixed. Ascanius then,
Now called Iulus, shall begin his reign. . . .
Then Romulus his grandsire's throne shall gain,
Of martial towers the founder shall become,
The people Romans call, the city Rome.
To them no bounds of empire I assign,
Nor term of years to their immortal line. . . .
The subject world shall Rome's dominion own,
And, prostrate, shall adore the nation of the gown.
An age is ripening in revolving fate
When Troy shall overturn the Grecian state,
And sweet revenge her conquering sons shall call,
To crush the people that conspired her fall.
Then Caesar from the Julian stock shall rise,
Whose empire ocean, and whose fame the skies
Alone shall bound; whom fraught with eastern spoils,
Our heavens, the just reward of human toils,
Securely shall repay with rites divine;
And incense shall ascend his sacred shrine.
Then dire debate and impious war shall cease
And the stern age be softened into peace:
Then banished Faith shall once again return,
And Vestal fires in hallowed temples burn;

And Remus with Quirinus shall sustain
The righteous laws, and fraud and force restrain.
Janus himself before his fane shall wait,
And keep the dreadful issues of his gate,
With bolts and iron bars: within remains
Imprisoned Fury, bound in brazen chains;
High on a trophy raised, of useless arms,
He sits, and threats the world with vain alarms.

(I, 357–65; 375–9; 384–407,
translating 262–8; 276–9; 282–96)

The wars to be waged in Italy by Aeneas in the second half of the poem are a prelude to endless Roman power: *imperium sine fine dedi* (279) 'I have given dominion without end' says Jupiter. Through the Roman conquest of Greece, the heirs of Trojan Aeneas will be avenged. Though Virgil mentions the Julian stock (to make clear the relation to Iulus, another name of Ascanius, the son of Aeneas) the allusion is to Augustus Caesar who in 27 BC ordered the gates of the temple of Janus, which were always open in times of war, to be ceremonially closed for only the third time in Roman history, thus inaugurating the new age of the *pax Augusta*. The Augustan settlement (which endured for four centuries) put an end to the civil strife that had bedevilled Rome in the years of the late Republic; hence the twins Romulus (here given his divine name Quirinus) and Remus, who had themselves fallen out over the founding of Rome, will now be acting in concert. Jupiter looks forward to the Augustan religious revival and the restoration of order to the Roman state.

Aeneas is to accomplish his part in the grand design by virtue of his piety (*pietas*), most famously demonstrated in the scene alluded to by Jonson in which we see him on Troy's last night, bearing upon his shoulders his aged father Anchises, as he makes his escape through the burning city. He also leads his small son Ascanius by the hand, and Anchises carries with him the images of Troy's gods, the *penates*, so that here concentrated in a single image is the patriarchal ideal of Roman society, the gods, the fatherland, the grandfather and father, the father and son, the son and grandson bound each to the other in the closest relation, thereby ensuring the survival and continuous life of the family and the city. The ultimate sanction of all this is, of course, Jupiter himself, *pater Romanus* in the heavenly sphere, who ratifies the decision to leave Troy and sends an omen in the form of a shooting star to guide them on their way.

To Aeneas, on the ground, the grand design is only gradually revealed; he has to learn his task. As the chosen instrument of the gods and of the fates that lead inexorably to the foundation of Rome, he finds that he is required to subdue his personal inclinations at every stage. When he is disposed to linger with Dido at Carthage, Jupiter sends Mercury with a stern message to remind him of his duty. Terrified into leaving, Aeneas tells Dido that if the fates had allowed him to follow his own pleasure he would return to Troy and rebuild it. But Apollo has ordered him to seek Italy. There lies his love and his fatherland. The spirit of Anchises has been terrifying him in dreams, and he thinks of Ascanius whom he is cheating of his Italian inheritance. Jupiter's messenger had appeared in person. He does not seek Italy of his volition (IV, 333–61): *Italiam non sponte sequor* (361).

The sacrifice of self made here is consummated in the journey undertaken to meet the spirit of Anchises in Hades. Anchises welcomes his son:

'Welcome', he said, 'the gods' undoubted race!
O long expected to my dear embrace!
Once more 'tis given me to behold your face!
The love and pious duty which you pay
Have passed the perils of so hard a way. . . .
How have I feared your fate! but feared it most
When love assailed you on the Libyan coast'.
To this, the filial duty thus replies:
'Your sacred ghost before my sleeping eyes
Appeared, and often urged this painful enterprise.'
    (VI, 931–5; 940–4, translating VI, 687–8; 694–6)

The proud father then reveals to Aeneas the roll-call of his illustrious Roman descendants first highlighting the Caesars:

Now fix your sight and stand intent, to see
Your Roman race, and Julian progeny
The mighty Caesar waits his vital hour,
Impatient for the world, and grasps his promised power.
But next behold the youth of form divine,
Caesar himself, exalted in his line;

Augustus, promised oft, and long foretold,
Sent to the realm that Satum ruled of old;
Born to restore a better age of gold.
                    (VI, 1073–81, translating VI, 788–96)

After praise of Augustus, who will restore the golden age to Italy
(a mythical time of peace and virtue) and at the same time extend
Roman power and influence to the utmost limits of the earth,
Anchises then goes back in time to the heroes of early Rome.
Paternal pride in the achievements of the sons of Rome is mingled
with paternal sorrow at the prospect of the wounds which the
sons of Rome are to inflict upon their fatherland in the civil war of
Caesar and Pompey (826–35). The note of pride returns as
Anchises then looks to the heroes of foreign conquests over the
Greeks and the Carthaginians, at the same time pointing to those
noble figures of uncorrupted Roman virtue whose stern devotion
to duty and austere personal integrity later Romans believed to be
the source of Roman strength and power (836–46). Then comes
the proud assertion of Rome's imperial mission:

> excudent alii spirantia mollius aera
> (credo equidem), vivos ducent de marmore vultus,
> orabunt causas melius, caelique meatus
> describent radio et surgentia sidera dicent:
> tu regere imperio populos, Romane, memento
> (hae tibi erunt artes), pacique imponere morem,
> parcere subiectis et debellare superbos.
>   (VI, 847–53)

> Let others better mould the running mass
> Of metals, and inform the breathing brass
> And soften into flesh a marble face;
> Plead better at the bar; describe the skies,
> And when the stars descend and when they rise.
> But, Rome, 'tis thine with awful sway
> To rule mankind and make the world obey,
> Disposing peace and war thy own majestic way;
> To tame the proud, the fettered slave to free:
> These are imperial arts, and worthy thee.
>   (1168–77)

Others, like the Greeks, may excel in the arts and the sciences, but
Roman arts are to be the arts of government and rule. Here the

civilising mission of Rome is most clearly expressed; it is the imposition of Roman order (earlier identified with the imposition of Roman law in Jupiter's speech at IV, 231); Roman power is morally justified in the peace that it imposes.

The Trojans then reach the mouth of the Tiber, the site of the destined city to be named Lavinium after Aeneas' future wife, Lavinia, daughter of Latinus, king of the Latins. This marriage, which will eventually confirm the union of the Trojans and the Latins, is at first welcomed by Latinus, who, from earlier prophecies, recognises in Aeneas the stranger who is destined to be his son-in-law. However, Juno, who opposes the Roman destiny at every stage, tries to prevent the match and provokes Turnus, prince of the neighbouring Rutulians and Lavinia's suitor, to oppose the incoming Trojans. In preparations for war, Aeneas sails up the Tiber to Pallanteum, the site of the future Rome, to seek allies from peoples disaffected with Turnus. Their king, Evander, entrusts his son Pallas to Aeneas' cause. Here arms are provided by Venus for Aeneas. On the shield, Vulcan depicts famous scenes illustrating the martial character of the Romans beginning with the image of the infants Romulus and Remus fearlessly being suckled by their foster-mother, the she-wolf, in the cave of their father Mars (their mother Ilia is a descendent of Aeneas), and culminating with the climactic scene at the centre of the shield in which Augustus defeats Antony and Cleopatra at the battle of Actium, for which he celebrates a Roman triumph.

In the subsequent war Aeneas experiences none of the joy of battle that sustains the heroes of Homer, nor is he motivated by the desire for personal honour and glory. For him events bring only misery and loss. Before the final contest with Turnus, as he raises the great shield bearing upon it the fame and fortune of his Roman descendants, *pater Aeneas Romanae stirpis origo* (XII, 166), 'Aeneas the father and source of the Roman race' addressing his son Ascanius *magnae spes altera Romae* (168) 'the other hope of Rome's greatness', though he anticipates the fated victory nevertheless moralises on his own misfortune. After he has been defeated, Turnus begs for mercy in the name of Anchises but Aeneas catches sight of the belt of Pallas taken by Turnus as a spoil of war after he had killed the youth, and in a fit of anger Aeneas kills the prostrate Turnus, so that the poem ends not with a Roman triumph or with magnanimity in victory, but on a bitter note: for Aeneas does not feel even the sweetness of revenge but rather the pain of loss. Virgil emphasises the cost imposed by the Roman destiny not only to those who are the obvious victims of it (Dido and Turnus) but also to the victors themselves:

> tantae molis erat Romanam condere gentem.

Virgilian influence in the early Renaissance

Because of the connection of poet and the poem's hero to the *civitas*, it was Virgil rather than Homer who could be used to dignify civic occasions, as when Jonson addresses King James:

> Think on thy loved Aeneas, and what name
> Maro, the golden trumpet of his fame
> Gave him, read thou in this. A Prince that draws
> By example more than others do by laws;
> That is so just to his great art and thought,
> To do, not what Kings may, but what Kings ought.
> Who out of piety unto peace is vowed
> To spare his subjects, yet to quell the proud
> And dares esteem it the first fortitude
> To have his passions, foes at home, subdued.[31]

In acting as interpreter of Roman history and experience and in dedicating his art to the service of the *civitas*, Virgil seemed a more apposite model than the Homeric bard who worked in social circumstances alien to any Renaissance court. As the uncrowned laureate of Rome, Virgil who accepted the patronage of Maecenas, Augustus's minister of the arts, and was able to identify himself with the ruling powers, represented a model for the poet contemplating the highest calling. In the way that he fulfilled his laureate role as in the order of his values reflected in the character of his epic hero, Virgil was nearer to the Christian Renaissance than Homer, quite apart from linguistic considerations. But it was what was perceived as his achievement in refining and perfecting the Latin language that made Virgil central

31. Herford, C.M., Simpson, P. (1941) *Ben Jonson*, vol. VII, p. 256.

to the humanist poetics of the Renaissance. In the chapter 'Of Imitation' in his *Schoolmaster* (1570) Roger Ascham writes:

> And therefore even as Virgil and Horace deserve most worthy praise that they, spying the imperfitness in Ennius and Plautus by true imitation of Homer and Euripides brought poetry to the same perfitness in Latin as it was in Greek, even so those that by the same way would benefit their tongue and country deserve rather thanks than dispraise in that behalf.[32]

Much Tudor criticism is preoccupied with discussion concerning the best means of attempting this. Some, like Gabriel Harvey, thought the best way forward lay in perfection of the English hexameter in direct imitation of the dactylic hexameter which had been the metre of Homer adopted by Roman writers of epic and perfected by Virgil. Direct transposition of classical metres which are determined by quantity (length of syllable chiefly determined by vowel sounds) into English in which metre was traditionally determined by stress or accent was not successful. If we look at the version of Virgil by Richard Stanyhurst, it is not difficult to understand why:

> Now manhood and garboils I chant and martial horror.
> I blaze thee captain first from Troy city repairing,
> Like wand'ring pilgrim to famosed Italy trudging
> And coast of Lavyn: soust with tempestuous hurlwind,
> On land and sailing by God's predestinate order:
> But chief through Juno's long fostered deadly revengement. . . .
> My muse show the reason, what grudge or what fury kindled
> Of gods thee princess through so cursed mischievous hatred
> With sharp sundry perils to tug so famous a captain
> Such festered rancour do saints celestial harbour?[33]

The inadequacy of this attempt was apparent to his contemporaries. Commenting on the line 'what moved Juno to tug so great a captain as Aeneas', Puttenham is eloquent on the indecency of the word 'tug', and is highly critical of Stanyhurst's metrics.[34] In his preface Stanyhurst says that he had been prompted by

32. Smith, G.G. (1904) vol. 1, pp. 33–4.
33. Stanyhurst, R. (1583) *The First Four Books of the Aeneid . . . in English Heroic Verse etc*, H. Bynneman.
34. Smith, G.G. (1904) vol. 2, p. 178 and p. 122.

Ascham who in his *Schoolmaster* 'doth wish the University students to apply their wits in beautifying our English language with heroical verses',[35] but Ascham there, though he is in favour of the naturalisation of the iambic measure into quantitative verse, found that the hexameter 'doth rather trot and hobble than run smoothly in our English tongue'. The reasons for this he gives as follows:

> Indeed, our English tongue, having in use chiefly words of one syllable which commonly be long, doth not well receive the nature of the *carmen heroicum* because *dactylus*, the aptest foot for that verse, containing one long and two short, is seldom found in English; and doth also rather stumble than stand upon *monosyllabis*.[36]

Curiously enough, there is an analogous reason that caused the Romans difficulty in naturalising the Greek hexameter, for Latin, a much less polysyllabic language than Greek, is predominantly trochaic in rhythm (tum ti) rather than dactylic (tum ti ti) so that there are many Latin words that cannot be fitted into the pattern of the dactylic hexameter, with the result that it is much more difficult to compose fluent and flexible hexameters in Latin than it is in Greek. Virgil mastered the form with results that make previous Latin hexameter writers (such as Ennius, Lucretius and Catullus) sometimes seem clumsy in their handling of the caesura, abrupt in their sense and rhythm, awkward in their connection of syntactical units within and between lines and insufficiently varied in their rhythmical patterns. His periodic style, extending the sense over many lines and not necessarily concluding it at the end of a line, was a model not only for modern writers using Latin but also for vernacular poets.

In his crusade to raise the standard of vernacular literature and reform English versifying, Ascham makes common cause with earlier writers who had appealed to the example and authority of Virgil and Horace in attacking the prevalent practice of rhyming:

> They wished as Virgil and Horace were not wedded to follow the faults of former fathers . . . but by right imitation of the perfit Grecians had brought poetry to perfitness also in the Latin tongue, that we Englishmen likewise would acknowledge and understand rightfully

35. Smith, G.G. (1904) vol. 1, p. 137.
36. Smith, G.G. (1904) vol. 1, p. 30.

our rude beggerly rhyming brought first into Italy by Goths and Huns, when all good verses and all good learning too were destroyed by them, and after carried into France and Germany, and at last received into England by men of excellent wit indeed, but of small learning and less judgement in that behalf.[37]

In the approving list that follows of those few modern poets who have followed the Greeks and Romans in avoiding rhyme comes the Earl of Surrey, who, in his translations of the second and fourth books of the *Aeneid* (favourite school texts recounting the sack of Troy and the encounter with Dido), used for the first time in English the unrhymed iambic pentameter. The introduction of blank verse, therefore, may reasonably be said to have been prompted by the desire to raise the dignity of the English language in providing a workable English equivalent of the Latin hexameter as perfected by Virgil. The translation is not wholly successful but in the narrative, through the use of enjambment between lines and variation of pauses within lines, Surrey is able to convey something of the rhythm and movement of Virgil's periodic style:

As wrestling winds, out of dispersed whirl
Befight themselves, the west with southern blast,
And gladsome east proud of Aurora's horse;
The woods do whiz; and foamy Nereus
Raging in fury, with three forked mace
From bottom's depth doth welter up the seas;
So came the Greeks.
(*Aeneid* II, 531–7, translating 416–9)[38]

In the speeches there are intimations of rhythmical flexibility and rhetorical power later to be achieved by subsequent dramatists perfecting the medium:

O wretched citizens!
What so great kind of frenzy fretteth you?
Deem ye the Greeks our enemies to be gone?
Or any Greekish gifts can you suppose
Devoid of guile? Is so Ulysses known?
Either the Greeks are in this timber hid;

37. Smith, G.G. (1904) vol. 1, pp. 29–30.
38. Jones, E. (ed.) (1964) *Henry Howard, Earl of Surrey: Poems*, Oxford University Press.

Or this an engine is to annoy our walls,
To view our towers, and overwhelm our town.
Here lurks some craft. Good Trojans! give no trust
Unto this horse; for what so ever it be,
I dread the Greek; yea! when they offer gifts.
                    (*Aeneid* II, 56–66, translating 42–9)

Here it may be noted that the poet who is usually accredited with
the achievement of making blank verse a truly flexible medium
for the stage made an early dramatic adaptation of the encounter
between Aeneas and Dido. In the prologue to *Tamburlaine*,
Marlowe distances himself from 'the jigging veins of rhyming
mother wits',[39] conscious no doubt of his own achievement in
making English resound heroically like his classical models.

The humanist Virgil: Jonson

The deeper significance of Virgil's meaning in the Renaissance is
evident in Jonson's comical satire *The Poetaster* (1601) in which the
Roman poet appears as a character alongside Horace, Maecenas
and Augustus. In an apologetical dialogue to the reader, Jonson
explains that he has endured critical attack for some three years:

    And I at last, unwilling
But weary, I confess, of so much trouble,
Thought I would try if shame could win upon them
And therefore chose Augustus Caesar's times
When wit and arts were at their height in Rome,
To show that Virgil, Horace and the rest
Of those great master-spirits did not want
Detractors, then, or practisers against them.
                                    (98–105)

His particular targets in a personal war are Marston and Dekker,
who figure as Crispinus and Demetrius. They are indicted on the
charge that they have 'most ignorantly foolishly and . . .
maliciously gone about to deprave and calumniate the person and

---

39.   Steane, J.B. (ed.) (1969) *Christopher Marlowe: The Complete Plays*, Penguin
      p. 105.

writings of Quintus Horatius Flaccus here present [as Jonson himself] poet and priest of the muses; . . . taxing him falsely of self love, arrogancy, impudence, railing, filching by translation etc' (V, iii, 224–8; 231–2). Augustus appoints Virgil as judge, and he represents the ideal of the true poet against whom the poetaster (Crispinus) is judged. Before the trial scene he is introduced in conversation with Augustus, who, as the ideal prince, honours the poet for his creative talent and in recognition of the role to be played by poetry in the *civitas*. The poet sits on the right hand of Caesar and recites to him an extract (translated by Jonson) from the fourth book of the *Aeneid*. (There is a tradition that Virgil read parts of his epic in the presence of the emperor.) Before Virgil enters there is an extended eulogy of him put into the mouths of three fellow-poets:

> *Horace.* I judge him of a rectified spirit
>   By many revolutions of discourse
>   (In his bright reason's influence) refined
>   From all the tartarous moods of common men;
>   Bearing the nature and similitude
>   Of a right heavenly body: most severe
>   In fashion, and collection of himself,
>   And then as clear, and confident, as Jove.
> *Gallus.* And yet so chaste and tender is his ear
>   In suffering any syllable to pass
>   That he thinks may become the honoured name
>   Of issue to his so examined self
>   That all the lasting fruits of his full merit
>   In his own poems, he doth still distaste:
>   As if his mind's peace, which he strove to paint
>   Could not with fleshly pencils have her right.
> *Tibullus.* . . . That which he hath writ
>   Is with such judgement laboured and distilled
>   Through all the needful uses of our lives
>   That could a man remember but his lines
>   He should not touch at any serious point
>   But he might breathe his spirit out of him.
> *Horace.* His learning labours not the school-like gloss
>   That most consists in echoing words and terms,
>   And soonest wins a man an empty name:
>   Nor any long or far-fetched circumstance

Wrapped in the curious generalities of arts:
But a direct and analytic sum
Of all the worth and first effects of arts.
And for his poesie, 'tis so rammed with life
That it shall gather strength of life, with being
And live hereafter, more admired, than now.
                (V, i, 100–15; 118–23; 129–38)

In the play the poets are speaking of Virgil the man, but in such a way that the man and the poet are interchangeable and inseparable. Jonson's audience is being instructed (or reminded) of a central humanist proposition: that good art is the product of a good life in which self-examination and knowledge of the world are equally vital. The refinement of language with which Virgil has always been associated is also the expression of a refinement of sensibility and spirit. The judgement in which Virgil was deemed to have excelled is not only that of the disciplined artist but also of the man who knows about life and manners. Virgil is both *arbiter elegantiae* and *arbiter morum*, and this is reflected in his role in the play. After Horace has administered pills to Crispinus which cause him to vomit up his 'crudities' (words actually derived from Marston's plays), Virgil pronounces as his sentence 'a strict and wholesome diet' of good reading with which to refine his style:

> Look, you take
> Each morning of old Cato's principles
> A good draught, next your heart; that walk upon
> Till it be well digested: then come home
> And taste a piece of Terence, suck his phrase
> Instead of licorice; and at any hand,
> Shun Plautus and old Ennius, they are meats
> Too harsh for a weak stomach. Use to read
> (But not without a tutor) the best Greeks: . . .
> You must not hunt for wild outlandish terms
> To stuff out a peculiar dialect;
> But let your matter run before your words . . .
>   (V, i, 536–44; 549–51)

The Greek and Latin references represent the humanists' idea of the reading that might have been the basis of Virgil's own, beginning with the chaste speech of Cato the censor, the very incarnation of the old Roman virtue, whose doctrine *rem tene verba sequentur* ('hold to your matter, the words will follow') underlies the injunction 'let your matter run before your words', which turns up again in Horace's *Art of Poetry*:

> verbaque provisam rem non invita sequentur.
>
> (311)

And, where the matter is provided still,
There words will follow, not against their will.

(Jonson's translation, 443–4)

Style is not to be cultivated as an end in itself but is to be clear and pure. It may seem in all this that Virgil for the most part is being associated with contemporary ideas, but in reality Jonson is giving back to the poet ideas which he above all embodied for the humanists of the Renaissance.

Jonson's idealisation of Virgil is symptomatic of a general humanist tendency that has its origin in the Italian drive towards elegant Latinity. When they desired to purge Latin of what they regarded as its barbarous medieval accretions, the humanists from Petrarch onwards turned to classical authorities, pre-eminently to Cicero for Latin prose and Virgil and Horace for poetry. For Renaissance humanists the beauty of Virgil's art was the practical embodiment of their aspiration to a pure Latinity regarded as reaching its highest manifestation in the *Aeneid*, his last work representing the maturity of his genius to which his pastorals and georgics were by way of prelude and preparation (hence the propriety of treating this fundamental aspect of the classical tradition in a foundation chapter on epic). In Virgil's poetry, as presented in Renaissance editions and taught in schools, was a veritable Art of Poetry embodying classical principles to be found in Aristotle[40] and Horace, and reflected not only in the beauty of the end product but also in what could be divined of the method by which he had achieved his poetic effects and purity of style. Since Latin literature was the basis of the grammar school curriculum (until comparatively recent times) and since every schoolboy (inevitably school*boy*), however little he might know of English literature, which was not taught in school, knew at least a smattering of Virgil, while the more advanced pupils composed their own Latin verses using Virgil as the classical

40. In Aristotle's *Rhetoric* as well as his *Poetics*.

standard (rather as Cicero tended to be the model for Latin prose) his influence is fundamental, pervasive and incalculable.

First of all let us consider poetic method. In Jonson's commonplace book, *Discoveries*,[41] *ingenium* the 'goodness of natural wit' (2987) is to be disciplined by exercise and imitation, in description of which Jonson again uses the digestive metaphor that occurs throughout *The Poetaster*:

> The third requisite in our poet [after *ingenium* and *exercitatio*] or maker is imitation, to be able to convert the substance, or riches of another poet, to his own use. To make choice of one excellent man above the rest, and so to follow him, as the copy may be mistaken for the principal. Not, as a creature that swallows what it takes in, crude, raw or indigested; but that feeds with an appetite, and hath a stomach to concoct, divide and turn all into nourishment. Not to imitate servilely, as Horace saith, and catch at vices, for virtue: but, to draw forth out of the best and choicest flowers with the bee, and turn all into honey, work it into one relish and savour: make our imitation sweet: observe how the best writers have imitated, and follow them. How Virgil and Statius have imitated Homer; how Horace, Archilochus; how Alcaeus and the other lyrics: and so of the rest.
>
> (3056–74)

Imitation is to be creative not servile:

> For being a poet, thou mayst feign, create
> Not care, as thou wouldst faithfully translate
> To render word for word, nor with thy sleight
> Of imitation, leap into a strait
> From whence thy modesty or poem's law
> Forbids thee forth again thy foot to draw.
> (*The Art of Poetry*, 189–94)

So Jonson translated the famous passage in Horace's *Art of Poetry* (used as an epigraph to this book) to which he alludes in *Discoveries*. John Oldham has an easier version published in 1683:

> Be not too nice the author's words to trace,
> But vary all with a fresh air and grace;

---

41. Conveniently available with line numbers in Parfitt, G. (1975) pp. 374–458. All subsequent references are to this edition which also has Jonson's translation of Horace's *Art of Poetry*.

Nor such strict rules of imitation choose,
Which you must still be tied to follow close.[42]

(226–9)

In *The Poetaster*, where one of the charges against him was filching by translation and where in addition to translating Virgil directly he had also dramatised a whole satire of Horace (I, 9 in which the Roman poet encounters the bore)[43] Jonson's Virgil pronounces:

And for his true use of translating men
It still hath been a work of as much palm
In clearest judgement, as t'invent or make.

The authority and decorum of this judgement from Virgil are clear when we recall that, according to the ancient lives, Virgil had been accused of filching from Homer, and that a Roman grammarian had compiled a book of his 'thefts'. Virgil is reported to have replied that it was easier to steal Hercules' club than to steal one of Homer's verses.[44]

The practice of juxtaposing passages from Virgil and Homer began in Roman times. The fifth-century grammarian Macrobius has over 200 such juxtapositions in his *Saturnalia*.[45] Renaissance commentators had eagerly recorded Virgil's sources, chiefly Homeric, in their editions of the poet, noting both larger debts such as the Aristotelian form of the poem of which the first half, when Aeneas is shipwrecked and recounts his wanderings, is Odyssean and of which the second half, in which he fights his battles and kills Turnus (as Achilles had killed Hector), is Iliadic, and the use of the divine machinery of gods and goddesses; and also noting specific motifs such as invocation of the muse, the epic catalogue, the description of the shield, the journey to Hades and the funeral games in honour of dead heroes; and finally illustrating Virgil's debt to Homer in his epic style (affecting one in three lines of the poem) in the use of formulaic language, formal epithets and the extended simile. One such commentator, J.C. Scaliger, made

42. Brooks, H.F. (ed.) (1987) *The Poems of John Oldham*, Oxford University Press, p. 97.
43. Jonson's adaptation is discussed below on pp. 343ff.
44. See Brummer, J. (ed.) (1912) *Vitae Vergilii*, Teubner, Leipzig.
45. Willis, J. (ed.) (1963) *Macrobii Saturnalia*, Teubner, Leipzig; Davies, P.V. (translator) (1969) *The Saturnalia*, Columbia University Press, London and New York.

the comparison with the highly partisan aim of showing that in Virgil the raw material of Homer had been refined and improved.[46] For Scaliger, Homer is a primitive child of invention, Virgil the artist of mature judgement. A juster version of what became a Renaissance commonplace is Dryden's application of the terms of the comparison to Jonson himself and Shakespeare: 'If I would compare him with Shakespeare, I must acknowledge him the more correct poet, but Shakespeare the greater wit. Shakespeare was the Homer or father of our dramatic poets; Jonson was the Virgil, the pattern of elaborate writing.'[47]

When he composed, the Homeric bard had behind him a continuous oral tradition which had been refined over several centuries; he was the heir of the blind bard in the *Odyssey* who sings from memory with unpremeditated art and immediate inspiration as the god prompted (*Odyssey* VIII, 44–5). For the allusive and literary Virgil, the writing of heroic poetry and the evocation of a mythical world involved a great labour of reconstruction from secondary sources, the chief of which was Homer. Nor did he inherit in the Latin language a style fashioned and refined for his purposes. It is little wonder that he is the type of poet who triumphs through exercise of his craft: 'It is said of the incomparable Virgil that he brought forth his verses like a bear and after formed them with licking. Scaliger the father writes it of him, that he made a quantity of verses in the morning which afore night he reduced to a less number' (*Discoveries*, 3034–9, 'Exercitatio'). Elaborate writing required what Horace in his *Art of Poetry* called *limae labor* (291) 'the labour of the file'.

It is therefore something of a disappointment that Jonson, though giving us an idea in *The Poetaster* of the central place of Virgil in humanist poetics, does not in his own language, when actually translating Virgil, succeed in capturing the qualities that made Virgil's style an ideal to be admired and emulated. For he did not adopt the method of Horace that he recommends in his

---

46. Scaliger, J.C. (1561) *Poetics Libri Septem*, Lyons Liber V, 'Criticus'. There is a facsimile reprint published by Frommann, Stuttgart (1964). See also Shepherd, S. (1961) 'Scaliger on Homer and Virgil: A Study in Literary Prejudice', *Emerita* **29**: 313–40.
47. *Of Dramatic Poesy: An Essay* (1668) in Watson, G. (ed.) (1962) *Dryden: Of Dramatic Poesy and Other Critical Essays*, Everyman's Library, 2 vols, J.M. Dent, vol. 1, p. 70.

Discoveries for imitation in his formal translation, confining himself too much to servile rendering of the sense word for word. For on approximation of the stylistic ideal embodied in Virgil we must look elsewhere.

Virgil and Dryden

Virgil continued to represent a poetic ideal throughout the seventeenth century. Dryden, for example, rejected the conceited metaphysical style of his youth in favour of a style that aspired to emulate classical values in English.

> I drew my definition of poetical wit from my particular observation of him; for propriety of thoughts and words are only to be found in him, and where they are proper they will be delightful. . . . This exact propriety of Virgil I particularly regarded as a great part of his character. . . . And indeed what I have already written in justification or praise of Virgil is against myself for presuming to copy in my coarse English the thoughts and expression of this inimitable poet, who flourished in an age when his language was brought to the last perfection for which it was chiefly owing to him and to Horace . . . Spenser and Milton are the nearest in English to Virgil and Horace in the Latin; and I have endeavoured to form my style by imitating their masters.[48]

This imitation involved emulation of metrical harmony, elegance of expression and judicious management of the rhetorical figures. In the art of Virgil, of course, all these elements are naturally compounded together, but it will be useful to deal first with his use of the figures, since what has previously been said of his metrical refinement differentiates Virgil from those who came before him, while what Dryden has to say about his use of the figures serves to suggest ways in which he differs from other Roman poets who followed him.

Like all ancient poets Virgil is a rhetorical poet in that he makes use of the various figures of rhetoric which can be found, for example, in any of the Elizabethan rhetorical handbooks.[49] The ancient lives record that he studied rhetoric at Rome under the

48. 'Preface to *Sylvae*' (1685) in Watson, G. (1962) vol. 2, p. 22.
49. As included in Smith, G.G. (1904).

best teachers of the day. Training in rhetoric, the art of expressing oneself most effectively, was basic in all Roman education. The civic ideal of Cato the censor in early Rome had been the *vir bonus dicendi peritus* 'the good man skilled in speaking' who devoted his oratory to the service of the *senatus populusque Romanus*. For Cicero, the whole point of a liberal education in the humanities is to produce a philosophic orator. The same can be said of Quintilian.[50] Renaissance commentaries upon Virgil's poems drew attention to rhetorical devices which might relate to word order, euphony or rhythm (figures of sound) or to non-literal ways of using language such as metaphor, metonymy and hyperbole (figures of sense and meaning). Virgil was always praised for what Dryden calls his 'judicious management' of these figures. In the preface to the *Sylvae* (1685), where he published his first translations of Virgil, he finds himself guilty of a conceit in one line of his translation that he considers typical of Ovid but beneath the dignity of Virgil:

> When Lausus died, I was already slain.
> This appears pretty enough at first sight, but I am convinced for many reasons that the expression is too bold; that Virgil would not have said it, though Ovid would.[51]

Characterising Virgil in the same preface, he had declared:

> He is everywhere above conceits of epigrammatic wit and gross hyperboles: he maintains majesty in the midst of plainness, he shines but glares not and is stately without ambition which is the vice of Lucan.[52]

The vice of Lucan, author of the historical epic on the civil wars of Pompey and Caesar, the *Pharsalia*, written after Virgil in the reign of Nero, is overuse of his favourite figure of hyperbole as he strives to keep his style at a constant pitch of elevation. An example from the translation of the first book made by the young Christopher Marlowe may illustrate Dryden's point:

> Romans, what madness, what huge lust of war
> Hath made barbarians drunk with Latin blood?

50. See Cicero's *Orator* and Quintilian's *Institutio Oratoria*, 'The Education of an Orator'.
51. 'Preface to *Sylvae*' (1685) in Watson, G. (1962) vol. 2, p. 24.
52. Watson, G. (1962) vol. 2, p. 22.

Now Babylon (proud through our spoil) should stoop,
While slaughtered Crassus' ghost walks unrevenged,
Will ye wage war, for which you shall not triumph?
Aye me, O what a world of land and sea
Might they have won whom civil broils have slain! . . .
That now the walls of houses half reared totter,
That rampires fallen down, huge heaps of stone
Lie in our towns, that houses are abandoned
And few live that behold their ancient seats,
Italy many years hath lain untilled
And choked with thorns, that greedy earth wants hinds,
Fierce Pyrrhus, neither thou nor Hannibal
Art cause; no foreign foe could so afflict us;
These plagues arise from wreak of civil power.

(8–14; 24–32)[53]

Marlowe continued to be fond of this hyperbolic style, and what Jonson called 'his mighty line'[54] owes as much to the cruder Roman poet as it does to Virgil whose more refined sensibility eschewed what Dryden well calls 'ambition'.

Even more hyperbolic and heated in style is Aeneas' speech to Dido, especially where he speaks of Priam's slaughter, as recalled by the overwrought Hamlet in conversation with the players:

The rugged Pyrrhus, he whose sable arms,
Black as his purpose, did the night resemble
When he lay couched in the ominous horse,
Hath now this dread and black complexion smeared
With heraldry more dismal; head to foot
He is now total gules, horridly tricked
With blood of fathers, mothers, daughters, sons,
Baked and impasted with the parching streets,
That lend a tyrannous and damned light
To their lord's murder. Roasted in wrath and fire,
And thus o'ersized with coagulate gore,
With eyes like carbuncles, the hellish Pyrrhus
Old grandsire Priam seeks.[55]

(II, ii, 446–58)

53. Orgel, S. (ed.) (1971) *Christopher Marlowe: The Complete Poems and Translations*, Penguin, p. 189.
54. 'To the Memory of My Beloved, the Author Mr William Shakespeare', 30.
55. Quotations from Shakespeare are from Alexander, P. (ed.) (1951) *William Shakespeare: The Complete Works*, Collins.

Though not a translation, the speech is ultimately derived from Aeneas' account of the death of Priam at the sword of Pyrrhus, the son of Achilles, in the second book of the *Aeneid*. The contrasting refinement and restraint of Virgil's majestic heroic style may be suggested in the energetic rendering of Pyrrhus' entrance by Dryden:

> Before the gate stood Pyrrhus, threat'ning loud,
> With glittering arms conspicuous in the crowd.
> So shines, renewed in youth, the crested snake,
> Who slept the winter in a thorny brake,
> And, casting off his slough when spring returns,
> Now looks aloft, and with new glory burns;
> Restored with pois'nous herbs, his ardent sides
> Reflect the sun; and raised on spires he rides;
> High o'er the grass, hissing he rolls along,
> And brandishes by fits his forky tongue.
>
> (II, 639–48, translating 469–75)

Virgil's refinement is most obviously seen in his handling of the hexameter, and on this subject and on his choice of words Dryden is eloquent indeed.

> Virgil . . . is everywhere elegant, sweet and flowing in his hexameters. His words are not only chosen but the place in which he ranks them for the sound . . . I cannot boast that I have been thus exact in my verses but I have endeavoured to follow the example of my master and am the first Englishman perhaps who made it his design to copy him in his numbers, his choice of words, and his placing of them for sound . . . we must not only choose words for elegance, but for sound to perform which a mastery in the language is required; a poet must have a magazine of words and have the art to manage his few vowels to the best advantage, that they may go further. He must also know the nature of the vowels which are more sonorous and which more soft and sweet and so dispose them as his present occasions require; all which, and a thousand secrets of versification beside, he may learn from Virgil . . ..[56]

It might be expected that as a disciple of Virgil Dryden would have favoured blank verse and dispensed with rhyme, which was generally regarded by the humanists as a barbarous invention

---

56. 'The Dedication of the *Aeneis*' (1697) in Watson, G. (1962) vol. 2, pp. 234–5.

since it was not used in antiquity. In his *Essay on Translated Verse*
(1684) the Earl of Roscommon hopes for a time when the British
Muse might appear without rhyme in true 'Roman majesty';[57] in
the second edition in the following year he actually added an
imitation of the war in heaven from the sixth book of *Paradise
Lost*, written in blank verse, though the Earl wrote the rest of the
Essay in heroic couplets. As if in answer to Roscommon, and
perhaps to Milton himself, who in his preface to *Paradise Lost*
(1667) had severely castigated the use of rhyme, Dryden offers
what seems like a vigorous defence:

> For conquering Rome
> With Grecian spoils brought Grecian numbers home,
> Enriched by those Athenian muses more
> Than all the vanquished world could yield before.
> Till barb'rous nations and more barb'rous times
> Debased the majesty of verse to rhymes.
> Those rude at first: a kind of hobbling prose
> That limped along and tinckled in the close.
> But Italy reviving from the trance
> Of Vandal, Goth and monkish ignorance
> With pauses, cadence and well-vowelled words
> And all the graces a good ear affords
> Made rhyme an art . . .
> ('To the Earl of Roscommon on his Excellent Essay
> on Translated Verse', 7–19)[58]

Taken together, what Dryden has to say of Virgil's versification
and of the art of rhyme shows how the use of rhyme did not itself
preclude the influence of the classical model. Indeed it can be no
accident that the two poets recognised by later Augustans as
precursors in their drive towards refinement of expression and
perfection of form, John Denham and Edmund Waller, both
translated substantial portions of Virgil's *Aeneid*, also into heroic
couplets.

57. Dillon, Wentworth [The Earl of Roscommon] (1971) *An Essay on Translated
Verse* (1685) and *Horace's Art of Poetry Made English* (1684) Scholar Press,
Menston, p. 26. All quotations from Roscommon are made from this
reprint. There are no line numbers. Though bound together, the two works
are paginated separately.
58. In the same poem Dryden goes on to describe rhyme as 'At best a pleasing
sound and fair barbarity' (23). Printed in Watson, G. (1962) vol. 2,
pp. 14–17.

What Dryden has to say about Virgil's versification is inextricably bound up with what he has to say about sound and diction:

> There is an inimitable grace in Virgil's words, and in them principally consists that beauty which gives so inexpressible a pleasure to him who best understands their force. . . . For Virgil above all poets had a stock which I may call almost inexhaustible of figurative elegant and sounding words. . . . There is a beauty of sound, as Segrais has observed, in some Latin words which is wholly lost in any modern language. He instances in that *mollis amaracus* in which Venus lays Cupid in the *First Aeneid*. If I should translate it *sweet marjoram* as the word signifies, the reader would think I had mistaken Virgil, for those village words, as I may call them, give us a mean idea of the thing, but the sound of the Latin is so much more pleasing by the just mixture of vowels with consonants, that it raises our fancies to conceive somewhat more noble than a common herb, and to spread roses under him and strew lilies over him, a bed not unworthy the grandson of a goddess.[59]

In his translation, Dryden dispensed with sweet marjoram altogether, substituting in its stead the more dignified myrtle.

> The goddess then to young Ascanius flies,
> And in a pleasing slumber seals his eyes;
> Lulled in her lap, amidst a train of Loves,
> She gently bears him to her blissful groves;
> Then with a wreath of myrtle crowns his head,
> And softly lays him on a flow'ry bed.
>   (I, 969–74, translating 691–4)

In the lulling rhythms and sweet music of this passage is a English equivalent of the sonorous beauty and sweet harmony of numbers that Dryden so admired in the original.

But Virgil is admired not only for his fluent harmony but also for his great metrical variety and for the propriety with which he can adapt his numbers to the differing requirements of his subject matter:

> His verse is everywhere sounding the very thing in your ears whose sense it bears; yet the numbers are perpetually varied to increase the delight of the reader, so that the same sounds are never repeated twice

59. 'Preface to *Sylvae*' (1685) and 'The Dedication of the *Aeneis*' (1697) in Watson, G. (1962) vol. 2, pp. 24, 250, 251.

together . . . though he is smooth where smoothness is required, yet he is so far from affecting it, that he seems rather to disdain it.[60]

When, for example, Aeneas comes upon the Titan Salmoneus in Hades, the musical effects and metrical management are altogether different:

> Salmoneus suff'ring cruel pains, I found,
> For emulating Jove; the rattling sound
> Of mimic thunder, and the glitt'ring blaze
> Of pointed lightnings and their forky rays.
> Through Elis and through Grecian towns he flew
> Th' audacious wretch four fiery coursers drew:
> He waved a torch aloft, and, madly vain,
> Sought godlike worship from a servile train.
> Ambitious fool, with horny hoofs to pass
> O'er hollow arches of resounding brass;
> To rival thunder in its rapid course
> And imitate inimitable force.
> But he, the king of heaven, obscure on high
> Bared his red arm, and launching from the sky
> His writhen bolt, not shaking empty smoke,
> Down to the deep abyss the flaming felon strook.
>
> (VI, 788–803)

Here it may be appropriate to cite the verdict of Dr Johnson, who shared Dryden's classical values, upon his contribution to English poetry: 'What was said of Rome adorned by Augustus may be applied by easy metaphor to English poetry embellished by Dryden . . . "He found it brick and left it marble." '[61] It is perhaps superfluous to add that the polish and refinement of Virgilian art is not simply the cultivation of smoothness and fluency for its own sake. Indeed these passages bring to mind Pope's account of Dryden's versification:

> Wit grew polite and numbers learned to flow;
> Waller was smooth, but Dryden taught to join
> The varying verse, the full resounding line,
> The long majestic march and energy divine.[62]

60. 'Preface to *Sylvae*' (1685) in Watson, G. (1962) vol. 2, pp. 21–2.
61. 'Dryden' in Hill, G.B. (ed.) (1905) *Lives of English Poets by Samuel Johnson*, 3 vols, Oxford University Press, vol. 1, p. 469.
62. 'The First Epistle of the Second Book of Horace Imitated' ['To Augustus'] 266–6.

And it was by virtue of this energy that Walter Scott believed Dryden's Virgil to be superior to all others: 'It is in this art of communicating the ancient poet's ideas with force and energy equal to his own that Dryden has so completely exceeded all who have gone before, and all who have succeeded him.'[63] Dryden's own hope was that he had captured 'the clearness, the purity, the easiness and the magnificence of his style'.[64] And if this claim is to be allowed, then it is clear that for the success of his poetry in English, Dryden needed all the artistic judgement for which Virgil is famous in the Latin.

In Dryden's poetry is the culmination of that linguistic phase which had begun in the early Renaissance wherein the poetic stock was gradually increased and enriched by commerce with the ancients. Dryden's defence of his own contribution makes us realise what English poetry at its most basic level owes to the classics in general and to those poets who, like himself, had the judgement and capacity to naturalise the foreign to enrich the native:

I will not excuse but justify myself for one pretended crime with which I am liable to be charged by false critics not only in this translation but in many of my original poems, that I latinise too much. 'Tis true that when I find an English word significant and sounding I neither borrow from the Latin or any other language, but when I want at home, I must seek abroad. If sounding words are not of our growth and manufacture, who shall hinder me to import them from a foreign country? I trade with both the living and the dead for the enrichment of our native language. We have enough in England to supply our necessity but if we will have things of magnificence and splendour we must get them by commerce. Poetry requires ornament, and that is not to be had from our old Teuton monosyllables; therefore if I find any elegant word in a classic author I propose it to be naturalised by using it myself . . . . A poet must first be certain that the word he would introduce is beautiful in the Latin and is to consider in the next place whether it will agree with English idiom . . . let him use this licence sparingly for if too many foreign words are poured in upon us, it looks as if they were designed not to assist the natives but to conquer them.[65]

63. Scott, W., Saintsbury, G. (eds) (1882–93) *The Works of John Dryden*, 18 vols, Paterson, Edinburgh, vol. 1, p. 431.
64. 'The Dedication of the *Aeneis*' (1697) in Watson, G. (1962) vol. 2, p. 247.
65. 'The Dedication of the *Aeneis*' (1697) in Watson, G. (1962) vol. 2, p. 252.

It is a tribute to Dryden's judgement that his Latinisms rarely
stand out (unlike those of Chapman who had neither Dryden's
judgement nor his fondness for Virgil) as so many of them have
become part of what we regard as our native tradition, so that, to
a very different poet two hundred years later, in Dryden could be
seen 'the native thew and sinew of the English language'.[66]
    In his translation of Virgil, Dryden sought to repay a debt that
he had incurred when he first began to write his laureate poems,
such as *Astraea Redux* where Charles II is the new Augustus:

> O happy age, O times like those alone,
> By fate reserved for great Augustus' throne,
> When the joint growth of arms and arts foreshew
> The world a monarch and that monarch you.
>
> (320–3)

or *Annus Mirabilis* of which he declared: 'Virgil . . . has been my
master in the poem: I have followed him everywhere . . . my
images are many of them copied from him and the rest are
imitations of him. My expressions also are as near as the idioms of
the two languages would admit of in translation.'[67] Here he first
defends the practice of introducing into poetry words 'which I
have innovated . . . upon his Latin', appealing to the authority of
Horace:

> et nova fictaque nuper habebunt verba fidem, si
> Graeco fonte cadent parce detorta.
>
> (*Art of Poetry*, 52–3)

> [But he that hopes to have new words allowed,
> Must so derive them from the Grecian spring,
> As they may seem to flow without constraint.
>
> (Roscommon)]

The inference is exceeding plain; for if a Roman poet might have
liberty to coin a word, supposing only that it was derived from the
Greek, was put into the Latin termination, and that he used this liberty

---

66. The words of Gerard Manley Hopkins: see Abbott, C.C. (ed.) (1935) *The
    Letters of Gerard Manley Hopkins to Robert Bridges*, Oxford University Press,
    Letter CLV, 6 Nov. (1887) pp. 265–6.
67. Watson, G. (1962) vol. 1, p. 100.

but seldom, and with modesty; how much more justly may I challenge that privilege to do it with the same prerequisites from the best and most judicious of Latin writers?[68]

In context, Horace is defending contemporary Augustan practice (he goes on to mention Virgil specifically in the next sentence) against conservative Roman opinion that deplored innovation. For Renaissance readers the Horatian doctrine of poetic diction insisting that in the general cultural flux the only authority is usage (*Art of Poetry*, 44–72) served as a reminder that Augustan purity of diction was not achieved by attempting to preserve traditional 'classical' expression but by the individual poet's mixing of ancient with modern and native with foreign elements in response to the current speech of the time. In the preface to *Annus Mirabilis*, the poetry of Virgil, reinforced by Horatian precept, is the authority to sanction vernacular imitation, the actual model from which the English poet works and the standard by which the end product is to be judged, 'at once the source, and end, and test of art'.[69]

Virgil set an ideal standard for poets who like Dryden, following Spenser and Milton, believed that poetry requires ornament and in its highest manifestation is a disciplined art whose end is not fully achieved without the effect of beauty:

What I have done . . . will be judged in after ages and possibly in the present to be no dishonour to my native country whose language and poetry would be more esteemed abroad if they were better understood. Somewhat (give me leave to say) I have added to both of them in the choice of words and harmony of numbers which were wanting (especially the last) in all our poets even in those who being endued with genius yet have not cultivated their mother tongue with sufficient care, or relying on the beauty of their thoughts, have judged ornament of words and sweetness of sound unnecessary.

('Postscript to the reader')[70]

68. Watson, G. (1962) vol. 1, p. 101.
69. Pope, *An Essay on Criticism*, 73, said of Nature. At line 135, 'Nature and Homer were, he found, the same', he being Virgil.
70. Watson, G. (1962) vol. 2, p. 258.

Chapter 2

Drama

Tragedy

omne genus scripti gravitate Tragoedia vincit.
(Ovid, *Tristia* II, 381)

(Tragedy outdoes every other kind of writing in its seriousness.)

Tragedy seems to have been an Athenian invention (little is recorded of drama in other Greek states), coming into being in the latter part of the sixth century at a time when the Athenian state was experiencing changes in the old aristocratic order that were to lead eventually to the establishment of radical democracy in the age of Pericles in the mid fifth century. The earliest extant tragedy, the *Persians* of Aeschylus, concerns an event without which that transformation, which made the fullest development of tragedy possible, could not have taken place: the triumph of Greece in the Persian wars of the 490s and 480s. All the remaining thirty-one extant plays were written in the period of Athenian greatness and power that extended from the Persian wars to the defeat of Athens by Sparta after the long Peloponnesian war in 404 BC.

Little is known about the origins or even about the immediate antecedents of tragedy. The word means 'goatsong', but the form had long lost any connection it may have had with rituals involving goats by the classical period. In the beginning, we may believe, the choral element was dominant. A major advance is associated with the name of Thespis the actor/dramatist who separated himself from the singing and dancing chorus to converse with the chorus leader. Aristotle accredits Aeschylus with reducing the part of the chorus and with the introduction of a second actor, and accredits Sophocles with the introduction of a third actor (*Poetics* IV, 16).

The plays were performed at the annual festival of the god Dionysus (held in March) and known as Great Dionysia. By the time of its earliest extant play, the city Dionysia consisted of a day's procession followed by a contest in dithyrambic odes involving ten choruses, a day given over to comedy (five in number) and then three days of tragedies presented on a competitive basis. On each day, one playwright presented three tragic plays which might be linked like the three plays that make up the Oresteian trilogy, but usually were not related in their plot (though it is difficult to believe that they did not form some kind of sequence in mood or theme). These were followed by something completely different: a grotesque satyr–play, a kind of bawdy phallic romp which doubtless had the function and certainly had the effect of providing comic relief at the end of the day. On the next day, judges elected by lot gave their verdict.

The dramatic festival was the responsibility of the civil authorities who bore some of the expenses (including the cost of entry for citizens) while appointing from the wealthiest citizens a number of *choregoi* who were required to pay for the equipping and training of a chorus. The role of the *choregos* like that of the modern producer was largely financial; the playwright in addition to writing the play and providing music for the chorus was responsible for the direction and for the choreography. The dramatist had remarkable freedom and was not subject to any priestly control. If Greek drama developed from some kind of religious ritual, it quickly freed itself from the restriction implied in the word ritual, so that ritualistic is not a word to describe classical tragedy.

However, the form is stylised, and the style is determined by the production of the plays for the city festival. They were performed in the open air in a vast amphitheatre estimated to have held about 14,000 people. The scale of the proceedings precluded the development of naturalistic techniques in writing, acting or direction. Actors wore masks, and the principal figures were later distinguished by special buskins or *cothornoi*. All plays consist of a number of episodes or scenes involving the principal characters written in the iambic trimeter divided by choral interludes called *stasima* written in a variety of metrical forms. The division of the choral odes into *strophe* (turn) *antistrophe* (counter-turn) and *epode* (after-song) probably reflects the physical movement of the chorus through the *orchestra*, the large dancing circle of about 60 feet in diameter. The complicated choral metres may be related to particular steps. In Aeschylus, the chorus (ten in number) amounts to a third of the play, and in the third part of the *Oresteia*, the chorus of Furies, the Eumenides, who give their name to the play, is central to the action itself. Sophocles and Euripides (who have a chorus of fifteen) reduced the proportional part of the chorus, though in particular plays it might still play a special role in the action as in the case of Euripides' *Bacchae*, where the chorus of Bacchanals bear witness to and define the nature and benefits of the Dionysiac experience. More commonly the chorus is detached from the main action involving the heroic figures of myth, but in comment and response is usually fully integrated into the emotional and thematic pattern of the play as a whole. The need to integrate the chorus with the main action, and the comparative brevity of a Greek play when compared to modern drama (approximately 1,500 lines in length including the chorus) determined by the festival production of four plays in one day, precluded the development of complicated plots involving more than one strand of action or variety of scenes (there is a scene change from Delphi to Athens in the *Eumenides* but this is rare) or complicated time sequences. Concentration of effect and a concern for unity of design are principles endemic in Greek art from Homer onwards. In drama, simplicity and economy were further encouraged by limitations of time and form outside the individual playwright's control.

For the Renaissance, classical tragedy meant not Aeschylus, Sophocles or Euripides, but the Roman reworking of the Greek myths in the nine plays of Seneca, otherwise known as a Stoic philosopher and political adviser to the emperor Nero.

Tragedy was not a state institution and did not have the civic importance at Rome that it had enjoyed in Athens. The earliest Roman tragedies had in fact been translations and adaptations of Greek originals. They seem to have been performed during the Games held in the circus at which a major attraction had been gladiatorial spectacles. The latter were an important part of Roman life from the beginning and continued to be so; in Seneca's time, Nero is accredited with devising a new entertainment whereby Christians were thrown to the lions. It was not until 55 BC that there was a permanent theatre in Rome. Some hostility to drama is reflected in strict Roman laws prohibiting the representation of Roman families on stage, which probably accounts for the persistent tendency in all Roman drama to keep to Greek subject matter. Nor did the acting profession always enjoy at Rome the high esteem it had in Greece, where there had been prizes for acting as well as for the playwrights. The early tragedians Accius and Pacuvius, of whom only fragments survive, were held in high esteem by later writers like Cicero and Quintilian, but the form seems subsequently to have attracted no inspired practitioners. The marked emphasis in Horace's *Art of Poetry* upon drama in general and tragedy in particular has sometimes been regarded as indicative of the hope of an Augustan revival. The two Augustan tragedies of which anything is known, Ovid's *Medea* and Pollio's *Thyestes*, have not survived. Like these Roman adaptors, Seneca keeps close to the original Greek form and retains the chorus, although his interludes often have little immediate connection with what is happening in the main action. His subjects overlap with those of the Greek dramatists, making possible a comparison with each.

Seneca and Aeschylus: *Agamemnon*

The *Agamemnon* of Aeschylus, unlike that of Seneca, is the first part of a trilogy involving two generations of the house of Atreus locked in a blood feud of crime and counter-crime that is only resolved at the end of the third play with the acquittal of Orestes by the judgement of Athene in a trial on the hill of Ares. Here he is prosecuted by the Furies seeking vengeance for matricide and defended by Apollo who, through his oracle, had ordered the son to kill his mother Clytemnestra in retribution for her killing of her husband Agamemnon, father of Orestes. In the Aeschylean *Agamemnon*, the opening chorus sets the scene by relating Agamemnon's sacrifice of his daughter Iphigeneia demanded by the goddess Artemis at Aulis before she would grant favourable winds to the fleet bound for Troy. It is this sacrifice that motivates Clytemnestra who has taken Aegisthus, Agamemnon's cousin, as her paramour. She is a character of strong will who acts without hesitation despatching her husband as soon as he has returned from Troy by throwing a net over him at a welcoming banquet and stabbing him repeatedly. She never doubts the justice of her act.

The trilogy has both political and religious dimensions, and these are not easily separable. In the midst of their first song, the chorus of the *Agamemnon* invokes Zeus 'whoever he is' (160), he who has overthrown Cronos and the old order and he who has ordained that through suffering comes wisdom and knowledge *pathei mathos* (177). In the victory of the Olympian gods of the upper world, Apollo and Athene, together with the mitigation of the older Furies (deities from the nether world) which is attributed to the unseen workings of Zeus, there is a clear symbolic force. The trilogy ends with a celebration of Athens, and the court scene on the Athenian Areopagus is clearly designed to represent what was historically the solution to the old tribal system of justice through blood-feud in the laws and institutions of the developed *polis*.

The poet of metropolitan Rome is not concerned with this larger religious and political perspective. In the single play we are left to contemplate the appalling crimes of the house of Atreus without the consolation of any ameliorating social or political consequences. The issue becomes more straightforwardly one of revenge, a favourite Senecan theme. Seneca shifts the focus onto Aegisthus, the ghost of whose father, Thyestes, in a prologue to the action, reminds us of a fact not mentioned by Aeschylus: that Aegisthus was the product of an incestuous union of Thyestes with his daughter. As a result of this Thyestes had been told by an oracle that he would avenge himself upon his brother Atreus (Agamemnon's father) for the 'Thyestean feast' served up by Atreus, in which Thyestes had unwittingly eaten the flesh of his own sons. As the figure of Clytemnestra might be regarded as a distant literary ancestor of Lady Macbeth, so the ghost of Thyestes might put us in mind of the ghost of Hamlet's father, with this difference: that Thyestes comes both burdened with the consciousness of his own crimes and eagerly anticipating the prospect of more to come:

Now mischief marcheth on a pace, now falsehood doth appear,
Now butcher's slaughter doth approach, and murther draweth near.[1]

(II, 103, translating 44–5)

The question that the ghost puts to Aegisthus might have
provided the basis of a great play:

Fie, what doth shame abash thee so, and cause thy courage quail?
Why doubts thy right hand what to do? to smite why doth it fail?
What he forecasting might suspect, why shouldst thou take advice?
Why frettest thou, demanding if thou may it enterprise?

(II, 103, translating 49–52)

The protagonists like Hamlet do hesitate, but their hesitation is
prompted not by moral scruples about homicide but more by
considerations of expediency and their personal safety; Clytemnestra is not the single-minded embodiment of will and resolution
that she is for Aeschylus, but a figure who recognises that she has
fallen from grace and is in a tight spot. Her first thoughts are that
it is too late to turn back: *per scelera semper sceleribus tutum est iter*
(116): 'The safest path to mischief is by mischief open still' (II,
106). This line was one of Seneca's most famous;[2] it appears, for
example (in Latin) in a central soliloquy spoken by Hieronymo in
The Spanish Tragedy (III, xiii, 6). The feature of Seneca's style that
it exemplifies was much imitated. By 1589 Thomas Nashe
ridiculed the habit:

English Seneca read by candlelight yields many good sentences, as
'Blood is a beggar' and so forth; and if you entreat him fair in a frosty
morning, he will afford you whole *Hamlets*, I should say handfuls of
tragical speeches . . .. Seneca, let blood line by line and page by page,
at length must needs die to our stage.[3]

---

1. Whibley, C. (ed.) (1927) *Seneca: His Tenne Tragedies translated into English edited
by Thomas Newton anno (1581)* with an introduction by T.S. Eliot, 2 vols, The
Tudor Translations: second series XI–XII, Constable, London; Knopt, New
York. The reference is to volume and page number; no line numbers are
given. The text in this edition has not been modernised.
2. See Cunliffe, J.W. (1893) *The Influence of Seneca on Elizabethan Tragedy*,
Macmillan, esp. Appendix I, p. 127. Knowledge of Seneca was not necessarily
direct but may have come through florilegia or collections of sententiae: see
Hunter, G.K. (1967) 'Seneca and the Elizabethans: a case-study in 'influence'',
Shakespeare Survey **20**, pp. 17–26.
3. From the preface 'To the Gentleman Students of both Universities' prefixed to
Robert Greene's *Menaphon*, 1589 in Smith, G.G. (1904) vol. 1, p. 312.

This *sententia* of Clytemnestra, however, could never have been uttered by her Aeschylean counterpart who regards her deed not as a crime but as an entirely justifiable act of retribution which is supported by Zeus. A further diminution of her heroic status occurs when she is seen to be merely a feeble stereotype:

> Now put in practice, seek about, search out and learn to find
> The wily trains, and crafty guiles of wicked womankind:
> What any devilish traiterous dame durst do in working woe,
> Or any wounded in her wits by shot of Cupid's bow.
>
> (II, 106, translating 116–20)

In Aeschylus she acts 'with the heart and soul of a man' (*Agamemnon*, 351). To her nurse who urges restraint, the Senecan Clytemnestra confesses that she is borne upon a tide of conflicting emotions, and to Aegisthus she even admits to pangs of conjugal love at the prospect of the approaching Agamemnon. Aegisthus who has conquered his own hesitations persuades her to the deed.

The focus then switches after the second act to the returning Greeks with the messenger's long account of their shipwreck on the return journey from Troy and of the heroic death of Ajax – Agamemnon is only on stage briefly and there is nothing to match the famous scene in Aeschylus where Clytemnestra masters Agamemnon psychologically in tempting him to walk upon the purple carpet into the palace. We experience the murder by way of the prophecy of Cassandra, a daughter of Priam allotted to Agamemnon in the distribution of spoils. Clytemnestra's daughter Electra then makes provision for the escape of her younger brother Orestes. In the final scene Clytemnestra threatens Electra with immediate death. Aegisthus enters and decrees imprisonment for Electra. Clytemnestra then seals the fate of Cassandra who has the last prophetic word: 'The frenzy fits of fury fell on you shall also light' (II, 141).

The Elizabethan translator evidently felt the ending to be somewhat abrupt, and added a seventy-line epilogue in which the Greek messenger first asks why Thyestes could not have been content with his own crimes in life rather than stirring up more after death. He then pronounces the moral:

> Lo hear how fickle fortune gives but brittle fading joy.
> Lo, he who late a conqueror triumphed over Troy,
> Enduring many sturdy storms with mighty toil and pain

To sow the seed of fame, hath reapt small fruit thereof again.
When as his honour budding forth with flower began to bloom,
(Alas) the stock was hewed down and sent to deadly doom.
And they that of his victory and coming home were glad,
To sudden mourning change their mirth with heaviness bestad.
The lusty pomp of royal court is dead: (O doleful day)
The people moan their prince's death with woe and weal away:
With howling, crying, wringing hands, with sobs, with sighs, and tears,
And with their fists they beat their breasts, they pull and hale their
ears.

(II, 139–40)

In the *Oresteia*, Aeschylus puts us in raw contact with the primitive roots of human behaviour which the social and legal institutions of the *polis* are designed to restrain, while at the same time expressing faith in those institutions and the new religious order which underpins them. In his handling of the same mythical material in his *Electra*, Sophocles portrays his central figure of suffering as the heroic agent of justice whose strength of will encourages Orestes in the act of retribution which he undertakes on Apollo's orders to cleanse and to restore order to the house of Agamemnon. In his *Electra*, the sceptical Euripides subjects the mythical material to a rigorous scrutiny, questioning the morality of the oracle and showing how the god's command and the act of matricide unhinge the protagonists. But it is difficult to discern any comparably coherent unifying dramatic design in the Senecan play, which virtually splits into two halves (there are even two choruses one of Argive and one of Trojan women) with no real dramatic climax and no resolution. As for the Elizabethan moral, Seneca does not concentrate upon Agamemnon at all. After the initial vacillation, Clytemnestra and Aegisthus do not reflect upon their actions, nor does Seneca invest them with any moral force or much human interest.

Seneca and Sophocles: *Oedipus*

There is a similar lack of dramatic coherence in Seneca's version of *Oedipus*. The Sophoclean *Oedipus* has always been regarded as fulfilling the requirements of Aristotle for the well-made play with a clear beginning, middle and end connected by a chain of cause and effect in a necessary or probable sequence. 'There must

be nothing inexplicable in the incidents, or if there is, it must lie
outside the tragedy. There is an example in Sophocles' *Oedipus* (as
for instance Oedipus not knowing how Laius died)' (*Poetics*
XXIV, 20). It has often been thought that in describing the best
sort of tragedy, Aristotle has this play particularly in mind. He
mentions it when defining three of his most famous terms:
discovery (*anagnoresis*), reversal (*peripeteia*) and error (*hamartia*):

> ... by a complex action I mean one wherein the change of fortune
> coincides with a discovery or a reversal or both. These should result
> from the actual structure of the plot in such a way that what has
> already happened makes the result inevitable or probable. . . . A
> reversal is the change of the situation into the opposite, this change
> being probable or inevitable like the man in *Oedipus* who came to cheer
> Oedipus and rid him of his anxiety about his mother by revealing his
> parentage and changed the whole situation . . .. A discovery (a change
> from ignorance to knowledge) is most effective when it coincides with
> reversals such as that involved by the discovery in *Oedipus*. Best of all
> is the discovery which is brought about directly by the incidents, the
> surprise being produced by means of what is likely – take the scene in
> Sophocles's *Oedipus*. Such a discovery or reversal will involve either
> pity or fear. . . . Since then the structure of the best tragedy should not .
> be simple, but complex and one that represents incidents arousing pity
> and fear, a good man should not be shown passing from prosperity to
> misery. That does not arouse pity or fear but shocks our feelings. Nor
> again wicked people passing from bad fortune to good. That is most
> untragic of all; it does not appeal to our humanity or awaken pity and
> fear in us. Nor again the passing of a thoroughly bad man from good
> fortune to bad fortune. Such a structure might satisfy our feelings but
> it arouses neither pity nor fear: for our pity is awakened by undeserved
> misfortune, and our fear is for the man who is like ourselves. There
> remains a mean between these two extremes. This is the sort of man
> who is not conspicuous for virtue and justice, and whose fall into
> misery is not due to vice and depravity but rather to some error, he
> being one of those who are in high station like Oedipus.
>
> (*Poetics* X, XI, XIII)[4]

Oedipus in its plot and in its presentation of the character of the
protagonist (plot 'the soul of tragedy' comes before character in

---

4.   Adapted slightly from the Loeb translation: see Fyfe, W.H. (translator) (1927),
     Aristotle: The Poetics; '*Longinus*': *On the Sublime*; *Demetrius: On Style*, Loeb
     Classical Library, Heinemann London, Harvard University Press, Cambridge,
     Mass.

the Aristotelian analysis) exemplifies what is necessary to produce the most tragic effect, in accordance with the famous Aristotelian definition of its function:

> Tragedy then is a representation [*mimesis*, sometimes translated imitation] of an action that is serious, complete and of a certain magnitude, by means of language enriched with all kinds of ornament, each used separately in the different parts of the play: it represents men in action and does not use narrative, and through pity and fear it effects relief [*catharsis* sometimes translated as purgation or purification] of these and similar emotions.
>
> (*Poetics* VI, 2)[5]

Certainly no play in its plotting, whether in the larger management of incidents or in the details of language and imagery, has so ruthlessly exploited the possibilities of dramatic irony present in all ancient drama in which the basic elements of the play were well known to the audience. When the self-confident king, eager to find out for himself the cause of the plague afflicting Thebes, says in the opening speech of the play: 'I am here to learn for myself, I Oepidus, whose name is known from far' (6–8), he is thinking of the fame he has acquired from solving the riddle of the sphinx, whereas his greater fame from Homer onwards (see *Odyssey* XI, 271–80) stems from parricide and mother-marrying. Much of the play's impact and symbolic force stems from this irony, most obviously brought to play in the confrontation between the blind prophet Tiresias who can see the truth and the sighted king who cannot, and in the reversal in the play's climax when the knowing Oedipus blinds himself as he cannot bear to look upon the light of day.

In Seneca, Oedipus opens the play with an eighty-line monologue in which he laments his burdensome royal fate. He expresses his fear of the oracle that he would kill his father and marry his mother, the truth of which he knows in full. Why is he alone spared from the ravages of the plague? He dwells at length and in hyperbolic language on its horrors, praying for death. He is full of frightful foreboding. Jocasta enters and urges the abject and fearful Oedipus to face adversity with firmness of purpose and with stoic resolve. After a further description of the physical symptoms of the plague in a hundred-line chorus, Creon enters

5. As above.

with news of the oracle. In Sophocles the oracle delivers a Delphic utterance, laying blame for the plague on the pollution caused by the murderer of Laius. In Seneca the oracle clearly requires the expulsion of a fugitive stranger who has killed a king and returned once more to the womb of his mother. We may wonder how it is that Oedipus who could solve the riddle of the sphinx does not immediately see that he is the object of the god's anger and take steps to solve the greater riddle. This potential pitfall in the story of Oedipus, which as a story is full of absurdities, many of which are present in Seneca, is avoided by Sophocles through a cunning sleight of hand in the play's plotting. For in Sophocles not only does the truth emerge gradually for Oedipus, but through skilful use of oracles and suppression of information the audience only gradually comes to know how much Oedipus knows. The scene of confrontation between Oedipus and Tiresias, which occurs early in Sophocles and in which the prophet in anger tells Oedipus that the killer of Laius is present and will be found to be the son and husband to the mother who bore him, is only credible on the assumption that Oedipus is ignorant of his own predicted fate. It is only later in the play that we learn of Oedipus's knowledge of this oracle when he tells Jocasta of his reasons for leaving Corinth. That Jocasta should then seek to deny the validity of oracles by telling of another oracle that Laius would die by the hand of his own child (which we know to be true but which she believes to be false because she supposes that the child of Laius had been exposed at birth and because it is widely believed through Thebes that Laius had been killed by *robbers*, in the plural) is another of the many powerful ironies of Sophocles' plot ignored by Seneca or simply beyond his dramatic skills.

Whereas the intricate plotting of Sophocles is unerringly directed to give maximum impact to the discovery of truth in the play's climax, in Seneca there is no overall subordination of the parts to one great end that is the hallmark of a classic structure, rather a recurring dissipation of dramatic intensity at every stage in the interests of horrific sensation and macabre atmospherics. To the long-drawn-out descriptions of the horrors of the plague are to be added the frisson induced by Creon's account of his consultation of the oracle, the long scene in which Manto reports to the blind Tiresias the results of a sacrifice, which she actually makes on stage, to read the entrails of a heifer which turn out to be twisted and deformed, and the long report by Creon of the necromantic rites with which the aged prophet, unable to make head or tail of the entrails, summons up the ghost of Laius. When Odysseus raises the dead in Homer, he digs a trench, pours blood into it and up come the spirits to talk to him in a very matter-of-fact way (*Odyssey* XI, 24ff.). In *Oedipus*, of course, the whole operation is much more frenzied and ghoulish. After the raising of the dead, the chorus sing of the various monsters that have afflicted Thebes in the past. In the next scene the old Theban shepherd vividly recalls the swelling engendered by the wound to the infant Oedipus. After the discovery, the horror reaches its climax in the punishments inflicted upon themselves by Oedipus and Jocasta.

The handling of the response to the discovery is equally different in the two dramatists. In Sophocles, Oedipus prays never to look upon the light again. The chorus sing that man is nothing and happiness illusory. They had hailed Oedipus as the great saviour of the city when he freed them from the terror of the sphinx, now they wish they had never known him. A palace attendant tells how the tormented king had rushed inside in search of Jocasta with drawn sword (his first instinct being to kill them both) only to find that she has already hanged herself. After cutting her down, he seizes the brooches on her dress and blinds himself. He then gropes his way on stage crying of the horror of the dark, and converses with the chorus who are both repelled by and sensitive to his fate. When they ask how he could have endured to mar his sight he replies:

> Apollo, friends, brought my sufferings to fulfilment
> But no other hand struck the blow but mine
> For why should I see, when nothing is sweet to the eyes?
>   (translating, 1329–33)

Here is the noble Oedipus who seeks to take his fate upon himself, the character who throughout the play has consistently dominated the action by force of individual will, and who, when others, fearing the truth, try to deflect him from the discovery, had persisted in his quest to know who he is. As the play ends, he can even look beyond himself to the fate of his children as he makes arrangements for the future. His spirit is not entirely broken by the appalling self-knowledge that causes his fall from greatness and his suffering evokes more than pity and more than the chastening fear that but for the grace of inscrutable gods go we. If Aristotle's theory of catharsis (whatever precisely it might mean) – which seems to have been devised to assign to tragedy a wholesome psychological and ethical effect in reply to Plato, who had banished the tragic poets from his ideal *Republic* – does not fully account for the tragic effect of *Oedipus*, we can perhaps appreciate the meaning of the remark that he cites from Sophocles that, while Euripides portrayed men as they are, he portrayed them as they ought to be (*Poetics* XXV, II). For Oedipus manages to hold on to his humanity despite the horror he experiences as a civilised being in learning that he has violated the most sacred taboo upon which civilisation is founded.

The effect of the climax in Seneca is altogether different. Oedipus's initial reaction culminates in a self-addressed imperative to dare something worthy of his crimes and in a sarcastic taunt that he congratulate his mother on her house enriched by children. The chorus shows no sensitivity towards Oedipus but are prompted to reflect stoically (but without great relevance) that a life in moderate station is the safest, pointing to the example of Icarus who flew too near the sun, as if the fate of Oedipus himself (which they do not mention) were not a sufficiently cogent example to bear witness to any moral that might be deemed appropriate at this moment. The messenger reports Oedipus's words as he searches for a suitable punishment for himself. The climax of the messenger's account is a grotesquely detailed description of the self blinding; in one hyperbole the eyes start out to meet the advancing nails of his incoming hands and rush upon their wound. The blinding in Sophocles immediately follows the discovery of Jocasta and is not represented as a conscious act to which Oedipus must summon up courage but is part of an unconscious instinctive response that follows from his first desire not to see the light any more, which is later rationalised in conversation with the chorus. In Sophocles the physical horror is part of the more basic horror and is fully integrated into the dramatic action. Moreover it has clear symbolic force and completes a chain of imagery relating to seeing and not seeing and to light and dark that is basic to the linguistic texture of the play.

After the messenger's speech, the Senecan chorus give what is perhaps its most significant utterance in the play which has been

seen as the key to the main spring of Seneca's interest in the myth
of Oedipus:

> fatis agimur, cedite fatis
> non sollicitae possunt curae
> mutare rati stamina fusi.
> quicquid patimus mortale genus,
> quicquid facimus venit ex alto,
> servatque suae decreta colus
> Lachesis nulla revoluta manu. . . .
>   multis ipsum
> metuisse nocet, multi ad fatum
> venere suum dum fata timent.
>   (980–6, 992–4)

(We are driven by the fates; yield to the fates. No anxious cares can
change the thread of its fixed spindle. Whatever we mortal race suffer,
whatever we do, comes from above, and Lachesis keeps the decrees of
her distaff which cannot be unravelled by any hand . . .. Fear itself
harms many, and many have come to their fate while they feared their
fate.)

Having confronted his fate, Oedipus then enters not with his
consciousness overwhelmed as in Sophocles but in a calm mood
of self-congratulation now that in the self blinding he has paid a
debt to his father. Reversing Sophocles, he says that he owes
nothing to his own hand. Some god has plunged him in merciful
night. But his equilibrium is immediately disturbed by the
entrance of Jocasta whom he is unwilling to face. She absolves
him from guilt putting the blame on fate. In a soliloquy she
addresses herself *quid, anime, torpes?* (1024): 'why are you numb,
my soul?' determining on death, and seizing the sword which
killed Laius, in an act of explicit symbolism she kills herself on
stage by stabbing herself in the womb that has borne her children
and her husband. In the last words of the play, Oedipus upbraids
Apollo for not prophesying that he would cause the death of his
mother too:

> O Phoebe mendax, fata superavi impia.
>   (1047)

(O lying Phoebus, I have outdone the impious fates.)

Such rhetorical bravado is too superficial to be an effective protest or to reveal deeper feeling. Given that Jocasta has stabbed herself only seven lines previously, it is a jarringly egotistical claim even if we take it to be sarcastic. The moment demands more, or less, than sarcasm. The blind Oedipus thinks of Jocasta in his next breath, however, when with similar jarring infelicity he tells himself

> I profuge vade, – siste ne in matrem incidas.
>
> (1051)

(Go flee hurry – stop lest you stumble over your mother.)

Finally he sees the horrific burden of the plague being lifted from the city with his departure:

> mortifera mecum vitia terrarum extraho.
> violenta Fata et horridus Morbi tremor,
> Maciesque et atra Pestis et rabidus Dolor,
> mecum ite, mecum. ducibus his uti libet!
>
> (1058–61)

(I take with me the pestilential humours of the land. Violent fates, the horrific trembling of disease, wasting, black plague and mad despair, come with me, with me. It is a pleasure to have such guides.)

These last words, culminating in sarcasm, are a far cry from the final pitiful humanity of the Sophoclean Oedipus contemplating the wretched future of his children and begging Creon to let them accompany him into his self-imposed exile. Creon's dismissal of the Sophoclean Oedipus at the end leaves him speechless, impotent, defeated and emptied of ego. Conversely, in the Roman play, Jocasta dies and Oedipus departs with something of the egotistically defiant pride in the face of fate which is characteristically Senecan. The presentation of Jocasta's suicide on stage and of Oedipus's acquiescence in the role of scapegoat perhaps also show 'a kind of self-consciousness' and 'an attitude of self-dramatisation at moments of tragic intensity' that T.S. Eliot believed to have been the main influence of Seneca on Shakespeare and other Renaissance dramatists.[6]

---

6. Eliot, T.S. (1927) 'Shakespeare and the Stoicism of Seneca' in (1951) *Selected Essays*, Faber & Faber, p. 129.

The Elizabethan translator evidently felt that the ending should be made more of, and doubles the length of Oedipus's final speech, making him even more self-conscious, and, despite the diffuseness, giving an example of the kind of hyperbolic rhetoric common in Seneca in which, according to Stoic doctrine, the macrocosm reacts sympathetically to disorder in the microcosm:

> The skies do blush and are ashamed, at these thy mischiefs great:
> The earth laments, the heavens weep, the seas for rage do fret,
> And blustring rise, and storms do stir, and all thou wretch for thee,
> By whose incest, and bloody deeds all things disturbed be.
> Quite out of course, displaced quite, O cursed fatal day,
> O mischiefs great, O dreadful times, O wretch, away, away.
>
> (I, 230)

Surveying the Elizabethan Seneca, we may reflect how easily the Roman could be accommodated to existing ideas about tragedy that the Renaissance inherited from the Middle Ages. The translator of *Oedipus* substitutes for the chorus describing the various monsters that have afflicted Thebes an interlude of his own devising, but very much on a Senecan theme:

> See, see the miserable state of princes' carefull life.
> What raging storms? what bloody broils? what toil? what endless strife
> Do they endure? (O God) what plagues? what grief do they sustain?
> A princely life: No. No. (No doubt) an ever-during pain.
> A state e'en fit for men on whom Fortune would wreak her will.
> A place for cares to couch them in. A door wide open still
> For griefs and dangers all that ben to enter when they list. . . .
> Thus he that princes' lives, and base estate together weighs,
> Shall find the one a very hell, a perfect infelicity:
> The other eke a heaven right, exempted quite from misery.
> Let Oedipus example be of this unto you all,
> A mirror meet, a pattern plain, of princes' carefull thrall.
>
> (I, 215–16)

As well as being a mirror for magistrates Oedipus is also 'a dreadful example of god's horrible vengeance for sin'.[7] The overburdening sense of guilt felt by the Senecan Oedipus from the beginning meant that this version could seem to fit more readily into a Christian framework of reality whether Catholic or

7. From the translator's 'Preface to the Reader', Whibley, C. (1927) vol. 1, p. 190.

Protestant. Oedipus is guilty of original sin in a dramatic way and not predestined to be one of the elect. Seneca, unlike Sophocles, invites little reflection on the justice of Oedipus's fate. There is no direct suggestion in Sophocles that the gods are unjust, but the play insists on the limitations of human reason in our attempts to understand the world and the order that governs it, for despite the words of the chorus '*hubris* breeds the tyrant', etc. (870ff.), no one can believe that in *Oedipus Tyrannos* the king is being punished in any straightforward way for *hubris* shown in his treatment of Creon and Tiresias or even for his quick temper in response to provocation from Laius at the crossroads. The issue of injustice is more difficult to ignore in Sophocles than in Seneca, who is less alien than the Greeks to the cultural milieu of Tudor England, where the medieval morality tradition was still strong. Some time after the translation of Seneca, and ten years before the first flowering of English tragedy in the late 1580s, the idea of tragedy invoked by Sidney in his defence of poetry against its Puritan detractors is very much that of the morality tradition with a dash of Aristotle and a quotation from Seneca thrown in:

> high and excellent tragedy, that openeth the greatest wounds, and showeth forth the ulcers that are covered with tissue; that maketh kings fear to be tyrants, and tyrants manifest their tyrannical humours; that, with stirring the affects of admiration and commiseration, teacheth the uncertainty of this world, and upon how weak foundations gilden roofs are builded; that maketh us know

> Qui sceptra saevus duro imperio regit
> timet timentes: metus in auctorem redit.
> (705–6)

> [Who cruelly wield the sceptre with tyrannic power fears those who fear; terror recoils upon its author.][8]

This *sententia* uttered by Creon to Oedipus after the king has falsely accused him of treachery is pithily expressed though its message is only incidental to the play as a whole. Seneca is the touchstone for the Renaissance humanist but the underlying conception here is medieval. The morality tradition again seems

8. 'The Defence of Poesy', 744 in Duncan-Jones, K. (1989) p. 230.

intact when Sidney later in the *Defence* criticises *Gorboduc* (1561), praising its Senecan style but finding it defective in its violation of the unities of time and place:

> Our tragedies and comedies (not without cause cried out against), observing rules neither of honest civility nor skilful poetry – excepting *Gorboduc* (again, I say, of these that I have seen), which notwithstanding as it is full of stately speeches and well-sounding phrases, climbing to the height of Seneca's style, and as full of notable morality, which it doth most delightfully teach, and so obtain the very end of poesy, yet in truth it is very defectuous in the circumstances, which grieveth me, because it might not remain as an exact model of all tragedies. For it is faulty both in place and time, the two necessary companions of all corporal actions. For where the stage should always represent but one place, and the uttermost time presupposed in it should be, both by Aristotle's precept and common reason, but one day, there is both many days, and many places, inartificially imagined.[9]

Humanist thought about tragic drama often failed to go beyond the externals of form.

Seneca and Euripides: *Medea*

If comparison of the two Oedipus plays serves to suggest how readily Seneca might fit into inherited ideas about tragedy and into a Christian framework, then comparison with Euripides may suggest the fascination of the Renaissance for a new kind of drama that went beyond anything in the late medieval world. For in their energy and will, and in their going to the ultimate in the cause of self affirmation, Seneca's hero-villains are not in the least like the cardboard figures of the *De Casibus* tradition, nor are they inhibited by Christian codes of restraint or humility. This can be illustrated in a comparison of the Senecan *Medea* with its Greek predecessor.

In Euripides, the nurse acting as prologue tells how Medea out of love for Jason had helped him gain the golden fleece and been involved in the murder of his uncle Pelias, as a result of which

---

9. 'The Defence of Poesy', 1257 in Duncan-Jones, K. (1989) p. 243.

they had fled to settle in Corinth. After some years together, in which they had had children, Jason betrays Medea in secretly arranging a marriage to Glauce, daughter of Creon, King of Corinth. The play opens with Medea's sufferings as she bitterly records the solemn oaths given to her by Jason. This sense of injustice is fundamental to the play being still present in her mind at the end. The dramatic action concerns the gradual change from suffering to doing, and at the opening of the play Medea's plight is presented sympathetically and in fully human terms. Through her Euripides shows great understanding of the actual position of women in Greek society in his times and of a foreign woman in particular. The chorus agrees that her desire to punish Jason is quite justified. Creon then enters and orders Medea to take her sons into exile; in spite of his fear of her, he grants her request that the sentence be delayed for a day. In a remarkable ode, the chorus see a great reversal of roles: it is man who breaks oaths; woman's reputation for faithlessness will be ended. If Apollo had granted his gifts to women, women would answer the male sex, for time has as much to say of them as of men (410–30).

Seneca's starting point is the day of the marriage itself with Medea invoking the presence of the marriage gods and other deities (including Hecate, the underworld goddess of witches) by whose divinity Jason had sworn loyalty to her as she girds herself up for some terrible deed in words that bring to mind Lady Macbeth:

If any lusty life as yet within thy soul do rest,
If aught of ancient courage still do dwell within my breast,
Exile all foolish female fear, and pity from thy mind,
And as th' untamed tigers use to rage and rave unkind,
                    . . . permit to lodge and rest
Such savage brutish tyranny within thy brazen breast.
What ever hurly burly wrought doth Phasis understand
What mighty monstrous bloody feat I wrought by sea or land,
The like in Corinth shall be seen in most outrageous guise,
Most hideous, hatefull, horrible, to bear or see with eyes,
Most devilish, desperate, dreadfull deed yet never known before,
Whose rage shall force heaven, earth, and hell to quake and tremble
    sore.
My burning breast that rolls in wrath, and doth in rancour boil,

Sore thirsteth after blood, and wounds with slaughter, death and spoil,
By renting racked limbs from limbs to drive them down to grave.

(II, 57, translating 41–8)

The much more emotional Senecan figure of fury soon loses sight
of the issue of justice, and the dramatic action is essentially static;
she is intent on some dreadful deed from the start, and all her talk
is of sacrifices and horrors. This is the demon-witch of popular
mythology. Hearing the marriage hymn sung by the chorus she is
further inflamed. The nurse, as in the *Agamemnon*, urges restraint
and caution to no avail. The *stichomythia*, speaking in alternate
lines, that Seneca took over from the Greeks becomes particularly
pointed, epigrammatic and sententious:

Medea. fortuna fortes metuit, ignavos premit.
  (Fortune favours the brave, the cowardly overwhelms.)
Nurse. tunc est probanda, si locum virtus habet.
  (If there is a place for courage, then it can be approved.)
Medea. numquam potest non esse virtuti locus.
  (It can never be that there is no place for courage.)
Nurse. spes nulla rebus monstrat adflictis viam.
  (No hope shows a way out of this affliction.)
Medea. qui nil potest sperare, desperet nihil.
  (Who can hope for nothing, let him despair of nothing.)
Nurse. abiere Colchi, coniugis nulla est fides
  nihilque superest opibus et tantis tibi.
  (The Colchians have gone, your husband is untrustworthy and there
  is nothing left of all your great wealth.)
Medea. Medea superest – hic mare et terras vides
  terramque et ignes et deos et fulmina.
  (Medea is left and here you see the earth and sea and sword and fire
  and gods and thunderbolts.)

(159–67)

The many imitations of this stoic affirmation of personal identity
in the face of a hostile world ('I am Antony still', 'I am Duchess of
Malfi still') suggest another Senecan feature found attractive in the
Renaissance. The competitive cut and thrust becomes staccato in
effect.

Nurse. rex est timendus.
  (The king is to be feared.)
Medea.   rex meus fuerat pater.
  (My father was a king.)

Nurse. non metuis arma?
　　　(Do you not fear arms?)
Medea.　　　　　　　sint licet terra edita.
　　　　　　　(Not though they were sprung from the earth.)
Nurse. moriere.
　　　(You will die.)
Medea.　　　cupio.
　　　　　(I wish to.)
Nurse.　　　　profuge.
　　　　　　(Flee.)
Medea.　　　　　　　paenituit fugae.
　　　　　　　(I have changed my mind about flight.)
Nurse. Medea,
Medea.　　　fiam. . . .
　　　　　(I shall be.)
　　fortuna opes auferre, non animum potest.
　　(Fortune can take away my wealth but not my spirit.)
　　　　　　　　　　　(168–71, 176)

Hamlet's doubtful question:

> Whether 'tis nobler in the mind to suffer
> The slings and arrows of outrageous fortune,
> Or to take arms against a sea of troubles
> And by opposing end them?
> 　　　　　　(III, i, 57–60)

could never be entertained by this proud and defiant Senecan protagonist who, with no benumbing fear of something after death, furiously threatens the terrors of the earth to assert the triumph of the will over the outrages of fortune, however iniquitous the devastation that ensues.

In the ensuing confrontation between husband and wife the Jason of Euripides cuts a sorry figure. If only she had accepted things and kept quiet, he says, she need not have been banished. In the face of Medea's recriminations he recognises that he will need all his powers of speech. Euripides has been criticised for making his characters indulge in clever-talking or sophistry. Jason may be a case in point, but if so, then the case has a dramatic point as Medea is able persuasively to denounce him for cloaking his base conduct in specious words. Jason asserts that she did what she did for him through *eros*, though he recognises a debt. Nevertheless, he (the oath-breaker) claims in bringing her to

Greece to have given her a foreigner, the benefits of Greek life under the rule of law where she is now famous. If it was not for her sexual jealousy, she would see that the marriage is in everybody's best interests. What a pity, he goes on, that children cannot be got in some other way, then men could do without women altogether. The chorus admire his verbal prowess, but tell him to his face that he was wrong to betray his wife. He then claims that the marriage will bring prosperity and security not just for him but for Medea and her children.

In the same confrontation in Seneca, where she sees in Jason's love for his children the way to revenge, Medea shows little of the coolly rational argument with which she had demolished Jason's case in Euripides. Just rebuke gives way to bitter sarcasm and emotional pleading, as Medea tries to persuade Jason to leave Corinth with her. Seneca has tried to save Jason's reputation by representing him as acting under duress in fear of Creon. After the confrontation, the chorus of Corinthian men reflect that there is no natural force as great as the hatred of a woman robbed of love: 'hell hath no fury like a woman scorned'. In fact, Seneca's men show none of the sympathy for Medea expressed by Euripides' women of Corinth. The political dimension of the Greek gives way to a conservative Roman ethos that does not seek to question the rights of the *paterfamilias*.

Having gained political asylum from the visiting Athenian Aegeus, who also deplores Jason's conduct, the Euripidean Medea now reveals her terrible plan of revenge. She will send her children to Glauce with the gift of a poisonous dress in which she will expire in agony. Then she will kill her sons, preferring guilt to the mockery of her enemies. The climax of the play is a long monologue in which Medea wavers over her intention to kill her children: 'Oh, what am I to do?' (1042). In Aeschylus, Orestes, when face to face with the mother he has come to kill, asked the same question of Pylades whose answer invoked the command of Apollo. Here, although Medea is in the presence of the chorus, she is really addressing herself, her *thymos*, her own heart or spirit, and there is no interplay between human and divine. In a long self-analysis her maternal feelings struggle against her desire for revenge against Jason (in particular her desire not to be made a laughing-stock). Although she recognises that her sons are doomed anyway, as they will be killed for their part in the murder of Glauce, she is fully conscious of the wickedness of her action, as she makes clear in the last words she speaks before she goes off stage to kill them: 'Let not Medea slay her children in front of the people' (Horace, *Art of Poetry*, 185).

> I learn what evils I am about to do
> But my passion is stronger than my mind's deliberations
> And this is the cause of direst ills to human beings.
>
> (1978–80)

This is a chillingly calm expression of clear self-knowledge. Medea is alarmingly rational, knows what she is doing and passes judgement on herself. The judgement upon her is never in doubt. After she has revealed her plans, the chorus tries to dissuade her, and in a famous ode in praise of Athens, asks how the city of wisdom and beauty can give asylum to one who has murdered her children. In making Medea pronounce so consciously upon her own wrong-doing it has been suggested that Euripides had in mind the Socratic doctrine that wrong-doing results from a faulty perception of the good, that virtue is knowledge, that 'no one willingly does wrong' *oudeis hekon hamartenai*.[10] The Greek word here brings to mind the *hamartia*, or error, the word made famous by Aristotle in his *Poetics*. Oedipus makes his error unconsciously and unwittingly, though, in Sophocles' play, with apparent freedom of the will; Medea makes hers consciously and with similar freedom of the will, nor does she repent of it as she confronts the hapless and helpless Jason in bitter triumph at the end of the play in a chariot drawn by dragons above the stage. Certainly Euripides' dramatic representation of human beings in action is radically different from the theoretical ideal of it made famous by Plato's Socrates, stressing as it does the intractable power of irrational forces in human affairs, often represented by gods in other plays, and here manifested in the extremity of Medea's revenge intensified by Euripides, for the motif of infanticide is believed to be his own addition to the myth. At the same time the rationalist poet and liberal humanist of Periclean Athens seeks understanding of the cause of that irrationality, and takes pains to make Medea's initial motives sympathetically comprehensible.

10.   See Xenophon, *Memorabilia* III, 9, 4; Plato, *Protagoras*, 358cd.

Cool rationality in Euripides is replaced by an almost Satanic madness in Seneca. The interview with Aegeus is dispensed with; instead the nurse appears on stage reporting at length on Medea's resort to the occult as she summons up poisonous snakes and gathers her store of baleful herbs. She then enters in a state of frenzy and invokes the powers of hell offering a varied assortment of unpleasant things to Hecate. At the climax of the lurid incantation (which extends over a hundred lines) she slashes her arm and lets the blood flow over the altar. She then goes off with her children. Little wonder that the chorus reflect that the sooner they are rid of this demonic barbarian witch the better.

The climax is again in the fluctuation in Medea's mind, an extension of that experienced by Clytemnestra and Aegisthus in the *Agamemnon*. Like them, but unlike her Euripidean counterpart, the Senecan Medea is conscious of previous crimes including the gruesome murder of her brother (by which she had effected her own and Jason's escape from Colchis with the golden fleece) which she is now to outdo in a crowning deed that will make her truly Medea. Then anger subsides before maternal feeling only to return again expressed in the image of a possessing Fury and giving rise to a monstrous hyperbole in her wish that, like Niobe, she had fourteen children to kill. Nevertheless, the two she has will answer for the deaths of her father and husband. In her deranged state she has a vision of a whole horde of furies preceding the shade her mangled brother seeking punishment. She slays the first son (on stage, ignoring the Horatian rule) to appease his ghost. Immediately after the first infanticide she triumphantly feels that the crime has restored her regality, the lives of her brother and father, the golden fleece to the Colchians and the virginity she lost to Jason. This is not self-knowledge but manic self-delusion on a grand scale, by which Medea seeks to obliterate the past and assert her old self. In a state of great confusion after confronting Jason, she kills the second son and throws down their bodies to Jason below, who utters the famous last words:

Per alta vade spatia sublimi aethere;
testare nullos esse, qua veheris, deos.
(1026–7)

(Go through the lofty spaces of high heaven and bear witness where you ride that there are no gods.)

In the hotted-up Senecan version, therefore, Medea is in a state of raging *furor*, fury or madness, throughout. In this play, as in others, much effort is expended in working up an atmosphere of horror; there is much of the grotesque in the conception of character and in the incidents of the fable; on the other hand, the Senecan conception that Medea is driven by deep sexual jealousy, that she is the victim of demons from her past experience that rise up from the murky depths of her unconscious demanding appeasement, and that the crime of infanticide could only be committed hot-bloodedly by someone who is in a state of blind demonic fury (the killing on stage has thematic point) is fully coherent and shows an unleashing of Satanic energy which, when it carries conviction, threatens the moral order (which in Euripides, is left intact) with wholesale devastation. More successfully than in his *Agamemnon* or *Oedipus*, Seneca has taken over an old fable in his *Medea* and made it new with something of his own. Because like other Senecan hero-villains Medea is so far beyond the bounds of common humanity, her story as told by Seneca does not have the chilling effect that it does in Euripides' where, even if we believe that we could never cold-bloodedly murder our children, Medea is too disconcertingly, in Sophocles' phrase as reported by Aristotle, like human beings as they are (*Poetics* XXV, 11).

The Senecan Hercules: Stoicism

Seneca's penchant for hyperbole and excess found an appropriate vehicle for expression in the figure of Hercules, who features in two plays: *Hercules Furens*, based on the *Heracles* of Euripides, and *Hercules Oetaeus*, based on the *Woman of Trachis* of Sophocles, though Senecan authorship of the latter has been questioned. In the first play, Hercules rescues his wife and children from the tyrant Lycus and then in a fit of madness sent upon him by Juno murders them mistaking their identity. Upon recovering from his madness he is in despair and helped to reconcile himself to his actions by his father Amphitryon and his friend Theseus. In the second play, Hercules after a bloody campaign is about to return home to his wife Deianara who has learnt that he has fallen in love with one of his captives, Iole. She sends him a shirt impregnated

with a poison which had been given to her by the Centaur
Nessus. Her son Hyllus returns to describe the agony of Hercules
and denounces his mother as a murderess. She then kills herself.
The dying Hercules is brought in and orders Hyllus to prepare his
pyre on Mount Oeta. The final scene shows Hercules' death and
deification. In both plays Hercules is represented as a supreme
hero of achievement: he is a son of Jupiter and a figure of great
strength by virtue of which he has benefited mankind. At the
same time, this ardent and exceptional figure of aspiration and
achievement is not, conventionally speaking, good; for his great
qualities are perilously close to their opposites: brutality, mono-
mania and self-regarding pride.[11] In the second play he is also
lustful and rapacious. In both plays he suffers greatly, in the first
more humanly, in the second with a Herculean indifference to
physical pain:

> If ugly grested Caucasus in chain of iron link
> Should bind me as a groaning prey the greedy gripe to feed,
> Yet from mine eyes it should not strain a broken tear indeed.
> If wandering Symplegads would me with either rock assail,
> To bide the brunt of double wrack my courage would not quail.
> Let Pindus tumbled be on me, huge Aemus let me have
> Or Athos rock in Thracian seas that breaks the weltring wave,
> And bode the bolts of thundring Jove although th'unweildy mass
> Of all the world should fall on me and might be brought to pass
> That Phoebus flaming apeltree should burn upon my grave,
> No uncouth cry should force the mind of Hercles thus to rave.
>   (II, 239, translating 1376–88)

In the Elizabethan translation, this sounds as if it might be what
Shakespeare had in mind when he makes Bottom speak of 'Ercles'
vein' (A Midsummer Night's Dream I, i, 33). Whatever may be the
truth of that, like other Senecan protagonists, but perhaps more
obviously, Hercules transcends the clear categories of the morality
tradition in a way that the pagan Tamburlaine was to do in
Marlowe's play. It has sometimes been said that he has been
reclaimed for the Christian tradition by Milton in Samson
Agonistes. In his fortitude at the end he not only accepts his fate
but wills it when he recognises in the shirt of Nessus the

11.   See Waith, E.M. (1962) The Herculean Hero in Marlowe, Chapman, Shakespeare
      and Dryden, Chatto & Windus.

fulfilment of a prophecy. He is therefore the supreme example in Seneca of the self-sufficient, self-conscious and self-dramatising Stoic, boldly embracing death with his spiritual integrity intact, confident of past virtue and future fame, and master of a poetic grandiloquence matching and sustaining his transcendent sense of his own worth. Chapman's Bussy d'Ambois echoes the language of *Hercules Oetoeus* in his dying speech:

> Prop me, true sword, as thou hast ever done:
> The equal thought I bear of life and death,
> Shall make me faint on no side; I am up
> Here like a Roman statue; I will stand
> Till death hath made me marble: O my fame
> Live in despite of murder: take thy wings
> And haste thee where the grey-eyed morn perfumes
> Her rosy chariot with Sabæan spices;
> Fly, where the evening from th' Iberian vales
> Takes on her swarthy shoulders Hecate
> Crown'd with a grove of oaks; fly where men feel
> The burning axletree, and those that suffer
> Beneath the chariot of the Snowy Bear:
> And tell them all that D'Ambois now is hasting
> To the eternal dwellers; that a thunder
> Of all their sighs together (for their frailties
> Beheld in me) may quit my worthless fall
> Worth a fit volley for my funeral.
>
> (V, iii, 141–58)[12]

Chapman here gives a much better idea of Seneca's 'gravity and height of elocution' than do the Elizabethan translators.

At the moment of his death, Hercules assumes an attitude that might be called stoical; otherwise, of course, he is hardly the embodiment of the reasonable Stoic. The prevalence of stoic sentiments in the utterances of characters and choruses has prompted debate about the relation between the plays and the prose works, such as the *De constantia* and the *De ira*, in which Seneca expounds the main tenets of stoic ethics.

Stoicism had originated in the third century BC at Athens, where it has often been said its saving grace had been to offer philosophic consolation for the loss of identity and sense of

---

12.   Brooke, N. (ed.) (1964) *George Chapman: Bussy D'Ambois*. The Revels Plays, Methuen: Appendix B gives the Senecan passages, here lines 1518–27.

powerlessness experienced by the individual after the absorption of the classical *polis* into the larger unit of the Macedonian empire, itself later to be absorbed into the Roman empire in the mid second century. In the cosmopolitan world, the individual is offered not as in Plato and Aristotle a philosophic vision of the good life that takes for granted as its starting point that man is a political animal who can only achieve the highest actualisation of his human potential in the developed community of the *polis*, but one which finds positive virtue possible only when the individual has transcended the world around him and is wholly indifferent to the passions it excites. The goal that the Stoic seeks through the rule of reason is self-sufficiency (*autarcheia*, self-rule) and apathy, transcendence of the passions, *pathe*. It is perhaps something of a paradox that a Stoic, like Seneca, should have been attracted to the passionate genre of tragedy at all. Attempts to seek consistency between the philosopher and playwright and to find a stoic outlook coherently underpinning the plays have not proved convincing,[13] though the isolation of the individual from the surrounding world and his reliance for his own identity upon the inner resources of the self is strongly felt in the plays in the lack of communication between characters and chorus (there is a notable contrast here between the Oedipus plays of Sophocles and Seneca) in the development in Seneca of the soliloquy or interior monologue and in the frequent tendency of characters to give set speeches into a void even when they are ostensibly addressing one another.

The Senecan history play

If the plays of Seneca are not easily reconciled with the Stoic philosophy of the essays, then neither is his life. For Seneca did not act in accordance with the advice of his choruses when they praise the quiet life of moderate station; on the contrary, he actively sought power at the imperial court where he was first tutor to Nero, then his political adviser for the first eight years of

---

13. See the following thought-provoking article: Herington, C.J. (1966) 'Senecan Tragedy', *Arion* **5**, 422–71 and Braden, G. (1985) *Renaissance Tragedy and the Senecan Tradition: Anger's Privilege*, Yale University Press, New Haven.

his reign until ordered to commit suicide on suspicion of complicity in the conspiracy of Piso. His detractors point out that he was sufficiently enamoured of the things of this world to have amassed a huge fortune in his public career. The paradox of his position as courtier is apparent in the opening words given to the character Seneca in *Octavia*, the only surviving Roman play on a Roman theme which is included in the Senecan corpus but which a majority of the scholars who have investigated the matter now believe not to have been written by Seneca himself:

> On me with like consent why didst thou smile,
> With glozed looks deluding me a while,
> O fortune much of might and princely power?
> To lift aloft to noble royal bower?
> To th' end that I to honour's court extolled,
> From stately seat might have the greater fall,
> And round about in every place behold,
> Such dreadful, threating dangers to us all.
> (II, 163, translating 377–80)

He castigates the times in which he lives:

> The heaps of vice raked up in years long past,
> Abounding flow in these our days at last.
> And this same troublous time, and cumbrous age,
> Oppresseth all men sore, both young and sage.
> (II, 165, translating 430–3)

In dialogue with Nero, he attempts to dissuade the emperor from putting to death two distant relatives (a minor incident in the play) and from divorcing his wife Octavia in favour of Poppaea (the mainspring of the play's plot). Needless to say he fails, and Nero in conversation with the benign but ineffectual philosopher proves himself to be the wilful cynical tyrant, fearful and inspiring fear. In the next scene, the ghost of Agrippina, Nero's mother, makes an appearance to denounce her son for being instrumental in her own murder; she, in turn, prophesies his bloody end. In the previous scene the innocent Octavia and her nurse had set the moral tone by relating previous family crimes, notably the murder of Octavia's brother Britannicus. When there is public protest at the proposed marriage, the agitation is swiftly put down and Octavia is banished to a remote island where she is to be killed. The Julio-Claudians pursued their rivalries and sought satisfaction of their desires with an intensity almost equal to that in any of the familiar mythological fables. This historical context and the circumstances of Seneca's dangerous position on the fringes of power may account somewhat for characteristic emphases in Senecan drama: the overwhelming threatening presence of evil, the fearful insecurity of the powerful and the powerless and the impotence of the good who can only maintain their integrity and self-respect by dying well.

There is an even bleaker and thoroughgoing representation of political tyranny in Jonson's *Sejanus* (1603). Sejanus proves to be an aspiring Senecan villain whose fall when he overreaches himself is cunningly engineered by the emperor Tiberius; but the engineer is an altogether more sinister Machiavellian figure who prospers on the principle that 'A prince's power makes all his actions Virtue' (III, ii, 717). The impotent Stoic opposition is exiled, executed or otherwise silenced. The change of fortune experienced by Sejanus changes nothing in the Roman state. Jonson's second tragedy *Catiline* (1608) is similarly untragic for different reasons. Replete with ghost and chorus, in its externals it is even more Roman than *Sejanus*. Here the threat to civilisation in the form of Catiline is defeated by the philosopher–consul Cicero, whose oratory saves the Roman state. The stark black-and-white antithesis is in marked contrast to the shaded subtleties of Shakespeare's Roman plays, and perhaps suggests the limitations of the humanist account of tragedy that Jonson inherited. Certainly his own account of the four offices of the tragic writer ('truth of argument, dignity of persons, gravity and height of elocution, fullness and frequency of sentence')[14] seems to rest with externals and to lack the engagement and penetration of his more extensive discussions of comedy.

Senecan style and transmission

The features of Seneca's style referred to by Jonson have already been illustrated but general Renaissance interest in Senecan Latin warrants further comment. In prose, Seneca is a representative of

14. 'To the Readers' prefixed to the play. See Bolton, W.F. (1966) *Sejanus: His Fall*, The New Mermaids, Benn, p. 5.

a style that is pointed, sententious and epigrammatic in reaction against the rounded and sometimes florid periodic style of earlier classical Latin of which the great representative is Cicero. Dryden's criticism is memorable: 'For his style . . . we may call it a shattered eloquence, not vigorous, not united, not embodied, but broken into fragments: every part by itself pompous but the whole confused and unharmonious. His Latin . . . has nothing in it of the purity and elegance of Augustus his times . . .'.[15] For Seneca is a writer in what literary historians have called the silver age of Latin literature, and shares in common with other writers such as Lucan and Statius a reaction against Augustan values. Subsequent history has given the period the sobriquet silver to mark a stage in a decline and fall from the golden age of refinement, urbanity, poise and restraint that are the hallmarks of the literature of the Augustan age. Of Seneca's dramatic style, Dryden has this to say: 'Seneca . . . as if there were no such thing as nature to be minded in a play, is always running after pompous expression, pointed sentences and philosophical notions, more proper for the study than the stage.'[16] Scholars still question whether the plays were written for the stage at all, and if such was the case, then the idea of a dramatic performance in Nero's Rome seems to have been a decadent one amounting to little more than recitation, encouraging the declamatory tendencies fostered in the rhetorical exercises practised in the schools. Nevertheless, Seneca's style, though it is the expression of a cruder sensibility than we find in Virgil and Horace, is not consistently tumid, exaggerated and feverish. His quieter choral odes on stoic themes have inspired notable imitations, this by the Tudor courtier and humanist Sir Thomas Wyatt:

> Stand whoso list upon the slipper top
> Of court estate, and let me here rejoice
> And use me quiet without let or stop,
> Unknown in court, that hath such brackish joys.
> In hidden place so let my days forth pass
> That when my years be done withouten noise,
> I may die aged after the common trace.

---

15. 'The Life of Plutarch' (1683) in Scott, W., Saintsbury, G. (eds) (1882–93) *The Works of John Dryden*, 18 vols, Paterson, Edinburgh, vol. 17, p. 76.
16. 'Preface to Oedipus' (1679) in Watson, G. (1962) vol. 1, p. 233.

For him death grippeth right hard by the crop
That known of all, but to himself, alas
Doth die unknown, dazed with dreadful face.[17]

The Renaissance preference for Seneca should not be thought of as a choice between two traditions equally available. In the Latin culture of the Renaissance it was a comparatively easy matter to master Seneca's Latin, which is not difficult. He was sometimes a school text, and there were aids available in commentaries and vernacular translations. The Greek of Aeschylus and Sophocles, and of Euripides too in his choruses, was a much more difficult proposition. The Greek dramatists were rarely edited and chiefly available in expensive editions. These editions did not, in fact, offer the reader much help. The testimony of a scholar who has investigated Renaissance editions of the Greek comic poet Aristophanes is relevant here. 'But an examination of the editions shows the editors were concerned with his plays only as Greek texts, not as drama nor even as literature. They were still striving to attain mastery over the language itself.'[18] Erasmus translated Euripides' *Hecuba* and *Iphigeneia in Tauris* into Latin,[19] but Greek plays were scarcely translated into the vernacular at all. For the most part the only translations available were to be found in the bilingual editions providing literal Latin versions opposite the Greek text on the facing page. These versions, which followed the grammar, syntax and idiom of the Greek to which they were designed to be a key, if read independently, were unidiomatic and ungrammatical so that they could not adequately serve the needs of the Greekless. Moreover, they were often astonishingly inaccurate. It is not therefore surprising that, for the averagely educated, the Greek was simply not available. This prompts a

17. Text from Mason, H.A. (ed.) (1985) *Sir Thomas Wyatt: A Literary Portrait*, Bristol Classical Press. This is a translation of *Thyestes*, 391–403. It is appended with other versions including those of Jasper Heywood, Marvell and Cowley to Hunter, G.K., 'Seneca and English Tragedy' in Costa, C.D.N. (ed.) (1974) *Seneca, Greek and Latin Studies: Classical Literature and its Influence*, Routledge & Kegan Paul.
18. Baldwin, T.W. (1947) *William Shakspere's Five-Act Structure*, University of Illinois Press, Urbana, p. 153.
19. See Jones, E. (1977) *The Origins of Shakespeare*, Oxford University Press: Chapters 3 and 4, 'Shakespeare and Euripides'. Jones argues that Shakespeare may have known the two plays that Erasmus translated through the translation: see pp. 96–7.

more interesting question: Why did not the learned humanists put more effort into the understanding and dissemination of what are now regarded as the central classics of Greek literature? The dominance of Latinity in Renaissance humanism, and with it the failure to take the true measure of the more difficult and more alien literary inheritance of the Greeks, is nowhere more startlingly demonstrated than in the preference for Seneca often demonstrated by the most learned. J.C. Scaliger, the arch-priest of Renaissance formalism, thought Seneca not inferior to the Greeks in majesty and superior to Euripides in his cultivation and splendour.[20] Adherence to the name of Aristotle amongst such formulist critics in the later sixteenth century did not necessarily further the reception of the texts which Aristotle was thought to illuminate and from which the Greek philosopher and critic had made his observations in the first place.

Greek old comedy

The origins of comedy to Aristotle were obscure but he records the view that the word is derived from *kome*, a village, because comedians were turned out of towns and went strolling around the villages (*Poetics* III) rather than *komos*, revel, the preferred derivation of modern scholars. Revels which took place on festival days might end with the participants parading the streets, garlanded and with torches, singing, dancing, drinking and making merry. Aristotle also says that comedy came from improvisations connected with phallic songs (associated with fertility and the worship of Dionysus) still surviving in the institutions of many of the cities of his day, and that the earliest plot-makers were Sicilian.

In Athens comedy, like tragedy, was a state institution performed at the Great Dionysia and also at a special festival in January called the Leneia. The chorus (consisting of twenty-four members who might be divided into two half-choruses) was provided by a *choregos* whose responsibility it was to hire, train and fit out its members at his own expense. The actors, whose

---

20.   *Senecam nullo Graecorum maiestate inferiorem existimo, cultu vero ac nitore etiam Euripido maiorem: Poetics*, Lib V, Cap XVI.

number does not seem to have been restricted as in tragedy, wore masks of a grotesque kind, special footwear called the comic sock and often had a phallic emblem. Their costumes were extravagantly padded.

The only surviving comedies of the fifth century representing what was subsequently called by the ancients the old comedy are nine plays by Aristophanes written in late fifth-century Athens. A further two plays by Aristophanes, of a slightly different character, survive from the early fourth century. The first most striking feature of old comedy is its satirical character and the ridiculing invective against named individuals whether politicians like Pericles and Cleon, philosophers and thinkers like Socrates or poets like Euripides. Many other individuals (whose significance is often lost upon us now) are also named, including notable or newsworthy characters of the city presumably present in the audience. Hence the verb *komodein* meaning to represent in comedy is also used in this period to mean to satirise, ridicule, lampoon or libel. A second striking feature is a persistent and frank indecency with regard to sexual matters and bodily functions. In *Lysistrata*, for example, when the women of Athens and Sparta agree to bring the war to an end by withdrawing their sexual services until peace is concluded, their menfolk are in an acutely priapic state for much of the play. Aristophanic laughter acts as a kind of release from normal social embarrassment and inhibition.

Most plays involve some extravagant fantasy: the *Birds*, for example, concerns an attempt to establish an ideal city in the sky 'Cloudcuckooland' where the inhabitants can rule by controlling the food supply of both man and gods who are also treated irreverently in Aristophanic comedy. Despite the fantastic and highly imaginative elements, a realistic picture of the life of the ordinary Athenian citizen emerges through the distortion of the comic lens. In the *Wasps* and *Assemblywomen* we can see how the system works. Hence the anecdote that when the philosopher Plato was asked by the tyrant Dionysius of Syracuse about the Athenian constitution, his reply was to send him the plays of Aristophanes. A notable formal feature is the *parabasis* in which the poet uses the chorus to break the dramatic illusion midway through the play to speak in his own voice sometimes to harangue the spectators with advice of topical import that may or may not be connected with the issues of the play. Like tragedy, comedy is a poetic form, and many of the choral lyrics have an appealing delicacy and charm. Together with singing and dancing, the chorus (particularly the animal choruses) doubtless provided an extravagant visual spectacle, so that, considered as a whole, Aristophanic comedy is a remarkably varied and lively phenomenon, the like of which the world has never quite seen again.

Aristophanes' *Knights*

The *Knights*, the first play produced by Aristophanes himself in 424, is a quite savage attack upon the leading politician of the day, Cleon, Pericles' successor as leader of the Athenian *demos*. In the person of Cleon, the political leadership of Athens is being attacked on general grounds, and in particular for prosecuting the war against Sparta at all costs.

An oracle is discovered that Cleon, a seller of leather by trade, is to be ousted from the favour of Demos (the Athenian people) by a sausage-seller. One comes along and when told of his destiny feels unworthy because he was born in the gutter, has no virtues to speak of and can scarcely read or write. When told: 'Come off it, you don't think politics is for the educated do you or the honest? It's for the illiterate scum like you now!' (191–3)[21] he is still doubtful wondering how he can arrange the affairs of the city. He is then reassured: 'Dead easy; just carry on what you've always done. Mix all the city's policies into a complete hash, butter the people up a bit, throw in a pinch of rhetoric as a sweetener, and there you are' (213–16). He is supported by the chorus of Knights or cavalrymen who as men of education and social standing are the natural opponents of upstarts from the *nouveau riche* such as Cleon.

Cleon arrives, and a furious shouting match (the contest, or *agon*) develops between them. The sausage-seller contends that he is a bigger crook than Cleon; he has been cheating his customers in the market (the *agora* which can also mean assembly) for years. They compete for the favour of the irascible and stupid old man

21.   From Sommerstein, A.H. (translator) (1978) *Aristophanes: The Knights, Peace, Wealth, etc*, Penguin.

Demos by flattery, bribes and interpretation of oracles. The sausage-seller points out that though a tanner Cleon has never given Demos a pair of shoes, and he provides him with a pair, as well as a tunic and a chair for his comfort. Just before the final contest, old Demos, in conversation with the Knights, shows that he isn't quite as simple as he seems. He knows the thieving ways of politicians. Then there is a contest of hampers to appeal to Demos's appetite; the sausage-seller, by a clever trick he uses to cheat his customers, is able to steal Cleon's jugged hare while he is distracted, and wins by showing Demos that while his hamper is empty, Cleon has kept much of the food for himself (with the clear implication that the real Cleon lines his own pockets). Cleon now confesses that he has been outdone in shamelessness and sees the truth of the oracle. The sausage-seller is now revealed as Agoracritus, 'the choice of the assembly' or 'market haggler'. 'In the agora I thrived on my wrangling' (1257–8). This fits the sausage-seller both as purveyor of meat in the market place and as citizen of Athens schooled in the ways of the world in the assembly. In the wordplay here is concentrated the wit and design of the whole play. There may also be a third meaning 'I fed myself in the agora in judging' (in the law courts where in the developed democracy a citizen could earn three obols a day, almost a living wage. Here may be adduced the remark in the *Gorgias* of Plato 'For I am told that Pericles made the Athenians idle and cowardly and talkative and covetous, because he was the first to establish pay for service among them' 515e).[22]

Then, following Medea's example, the sausage-seller boils Demos to rejuvenate him so that he appears as he was in the good old days of Miltiades, the general who had commanded the Athenians in their finest hour when they had defeated the Persians at Marathon. Demos is then amazed at his stupidity and vows to reform the politics and manners of the city. He is pleased to be shown two sweet thirty-year-old treaties (in female form presumably) whom Cleon has hidden away and whom Demos can take back to his farm in the country. In a neat reversal Cleon is given Agoracritus's old job, selling sausages (a mixture of dog and donkey) at the city's gates.

22. Hamilton, E., Cairns, H. (eds) (1971) *The Collected Dialogues of Plato*, Princeton University Press, Princeton.

As Cleon had successfully prosecuted Aristophanes a year earlier for bringing the city into disrepute before foreigners, the *Knights* was a defiant reply as the *parabasis* makes clear. Aristophanes judged the audience well, for the judges awarded him first prize. Addressing the judges in the *Assemblywomen*, the poet has this suggestion to offer: 'Let the intellectuals choose me for my intellectual content, to those who enjoy a good laugh, judge me on my jesting. That should get most of the votes' (1155–7). Those who came simply for the entertainment doubtless enjoyed seeing their leaders brought down to size, revelling in the caricature, the burlesque and the reduction to absurdity. In the Athenian democracy Jack was as good as his master, or perhaps the Jacks had taken the place of the master. The more discerning doubtless appreciated the playwright's wit in pressing the resemblance between the politician who sells himself and the sausage-seller haggling in the market place and indulging in a spot of male prostitution on the side (1242).

The comparison entails a withering political analysis that is not wholly mitigated by the general air of mirth and absurdity or by the wishful ending. The clear implication is that Demos gets the politicians he deserves. As for Aristophanes' relation to the real Athenian *demos*, this may be likened to the jester at the court of the king; he is allowed a fool's licence to insult them with the unflattering truth. Paradoxically the *Knights* may be said to be a tribute to the maturity of the Athenian democracy (Cleon, of course, continued to be popular and Aristophanes to attack him to his death in 422) as well as a stringent criticism of it, as damning in its way as that of Thucydides in his history or that of Plato in his *Republic* and, unlike these, delivered directly at the time when the criticism might evoke a response.

Plato and Aristotle on comedy

Aristophanes took his comic role seriously, and in the plays the idea that poets, including comic poets, were the teachers of Greece is both implied and expressed.[23] Unexpectedly, perhaps, in view of his dismissal of poetry in the *Republic*, Plato, who includes

23. Particularly apparent in the *Frogs*.

Aristophanes as one of his speakers in the *Symposium*, defends
comedy in a later work, the *Laws*:

> It is necessary also to consider and know uncomely persons and
> thoughts, and those which are intended to produce laughter in
> comedy, and have a comic character both in respect to style, and song,
> and dance, or any other mode of imitation. For serious things cannot
> be understood without laughable things, nor opposites at all without
> opposites, if a man is really to have intelligence of either; but he cannot
> carry out both in action, if he is to have ever so small a share of virtue.
> And for this very reason he should learn them both, in order that he
> may not in ignorance do or say anything which is ridiculous and out of
> place – he should command slaves and hired strangers to imitate such
> things, and should never take any serious interest in them himself . . ..
> Let these then be laid down, both in law and in our narrative, as the
> regulations of laughable amusements which are generally called
> comedy.
>
> (VII, 816e)[24]

The Platonic argument lies behind most Renaissance defences of
comedy and satire.

Aristotle's treatise on comedy does not survive, but there are
scattered remarks in the *Poetics* that constitute part of the meagre
critical tradition from antiquity. Comedy is defined, and distinguished from tragedy. It represents the typical:

> Comedy as we have said is a representation (*mimesis*) of inferior people,
> not indeed in the full sense of the word bad, but the laughable is a
> species of the base or ugly. It consists in some blunder or ugliness that
> does not cause pain or disaster, an obvious example being the comic
> mask which is ugly and distorted but not painful.
>
> (V, 1–2)

> It is just in this respect that tragedy differs from comedy. The latter
> sets out to represent people as worse than they are today, the former as
> better.
>
> (II, 7)

> By a general truth I mean the sort of thing that a certain type of man
> will do or say probably or necessarily. This is what poetry aims at in

24. Jowett, B. (translator) (1871) *The Dialogues of Plato*, 4 vols, Oxford
    University Press, vol. 4, p. 330.

giving names to the characters. . . . In the case of comedy this has now become obvious, for comedians construct their plots out of probable incidents and then put in any names that occur to them. They do not, like the lampooners, write about individuals.

$$(\text{IX, } 4\text{--}6)^{25}$$

Since Aristophanes, whom he does not mention, and the old comedians did write about individuals, Aristotle must have had in mind the comedy of his own day. The *Poetics* is generally thought to have emanated from his later years (he died in 322), by which time comedy had probably acquired the characteristics that are associated with the new comedy of Menander (who was born in 342). That this is so is confirmed by an influential discussion in the *Nicomachean Ethics* about what it is that makes a man good or bad company. Aristotle seeks to define well-bred humour befitting a gentleman as a mean between vulgar buffoonery from the man who jokes at all costs without regard to his victim's feelings and the boorishness exhibited by the man who disapproves of humour:

> A man whose pleasantries do not go too far is called a 'wit'; that is to say, he is ready-witted or versatile, a witticism being thought of as the sally of a mobile temperament. . . . Then as to the middle state in dealing with the humorous, particularly characteristic of that is social tact or address, which may be defined as the gift of saying just the right things for a gentleman to say and of getting others to say such things to him. For there are things of this kind suitable for such a man to say and have said to him by way of pleasantry, the pleasantry of a man of liberal sentiments differing from that of a man of servile temper, and that of an educated from that of an uneducated person. You can see the difference if you compare the old with the new comedy. The masters of the old comedy thought obscenity was amusing, the masters of the new prefer innuendo, which is a great improvement from the point of view of decency.

$$(\text{IV, } 8)^{26}$$

---

25. In the translation of W. Hamilton Fyfe: see note 4 above.
26. Thomson, J.A.K. (1953) (translator), *The Ethics of Aristotle*, Penguin, p. 134. It has been argued that Jonson's character Carlo Buffone in *Everyman Out of His Humour* (1599) is based upon Aristotle's conception of the buffoon. See Campbell, O.Y. (1938) *Comicall Satyre and Shakespeare's Troilus and Cressida*, Huntingdon Library Publications, San Marino, p. 65.

Greek new comedy

Aristotle's gentleman might easily maintain his equilibrium at the performance of new comedy where the extravagant wit, indecency and caricature of the old was replaced by measured humour, decorum, and the realistic presentation of typical characters who no longer wore the padded costumes of old. The realism was such as to have prompted a famous question, 'O Menander, O life, which of you imitated the other?' The new comedy of general manners is no longer political, that is intimately concerned with contemporary events, public affairs and the workings of the city state, which lost its independence after the Macedonian conquest in 322.

One complete play by Menander survives, the *Dyskolos* ('The Peevish Man') which was performed in 316. It has a five-act structure, a chorus that is no more than a musical interlude between acts, and a prologue figure, as in Euripides, to set the scene. The central character is an obstacle in the way of the young man who has fallen in love at first sight with his daughter. Only when he has been rescued from near death after falling down a well does the peevish old man (who is much tormented by a garrulous cook and an impertinent slave) learn the error of his ways: 'Only disasters can educate us' (699–700) and accommodate his misanthropy to the common-sense norms of social living. Likewise, the young man is put to the test to prove himself worthy of the happy marriage that awaits him at the play's end.

Roman new comedy

The *Dyskolos*, which might suggest the comedy of Jonson or Molière, did not come to light until the twentieth century, so that Greek new comedy was directly known only through fragments. However, new comedy came to the Renaissance in its Roman form by way of the plays of Plautus and Terence[27] which were called *fabulae palliatae*, plays in Greek dress, from *pallium*, a Greek

---

27. See Duckworth, G. (1952) *The Nature of Roman Comedy*, Princeton University Press, especially Chapter 14, 'The Originality of Roman Comedy: A Recapitulation'; see also Chapter 15, 'The Influence of Plautus and Terence upon English Comedy'.

cloak, for the Romans preserved the Greek setting, the Greek names of the characters and the whole ethos and institutional order of the Greek world. The boastful soldier of Plautus, for example, is not a Roman veteran of the Punic war but an Athenian mercenary who had fought in Alexander's campaigns. Indeed, the slave Palaestrio introducing the plot of the play to the audience declares: 'In the Greek this play is entitled *Alazon* – *The Braggart* which in Latin we have translated *Gloriosus*'.[28] Similarly, of his *Eunuch* Terence says 'The play we shall present today is *The Eunuch* of Menander.' Comedy proper, like tragedy at Rome, began by way of translation from the Greek, and these remarks of both Plautus and Terence suggest that their plays were close reworkings, if not actual translations. In the absence of the Greek originals there is a scholarly debate about the nature and extent of the Roman debt. There are interesting signs of a debate about the proprieties of translation amongst the Roman practitioners themselves. Unlike Menander and Plautus who used the prologue for expository purposes in introducing the plot, Terence used his prologues as Jonson was to do later in self-defence as an *apologia pro arte sua*. In the prologue to his *Brothers* he defends himself against an anticipated charge of plagiarism:

> *Joined in Death* is a comedy by Diphilus: Plautus made a Latin play out of it with the same name. In the beginning of the Greek play there is a young man who abducts a slave girl from a slave dealer. Plautus left out this incident altogether so the present author took it for his *Brothers* and translated it word for word. This is the new play we are going to act; watch carefully and see if you think the scene is a plagiarism or the restoration of a passage which had carelessly been omitted.

On his own admission Terence has used more than one Greek source for his *Brothers*, and he was criticised for this method of combining or blending different comedies (*contaminatio*), thereby spoiling them for other, more straightforward translators. He defends his practice in the prologue to the *Girl from Andros*: 'In attacking the present author, they are really attacking Naevius, Plautus and Ennius whom he takes for his models and whose carelessness he would rather imitate than his critics' dreary accuracy.' Of one critic he says 'for all his competence as a

28. Quotations from Terence's prologues are from Radice, B. (translator) (1975) *Terence: The Comedies*, Penguin.

translator, his poor style of writing has turned good Greek plays into bad Latin ones'. In the same prologue (to his *Eunuch*) we also find Terence defending himself against the charge that he had stolen the character of the sponger and the soldier from a previous Latin play, called the *Flatterer*, by Plautus and Naevius:

> The author admits that he has transferred these characters from the Greek play into his *Eunuch*, but the suggestion that he knew these plays had already been translated into Latin he absolutely denies. If he is not allowed to make use of the same characters as other writers, how can he still bring on a running slave, virtuous wives and dishonest courtesans, greedy spongers and braggart soldiers? How can he show the substitution of a child, deception of an old man by his slave, love, hatred and suspicion? Nothing in fact is ever said which has not been said before.

Roman dependence upon Greek originals evidently prompted a vigorous debate about the limits of translation and the lines to be drawn between plagiarism on the one hand and legitimate imitation on the other. Terence takes the view that the plot devices and stock characters of new comedy are public material, and evidently preferred the freedom exercised by the earlier dramatists in relation to their Greek originals against stricter ideas of translation. Given his favourable citation of Plautus as a model to be followed, and given the marked differences in technique and comic effect displayed and achieved by the two dramatists, it may be supposed that each allowed himself a measure of freedom in adapting the themes, characters and conventions of Greek new comedy.

Plautus and Terence compared

Differences between the two Roman comedians may be illustrated in a comparison of the *Miles Gloriosus* ('The Boasting or Swaggering Soldier') of Plautus and the *Eunuch* of Terence, his most Plautine play, which includes amongst its characters a boasting soldier called Thraso. In *As You Like It*, Rosalind refers to Caesar's 'thrasonical brag of I came, saw and overcame' (V, ii, 34). The stock character of the boasting soldier in new comedy is the prototype of Jonson's Bobadill in *Everyman in his Humour*,

Shakespeare's Armado in *Love's Labour's Lost* and his Falstaff in *The Merry Wives of Windsor* and in the two parts of *Henry IV*. The *Miles* has proved a popular and entertaining play, even if it is haphazard in its dramatic construction. For instance, the opening scene between the soldier Pyrgopolynices and his satellite Artotrogus, which characterises the ridiculous soldier who has a high opinion not only of his military prowess but also of his attractiveness to women, proves to be detached from the main action but is necessary to introduce the main character of the plot who otherwise would not appear until well into the second half of the play. Horace, judging Plautus by classical standards, found him wanting in his loose plotting and in his readiness to sacrifice consistency of character for local effect:

> It is thought that comedy because it takes its subjects from everyday life, calls for less labour, but it carries a heavier burden as the indulgence allowed is less. See how poorly Plautus maintains the part of the youthful lover, or that of the watchful father or of the tricky pander; what a Dossenus he is among his greedy parasites, with what a loose sock he trips across the stage.
>
> ('Epistle to Augustus', 168–74)[29]

Jonson, however, commenting on this judgement in his *Discoveries* calls Plautus 'the parent of all conceit and sharpness' (3221). His own first comedy, *The Case is Altered* (written about 1597), takes its plot largely from the *Aulularia* and the *Captivi* of Plautus. It is well known that Shakespeare in one of his earliest plays drew upon the plot of the *Menaechmi* of Plautus for *The Comedy of Errors*, with additional material from the *Amphitryo*. Polonius, who in his saws and his silliness has something of the Plautine *senex*, puts Plautus at one end of the dramatic spectrum: 'Seneca cannot be too heavy nor Plautus too light' (II, ii, 396). *Hamlet*, of course, has both Plautine and Senecan elements within the one play. Overall, Plautus was the most popular of all the ancient dramatists in the Renaissance.

After the introduction of Pyrgopolinices (who like many Plautine characters has a tell-tale name, something like 'Towerbattler'), in comes his slave Palaestrio, the engineer of the plot, to address the audience: 'If you don't want to listen, you'd better get

---

29.   Dossenus 'hunchback', a lumbering buffoon.

up and go / And leave room for those who do. All right? . . .
very well, then' (81–2).[30] He proceeds to fill in the complex
background to the start of the action in the manner of a prologue,
telling us that he had formerly been the slave of a young Athenian
of good character called Pleusicles. The young man had been in
love with an Athenian girl, Philocomasium, but while he had
been away on military service, Pyrgopolinices on a visit to Athens
had inveigled himself into the girl's house by paying court to her
mother and managed to abduct Philocomasium who is now in
Pyrgopolinices' house in Ephesus where the play is set. Palaestrio,
attempting to reach Pleusicles, had been captured by a pirate who
had then given him as a present to Pyrgopolinices. Palaestrio has
managed to let Pleusicles know of the situation by letter, and the
young man has just arrived in Ephesus and is staying next door in
the house of Periplectomenus, an old family friend who is
sympathetic to attempts to reunite the lovers. Palaestrio has
devised a cunning scheme to enable the lovers to meet by cutting
an opening in the girl's private room that leads to the adjoining
house. It is given out that Philocomasium's twin sister has
arrived, and this explains the girl's appearance now in one house
now in the other. Much of the first half of the play concerns the
long-drawn-out (and successful) attempts of Palaestrio to persuade
the rather dimwitted slave who is supposed to be guarding
Philocomasium that there are two girls:

> . . . we're going to play some laughable tricks on him –
> Oh, some very ingenious japes – and throw dust in his eyes,
> And persuade him he hasn't seen what he thinks he has seen.
> But we don't want *you* to be deceived; so don't forget,
> One girl is going to pretend to be two girls,
> One from this house and one from that: same girl,
> But pretending to be a different one – all right?
> That's how the jailor is going to be bamboozled.
>
> (147–54)

Palaestrio is then both master of ceremonies and popular
entertainer, as the playwright goes to farcical extremes in
exploiting the hoariest of comic motifs: the gap between illusion

---

30. Quotations from Watling, E.F. (translator) (1965) *Plautus: The Pot of Gold and
Other Plays*, Penguin. There is no Renaissance English translation of the
Miles.

and reality. The audience is safe in its superior knowledge, and can enjoy the resulting absurdities of the comic irony. This basic comedy of intrigue and error is typically Plautine.

After this clowning, there follows a digressive conversation between Palaestrio, Pleusicles and Periplectomenus in which the main entertainment arises from the jovial misogyny of Periplectomenus who speaks at length about the ghastliness of women and the burdensomeness of family life. In strict logic it could be said that, holding the views he does, Periplectomenus should do all in his power to frustrate the plans of Pleusicles. After the scene has been going for about 200 lines, and just at the halfway point in the play, Palaestrio comes to the point: 'perhaps we ought now to turn our attention to the business in hand. Please listen to me, gentlemen; I shall need your help to carry out the ingenious ruse which I have devised for trimming Captain Curlylocks and assisting our loving friend in his design of abducting and possessing his beloved Philocomasium' (767–71).

Periplectomenus is to invite into his house an attractive woman who is to masquerade as his wife. The captain is to be deceived into thinking that she is desperately in love with him. Palaestrio, with the help of the woman's maid, will act as go-between. The captain is to be induced to dismiss Philocomasium in order to pursue this new love and is to be lured into the neighbouring house where he can be denounced as a fornicator. Two-thirds of the way through the play, Pyrgopolinices makes his second appearance, to be given a love token by Palaestrio, ostensibly from his neighbour's wife. The gulling of the captain occupies the rest of the play. The humour is increased when he is persuaded to allow Philocomasium to take all the jewels and presents he has given her, supposedly to keep her goodwill. He gives her all she asks for, including Palaestrio himself. Pleusicles poses as a sailor who has come to take her back to her mother in Athens. As soon as the lovers depart, the captain enters his neighbour's home to be caught by Periplectomenus. He is beaten, utterly humiliated and forced to take an oath promising good behaviour in future. In the end he repents: 'Well it was a fair catch, and justice has been done. Serve all lechers so, and lechery would grow less rife; the sinners would have more fear and mend their ways' (1434–6).

The *Miles* is typically Plautine in its exaggerated characters and its tendency to clowning and farce. (Indeed Plautus' *nomen*,

Maccius, may be derived from a stock comic character, *maccus*, the buffoon.) Its language is lively and its humour broad. Horace thought his wit inurbane (*The Art of Poetry*, 270–3), but Cicero enjoyed it (*De Officiis*, I, 104) and probably more accurately reflects Roman taste for his plays were popular and frequently revived. The *Miles* is untypical in that it has no musical interludes. Elsewhere, Plautus increased the musical element and gave what are sometimes called operatic parts to some characters, so that his kind of comedy has been likened to, and has indeed inspired, modern musical comedy.[31]

The *Eunuch* of Terence has the love intrigue that is basic to all new comedy, but is a more sophisticated dramatic construction than anything in Plautus. At the start, for example, information that would be given by Plautus in a prologue directly addressing the audience is imparted by the characters as they interact with one another in the course of the drama. While Plautus exploited incongruities between his Greek material and the contemporary Roman world for comic effect and frequently breaks the dramatic illusion to remind his audience that they are only watching a play, Terence maintains artistic decorum throughout, eliminating as far as possible intrusive Roman colouring. Although particular situations may be complicated in Plautus, his overall plotting is simple. In the *Miles* he has two intrigues in succession, both conducted by the central schemer Palaestrio, in whom the play finds its unity. By contrast, the Terentian double plot, with its two closely integrated love affairs that develop side by side, has its own dynamic achieved by the complex interaction of characters and incident, and is not in the control of a single omnipotent schemer like Palaestrio. There are in fact four schemers (two slaves, a courtesan and a sponging parasite) with diverse methods, characters and motives, and the central schemer is successfully outwitted by his counterpart from the women's quarters. In Terence there is comic irony as in Plautus, but also many surprising turns that keep the audience guessing. Horace, who criticised Plautus, refers to the commonplace commendation of Terence for his artistry (*Epistle* II, i, 59). The *Eunuch* is typically Terentian in being an example of an ingeniously well-made play.

31.   The Rodgers and Hart musical *The Boys from Syracuse* is a modern version of the *The Brothers Menaechmus*.

The play opens with the young Athenian Phaedria coming out of his father's house and conversing with his middle-aged slave, Parmeno. He has been repulsed by his beloved Thais, a courtesan who lives next door, and asks Parmeno what he is to do about it. Parmeno reasons with Phaedria and urges him to use his sense, but to no avail. Thais comes out of her house and explains her behaviour towards Phaedria. Her mother had been given a baby girl, Pamphila, by a merchant. She had been brought up as Thais' sister, but on the mother's death had been sold by her uncle to a soldier, Thraso, who had bought the girl to curry favour with Thais. Having found out about Thais' relationships with Phaedria, the soldier is making excuses not to hand her over. Thais wants the chance to restore her to her family, and asks Phaedria to go away for a short time so that she can secure the girl. Then Gnatho, the satellite of Thraso, enters with Pamphila to hand her over to Thais and to ask her to dine with Thraso. He delivers a monologue explaining his attitude to life:

> There's a sort of jolly companions in the world, that desire to bear all the sway and rule the roost where they come in everything: yet they are but bragging fellows and nothing so they would be reputed. These I follow at the heels and am ready at a beck, and yet I do not so fashion myself to them as that they may make all their jests on me: but I show them a smiling countenance for the nonce, and withal I fall a wondering at their high wits: whatsoever it be that they say, I say too, and commend it . . . this order have I taken with myself to give them the applause in everything. It's the best way in the world nowadays; by doing this, a man shall reap most commodity . . . even as sects receive their names from philosophers themselves, so from me in the same manner parasites might be called Gnathos.[32]
>
> (translating 248–53, 262–4)

Gnatho had his wish. At the end of a list illustrating the efficacy of the poet in offering 'speaking pictures' of virtues and vices, Sidney in *The Defence of Poesy* mentions 'the Terentian Gnatho and our Chaucer's Pandar, so expressed that we now use their names to signify their trades' (435–6). This is confirmed by a cluster of references in the *OED*, but while 'Pandar' through Chaucer and Shakespeare (in *Troilus and Cressida*) is still in general conscious-

---

32. In the version contained in Bernard, R. (1598) *Terence in English*, John Legat, Cambridge.

ness, Gnatho's afterlife was confined to the classically-educated Renaissance.

Phaedria's younger brother Chaerea enters to tell Parmeno that he has just been smitten by love at first sight for a girl in the street. She turns out to be Pamphila. Then comes the central intrigue of the play. Not to be outdone in the matter of courting gifts, Phaedria has instructed Parmeno to give Thais the present of a eunuch for her household. Pressed for help by Chaerea, Parmeno suggests that the boy dress up as the eunuch to go in his place, thereby gaining intimate access to the women's quarters where Pamphila will reside. When Chaerea is enthusiastic, Parmeno has second thoughts: 'Ay, but this mischief will all light upon my neck; ah, it is a sinful deed and heinous act Chaerea that we do.' Chaerea is unmoved. Thraso enters and is played along by Gnatho. The soldier asks advice about the best way to conduct his suit of Thais. Gnatho points out that Thais loves the presents given to her by Thraso and that this is the route to her heart. Thais comes out and Thraso invites her to dinner, but has to watch indignantly as Parmeno hands over to her Phaedria's gift of the eunuch. Thais now departs for dinner at Thraso's, leaving instructions with her maid Pythias that if the Athenian Chremes arrives whom she believes to be related to Pamphila, he is to wait or follow her to Thraso's. Chremes then enters, nonplussed at Thais' invitation. He goes off to Thraso's in search of her. Chaerea comes out of Thais' house and to one of his friends who has come looking for him he explains the trick and ecstatically announces that he has taken advantage of (i.e. raped) Pamphila. One of Thais' maids returns, telling of a quarrel between her mistress and Thraso occasioned by the presence of Chremes (whom Thraso believes to be a rival) and by Thraso's counter-action in demanding the presence of Pamphila at the banquet to sing. Then Phaedria unexpectedly returns from the country. The maid Pythias emerges from Thais' house to complain to Phaedria about his 'eunuch's' behaviour. Phaedria catches Dorus (the real eunuch) and is mystified to find him dressed in Chaerea's clothing but thinks it is a disguise designed to make good his escape.

First Chremes and then Thais return from Thraso's, expecting that the soldier will follow any minute to reclaim Pamphila. Thais attempts to stiffen Chremes' resistance without much success. Thraso enters with his kitchen army, consisting of his cook and his servants, with the intention of storming Thais' house. Eventually Chremes stands up to Thraso, announcing that Pamphila, whom Thraso believes to be a slave and therefore his property, is his sister and a free-born citizen of Athens. He goes to fetch their old nurse to show tokens of proof. Thraso retreats.

In conversation with her maid, Pythias, who suspects Chaerea, Thais now discovers the awful truth about Pamphila's rape. Chaerea enters to be confronted by the women. He is repentant and desires to marry Pamphila, a solution that appeals to Thais. Chremes returns with the nurse who confirms Pamphila's identity. Pythias, enraged at the conduct of Parmeno, plans revenge.

Parmeno then enters, complacently congratulating himself on his part in securing a marriage for Chaerea easily and without expense. Then come the famous lines of Parmeno that were cited by sixteenth-century commentators to point to the moral wholesomeness of this play and to the utility of comedy in general, here summarised in a version made by Sir Thomas Elyot in *The Book Named the Governor* (1530):

> In this thing I triumph in my own conceit
> That I have found for all young men the way
> How they of harlots shall know the deceit,
> Their wits, their manners, that thereby they may
> Them perpetually hate; for so much as they
> Out of their own houses be fresh and delicate,
> Feeding curiously; at home all the day
> Living beggarly in most wretched estate.[33]

His moment of triumph is short-lived, however, and his complacency shattered when Pythias tells him the false story that Chremes has tied up Chaerea and is threatening him with the penalty for fornicators allowed by Greek and Roman law (castration). At this moment, Laches, Chaerea's father, returns home from the country. The now distraught Parmeno sees no way out but confession. Laches storms into Thais' house. Pythias comes out laughing and enjoying the discomfiture of Parmeno.

---

33. See Gilbert, A.H. (ed.) (1962) *Literary Criticism: Plato to Dryden*, Wayne State University Press, Detroit, p. 239.

Chaerea comes out of the house ecstatic at the prospect of marriage:

> What should I speak of first, or whom may I most of all commend, either him that gave me counsel to do it, or myself that durst begin it? Or shall I withal extoll fortune, which had the guiding of it, which hath brought so many matters so great and so fitly to pass in one day? Or shall I magnify in this matter my father's pleasantness in his speech, and his mildness and courtesy in his behaviour? O great God, keep and continue us in this good prosperity.

He also announces that Laches has agreed to take Thais under his protection, so allowing Phaedria the undisputed attention of Thais who can now dispense with the services of her rich soldier.

An exultant Phaedria comes out of the house, and a desperate Thraso appeals to Gnatho to put him on some sort of footing with Thais. In the final move Gnatho, acting primarily to secure his own interests as he tells Phaedria, persuades him on economic grounds to put up with Thraso as a rival. Thraso will be useful for his money, and for the entertainment they can all have at his expense in every way. And so, there is happiness all round.

The Terentian double plot allows greater complication of incidents with a greater number and variety of players in the game. (There are eighteen characters in the *Eunuch*, only ten in the *Miles*, despite the fact that the latter is 300 lines longer.) These players have contrasting parts and make different moves. In the relationship between Thais and Phaedria, the scheming courtesan has the upper hand while the lovelorn Phaedria is forced into impotent passivity. By contrast, his brother Chaerea brashly makes all the moves in pursuit of Pamphila who is conceived in so passive a role that she is not even given a speaking part. This complementary contrast in the playwright's conception and conduct of the principals is also to be found in the handling of their underlings. The active part of Parmeno, the chief slave of the young brothers, is complemented by that of the reactive Pythias who, like her mistress, gains the upper hand.

As Terence's plots are more complicated than those of Plautus, so his characters are less stereotypical. In the *Miles*, Plautus has a very clever, witty and, in this case, entirely well-intentioned slave, a very stupid jailor and a very swaggering and reprehensible soldier. The *Eunuch* is regarded as Terence's most Plautine play because of the absurd character of Thraso and the farcical element he and Gnatho add to the play (particularly in the highly amusing attack on the house of Thais). Even here, though, Thraso is less exaggerated than Pyrgopolynices and he is intermittently aware that he is not irresistibly attractive to Thais. There is more psychological interest too, invested in Gnatho than in Artotrogus, his Plautine equivalent. Gnatho's monologue on sponging (which may be compared to Mosca's on parasites at the beginning of the third act of Jonson's *Volpone*) is unique in Terence in that it is the only extended passage in his plays that does not seem directly to advance the plot. Compared with the Plautine digression in which Periplectomenus inveighs against women, however, the relevance of Terence's apparent digression is clear. It establishes him as an important character (more so than Artotrogus) and it prepares us for the ending in which Phaedria and Thais are persuaded by him to be content to sponge off Thraso. His cynical view of the world is shown to rest on psychologically credible foundations and is to some extent vindicated by the outcome of the action. In the case of the trickster slave, Parmeno is less sure of himself than Palaestrio, and less successful; nor are his views of the world infallible. Despite his sixteenth-century commentators, his judgement of Thais is only partially true, for she is allowed a soliloquy in which she declares genuine love for Phaedria (even if she also loves the good things of life that Thraso can provide). Her intentions towards Pamphila are not only self-serving, and she is appalled at the rape. Admittedly her first reaction is to express shame that she has been taken in (her self-esteem has taken a blow) and she is indignant that her plans have been frustrated, but there is also genuine concern for the girl herself. Confronting the repentant Chaerea, she is inclined to forgiveness, saying that she is not altogether lacking in human feeling or experience and that she knows something of the power of love. This inclination to tolerance and reasonableness, typically Terentian whether or not we think it to be appropriate in this particular instance, is consistent with the rest of her character, and not the sort of thing to be found in Plautus. Thais, therefore, does not simply function as the hard-nosed *meretrix* of the comic tradition, nor is she simply a vehicle for the Roman misogyny of Parmeno, whose gloating speech about the iniquity of harlots immediately becomes the occasion of comedy when he is ridiculed by Pythias. She is sympathetically presented as an attractive character exhibiting a number of traits that make up a psychologically credible mixture.

With ingenious plotting and less stereotypical characterisation comes a more complex resolution. In the *Miles*, the devastating poetic justice is satisfyingly uncomplicated. The twofold denouement in *The Eunuch* is surprisingly neat and unexpected, but also problematic, at least for a modern audience. The actuality as distinct from the threat of rape is rare in comedy. In this Roman comic world, however, characters are let off the hook when it is revealed that Pamphila is a freeborn citizen and that Chaerea can marry her. By implication the honour of a slave has no value. This doubtless reflects a Roman reality. Though we hear of Pamphila's distress, there is no word of her consent to the marriage, another Roman reality. Unease has also been felt at the Gnathonical arrangement whereby Phaedria agrees to share Thais with Thraso. In a safer play, the violation would have fallen short of actual rape, and in a more conventionally moralised but less artistically decorous ending, Thraso would have been thoroughly disillusioned and discarded, while Gnatho would have been punished for his cynical philosophy of manipulation. Terentian comedy does not seek earnestly to correct the reality of the world it represents. That reality is far from idealised; hence the ending and the inclusion of passages like that in which Chaerea explains how he was encouraged to make advances against Pamphila by the sight of a picture in her room showing the story of Jupiter pouring the shower of gold into Danae's lap – a psychologically convincing touch which met with the disapproval of St Augustine who thought it likely to corrupt schoolboys.[34] In this detail, as in the whole, Terentian comedy offers Menandrian verisimilitude, fulfilling the Ciceronian demands of comedy that it should be *imitatio vitae, speculum consuetudinis, imago veritatis*[35] 'an imitation of life, mirror of custom, and image of truth'. Time has rendered obsolete many of the actual customs, attitudes and habits of the Graeco-Roman world, but Terence's artistry is such that we suspend our disbelief in the reality he presents, and the idea of comedy underlying the plays has been one of the most persistent,

34. Augustine *Confessions* I, 16 and *City of God* II, 7 noted in Radice, B. (1975) p. 191.
35. Transmitted by Donatus: see note below.

and has extended beyond comedy to dramatic performance generally, as in the advice of Hamlet to the players:

> Suit the action to the word, the word to the action; with this special observance, that you o'erstep not the modesty of nature; for anything so o'erdone is from the purpose of playing, whose end, both at the first and now, was and is to hold as 'twere, the mirror up to nature; to show virtue her own feature, scorn her own image, and the very age and body of the time his form and pressure.
>
> (III, ii, 16–26)

Terence's refinement of Roman comedy encompasses its language. In the words of the prologue to the *Self-Tormenter, in hac est pura oratio* (46) 'in this play is pureness of speech'. Paring down the more flamboyant language of traditional Roman comedy used by Plautus, he cultivated a spare terse style devoid of tricks and verbal display something like that which Jonson had in mind when he remarked in his *Discoveries*, 'Pure and neat language I love, yet plain and customary' (2315–16); this was the essential medium for his realistic characterisation.

This was also his distinctive achievement, according to the famous testimony of Cicero and Julius Caesar as given in epigrammatic form in an ancient life of Terence:

> You too who alone with your choice speech, Terence, bring Menander to us translated and expressed in the Latin tongue with gentle measures, always speaking affably and saying everything sweetly.
>
> (Cicero)

> You too will be placed with the highest, O halfsized Menander, and justly, lover of pure speech (*puri sermoris amator*). If only some vigour (*vis*) had been added to your gentle writings, so that your comic strength might have power equal to the Greeks.
>
> (Caesar)[36]

Caesar himself, from all we know of him as general, politician, orator and writer of unerringly clear prose, was greatly possessed of *vis*, and it is not altogether surprising that he finds Terentian comedy lacking in this respect. However, Menander is the

---

36. *Vita Terenti* 7 prefacing the commentaries on Terence in Wessner, P. (1902) *Aeli Donati quod fertur commentum Terenti*, Teubner, Leipzig.

touchstone for him and for Cicero, so that it may be appropriate
to cite the verdict of the rhetorician Quintilian on the virtues of
Menander as a model for the would-be stylist:

> The careful study of Menander alone would, in my opinion, be
> sufficient to develop all those qualities with the production of which
> my present work is concerned; so perfect is his representation of actual
> life, so rich is his power of invention and his gift of style, so perfectly
> does he adapt himself to every kind of circumstance, character and
> emotion.
>
> (*The Education of an Orator* X, i, 69)[37]

For Quintilian, Menander is the perfect model for the orator, as
his style is rooted in knowledge of human behaviour and
psychology which it has the resources to express in all its
versatility.

Commentators on Terence: classical dramatic theory

Although we are told that the *Eunuch* was highly successful when
first performed,[38] there are indications that Terence was running
against the tide of public taste in his day. In his prologue he
complains that the *Mother-in-Law* had been denied a hearing twice
on account of the rival attractions first of a tight-rope walker and
some boxers and second of a gladiator's show, and appeals to the
audience not to let the art of drama sink into the hands of a few.
His plots made considerable demands, and, unlike Plautus, he did
not seek a rapport with his audience. However, as the Roman
Menander, he had a rich after-life in the study and the schools,
where he attracted the attention of Roman grammarians who
sought to exemplify in detailed commentary the qualities praised
by Quintilian in relation to Menander. Commentaries accompanying the text survive from the fourth century and were
transmitted to the Renaissance with the manuscripts of the plays.
    The most notable is that of Donatus which includes two essays:
one entitled *De Fabula* (now ascribed to Evanthius) and another

37. Butler, H.E. (translator) (1922) *The Institutio Oratoria of Quintilian*, 4 vols,
    Loeb Classical Literary, Heinemann, London; Putnam's, New York.
    Subsequent quotations from Quintilian are in this translation.
38. *Vita Terenti* 10.

entitled *De Comoedia*. In the Renaissance they were usually combined under the title *De Comoedia et Tragoedia* and attributed to Donatus.[39] Donatus's essay on comedy transmits the well-known Ciceronian definition and other commonplaces, including the Greek definition of Diomedes: 'comedy is a treatment of private affairs that is without danger to life' (V, 1). Donatus emphasised the didactic function of comedy which shows what is useful and what is to be avoided in everyday life. In general comment on the origins of the drama, Evanthius remarks that the *Iliad* is the founding model for tragedy, the *Odyssey* for comedy. Old comedy represented contemporary events with the naming of individuals and was useful to the state when people sought to avoid blame in fear of being made a public spectacle. When poets abused this licence by attacking good people they were silenced by laws against slander. Another kind of comedy called the satyr play, which used scurrilous jokes without naming individuals, was considered suspect by the most powerful members of the community. And so new comedy came into being 'which with themes of a more general nature applicable to all persons who are of a less exalted station caused less bitterness to the spectators and gave much pleasure being well balanced in plot, fitting in its general manners, useful in its sentiments, pleasing in its wit, and neat in its metre' (II, 6). 'No one has more diligently preserved the rules about the habits, age, duties and manners of persons than Terence. Though he sought verisimilitude in his fictitious plots, he alone has ventured sometimes to introduce courtesans who are not ill-natured, giving a reason why they are good, and there is no diminution of pleasure because of this' (III, 4). Terence is praised for keeping the true decorum of comedy, neither veering towards tragedy nor, like Plautus, descending to farce. His plots are well-knit and maintain the dramatic illusion. In a final section he has general remarks on the differences between tragedy and comedy. They differ 'in the first place because in comedy are people of middle station with petty onsets of dangers and happy outcomes of the action, but in tragedy all is opposite, mighty personages,

39. The texts are included in the edition cited in note 36 above. The following account is particularly indebted to Baldwin, T.W. (1947) *William Shakspere's Five-Act Structure*, University of Illinois Press, Urbana, and Herrick, M.T. (1950) *Comic Theory in the Sixteenth Century*, University of Illinois Press, Urbana.

great fears and the outcomes are calamitous; in comedy the beginning is turbulent and the ending calm, in tragedy the opposite is true; then because in tragedy life is represented as something to be fled from, in comedy as something to be embraced; finally because all comedies are fictitious while tragedy often has historical truth' (IV, 2). Evanthius divides comedy into four parts: *prologue, protasis, epitasis* and *catastrophe*:

> The prologue is the preface to the play in which something over and above the plot may be presented or something to do with the author, the play itself, or the actor. The *protasis* is the first act and the beginning of the play proper. The *epitasis* is the rising of the forward progress of the turmoils (*incrementum processusque turbarum*) or, as I have said before, the knot of the confusion (*nodus erroris*); the *catastrophe* is the reversal (*conversio*) of affairs preparatory to the cheerful outcome; it reveals all by means of a discovery (*cognitio*).
>
> (IV, 5)

Evanthius is transmitting in commonplace prose some of the leading principles derived from usual classical practice that are better known in the neat poetic formulations of Horace in his *Art of Poetry*. In the first place there is the decorum of genre; tragedy and comedy are essentially distinct with no matching of 'hornpipes and funerals' (1326), as Sidney put in *The Defence of Poesy*, though Plautus called his *Amphitryo*, which features gods, heroic persons and servants, *tragico-comoedia*, and this play was regarded in the Renaissance as the classical archetype of tragi-comedy.[40] Horace does not admit the term, though his formulation represented here in Jonson's version allows for flexibility within the general framework of generic distinction:

> The comic matter will not be expressed
> In tragic verse; no less Thyestes' feast
> Abhors low numbers, and the private strain
> Fit for the sock: each subject should retain
> The place allotted it, with decent thews . . .
> Yet, sometime, doth the comedy excite
> Her voice, and angry Chremes chafes outright
> With swelling throat; and oft the tragic wight
> Complains in humble phrase. Both Telephus,

40. Herrick, M.T. (1965) *Tragicomedy: Its Origins and Development in Italy, France and England*, University of Illinois Press, Urbana.

And Peleus, if they seek to heart-strike us
That are spectators, with their misery,
When they are poor and banished, must throw by
Their bombard-phrase, and foot-and-half-foot words.
                    (121–5; 132–9, translating 89–98)[41]

Then there is decorum in two interrelated aspects of characterisation: the need to match language to character and to maintain
consistency in characterisation. This applies equally to the well-
known figures of traditional mythology used in tragedy and to
fictional characters newly created for comedy:

It much will differ if a God speak, then
Or a hero; if a ripe old man
Or some hot youth, yet in his flourishing course;
Where some great lady, or her diligent nurse;
A venturing merchant, or the farmer, free
Of some small thankful land: whether he be
Of Colchis born; or in Assyria bred;
Or, with the milk of Thebes or Argos fed.
Or follow fame, thou that dost write, or feign
Things in themselves agreeing: if again
Honoured Achilles chance by thee be seized,
Keep him still active, angry, unappeased;
Sharp and contemning laws . . .
If something strange, that never yet was had
Unto the scene thou bring'st, and create
A mere new person, look he keep his state
Unto the last, as when he first went forth
Still to be like himself, and hold his worth.
            (161–73, 178–82, translating 114–21, 125–7)

aetatis cuiusque notandi sunt tibi mores
mobilibusque decor naturis dandus et annis.
                                    (156–7)

(You must note the manners of each age and give what is becoming to
shifting natures and their years.)

41.   Chremes, a stock father in comedy. Telephus, king of Mysia, was wounded
       by Achilles and in desperation was driven to seek a cure from his enemies,
       the Greeks. Peleus, father of Achilles, was exiled twice before his marriage to
       Thetis. These stories were treated by a number of famous playwrights (in
       plays no longer surviving).

There follows the well-known thumb-nail sketch of the four ages of man from childhood through youth and maturity to old age. These precepts on character reflect general ancient practice in which characterisation is comparatively simple. Ancient characters may have a number of traits, like the hero of the *Odyssey*, but few if any ancient works are built around inner conflict or organised to explore growth of character. Odysseus remains the same from beginning to end. In the *Brothers* of Terence an over-harsh and an over-indulgent father both moderate their views at the end of the play in the light of experience, but this does not quite constitute character development in the modern sense. Nevertheless, the clarity with which the legislative critic crisply delivers his precepts, thus decorously fulfilling the requirement of a didactic *ars* and making his insistence upon typicality and self-consistency seem conservative to the point of inflexibility, can be offset by the practice of Terence (in the example of Thais, for instance), which shows how within the framework of the rules classical practice was in fact flexible, so that the typical need not mean the stereotypical.[42]

The ancient grammarians had divided Terence into five acts, in accordance with the Horatian precept (*The Art of Poetry*, 191–2). Renaissance commentators systematised the ancient inheritance by harmonising the Evanthian analysis (really tripartite, for the prologue in Terence is extraneous to the play) with the five-act structure. The typical scheme has the *protasis* extending over Acts I and II, the *epitasis* over Acts III and IV, with the *catastrophe* in Act V. Scaliger, in his *Poetics*, added another term *catastasis*, meaning the full development of the action, the counterturn which stirs up added difficulties.

In the *Eunuch*, the substitution of Chaerea for Dorus suggested by Parmeno at the end of the second act, takes place in the third. Here begins the *epitasis*. In the last scene of the act Chaerea tells of the violation of Pamphila. In the fourth act the confusion is increased with the quarrel between Thais and Thraso and the return of Phaedria. Here is the *catastasis*. In the fifth act the perturbation of Parmeno caused by the trick played upon him by Pythias brings upon the *catastrophe*, when Parmeno confesses the

---

42.   The limitations of ancient characterisation are noted in *An Essay of Dramatic Poesy* (1668) by Dryden: see Watson, G. (1962) vol. 1, p. 73.

truth to Chaerea's father. Recognition of the real identity of
Pamphila is fully confirmed to all the characters in the third scene
of the final act facilitating the final denouement.

In the chorus introducing Jonson's *The Magnetic Lady* (1632),
the boy of the playwright's house educates the ignorant Damplay
in these elementary facts of dramatic life:

> *Boy.* Now gentlemen, what censure you of our protasis, or first act?
> *Probee.* Well, boy, it is a fair presentment of your actors; and a
> handsome promise of somewhat to come hereafter.
> *Damplay.* But there is nothing done in it, or concluded: therefore I say
> no act.
> *Boy.* A fine piece of logic! do you look, master Damplay, for
> conclusions in a protasis? I thought the law of comedy had reserved
> them to the catastrophe; and that the epitasis, as we are taught, and
> the catastasis, had been intervening parts, to have been expected.

At the end of the second act, the final words of the Boy are 'Let us
mind what you come for, the play, which will draw on to the
epitasis now.' At the end of the fourth act, the bewildered
Damplay is again instructed by the Boy:

> *Damplay.* Troth, I am one of those that labour with the same longing,
> for it is almost pucker'd, and pulled into that knot by your poet
> which I cannot easily, with all the strength of my imagination,
> untie. . . .
> *Boy.* Stay, and see his last act, his catastrophe, how he will perplex
> that, or spring some fresh cheat, to entertain the spectators, with a
> convenient delight, till some unexpected and new encounter break
> out to rectify all, and make good the conclusion.

Jonson's plots may be considered to be elaborations of the
Terentian scheme, with Brainworm in *Everyman in his Humour*,
Mosca in *Volpone* and Face in *The Alchemist* acting the part of the
new comedy schemer like the Plautine Palaestrio or the Terentian
Parmeno. The appeal of the Jonsonian kind of plot is well
described by one of the speakers in Dryden's dialogue *Of Dramatic
Poesy* (1668):

> If then the parts are managed so regularly that the beauty of the whole
> be kept entire, and that the variety become not a perplexed and
> confused mass of accidents, you will find it infinitely pleasing to be led

in a labyrinth of design, where you see some of your way before you, yet discern not the end till you arrive at it.[43]

The speaker proceeds to illustration by way of an 'examen' of *The Silent Woman* (1609), otherwise known as *Epicene*. Much of what he says about it could equally well apply to the simpler Terentian scheme here perfected by Jonson:

> The intrigue of it is the greatest and most noble of any pure unmixed comedy in any language. . . . the business of it rises in every act. The second is greater than the first, the third than the second, and forward to the fifth. There too you will see till the very last scene new difficulties arising to obstruct the action of the play; and when the audience is brought into despair that the business can naturally be effected, then, and not before the discovery is made. . . . Thus like a skilful chess-player, by little and little he draws out his men, and makes his pawns of use to his greater persons.[44]

As the sixteenth-century commentators came to know the *Poetics*, the Roman inheritance was soon harmonised with the Greek. *Protasis*, *epitasis* and *catastrophe* were identified with the Aristotelian beginning, middle and end, and *epitasis* with Aristotle's *desis*, complication, and *catastrophe* with *lusis* denouement. The latter was also identified with Aristotle's change of fortune. Evanthius' *conversio* was related to *peripeteia* and *cognitio* to *anagnoresis*. The complex plot preferred by Aristotle, wherein a change of fortune coincides with a discovery or a reversal, or both, was easily found to be exemplified in Terence. The *duplex argumentum*, the twofold plot, might at first seem to clash with the Aristotelian requirement for unity of action, but the two aspects are so well integrated that this was not seen to be a problem, as it was so clearly an excellence in Terence. The other unities are well observed. The *Eunuch*, for example, has a single setting in a street in front of the two houses and the action falls well within the course of a day. The verisimilitude of Terentian comedy seemed to harmonise with all that Aristotle has to say about probability[45] as well as meeting the requirements of Horatian precept. 'Aristotle

43. Watson, G. (ed.) (1962) vol. 1, p. 71.
44. Watson, G. (1962) vol. 1, pp. 75–6. See also 'Shakespeare's New Comedy' in Nevo, R. (1980) *Comic Transformations in Shakespeare*, Methuen, esp. pp. 7–8.
45. For example *Poetics* VIII, 9ff.; XV, 10; XXIV, 19ff.

has now . . . been forced into conformity with the system which
had been conglomerated from the Latins. This harmonised
conglomerate is labelled Aristotle.'[46] For example, in Dryden's
dialogue *Of Dramatic Poesy* is to be found the following statement
'Aristotle indeed divides the integral parts of a play into four.
First, the *protasis* . . . Secondly, the *epitasis* . . . Thirdly the
catastasis . . . Lastly, the *catastrophe* . . .'[47] These terms derive
from Scaliger, who took them from Donatus (adding *catastasis*),
and are not in fact Aristotelian. The best-known 'Aristotelian'
doctrine concerning the unities is not, strictly speaking, Aristotelian at all. The Greek critic makes much of the unity of action,
but on time has the simple observation that 'tragedy attempts to
keep within a single revolution of the sun or to exceed it only a
little' (*Poetics* III, 8), while he has nothing to say about place.
Aristotle was very largely a Renaissance invention (or in a modern
parlance 'construction') in a way that Horace, Cicero and
Quintilian were not. It is one of the great ironies of literary
history that the *Poetics* only came to be distinctively appreciated as
the name of its author ceased to carry authority.[48] It was pre-
eminently through study of Terence that classical 'rules' came to
be transmitted, as the Greeks were too unfamiliar and Seneca
violated too many of them, notably decorum, in that all his
characters tend to orate in the same language and verisimilitude in
his inclusion of deeds of violence and horror on the stage (against
the precept of Horace in *The Art of Poetry* 182–8). To return to
The Magnetic Lady:

> *Damplay.* You have heard, Boy, the ancient poets had it in their
>   purpose still to please this people.
> *Probee.* Ay, their chief aim was –
> *Damplay. Populo ut placerent:* (if he understands so much)
> *Boy. Quas fecissent fabulas.* I understand that, sin' I learned Terence, i'
>   the third form at Westminster:
>
> ('Induction', 33–8)

46. Baldwin, T.W. (1947) p. 284. Also Herrick, M.T. (1946) *The Fusion of Horatian and Aristotelian Criticism 1531–1555*, University of Illinois Press, Urbana; Weinberg, B. (1961) *A History of Literary Criticism in the Renaissance*, 2 vols, University of Chicago Press, Chicago.
47. Watson, G. (1962) vol. 1, p. 33.
48. See Herrick, M.T. (1930) *The Poetics of Aristotle in England*, Cornell Studies in English **17**, Yale University Press, New Haven and London.

Damplay quotes the first part of the third line of Terence's prologue to the *Girl from Andros* 'to please the people'. The Boy caps him by adding the second half which gives the full sense of Terence 'to please the people by virtue of the *fabulae* they have made', and goes on to show that, unlike the ignorant Damplay, he understands the art of plotting to be inferred from the Evanthian analysis. Every attentive grammar schoolboy knew his Terence, and if, like Jonson, he was taught by a master like Camden, 'to whom I owe / All that I am in arts, all that I know',[49] he may also have been acquainted with much of the accompanying scholastic apparatus that was evidently not merely the remote property of the learned world. In the sixteenth-century grammar school Terence became a textbook of practical dramaturgy through which we may believe many a future playwright learned the basic grammar and syntax of his art.

The humanist Terence

The popularity of Terence as a school text (his plays along with those of Plautus were also performed in schools; the tradition of the Westminster Christmas play in Latin goes back to Jonson's days) was not entirely a consequence of his comic excellence. The humanists in their drive to revive classical Latin had been particularly interested in Terence from the beginning, for although he wrote before the classical period, on the testimony of Cicero, no less, and Caesar, he wrote Latin that was pure. Erasmus writes: 'Amongst Roman writers in prose and verse, Terence for pure terse Latinity has no rival, and his plays are never dull.'[50] Even though he writes in verse (iambics), his works are virtually unique among surviving texts, in that his Latin gives an idea of what decent ordinary conversation on everyday topics might have been like. Most of the rest of Latin literature is more formalised in a variety of ways. The ancient life records that Terence was a friend of Scipio Aemilianus, the great general, and cultivated phil-Hellene and of Laelius, surnamed Sapiens for his stoic inclinations, who both feature in Cicero's

49. Epigram XIV, 'To William Camden'.
50. Quoted by Baldwin, T.W. (1947) p. 162.

dialogues on old age and friendship as a result of which they have become cultural icons.[51] The language of Terence, therefore, has often been associated with the refined colloquialism of the great and the good. In an age when Latin was still spoken, this was not merely of academic or historical interest. Erasmus, for example, began his *Colloquies* with the aim of teaching good colloquial Latin. In this endeavour Terence seemed particularly useful. In the words of one of his early editors:

> This poet is profitable for the polishing of language, for the unlearning of rudeness, for the wealth and abundance of words and sentiments, for the invention of arguments for every kind of cause, for providing the knack of both speaking and writing. His speech is delightful and fitted above all to the understanding of boys – plain, simple, clear, never having anything obscure or ostentatiously affected.[52]

Mention here of 'the invention of arguments of every kind of cause' expresses the rhetorical interest common in Renaissance analyses of Terence. The German humanist Melanchthon, who made Terence a foundation author in his educational system, remarks of the *Brothers*: 'The whole play is like an oration of the persuasive type. For the old men, young men and servants consult variously about the whole cause.'[53] As well as finding different kinds of rhetoric in Terence and identifying its constituent parts, commentators pointed out the various figures of sound and sense used, as they were not in other authors, in the context of familiar discourse.

In England, the schoolmaster Nicolas Udall in 1533 brought out his *Floures For Latine Spekynge Selected And gathered oute of Terence, and the same tranclated in to Englysshe, together with the exposition and settynge forthe as welle of suche latyne wordes, as were thought nedeful to be annotated, as also of dyvers grammatical rules, very profytable & necessarye for the expedite knowledge of the Latin tongue.* Understanding Terence had practical contemporary application. Udall went on to write *Ralph Roister Doister* (1537), regarded as the first regular comedy in English, with its main character

51. *Vita Terenti* 2, 4.
52. From the editor's preface in Wagnerus, G. (ed.) (1550) *Terenti Fabulae*, Gesner, Zurich, quoted by Herrick, M.T. (1950) p. 215.
53. Scaliger, J.C. (ed.) (1552) *Terenti Comoediae*, Paris, p. 3a, quoted in Herrick, M.T. (1950) p. 14.

deriving from Terence's Thraso. More than knowledge of the rules, however, is necessary to produce a good play. Sadly Udall's doggerel verse is virtually unreadable. The first translation was produced in 1588 by Maurice Kyffin, *Andria, The First Comoedie of Terence, in English*. In his preface he translated directly from the preface of Melanchthon's edition of 1528:

> Among all the Roman writers, there is none (by the judgement of the learned) so much available to be read and studied, for the true knowledge and purity of the Latin tongue as Pub. Terence: for, sith the chiefest matter in speech, is to speak properly and aptly, and that we have not a more cunning craft-master of apt and proper speech than Terence, well worthy is he then, even with all care and diligence, to be both taught and learned before any other.[54]

The rest of Terence came in 1598, with Richard Bernard's bilingual *Terence in English*. There are sporadic lists of *sententiae* and *formulae loquendi* after the example of Udall's *Floures*, and also *ethicae seu morales expositiones* following each scene.

This ethical interest is typical of the sixteenth century. Defending comedy in *The Governor*, Thomas Elyot takes the line of Donatus that comedy is a mirror of life wherein evil is not taught but discovered. He then gives the abbreviated translation of Parmeno's speech, cited above.[55] Defending comedy, Sidney too in his well-known passage takes a strong moral line:

> . . . comedy is an imitation of the common errors of our life, which he representeth in the most ridiculous and scornful sort that may be, so as it is impossible that any beholder can be content to be such a one. Now, as in geometry the oblique must be known as well as the right, and in arithmetic the odd as well as the even, so in the actions of our life who seeth not the filthiness of evil wanteth a great foil to perceive the beauty of virtue. This doth the comedy handle so in our private and domestical matters as with hearing it we get as it were an experience of what is to be looked for of a niggardly Demea, of a crafty Davus, of a flattering Gnatho, of a vainglorious Thraso, and not only to know who be such, by the signifying badge given them by the comedian.
>
> (*The Defence of Poesy*, 724–35)[56]

54. Baldwin, T.W. (1947) p. 339.
55. On p. 106.
56. Duncan-Jones, K. (1989) pp. 229–30. Demea is the strict father in *The Brothers*, Davus a slave in *Phormio* and *The Girl from Andros*.

Sidney's touchstone is Terence, but his tone under pressure to defend represents him as more scornful than he is. Bernard in the preface to his translation calls Terence 'as ethical as Plato':

> he can play craftily the cozener and cunningly the clown: he will tell you the nature of the fraudulent flatterer, the grim and greedy old sire, the roisting ruffian, the mincing minion and beastly bawd; that in telling the truth by these figments men might become wise to avoid such vices and learn to practice virtue.[57]

Terence might have read this description of himself with a degree of surprise.

Jonson's classical practice

Bernard's Terence was published just about the time when Jonson was starting his dramatic career. With his much Latin and considerable Greek, the learned Jonson consciously sought to improve Elizabethan practice by bringing classical standards to bear upon the English stage. The prologue to the revised edition of his early play *Everyman in his Humour* (1601) castigates 'the ill customs of the age' where decorum and verisimilitude are disregarded:

> To make a child now swaddled, to proceed
> Man, and then shoot up, in one beard and weed,
> Past threescore years; or, with three rusty swords
> And help of some few foot and half-foot words
> Fight over York and Lancaster's long jars . . .

Usual theatrical devices are not to be expected:

> But deeds, and language, such as men do use,
> And persons, such as comedy would choose,
> When she would show an image of the times
> And sport with follies not with crimes.
>
> (7–11, 21–4)

Here is the humanist prescription drawn principally from new comedy. Asper's account of the humour character in *Everyman out of his Humour* (1599) may be related to the practice of typical

---

57. Bernard, R. (1598) *Terence in English*, John Legat, Cambridge, p. 10.

characterisation in new comedy (especially to Plautine caricature) whatever its basis in medieval psychology:

As when some peculiar quality
Doth so possess a man, that it doth draw
All his affects, his spirits, and his powers,
In their conflictions, all to run one way
This may be truly said to be a humour.

(105–9)

The prologue to *Volpone* (1605) offers the refinement of classical art in defiance of the crudity of theatrical productions pandering to contemporary taste:

Yet thus much I can give you as a token
    Of his play's worth, no eggs are broken,
Nor quaking custards with fierce teeth affrighted,
    Wherewith your rout are so delighted;
Nor hales he in a gull old ends reciting,
    To stop gaps in his loose writing;
With such a deal of monstrous and forced action,
    As might make Bethlem a faction:
Nor made he his play for jests stolen from each table,
    But makes jests to fit his fable;
And so presents quick comedy refined,
    As best critics have designed;
The laws of time, place, persons he observeth,
    From no needful rule he swerveth.

(19–32)

On the other hand, the introductory discussion of comedy prefacing *Everyman out of his Humour* between Cordatus 'the author's friend, a man inly acquainted with the scope of his plot' who has 'a discrete and understanding judgement' and 'the place of a moderator' and Mitis 'a person of no action . . . and therefore no character' is directed to a very different end:

Mitis. You have seen his play, Cordatus: pray you, how is it?
Cordatus. . . . 'tis strange, and of a particular kind, somewhat like *Vetus Comoedia* . . .
Mitis. Does he observe all the laws of comedy in it?
Cordatus. What laws mean you?
Mitis. Why, the equal division of it into acts and scenes, according to the Terentian manner; his true number of actors; the furnishing of

the scene with Grex or chorus, and that the whole argument fall within the compass of a day's business.

Cordatus. O no, these are too nice observations.

Mitus. They are such as must be received, by your favour, or it cannot be authentic.

Cordatus. Troth I can discern no such necessity.

Mitis. No!

Cordatus. No, I assure you, signior. If those laws you speak of had been delivered us *ab initio*, and in their present virtue and perfection, there had been some reason of obeying their powers; but 'tis extant, that that which we call *Comoedia*, was first nothing but a simple and continued song, sung by only one person, till Susario invented a second; after him Epicharmus a third; . . . Aristophanes, more than they; every man in the dignity of his spirit and judgement supplied something. And, though that in him this kind of poem appeared absolute, and fully perfected, yet how is the face of it changed since in Menander, Philemon, Cecilius, Plautus, and the rest! who have utterly excluded the chorus, altered the property of the persons, their names, and natures, and augmented it with all liberty, according to the elegancy and disposition of those times wherein they wrote. I see not then, but we should enjoy the same licence, or free power to illustrate and heighten our invention, as they did; and not be tied to those strict and regular forms which the niceness of a few, who are nothing but form, would thrust upon us.

This is an eloquent and dignified argument, supported by a common-sense appeal to the actual history of generic evolution and change, for the poet's right to freedom of invention against ideal notions of fixity of genre or timeless forms. Mitis, here the unthinkingly conservative proponent of mere classical 'form', is roundly rebuffed.

Here may be adduced two celebrated passages from Jonson's later *Discoveries* which show the same critical independence with regard to the past, a critical independence that particularly compels admiration because we know that he depended so much upon the ancients for guidance and inspiration:

I know nothing can conduce more to letters than to examine the writings of the ancients, and not to rest in their sole authority, or to take all upon trust from them . . . For to all the observations of the ancients we have our own experience, which if we will use and apply, we have better means to pronounce. It is true that they opened the gates, and made the way that went before us, but as guides not commanders. . . . Truth lies open to all; it is no man's several.

(160–73)

Nothing is more ridiculous than to make an author a dictator, as the schools have done Aristotle. The damage is infinite knowledge receives by it. For to many things a man should owe but a temporary belief, and a suspension of his own judgement, not an absolute resignation of himself, or a perpetual captivity. Let Aristotle and others have their due; but if we can make further discoveries of truth and fitness than they, why are we envied?

(2596–604)

In context Jonson is referring to Aristotle 'the philosopher' who dominated medieval scholasticism, but he could equally well have written something similar about Aristotle the literary critic whose 'rules' acquired such authority in the learned world of the late Renaissance, for the habit of mind revealed here is open, forward-looking and undogmatic.

In the course of the play, Mitis imagines another objection: to this particular kind of comedy.

> *Mitis.* That the argument of his comedy might have some other nature, as of a duke to be in love with a countess, and that countess to be in love with the duke's son, and the son to love the lady's waiting-maid; some such cross wooing, with a clown to their serving-man, better than to be thus near, and familiarly allied to the time.
>
> *Cordatus.* You say well, but I would fain hear one of these autumn-judgements define once *quid sit comoedia*? If he cannot, let him content himself with Cicero's definition till he have strength to propose to himself a better, who would have a comedy to be *imitatio vitae, speculum consuetudinis, imago veritatis*; a thing throughout pleasant and ridiculous, and accommodated to the correction of manners. If the maker have failed in any particle of this, they may worthily tax him.

To the objection that the play goes against the grain of expectation in being so closely related to the times rather than being a romantic comedy of error (a type already popular on the Elizabethan stage), Cordatus, while not actually defining its kind (new to England), associates the play with the familiar Ciceronian definition in such a way as to reinvigorate its meaning by accommodating it to satire. Mitis, whose name means gentle in Latin, is a contrasting foil in the opening sequence to Asper, the satirical presenter whose name means harsh. The image that the age will see in Asper's mirror is very different from the reflection of the world seen in Menandrian and Terentian comedy:

> *Asper.* Well, I will scourge those apes,
>   And to these courteous eyes oppose a mirror,
>   As large as in the stage whereon we act;
>   Where they shall see the time's deformity
>   Anatomised in every nerve and sinew
>   With constant courage, and contempt of fear.
>   (118–23)

Asper is 'an ingenious and free spirit, eager and constant in reproof, without fear controlling the world's abuses: one whom no servile hope of gain, or frosty apprehension of danger can make to be a parasite, either to time, place or opinion'. It is not difficult to see that the spirit of Asper is an essential ingredient in Jonsonian comedy (and one not wholly absent from his tragedy). In his 'comical satire', Jonson looked back beyond Plautus and Terence to the old comedy of Aristophanes when the comic poet had the role of public censor and functioned as a community scourge. Even if he had wished to do so, in semi-feudal England Jonson could not have assumed that role or exercised that function with the freedom allowed to and enjoyed by Aristophanes in democratic Athens when he directly pilloried men of power in the *Knights*. But there are indications that in some respects that freedom was uncongenial anyway. In the *Discoveries* he finds the wit of old comedy too readily appealing to our baser natures, and castigates Aristophanes for pandering to the multitude in his fantastic caricature of Socrates in the *Clouds*:

> So that, what either in the words, or sense of an author, or in the language, or actions of men, is awry, or depraved, doth strangely stir mean affections, and provoke for the most part to laughter. And therefore it was clear that all insolent, and obscene speeches; jests upon the best men; injuries to particular persons; perverse and sinister sayings (and the rather unexpected) in the old comedy, did move laughter; especially, where it did imitate any dishonesty; and scurrility came forth in the place of wit: which who understands the nature and genius of laughter, cannot but perfectly know. Of which Aristophanes

affords an ample harvest, having not only outgone Plautus, or any other in that kind; but expressed all the moods, and figures of what is ridiculous, oddly. In short, as vinegar is not accounted good, until the wine is corrupted: so jests that are true and natural, seldom raise laughter, with the beast, the multitude. They love nothing, that is right, and proper. The farther it runs from reason, or possibility with them, the better it is. What could have made them laugh, like to see Socrates presented, that example of all good life, honesty, and virtue, to have him hoisted up with a pulley, and there play the philosopher in a basket? . . . This was theatrical wit, right stage jesting, and relishing a play-house, invented for scorn, and laughter; whereas if it had savoured of equity, truth, perspicuity, and candour, to have tasten a wise, or a learned palate, spit it out presently; this is bitter and profitable, this instructs, and would inform us.

(3270–307)

Jonson's comical satire is perhaps more like the later plays of Aristophanes written in the fourth century, such as the *Ecclesiazusae*, 'Women in the Assembly', and *Plutus*, 'Wealth', which have been thought to exemplify 'middle comedy' because they are less overtly political and have satire not of individuals but of types and because in them the fantastic and the anarchic yield a little to probability and decorum in character and plotting, notably with the decline of the chorus and the abandonment of the *parabasis* in which the playwright breaks the dramatic illusion fearlessly to harangue the audience on some topic that may have little to do with the plot.

Asper alludes to the social and moral function of his satire when he says of would-be judicious gallants watching the play 'I would give them pills to purge / And make them fit for fair societies.' The imperceptible Renaissance blending of the Greek and Roman traditions gave rise to a body of doctrine embracing not only the means of dramatic representation but also its end. At the conclusion of *Cynthia's Revels* (1600), after a palinode in which a variety of affected, fantastic, swaggering, simpering and self-loving humours are renounced, comes the benediction of the final song, sung by Mercury and Crites (the judge):

Now each one dry his weeping eyes,
  And to the Well of Knowledge haste;
Where, purged of all your maladies,
  You may of sweeter waters taste:

And, with refined voice, report
The grace of Cynthia, and her court.

Aristotle's theory of catharsis, duly moralised in the usual Renaissance way, has been given practical expression in comic form. The serious moral catharsis is delightfully contrived in *The Poetaster* (1601), when, in a fantastic gesture reminiscent of Aristophanes, Horace administers emetic pills to the poetasters and plagiarists Crispinus and Demetrius (Marston and Dekker – this is as near as Jonson comes to naming individuals – who have been found guilty of falsely accusing Horace (Jonson) of 'arrogance, railing and filching by translation') so that they vomit up their 'crudities', a series of outlandish words and turgid expressions used in their plays. Poets are guardians of the language as well as of morals. Set in Augustan Rome, the play is designed to illustrate the ideal functioning of poets and poetry in the *civitas* in general, and in particular to demonstrate the wholesome corrective function of comical satire when it is used responsibly and with civilised moral restraint. This restraint, according to Horace's account in *The Art of Poetry* was forced upon old comedy when it abused its liberty:

> To these [early tragedians] succeeded the old comedy,
> And not without much praise; till liberty
> Fell into fault so far, as now they saw
> Her license fit to be restrained by law:
> Which law received, the chorus held his peace
> His power of foully hurting made to cease.
> (365–70, translating 278–84)

Jonson made this translation of Horace towards the end of his career (it was not published until after his death). *The Poetaster* written near the beginning is a dramatic *Art of Poetry* translating his Horatian ideals on to the Elizabethan stage. Old comedy (which Horace sees as one of the antecedents of his own formal satire) is to be artistically refined in accordance with the Horatian rules and to express the moral purpose that for the Augustan poet is embodied in the greatest literature:

> omne tulit punctum qui miscuit utile dulci
> lectorem delectando pariterque monendo.
> (*The Art of Poetry*, 343–4)

(But he hath every suffrage, can apply
Sweet mixed with sour, to his reader, so
As doctrine and delight together go.)

(514–17)

The familiar Horatian tag which neatly encapsulated a Roman (though not Aristotelian) attitude particularly useful for Renaissance defenders of poetry under Puritan attack, for all that it is a commonplace, presents one of Jonson's most deeply held convictions, often repeated: 'The parts of comedy are the same with tragedy, and the end is partly the same. For they both delight and teach; the Comics are called *didaskaloi* of the Greeks no less than the Tragics' (*Discoveries*, 3247–51).

It is perhaps futile, ultimately, to ask whether Jonsonian comedy is nearer to old, middle or new comedy or whether it is Aristophanic, Plautine or Terentian. It has elements of all these classical antecedents variously compounded. The Jonsonian bee, like the Horatian, foraged busily in a variety of pastures (and not all of them classical) before producing honey with its own distinctive tang. Nevertheless, we can to some extent trace the various elements of which it is compounded in its final form, and see that the classical input as variously described here was dominant, and that the final result was achieved by a vigorous critical intelligence applying classical theory as understood in the Renaissance to what Jonson believed was the ill-disciplined chaos of contemporary native practice.

Despite the popularity of Terence in schools, where schoolmasters had always approved of his good manners and pure style, it was perhaps not until after the Restoration, when the theatre became more exclusively the preserve of a sophisticated court, that Terence's artistry was generally appreciated by practising dramatists. He replaced Plautus in popularity, and more direct use was made of his plays. The intrigue of the *Eunuch*, for example, may have given Wycherley the germ of an idea for *The Country Wife* (1675). The character of Horner, who has given out that he has been rendered impotent by the pox and so effectively reduced to the status of a eunuch who can be no threat to the opposite sex, might be regarded as a lubricious and rakish transformation of the ebullient Chaerea. Sedley's *Bellamira* (1687) is a direct adaption of the *Eunuch*. Congreve, in a dedication to *The Way of the World*

(1695), hails Terence as 'the most correct writer' in terms that suggest an affinity between Terentian comedy and the English comedy of manners:

> The purity of his style, the delicacy of his turns, and the justness of his characters, were all of them beauties, which the greater part of his audience were incapable of tasting: some of the coarsest strokes of Plautus, so severely censured by Horace, were more likely to affect the multitude; such, who come with expectation to laugh out the last act of a play, and are better entertained with two or three unseasonable jests, than with the artful solution of the fable . . . and the further advantage which Terence possessed, towards giving his plays the due ornaments of purity of style, and justness of manners, was not less considerable, from the freedom of conversation, which was permitted him with Laelius and Scipio, two of the greatest and most polite men of his age. And indeed, the privilege of such a conversation, is the only certain means of attaining to the perfection of dialogue.[58]

58.   Davis, H. (ed.) (1967) *The Complete Plays of William Congreve*, University of Chicago Press, Chicago, p. 391.

Chapter 3

Lyric

Gods, heroes, conquerors, Olympic crowns,
Love's pleasing cares, and the free joys of wine,
Are proper subjects for the lyric song.
                (Horace, *The Art of Poetry*, 83–5)[1]

There thou shalt hear and learn the secret power
Of harmony in tones and numbers hit
By voice or hand, and various-measured verse,
Aeolian charms and Dorian lyric odes,
And his who gave them birth, but higher sung,
Blind Melisigenes thence Homer called
Whose poem Phoebus challenged for his own.
                (*Paradise Regained* IV, 254–60)

The Greek lyric

The Greek legacy in lyric is included and characterised amongst
the seductions of Greek culture with which Milton's Satan here
tempts Christ. In the generic hierarchy, lyric (unlike comedy,
elegy, pastoral, epigram or satire), though a lesser form, is
deemed worthy of mention alongside epic and tragedy in this
most solemn of contexts.

In ancient Greece, the lyric proper (derived from *lyros*, lyre, the
attribute of Phoebus Apollo, god of poetry) was called *melos*
(whence melody): a lyric poet was a *melopoios*, a maker of songs, a

---

1. Dillon, W. [Roscommon] (1684) p. 7.

musician as well as a wordsmith. (The word *lyrikos* occurs first in the second century BC.) The rise of Greek melic poetry, therefore, presupposes developments in music too. Many lyric performances also involved dancing. Music-making and dancing are activities central to Greek culture from Homer onwards. The Homeric bard sings to the accompaniment of the lyre in the great house; even in war, the toughest of the Greeks, Achilles, is to be found with his lyre, singing in his tent of the epic deeds of heroes (*Iliad* IX, 186–9). On the shield made for Achilles, Hephaestos depicts a scene with a marriage song (*Iliad* XVIII, 493) and a scene with a harvest song (usually said to be a dirge for Linos, perhaps a personification of the spring: 570). The description of the shield culminates in a celebration of the disciplined energy of the dance of young men and women as the bard sings to the accompaniment of the lyre (590–606). Homer also records the story of Polymele, a beautiful dancer, with whom Hermes fell in love as he saw her taking part in a chorus in honour of Artemis (*Iliad* XVI, 179–83). Homer incidentally records forms of artistic expression other than his own which were a natural part of early Greek culture and in which later developments had their origin.

Greek melic poetry, which came into being in the century after Homer, had two main branches. The Aeolian, which emanated from Aeolia in northern Asia Minor is monodic (composed for one voice) and monostrophic (written in stanzas that repeat the same metrical form). Its two great representatives, Sappho and Alcaeus, both came from Lesbos and wrote in the Aeolic dialect of Greek. They have given their names to their favoured metrical forms, the Sapphic and the Alcaic which they may have invented, though they used other metrical forms as well. Sappho seems to have been the centre of a kind of religious association dedicated to Aphrodite and the Muses which had young girls for its members. Much of her poetry is concerned with the lives and loves of these women.

> spirat adhuc amor
> vivuntque commissi calores
>   Aeoliae fidibus puellae
> (Horace, *Odes* IV, 9, 10–12)

(the love of the Aeolian girl still breathes, and her passion lives on committed to the lyre.)

Alcaeus composed a variety of monodies, including hymns to the gods, war-songs, political poems, love poems, encomia and drinking songs. In one of his own lyrics written in the metre of Alcaeus, the Roman poet Horace, after recording a lucky escape from accidental death, pays tribute to his Greek predecessors in lyric, giving Alcaeus precedence over Sappho.

> quam paene furvae regna Proserpinae
> et iudicantem vidimus Aeacum
>   sedesque discriptas piorum et
>   Aeoliis fidibus querentem
>
> Sappho puellis de popularibus
> et te sonantem plenius aureo,
>   Alcaee, plectro dura navis,
>   dura fugae mala, dura belli.
>
> utrumque sacro digna silentio
> mirantur umbrae dicere; sed magis
>   pugnas et exactos tyrannos
>   densum umeris bibit aure vulgus.
>   (II, 13, 21–32)

(How nearly we saw the realms of dark Proserpina and Aeacus giving judgement, and the seats set aside for the righteous and Sappho complaining on her Aeolian lyre of her countrywomen, and you singing with fuller strains, Alcaeus, with your golden plectrum [an instrument for plucking the lyre-strings] of the hardships of the sea, the appalling hardships of exile and the hardships of war. The shades marvel at both uttering words worthy of a reverent silence; but the dense crowd packed shoulder to shoulder drinks in more eagerly with listening ear the songs of battle and of tyrants expelled.)

The ancient scholiast explains that Alcaeus is the more robust poet because he wrote of war and his own journey by sea, when he had been expelled from Lesbos by the tyrants of Mitylene. Writing after Horace, Quintilian's verdict goes further than Horace in asserting traditional Roman values:

Alcaeus has deserved the compliment of being said to make music with *quill of gold* in that portion of his works in which he attacks the tyrants of his day and shows himself a real moral force. He is, moreover, terse and magnificent in style, while the vigour of his diction resembles that of oratory. But he also wrote poetry of a more sportive nature and stooped to erotic poetry, despite his aptitude for loftier themes.

(*The Education of an Orator* X, I, 63).

Elsewhere (*Odes* I, 32), Horace, in an invocation to his lyre, commends Alcaeus because in an active life as a soldier he had nevertheless sung of Bacchus, the Muses and Venus. Here the lyre is 'a sweet and healing consolation amidst troubles'.

The Aeolian monodic monostrophic *melos* is complemented by the Dorian choral *melos* that developed on mainland Greece at Sparta which in the archaic period had not become 'Spartan' in quite the later sense. The Dorian lyrics of an early practitioner, Stesichorus, contain a strong narrative element and he is commended for his handling of plot and character. He seems to have retold the stories of epic in lyric form, and in one of them records that Helen did not go to Troy at all. However, the predominance of a narrative element seems to have been untypical even of early lyric. Stesichorus is accredited with the introduction of the triadic structure with *strophe* (turn), *antistrophe* (counter-turn) and *epode* (stand). These terms suggest stages in both the music and the dance. Strophe and antistrophe had identical metrical patterns throughout the poem (they may have been sung and danced by different parts of the chorus) while the metrical pattern of the epode is different, but is similarly repeated throughout the poem. While the Aeolic lyric might be the expression of personal feeling (indeed its appearance has often been linked to the growth of individualism in the Greek world), the grander choral lyrics are invariably more public in character, though the poet might often make mention of himself (as Homer never does). There were many kinds of choral lyric (e.g. the hymeneal, the hymn, the dithyramb, in honour of Dionysus, the threnody, the encomium). The Theban poet Pindar (who used the Doric dialect and form) wrote in all these kinds, but only his epinician or triumphal odes celebrating the victories of competitors in the Greek games (Olympian, Pythian, Isthmian, and Nemean) survive in complete form. Most of these have a triadic structure.

In Athens, choral competitions were held in the Great Dionysia, and the vital role accorded to the choral *melos* in Athenian culture is suggested by the following extract from Plato's *Laws* (654):

A. May we not assume that our earliest education comes through the Muses and Apollo, or not?

B. We may make that assumption.

A. So by an uneducated man we shall mean one who has no choral training, and by an educated man whose choral training has been thorough?

B. Exactly.

A. And, mark you, the choric art as a whole embraces both song and dance.

B. No doubt.

A. Then it follows that a well-educated man can sing and dance well.[2]

Despite this, no information survives concerning the detail of Greek dance movements, nor have we any ancient musical settings.

The terms Aeolic and Doric denote the regional origin of the monodic and choral Greek *melos*. They also suggest the style of each as represented in the dialect form of the words, the kind of metre used and the musical mode. There were of course other styles, for example, the Ionic, the Phrygian and the Lydian, as well as styles that were mixtures, and with each style was associated a particular metrical form and musical effect. The Ionic was particularly relaxing, the Phrygian enthusiastic, while, in the words of Pindar, *Dorion melos semnotaton*[3] ('the Dorian song is the most solemn'). Aristotle is further illuminating:

> The musical modes differ essentially from one another and those who hear them are differently affected by each. Some of them . . . make men sad and grave . . . others enfeeble the mind like the relaxed harmonies, others, again produce a moderate and settled temper which appears to be the peculiar effect of the Dorian; the Phrygian inspires enthusiasm. . . . There seems to be in us a sort of affinity to harmonies and rhythms which makes philosophers say that the soul is a harmony, others that it possesses harmony. . . . All men agree that the Dorian is the gravest and manliest. And whereas we say that the extremes should be avoided and the mean followed, and whereas the Dorian is a mean

2. Hamilton, E., Cairns, H. (eds) (1961) *The Complete Dialogues of Plato*, Princeton University Press, Princeton, p. 1251. Translated by A.E. Taylor.
3. Sandys, J.E. (ed.) (1915) *The Odes of Pindar*, Loeb Classical Library, Heinemann, London; Harvard University Press, Cambridge, Mass. p. xxxv, note 3, quoted in the scholium on Olympian ode 1, 26.

between the other harmonies, it is evident that our youth should be taught the Dorian music.

(*Politics*, 1342)[4]

Plato, who had strong views about the ethical effect of music and poetry, had allowed the Dorian and Phrygian modes in his ideal *Republic*. The only kinds of poetry he will there countenance are the melic forms of the encomium and the hymn. Aristotle, whose whole philosophy, in contrast to that of Plato, worked with and not against the grain of Greek culture, is more liberal in his attitudes: he allows the beneficial effect of harmless pleasures and brings the idea of *catharsis* that he used in relation to tragedy to bear upon *melos* as well. Nevertheless, for the significance of the Greek *melos* in the actual life of the classical *polis*, we may let Plato's testimony in the *Protagoras* have the last word:

> The music masters by analogous methods instill self control and deter the young from evil doing. And when they have learned to play the lyre, they teach them the works of good poets of another sort, namely the lyrical, which they accompany on the lyre, familiarising the minds of the children with the rhythms and melodies. By this means they become more balanced, and better adjusted in themselves and so more capable in whatever they say or do, for rhythm and harmonious adjustment are essential to the whole of human life.
>
> (326)[5]

With the exception of the victory odes of Pindar, the Greek lyric tradition survives in a pitifully fragmented form. One complete poem of Sappho, addressed to the goddess Aphrodite, is cited by the Greek rhetorician Dionysius of Halicarnassus to illustrate what he calls the brilliant and finished style of composition, in his treatise *On Literary Composition*, written in Greek at Rome in the Augustan period. He comments: 'The verbal beauty and charm of this passage lie in the cohesion and smoothness of the joinery. Word follows word inwoven according to certain natural affinities and groupings of the letters.'[6]

4. Davis, H.W.C. (ed.) (1908) *Aristotle's Politics translated by B. Jowett*, Oxford, pp. 309–10, 316.
5. Hamilton, E., Cairns, H. (1961) p. 322. Translated by W.K.C. Guthrie.
6. 'On Literary Composition', 23: Usher, S. (translator) (1985) *Dionysius of Halicarnassus: The Critical Essays*, 2 vols, Loeb Classical Library, Heinemann, London; Harvard University Press, Cambridge, Mass., vol. 2, p. 199.

Dionysius' word for joinery is the Greek *harmonia*, derived from the verb meaning to fit or join together. Smooth verbal coupling is for Dionysius a source of what Milton calls the 'secret power of harmony' in the Greek lyric. A second substantial fragment, which is perhaps Sappho's most famous poem, is cited by Longinus in his treatise *On the Sublime*. By the sublime in poetry Longinus means that quality that elevates by its power to take us out of ourselves in *ecstasis* in the literal sense: 'we should find the source of the sublime in the invariable choice of the most suitable ideas, and the power to make these a simple whole by combining them together . . .. Sappho, for instance, always expresses the emotions proper to love-madness by means of its actual and visible concomitants.'[7] The poem he then cites, which was translated into Latin by the Roman poet Catullus, was adapted, probably from the Latin, by Sidney:

> My muse, what ails this ardour?
> My eyes be dim, my limbs shake,
> My voice is hoarse, my throat scorched,
> My tongue to this my roof cleaves,
> My fancy amazed, my thoughts dulled,
> My head doth ache, my life faints
> My soul begins to take leave,
> So great a passion all feel,
> To think a sore so deadly
> I should so rashly rip up.[8]

This bald list, culminating in the infelicitous expression and abrupt rhythm of the final two lines, offers a stark antithesis to Longinus's comment (as it does also to that of Dionysius):

> Is it not marvellous how she has recourse at once to spirit, body, hearing, tongue, sight, flesh, all as quite separate things, and by contraries both freezes and burns, raves and is sane, and indeed is afraid she is nearly dead, so that she expresses not one emotion but a concourse of emotions? Now all such things are characteristic of the lover, but it is the choice, as I said, of the best and the combination of

7. Longinus, *On the Sublime* X, quoted following the poem in Edmonds, J.M. (translator) (1922) *Lyra Graeca*, vol. 1, Loeb Classical Library, Heinemann, London; Putnam's, New York, p. 185.
8. Duncan-Jones, K, (ed.) (1989) *Sir Philip Sidney*, Oxford University Press, p. 94.

them into a single whole, that has produced the excellence of the
piece.[9]

Dionysius concentrates upon words, Longinus on ideas, but taken
together their complementary comments suggest the source of
what is attractive in Sappho.

How such harmony might best be achieved in English verse
was a question actively debated by Elizabethan metrists. Campion, in his *Observations on the Art of English Poetry*, argued against
the vernacular practice of rhymed verse, giving examples of
classical lines and forms, including the Sapphic, of which he says
'the number is voluble ['moving rapidly and easily especially with
a gliding or undulating movement', *OED*] and fit to express any
amorous conceit':

> Rose-cheeked Laura, come;
> Sing thou smoothly with thy beauty's
> Silent music, either other
>   Sweetly gracing.
> Lovely forms do flow
> From concent divinely framed;
> Heaven is music, and thy beauty's
>   Birth is heavenly.
> These dull notes we sing
> Discords need for helps to grace them,
> Only beauty purely loving
>   Knows no discord
> But still moves delight
> Like clear springs renewed by flowing
> Ever perfect, even in them –
>   selves eternal.[10]

Campion, who wrote madrigals and reflected long and hard on
the relationship between poetry and music, here, in a well-
controlled conceit, both likens and differentiates beauty and
music. The classical lyric is melodic, but the harmony is
necessarily made up of discordant elements; the result is far from
dull and shows what might be achieved when native wit (for the
sophisticated extension of the conceit is far from classical) submits

---

9.   Longinus quoted in Edmonds (1922) vol. 1, p. 185.
10. Vivian, P. (ed.) (1909) *Campion's Works*, Oxford University Press.

to a classical form that is seen to embody the ideals of smoothness, grace, clarity and fluency.

The fragmentary remains of the Greek lyric tradition were collected together and published in 1560 by Henri Etienne (Stephanus)[11] who also provided a Latin translation. However, for the Renaissance, the classical lyric meant primarily the Latin poems of Catullus and Horace, both of whom were an established part of the grammar school curriculum from Tudor England onwards.

The Roman lyric

At Rome the connection of the lyric with music is broken. Roman lyrics were composed for recitation, not for musical performance, and when Horace addresses his lyre (I, 32), the instrument is a metaphorical figure for poetic inspiration. We may say that Horace is a lyric poet because in his *Carmina* (poems, only later called odes) he revives the metres that were used by the Aeolic poets. Indeed, in the famous poem in which he prophesies his own immortality, *exegi monumentum aere perennius* (III, 30: 'I have built a monument more lasting than bronze'), it is his achievement in being the first to do this that he makes his chief claim to fame:

princeps Aeolium carmen ad Italos
deduxisse modos.
(13–14)

(that I first adapted the Aeolic song to Italian measures.)

The metre of this particular poem is one of several of similar composition which had been used by Sappho and Alcaeus, and which had been revived by a later Alexandrian epigrammatist called Asclepias (ff. 290 BC). Of Horace's 104 poems, thirty-four are Asclepiads, thirty-six in Alcaics and twenty-eight in Sapphics. His claim is hardly invalidated by the fact that Catullus, who came before Horace, had used the Sapphic metre in two of his poems. Catullus's Sapphics are, metrically speaking, irregular and rough.

11. Etienne, H. (ed.) (1560) *Pindari Olympia, Pythia, Nemea, Isthmia Ceterorum octo lyricorum carmina*, 2 vols, Geneva.

The singular achievement of Horace in naturalising Aeolic forms at Rome seems all the more remarkable when we reflect that he had no successors in the forms which he perfected. There are no other Roman Sapphics or Alcaics after him. In Greece the lyric had played a valued part in adult life, where it had been sung in the symposium (itself an important social institution) and in education, where, with music, it had a formative role. The Romans did not have the same feeling for music, and the testimony of Cicero, who is quoted by Seneca (*Epistle*, 49, 5) as saying that if he had a second lifetime he would not find time to read all the lyric poets (Greek, of course) on the grounds (according to Seneca) that they are trivial, suggests cause for the neglect of the genre at Rome.

With Catullus we are faced with a problem of definition and classification, for his favourite metre, the hendecasyllable (in which most of his short poems are written), is not one used by the Greek lyric poets but is an Alexandrian invention and used by epigrammatists in poems that were not sung. Technically, therefore, very few of his poems are written in lyric metres, though of all the Roman poets, including Horace, he is in the modern sense the most 'lyrical'. The 'lyric genius of Catullus' has been something of a cliché.

Catullus, writing in the late Republic sometime before the Augustan period in which Horace and Virgil flourished, is the only surviving representative of a group called by Cicero the new poets who consciously rejected the traditional Roman idea that literature should be public, impersonal and preoccupied with great national themes. Catullus's attitude to public affairs may be inferred from the following epigram:

Nil nimium studeo, Caesar, tibi velle placere
  nec scire utrum sis albus an ater homo.

(XCIII)

(I have no great desire, Caesar, to wish to please you, or to know whether you are a fair or dark fellow.)

Whereas earlier Roman writers had sought to create a national literature by modelling themselves upon the Greek masters of the classical period, the new poets turned away from the great forms of epic and drama in favour of the small-scale genres that had been revived or cultivated anew by the later Greeks of the Alexandrian age, when the classical *polis* had been absorbed into the Macedonian empire in the late fourth century, the capital city of which was Alexandria on the Nile delta. The Greek Alexandrians in their epyllia, didactic poems, pastorals, elegies and epigrams were characteristically scholars who wrote not for a general audience but for other *literati* in learned verse of formal elegance and cultivated artistic refinement. In literature, as in philosophy and sculpture, the ideal and the general yield to a greater concern for realism and for the personal interests of the individual who has now lost his political identity in the new metropolitan culture of the large city. In the mythological allusions and sometimes learned diction of his longer poems we can see traces of Alexandrian erudition, but perhaps it is because he had used his learning to extend the range of Roman literature by his mastery of hitherto unused metres and forms that later Roman poets called Catullus *doctus*, learned. Certainly the revival of small-scale Alexandrian forms to express personal concerns and the cultivation of Alexandrian ideals of formal perfection and artistic refinement, what Horace later in his *Art of Poetry* called *limae labor* (291), 'the labour of the file', are among the chief contributions of Catullus and his generation to subsequent Roman literature.

The opening poem of the collection, in which he self-deprecatingly calls his poems *nugae* (trifles), draws attention to their charm and polish:

Cui dono lepidum novum libellum
arido modo pumice expolitum?
                    (I, 1–2)

(To whom am I to present my pretty new book, freshly smoothed off with dry pumice-stone?)

The pumice-stone, used for smoothing books, metaphorically suggests metrical and stylistic polish. Trifles or no, he expresses the hope that they will last more than a hundred years.

In Catullus, for the first time in Roman literature, we encounter delicacy of feeling and grace of expression – a quality and a capacity neither of which we may suppose was naturally a part of the grave Roman inheritance. His tender poem lamenting the death of Lesbia's pet sparrow:

qui nunc it per iter tenebricosum
unde negant redire quemquam
(III, 11–12)

(who now goes through the shadowy way whence they say none returns)

has in its rhythms and expressions the very same grace and charm that Catullus sees as characteristic of those who might be expected to mourn:

Lugete O Veneres Cupidinesque
et quantumst hominum venustiorum
(1–2)

(Mourn, O Loves and Graces, and all you who are amongst the graceful.)

Grace, elegance, pleasure, such are the dictionary definitions of this favourite Catullan word *venustas* suggesting the values that guided the new poets in art and life.

The 116 surviving poems of Catullus are varied in form, metre and subject. The longer ones include an epithalamium in lyric metre (LXI), another very beautiful one in hexameters (LXII), a mythological poem in a galliambic metre on Attis, a devotee of Cybele (LXIII), an epyllion on the marriage of Peleus and Thetis (LXIV), and a version of the Alexandrian poet Callimachus's ingenious poem 'The Lock of Berenice', in which the lock recalls how it had been made a constellation. He wrote many elegiac poems, a number of short invectives, some wittily obscene, a poem in praise of the island of Sirmio (where he had a villa), poems of friendship, love and dislike. The latter are famously combined in a memorable short poem (an elegiac couplet):

Odi et amo. quare id faciam fortasse requiris.
   nescio. sed fieri sentio et excrucior.
(LXXXV)

(I hate and love: wouldst thou the reason know?
I know not; but I burn, and feel it so.)
(Lovelace)[12]

---

12. Lovelace's translations are included in Howarth, R.G. (ed.) (1931) *Minor Poets of the Seventeenth Century*, Everyman's Library, J.M. Dent. See p. 373.

Affectation, sentimentality and preciosity are the vices of Greek Alexandrian literature (indeed the sobriquet Alexandrian often carries the connotation of the second-rate), but here no one can mistake the virtues of simplicity, economy and directness. His love poems are admired for their intensity and variety of emotion. There are poems of tender feeling (like the sparrow poems V and VI), written in hendecasyllabics, poems of strong denunciation (like number XI in the Sapphic metre) and poems like the following (in elegiac couplets), which explores further the paradox of the conflicting emotions of *odi et amo*, and in a cool appraisal records the poet's recognition of an unwelcome truth about his feelings now that his relationship with Lesbia has changed as the result of some injury:

> Dicebas quondam solum te nosse Catullum,
>   Lesbia, nec prae me velle tenere Iovem.
> dilexi tum te non tantum ut vulgus amicam,
>   sed pater ut gnatos diligit et generos.
> nunc te cognovi: quare etsi impensius uror,
>   multo mi tamen es vilior et levior.
> qui potis est? inquis. quod amantem iniuria talis
>   cogit amare magis, sed bene velle minus.

(LXXII)

Here is the version of the Cavalier poet Richard Lovelace:

> That me alone you loved you once did say,
> Nor should I to the King of Gods give way.
> Then I loved thee not as a common dear,
> But as a father doth his children cheer.
> Now thee I know, more bitterly I smart,
> Yet thou to me more light and cheaper art.
> What power is this, that such a wrong should press
> Me to love more, yet wish thee well much less?[13]

Taken together the love poems have prompted much biographical speculation (there is little evidence for the life outside the poems) because they seem to be the realistic record of an actual relationship. They have been thought to meet the Romantic criterion of sincerity. However that may be, in their disciplined economy of expression and their realistic embodiment of complex

13.   Howard, R.G. (1931) p. 373.

feelings the amatory poems of Catullus, if we think of them as models and as a sequence, offer something very different from the sugared sonnets of the Elizabethans that took their cue from the lofty idealism and conceited style of Petrarch.

Jonson and the classical lyric

Catullus's most famous poem prompted an equally well-known adaptation by Ben Jonson:

> Vivamus, mea Lesbia, atque amemus,
> rumoresque senum severiorum
> omnes unius aestimemus assis.
> soles occidere et redire possunt:
> nobis cum semel occidit brevis lux,
> nox est perpetua una dormienda.
> da mihi basia mille, deinde centum, . . .
>
> (V, 1–7)

> Come, my Celia, let us prove,
> While we can, the sports of love,
> Time will not be ours for ever,
> He, at length, our good will sever;
> Spend not then his gifts in vain;
> Suns, that set, may rise again;
> But if once we lose this light,
> 'Tis with us perpetual night.
> Why should we defer our joys?
> Fame and rumour are but toys.
> Cannot we delude the eyes
> Of a few poor household spies?
> Or his easier ears beguile,
> Thus removed by our wile? –
> 'Tis no sin love's fruits to steal:
> But the sweet thefts to reveal;
> To be taken, to be seen,
> These have crimes accounted been.[14]

The lines of Jonson's metre with their seven syllables do not allow him the room that Catullus has with eleven in his hendecasyl-

14. Parfitt, G. (1975) p. 103. Sung by Volpone in *Volpone* III, 7, 165.

lables, so that he has sacrificed *dormienda*, where the force of the gerund '*must* be slept' underscores the choice that the lovers have to use their time well by sleeping together. The witty–serious wordplay, where *nox* and *dormienda* refer to the inevitability of the sleep of death while suggesting the counterpoise of the night in which the lovers might sleep together, allows maximum concentration of meaning and lifts the poem above the level of the charming and graceful. Jonson's adaptation of the poem to his own purposes in *Volpone* has not anything as intense as this (though the emphasis given to 'perpetual', the longest word in the poem, is finely managed), but it has long been an anthology piece admired for a combination of qualities, including lyric grace (for it is smooth, fluent and pleasing to the ear) directness of address without crudity (from which it is saved by a playful mischievousness akin to Catullan wit) and simple economy of phrase (for while the expression is poetic, the words are those of decent prose). The combination expresses a perfect decorum of style and content with nothing superfluous and nothing wanting. It is more urbane than courtly, that is to say it is the expression of a man of the world *vir urbanus*, rather than that of a gallant Elizabethan courtier. This clear-sighted Roman urbanity in the lyrics of Jonson, akin to but more restrained than the *sprezzatura* of the Renaissance courtly gentleman like Sir Philip Sidney, distinguishes them on the one hand from the simple magic of the faery songs of Shakespeare's plays with which they share simplicity, and on the other hand from the sometimes extravagant exuberance of more complicated Elizabethan lyric forms. Like Donne, Jonson reacted against the poetic habits of the late Elizabethans, but unlike Donne, who developed what has come to be known as the metaphysical manner, Jonson consciously turned to the classical tradition, and it is probably no exaggeration to say that he felt a greater affinity with Catullus and Horace than with his Elizabethan predecessors or early Jacobean contemporaries.

Catullus, of course, is only one of a number of influences flowing into Jonson's mind from antiquity. When, after the failure of his play *The New Inn*, in an 'Ode: To Himself', 'Come leave the loathed stage', he announces his intention to turn to the lyric; after four stanzas in which he denounces the taste of the age, the lyric inspiration and uplift come from a variety of sources:

> Leave things so prostitute,
> And take the Alcaic lute,
> Or thine own Horace, or Anacreon's lyre;
> Warm thee by Pindar's fire:
>
> (41–4)

Of the Greek tradition, Alcaeus, surviving only in fragments, is invoked symbolically as the founding father of lyric; the sixth-century Greek poet Anacreon wrote drinking songs in simple metres that were imitated by Jonson's successors. An example from Herrick is cited below. It is difficult to know the extent to which Jonson was conversant with Pindar,[15] but in the first poem of its kind in English, 'To the Immortal Memory of That Noble Pair Sir Lucius Cary and Sir H. Morison', he did imitate the triadic form of the Greek choral lyric, following Scaliger's division of it into *volta*, *rivolta* and *stanza*, which Jonson renders 'turn', 'counterturn' and 'stand' (equivalent to the Greek *strophe*, *antistrophe* and *epode*).[16] The turn and counterturn have identical ten-line metrical units which are repeated throughout; the stand has a twelve-line unit, again repeated throughout. Jonson did not call this poem a Pindaric, but it has been regarded as such subsequently.

Morison had died in 1629 on, or near, his twenty-first birthday. As the long title suggests, the ode has a dual subject: the consolatory celebration of a short life well lived (in contrast to mere length of years) (25–45):

> For what is life, if measured by the space
> Not by the act?
>
> (21–2)

> All offices were done
> By him so ample, full, and round,
> In weight, in measure, number, sound,
> As, though his age imperfect might appear,
> His life was of humanity the sphere.
>
> (48–52)

and in the second half, the celebration of an exalted friendship which, as it is immortalised in the poem, will be a fair example to

---

15. Jonson may have come to Pindar by way of the odes of Ronsard.
16. On this see the notes in Donaldson, I. (ed.) (1975) *Ben Jonson: Poems*, Oxford University Press, p. 233.

future generations. Jonson is discreetly celebrating his own immortalising power, and his consequent immortality through verse, and elevating his lyric vocation over his dramatic, making good his intention to leave the loathed stage and warm himself by Pindar's fire: 1629 is the date of his 'Ode: To Himself' of which there are clear echoes in the lines forming a climax to the first half of the poem, contrasting life with length of years:

> Go now, and tell out days summed up with fears;
> And make them years;
> Produce thy mass of miseries on the stage,
> To swell thine age;
> Repeat of things a throng
> To show thou hast been long,
> Not lived; for life does her great actions spell
> By what was done and wrought
> In season, and so brought
> To light: her measures are, how well
> Each syllabe answered, and was formed, how fair;
> These make the lines of life, and that's her air.
>   (53–64)

Here, and in every section after the first two, in the central conceit of the poem, Jonson's wit brings together life and poetry; a good life is like a good lyric, a matter of decorous performance 'what was done and wrought / In season' and self-knowledge or self-criticism 'so brought to light' with harmony and grace in the individual parts to form the whole. This decorum, clarity, harmony and grace are apparent in the contrasting images and in the dextrous art with which they are beautifully proportioned to the verse form in the poem's most famous lines:

> It is not growing like a tree
> In bulk, doth make man better be;
> Or standing long an oak, three hundred year,
> To fall a log at last, dry bald and sere:
> A lily of a day
> Is fairer far in May,
> Although it fall and die that night;
> It was the plant and flower of light.
> In small proportions we just beauty see,
> And in short measures life may perfect be.
>   (65–74)

The final couplet may make us think of the perfection of Jonson's shorter lyrics such as 'Drink to me only with thine eyes', 'Still he be neat, still to be dressed' or 'Queen and huntress, chaste and fair'. Why then did he attempt the grander lyric form of the Pindaric ode? It may be said that the dignified form of the poem is commensurate with Jonson's exalted conception both of the persons and values he is celebrating and of his own role as priest of the Muses who can pass on to the surviving world an evergreen poetic garland:

> Call, noble Lucius, then for wine,
> And let thy looks with gladness shine;
> Accept this garland, plant it on thy head;
> And think, nay know, thy Morison's not dead.
> He leaped the present age,
> Possessed with holy rage
> To see that bright eternal day,
> Of which we priests and poets say
> Such truths as we expect for happy men;
> And there he lives with memory, and Ben
>
> Jonson, who sung this of him, ere he went
> Himself to rest,
> Or taste a part of that full joy he meant
> To have expressed
> In this bright asterism;
>
> (75–89)

There are specific features reminiscent of the Pindaric ode, as in the use of historical example in the opening turn addressing the 'Brave infant of Saguntum' who, as reported by Pliny, retreated to the womb at the time when Hannibal was destroying the city. The opening allows both the expression of horror at premature death and a contrast with Morison who at least had lived and rather than retreating in the face of the horrors of life had 'stood a soldier to the last right end' (45). The mythological parallel with the Dioscuri, the twins Castor and Pollux, in the second half of the poem celebrates friendship and immortality in wittily lofty terms. Pindar celebrates his own muse in elevated language and puts his poetry at the service of aristocratic victors whom he crowns with poetic immortality. The greatness of Jonson's aristocrats stems from interior virtue and is a matter of 'brave minds and manners more than blood' (106). These features, the superficial characteristics of the Pindaric ode, might all be found in the less ambitious but nevertheless grand Stoic odes of Horace, but they are so handled here through the verse form and elaborate structure of the poem that they contribute to a grandeur of effect beyond the Horatian. The attraction and challenge of the Pindaric has always been its elevation; it has seemed to be the highest calling in the ode. In view of the later development of the irregular Pindaric, it is worth noting that Jonson is not carried away on the wings of enthusiasm, nor despite the grandeur of scale and conception, does he adopt the extravagant language of hyperbole; he sacrifices nothing of his habitual control. The regularity of his ode required discipline as well as energy, and the result is a remarkable technical feat rarely if ever repeated.

Jonson did not warm himself very often by Pindar's fire, but there can be no doubt of the influence upon him of the Roman poetic tradition represented by 'thine own Horace' in the 'Ode: To Himself'. The dignified ending of the poem, envisaging recognition for his success as a laureate lyrist, includes an echo of Horace's opening poem addressed to Maecenas:

> quodsi me lyricis vatibus inseris
> sublimi feriam sidera vertice.
>> (I, 1, 35–6)

> (But if you rank me among lyric poets, I shall hit the stars with my
>   head on high.)

>   Like ours
>   In sound of peace or wars
>   No harp e'er hit the stars,
>   In tuning forth the acts of his sweet reign:
>   And raising Charles's chariot 'bove his wain.[17]
>>   (56–60)

Unlike Catullus, Horace does not turn his back on national and political themes but incorporates them into his *carmina*, whether he is addressing Augustus or putting before his countrymen examples of the old Stoic virtue, the *prisca virtus*, in the Roman odes at the beginning of the third book – poems which would

17.   In the text of Donaldson, I. (1975) p. 356.

surely have earned the praise of Cicero had he lived to read them. In treating such public themes, Horace is fulfilling the laureate role of the poet that is so much a part of what the world has come to consider Augustan. This is the poetic possibility to which Jonson, poet laureate himself, is warming at the close of his ode.

Most of Horace's lyrics, however, in what is a varied collection of some hundred poems in four books covering so much that pertains to a full life, are not on public themes: there are *carpe diem* poems (the phrase is from Horace I, 9, 8), poems celebrating the pleasures of country life or the joys of wine, poems of moral reflection such as the ode on the golden mean (II, 10), poems of love and friendship and poems celebrating the supreme value of poetry itself. The mood varies from Stoic gravity to the gaily Epicurean, but the order in this variety of theme and mood is imparted by the regularity of Horace's metrical forms and by the artistry with which they are handled.

Unlike Campion, Jonson did not attempt direct imitation of classical forms such as the Sapphic or Alcaic, though in his three direct translations of Horace's shorter poems (Epode II, Odes IV, 1 and III, 9) the couplets he uses are related in length to the metrical lines of their originals. In these translations he does not freely adapt his originals, as he does in the case of Catullus, but follows the sense religiously as a *fidus interpres* so that they lack his characteristic grace and ease. Here is the opening of his translation of Horace's second epode, one of the main classical sources for the many seventeenth-century versions of 'The Happy Man',[18] to which he gave the title 'The Praises of a Country Life':

> Happy is he, that from all business clear
>   As the old race of mankind were,
> With his own oxen tills his sire's left lands,
>   And is not in the usurer's bands;
> Nor, soldier-like, started with rough alarms,
>   Nor dreads the sea's enraged harms;
> But flees the Bar and courts, with proud boards
>   And waiting-chambers of great lords.
> The poplar tall he then doth marrying twine
>   With the grown issue of the vine;

18. Rostvig, M. (1954) *The Happy Man: Studies in the Metamorphosis of a Classical Ideal*, vol. I, 1600–1700, Osto Studies in English no. 2, Oslo University Press; 1958, vol. 2, 1700–1760, Oslo Studies in English no. 8.

And with his hook lops off the fruitless race,
   And sets more happy in the place;
Or in the bending vale beholds afar
   The lowing herds there grazing are;
Or the pressed honey in pure pots doth keep
   Of earth, and shears the tender sheep.

(1–16)

The form seems to be an equivalent of the Horatian couplet made up of an iambic trimeter followed by an iambic dimeter.

Beatus ille qui procul negotiis
   ut prisca gens mortalium . . .

The poem is one that contrasts the peace and contentment possible in country living with the distractions and vexations of urban life, *otium* with *negotium*. Easier and more graceful is Jonson's handling of comparable themes in the same metrical form in 'To Sir Robert Wroth':

How blest art thou canst love the country, Wroth,
   Whether by choice, or fate, or both;
And, though so near the city and the court,
   Art ta'en with neither's vice nor sport;
That at great times art no ambitious guest
   Of sheriff's dinner or mayor's feast;
Nor com'st to view the better cloth of state,
   The richer hangings, or crown-plate;
Nor throng'st, when masquing is, to have a sight
   Of the short bravery of the night,
To view the jewels, stuffs, the pains, the wit
   There wasted, some not paid for yet!
But canst at home in thy securer rest
   Live with unbought provision blest;
Free from proud porches or their gilded roofs,
   'Mongst lowing herds and solid hoofs;
Alongst the curled woods and painted meads,
   Through which a serpent river leads
To some cool, courteous shade, which he calls his,
   And makes sleep softer than it is!

(1–20)

Whether these poems are strictly lyrical, despite their musical effects, is debatable. What is clear is that in couplet poems of moral reflection and idealising visions like 'To Sir Robert Wroth' and 'To Penshurst', Jonson is providing the kind of ethical and aesthetic blend that is to be experienced in many of Horace's odes. For example, there may be an echo in the opening lines of 'To Penshurst' of the ode in which Horace contrasts the vanity of riches and of 'proud ambitious heaps' with the contentment of a modest life on his Sabine farm:

> Thou art not, Penshurst, built to envious show
> Of touch or marble, nor canst boast a row
> Of polished pillars, or a roof of gold;
>
> (1–3)

> Non ebur neque aureum
> mea renidet in domo lacunar
> non trabes Hymettiae
> premunt columnas ultima recisas
>
> Africa . . .
>
> (II, 18, 1–5)

(Not ivory nor the gilded panel reflects the light in my home, nor do beams of Hymettian marble press on pillars quarried from farthest Africa.)

Jonson's affinity with Horace as the poet-critic of Augustan Rome goes deep; he actually takes his identity in *The Poetaster*. The identification is with the poet as guardian and upholder of civilised values through the proper exercise of his art in which the lyric vocation is but a part. Nevertheless, Jonson salutes Horace's lyric genius by giving him a song:

> Swell me a bowl with lusty wine,
> Till I may see the plump Lyaeus swim
> Above the brim:
> I drink as I would write,
> In flowing measure filled with flame and sprite.
>
> (III, 1, 8–12)

The example is brief, but in its evocation of Horace can suggest ways in which Jonson's classically inspired poetry differs from prevalent Elizabethan and metaphysical modes. The utterance is fluent and harmonious with something of what has been called

Horace's sinuous grace, but its rhythms are strong and it is pithy
and emphatic. The verse form and subject matter are finely
proportioned (as in the Cary/Morison ode). The imagery in the
swimming of the plump and lusty Bacchus is so fitting that it does
not draw attention to itself; the energy is achieved by a perfect
decorum of content, expression and form. Similarly, the wit
which brings together the drinking and writing in the flowing
measure of the poem's conclusion is simple and neat; the elements
which make the comparison are not far-fetched but their fusion
does produce something spirited. Every word counts; there is no
rhetorical excess, indulgence or display. The poem is direct, neat
and clear, yet subtle, energetic and sophisticated. The artistic
control and restraint serves to concentrate poetic energy. Though
it is complete in itself, after this aperitif, we could wish that the
poet had offered us more.

   Jonson was the presiding genius of a classically inspired lyric
revival in life and literature, and in both spheres the ancient form
was perfectly adapted to native habits, for, while the Greek
symposium had been held in the men's quarters in aristocratic
households, Jonson's sessions of the poets were held in that most
English of institutions, the local tavern:

    Ah Ben!
     Say how or when
     Shall we thy guests
   Meet at those lyric feasts
    Made at the Sun,
  The Dog, the Triple Tun?
 Where we such clusters had
As made us nobly wild, not mad;
  And yet each verse of thine
Outdid the meat, outdid the frolic wine.

    My Ben,
   Or come again
   Or send to us
 Thy wit's great over-plus;
  But teach us yet
 Wisely to husband it,
 Lest we that talent spend,
And, having once brought to an end

> That precious stock, the store
> Of such a wit the world should have no more.[19]

Herrick: Anacreon

Robert Herrick, a true son of Ben in his 'pure and neat language', his lucidity and in the graceful rhythms of his delicately turned stanzas, toasts Anacreon and Horace as the inspiring genii of the lyric feast of enticement that he offered his reader in 'An Ode to Sir Clipseby Crew':

> Here we securely live, and eat
>   The cream of meat;
>   And keep eternal fires,
> By which we sit, and do divine
>   As wine
>   And rage inspires.

> If full we charm; then call upon
>   Anacreon
>   To grace the frantic thyrse:
> And having drunk, we raise a shout
>   Throughout
>   To praise his verse.

> Then cause we Horace to be read,
>   Which sung, or said,
>   A goblet to the brim,
> Of lyric wine, both swelled and crowned,
>   A round
>   We quaff to him.

> Thus, thus, we live, and spend the hours
>   In wine and flowers:
>   And make the frolic year,
> The month, the week, the instant day
>   To stay
>   The longer here.

19. For Herrick's poems see Patrick, J.M. (ed.) (1968) *The Complete Poetry of Robert Herrick*, 2nd edn, Norton, New York. Herrick is one of the case studies in Braden, G. (1978) *The Classics and English Renaissance Poetry*, Yale University Press, New Haven and London. See also Mason, T. (1990) 'Cowley and the Wisdom of Anacreon', *Cambridge Quarterly* **19**, 103–37.

Come then, brave knight, and see the cell
      Wherein I dwell;
  And my enchantments too;
Which love and noble freedom is;
      And this
    Shall fetter you.

Take horse, and come; or be so kind,
    To send your mind
  (Though but in numbers few)
And I shall think I have the heart,
      Or part
    Of Clipseby Crew.

Herrick's ode in its content, spirit and form is a delightful
recreation in Cavalier fashion of the classically inspired Jonsonian
lyric.

Herrick may have had in mind Jonson's lines in 'Inviting a
Friend to Supper':

But that which most doth take my muse and me
Is a pure cup of rich Canary wine,
Which is the Mermaid's now, but shall be mine
Of which had Horace or Anacreon tasted,
Their lives, as do their lines, till now had lasted.
                                 (28–32)

However, since he wrote Anacreontics and translated Horace, his
invocation of the two ancient poets also signals direct classical
influence. Anacreon especially seems to have caught his fancy, as
recorded in 'The Vision':

Methought I saw (as I did dream in bed)
A crawling vine about Anacreon's head:
Flushed was his face; his hairs with oil did shine;
And as he spake, his mouth ran o'er with wine.
Tippled he was, and tippling lisped withal,
And lisping reeled, and reeling like to fall.
A young enchantress close by him did stand
Tapping his plump thighs with a myrtle wand:
She smiled; he kissed; and, kissing, culled her, too;
And being cup-shot, more he could not do.
For which (methought) in pretty anger she
Snatched off his crown, and gave the wreath to me;

Since when (methinks) my brains about do swim,
And I am wild and wanton like to him.

A few fragments of Anacreon's poetry from the sixth century
survive in quotations of him by later authors, but in 1554 Henri
Etienne (Stephanus) published an edition of just over fifty
Anacreontea[20] which he believed to have been the work of the
original poet but which modern scholars ascribe to imitators in
late antiquity. These poems are mostly amorous drinking songs
and together they suggest the picture of the poet envisaged by
Herrick above. In its sonnet form, however, 'The Vision' does
not resemble the Greek. Unlike more sophisticated lyric forms,
the Anacreontea are written in a simple short metrical line that is
repeated with little variation throughout the poem. The com-
monest of these metrical lines has been called the Anacreontic.
The simple form harmonises with the simple themes of this not
very exacting kind. The following two poems, both entitled 'On
Himself', are reworkings of poems in Etienne's edition:

I fear no earthly powers;
But care for crowns of flowers:
And love to have my beard
With wine and oil besmeared.
This day I'll drown all sorrow;
Who knows to live tomorrow?

Born I was to meet with age,
And to walk life's pilgrimage.
Much I know of time is spent,
Tell I can't, what's resident.
Howsoever, cares, adieu;
I'll have nought to say to you:
But I'll spend my coming hours
Drinking wine, and crowned with flowers.

Milton, Cowley and Horace

Herrick's *Hesperides*, containing these poems, appeared in 1648.
Not long after, Milton composed a more sober and virtuous *carpe*

20. Etienne, H. (ed.) (1554) *Anacreontis Teii ab Henrico Stephano luce et Latinitate
    nunc primum donatae*, Paris.

diem poem whose opening line, echoing in its form the opening line of an Horatian ode, *O matre pulchra filia pulchrior* (II, 16), 'O daughter more beautiful than your beautiful mother'), seems deliberately to invite classical comparison from his learned audience:

> Lawrence of virtuous father virtuous son,
>   Now that the fields are dank, and ways are mire,
>   Where shall we sometimes meet, and by the fire
>   Help waste a sullen day; what may be won
> From the hard season gaining: time will run
>   On smoother, till Favonius reinspire
>   The frozen earth; and clothe in fresh attire
>   The lily and rose, that neither sowed nor spun.
> What neat repast shall feast us, light and choice,
>   Of Attic taste, with wine, whence we may rise
>   To hear the lute well touched, or artful voice
> Warble immortal notes and Tuscan air?
>   He who of those delights can judge, and spare
>   To interpose them oft, is not unwise.[21]

Milton's readers would also have picked up the echo in his sixth line of the opening of one of Horace's most famous odes, *Solvitur acris hiems grata vice veris et Favoni* (I, 4), 'keen winter is breaking up at the welcome change to spring and the west wind'. In this poem Horace warns his addressee of the futility of making long-term plans as death is pressing upon him. Milton's echo brings with it the pagan gloom of *domus exilis Plutonia* (17), 'Pluto's insubstantial home', which is immediately dissipated by the New Testament allusion in 'The lily and the rose that neither sowed nor spun'. For Milton, the return of spring is reassuring evidence of divine Providence; as so often in *Paradise Lost* Milton echoes the classical to put it in a new perspective.[22] Here the biblical allusion comes at the climax of the octave, setting the context and mood in which the enjoyments to come in the sestet may be anticipated. There can be no question of an Anacreontic escape into irresponsible oblivion. The poet insists on the sobriety of individual judgement in his understated Horatian close.

---

21. For Milton's poem see Carey, J., Fowler, A. (eds) (1968) *The Poems of John Milton*, Longman.
22. See below, p. 231.

Milton's most famous encounter with Horace is his version of the ode to Pyrrha (I, 5), probably a youthful exercise in which the original is 'rendered word for word without rhyme according to the Latin measure as near as the language will permit'.[23]

What slender youth bedewed with liquid odours
Courts thee on roses in some pleasant cave,
   Pyrrha for whom bind'st thou
   In wreaths thy golden hair,
Plain in thy neatness; O how oft shall he
On faith and changed gods complain: and seas
   Rough with black winds and storms
   Unwonted shall admire:
Who now enjoys thee credulous, all gold,
Who always vacant always amiable
   Hopes thee; of flattering gales
   Unmindful? Hapless they
To whom thou untried seem'st fair. Me in my vowed
Picture the sacred wall declares t' have hung
   My dank and dropping weeds
   To the stern god of sea.

Quis multa gracilis te puer in rosa
perfusus liquidis urget odoribus
   grato, Pyrrha, sub antro?
     cui flavam religas comam,

simplex munditiis? heu quotiens fidem
mutatosque deos flebit et aspera
   nigris aequora ventis
     emirabitur insolens,

qui nunc te fruitur credulus aurea,
qui semper vacuam, semper amabilem
   sperat, nescius aurae
     fallacis. miseri, quibus

intemptata nites. me tabula sacer
votiva paries indicat uvida

23.   Milton's version is included in Storrs, R. (ed.) (1959) *Ad Pyrrham: A Polyglot Collection of Translations of Horace's Ode to Pyrrha*, Oxford University Press.

> suspendisse potenti
> vestimenta maris deo.

In its rhythm and movement Milton's English does indeed sound something like the Latin, even if close comparison forces us to recognise that the genius of English is not quite like that of Latin. When the later poet Ovid compliments Horace because his verbal music takes an inevitable hold of the ear *tenuit nostras numerosus Horatius aures* (*Tristia* IV, 10, 49) we may suppose that no Roman before him had been able to produce such melodic lyrics. For the Horatian ode has dignity (a natural Roman quality which is also in Milton), but also a melodic subtlety and charm that did not come so naturally. One of the difficulties encountered by the Romans adapting Greek metres had sprung from the nature of the Latin language itself, which is much less polysyllabic than Greek. How much more difficult was the task for Milton working with the Teuton monosyllables of English. He has one hundred words to Horace's sixty-five. The result is rhythmically heavier than Horace and less varied.

Milton faced another difficulty. One of Horace's achievements in the *Odes* is the incorporation into the lyric of the long oratorical period where, in Milton's phrase, 'the sense is variously drawn out from one verse into another'. In the Pyrrha ode, the sentence beginning *heu quotiens* extends sinuously over almost half the poem. Horace is helped in this by the very flexible word order he is able to exploit in a language that is highly inflected; the separation of adjectives and nouns in *aspera / nigris aequora ventis* allows an effect of neatness and compactness (like that of the 'golden line' in the hexameter)[24] that cannot be reduplicated in English. Such reduplications of sound in like case endings in the inflections of Latin and Greek are naturally so frequent that it is little wonder that ancient poets never adopted formal rhyme schemes. With no case endings 'who now enjoys thee credulous all gold' scarcely makes easy sense in English. In the Latin the separation of adjectives has the effect of allowing a contrast naturally to suggest itself between *aspera nigris* and *aurea*. The crowning incompatibility occurs in the final sentence. Only

---

24. Defined by Dryden in 'The Preface to *Sylvae*' (1685): 'that verse commonly which they call golden, or two substantives and two adjectives with a verb betwixt them to keep the peace'. Watson, G. (1962) vol. 2, p. 22.

someone with prior knowledge of the Latin could sort out the grammatical and syntactical relations of Milton's English.

The version has been greatly admired, for it has sustained the illusion that the effect of an original can be accurately reproduced in a literal version if the translator can find a fitting metrical and rhythmical correspondence. Yet what Milton has caught is superficial. What he has missed – the subtlety, the suggestiveness and the dramatic – is all that gives the poem its true meaning. The weakness of the version may be illustrated in Milton's translation of Horace's phrase describing Pyrrha as *simplex munditiis*. The dictionary equivalents of *munditiae* (the text printed by Milton has the singular form) are 'neatness', 'elegance' and 'fineness', while the synonyms given are *ornatus* and *cultus*. Although the phrase is not quite an oxymoron, for there is no sharp antithesis between *simplex* and *munditiis*, it is evident that it is what Horace calls in his *Art of Poetry* a *callida junctura* (47–8) 'a cunning conjunction', which suggests a good deal. How simple is Pyrrha's simplicity? (After all, the poem turns on the poet's presentation of her as *duplex*.) Or, put another way, how artful is she? This delightful expression, which has sometimes been regarded as a description appropriate to the art of Horace himself, is baldly translated by Milton in a flat and lifeless phrase 'plain in thy neatness'. For some clue as to the sparkling wit and dramatic charge carried by Horace's words, we may turn to the imitation of the poem by Abraham Cowley:

> To whom now Pyrrha art thou kind?
>   To what heart-ravished lover
> Dost thou thy golden locks unbind,
>   Thy hidden sweets discover,
>   And with large bounty open set
> All the bright stores of thy rich cabinet?

> Ah simple youth, how oft will he
>   Of thy changed faith complain?
> And his own fortunes find to be
>   So airy and so vain
>   Of so cameleon-like a hue;
> That still their colour changes with it too?

How oft, alas, will he admire
  The blackness of the skies?
Trembling to hear the winds sound higher,
  And see the billows rise;
    Poor inexperienced he
Who ne're, alas, before had been at sea!

He enjoys thy calmy sunshine now,
  And no breath stirring hears,
In the clear heaven of thy brow,
  No smallest cloud appears.
    He sees thee gentle, fair and gay,
And trusts the faithless April of thy May.

Unhappy! thrice unhappy he,
  T'whom thou untried dost shine!
But there's no danger now for me,
  Since o're Loretto's shrine
    In witness of the shipwreck past
My consecrated vessel hangs at last.[25]

Here it is the youth who is simple, and by implication, in the
opening stanza, Pyrrha (whose name suggests fire) is very far
from being a plain Jane. In his imitation (so-called by Cowley
who consciously modernises the poem and does not attempt to
reproduce the metrical effect of the original) the wit has been
intensified and indeed draws attention to itself as it does not in the
Horatian original. But Cowley has captured an aspect of the poem
that must be essential to any rendering. His views on translation,
quoted below in the preface to his Pindaric odes, offer a
counterpoint to those who believe that Milton's ode to Pyrrha
shows what a translator should aim for in a model version. As to
the original, its art is of a subtle and sophisticated kind without
the direct intensity of expression that has been felt in the surviving
fragments of the Greek monodists or in the poems of Catullus.
The poem is one of escape from involvement, but one that re-
enacts involvement through the imagined experience of the poet's
successor. That the imagined tumult at the centre of the poem
should prove to be the fruits of the poet's experience is a
surprising and artful turn. The plight of the unknowing youth is

25. For Cowley's poems see Waller, A.R. (ed.) (1905) *The Poems of Abraham
    Cowley*, Cambridge University Press.

treated sympathetically by the knowing poet, even if we are aware of something absurd about it and about the youth steeped in perfume and supposedly enjoying 'la vie en rose'. Nor, in spite of the interpretation of early commentators, is Pyrrha harshly condemned as a *meretrix*. Experience does not breed either complacency or contempt. The spirit in which this miniature drama is enacted in its beginning, middle and end (so delicately connected) is not cynical. If it is composed by a man of the world, then his wit and urbanity do not render him invulnerable to human concerns.

Marvell's 'Horatian Ode'

The most famous and intriguing allusion to Horace in the seventeenth century is by Andrew Marvell in 'An Horatian Ode upon Cromwell's Return from Ireland'. The title affords a very clear signal, but in the content of the poem itself there is nothing that directly and unequivocally invites comparison with Horace or even calls him to mind, so why did Marvell call his poem an Horatian ode? Or, put another way, what is Horatian about the poem?

The ode on Cromwell is not the only Horatian ode composed by Marvell. As a 'forward youth' he had produced an Horatian ode for inclusion in a collection of Greek and Latin poems by Cambridge students celebrating the birth of Princess Anne, the fifth child of Charles I in 1637. Latin odes in Horace's metres appeared in countless academic collections throughout Europe in response to victories, deaths, marriages and, as here, royal births. When poets turned to the panegyric, the Augustan odes of Horace were an obvious model. Marvell's poem *Ad Regem Carolem Parodia*[26] follows the Latin of Horace closely:

> Iam satis pestis, satis atque diri
> fulminis misit pater, ẹt rubenti
> dextera nostras iaculatus arces
>   terruit urbem.
>   (Marvell, 1–4)

26. McQueen, W.A., Rockwell, K.A. (eds) (1964) *The Latin Poetry of Andrew Marvell*, University of North Carolina Press, Chapel Hill, pp. 7–11.

(Already the father has sent enough of plague and enough of his dire thunderbolt; striking our citadels with his red right arm, he has terrified the city.)

Iam satis terris nivis atque dirae
grandinis misit Pater et rubente
dextera sacras iaculatus arces
    terruit urbem.
          (Horace, 1–4)

(Already the father has sent enough of snow and enough of his dire hail; striking our sacred citadels with his red right arm he has terrified the city.)

The poem of Horace, one of his most famous, is the second ode of his first book. In the opening poem, addressed to his patron Maecenas, he had asserted his vocation to poetry, the supreme value in Horace's life, in the lyric genre, while the second is addressed to the figure behind Maecenas who made that patronage and the poet's ensuing fame possible, Caesar Octavianus. It is usually dated to the year 27 BC, when the triumvir Octavian returned to Rome and took the name Augustus after the eastern campaigns in which he had defeated Antony and Cleopatra. The poem opens with what ancient scholiasts report to be descriptions of the portents sent by Jupiter in his displeasure at the murder of Julius Caesar. Horace then asks:

quem vocat divum populus ruentis
imperi rebus? . . .

cui dabit partes scelus expiandi
Iuppiter?
          (25–6, 29–30)

(Whom of the gods shall the people call to the needs of the falling empire? . . . To whom shall Jupiter give the part of atoning for our guilt?)

He then invokes the various gods as possible saviours or propitiators: Apollo, Venus, Mars and finally Mercury, if he will assume the guise of a mortal *patiens vocari / Caesaris ultor* (43–4) 'ready to be called the avenger of Caesar'. May he stay long on earth (*serus in caelum redeas*, 45):

    hic magnos potius triumphos
his ames dici pater atque princeps,
neu sinas Medos equitare inultos
    te duce, Caesar.

                    (49–52)

(Here may you prefer mighty triumphs, here to be hailed as father and
first citizen; nor allow the Medes to ride unpunished, under your
leadership, Caesar.)

Horace, who had fought against the triumvirs in the army of
Brutus and Cassius at Philippi, here, in the final word of the
poem, signals his accommodation to the new order of the
Caesars, expressing the weary hope that it will bring an end to
civil strife.

Marvell makes use of the recent plague that had closed the
university in 1636, and he too asks who will save the sinking
state, finding the answer in the prolific Charles, whose offspring
alone is able to make good losses sustained in the plague.

    hic magnos potius triumphos
hic ames dici pater atque princeps,
et nova mortes reparato prole
    te patre, Caesar.

(Here rather celebrate great triumphs; here may you delight to be
called prince and father, and with new birth make good our losses with
you as our father, Caesar.)

Marvell is not offering a parody of Horace in the modern sense,
but rather a witty adaptation in which he ingeniously turns the
grave matter of the original into a light-hearted compliment to the
king.

    The context of Horace's praise of Augustus, on the other hand,
is never trivial, his manner of praising never simply designed to
be ingeniously entertaining, nor is his style ever strained,
exaggerated or affected. In writing panegyric he may sometimes
be indirect, but there is usually little doubt about his attitude to
Augustus or about his assumption of the laureate role:

    Quem virum aut heroa lyra vel acri
    tibia sumis celebrare, Clio?
    quem deum?

                    (I, 12, 1–3)

(What man, what hero do you take to celebrate on the lyre or the clear-toned flute, Clio? what god?)

This is translated from Pindar and applied to the gods and heroes of Rome, culminating in the praise of Caesar:

gentis humanae pater atque custos,
orte Saturno, tibi cura magni
Caesaris fatis data: tu secundo
    Caesare regnes.

(49–52)

(O father and guardian of the human race, son of Saturn, to you by the fates has been given the care of Caesar; may you reign with Caesar next in power.)

The poet creates an august context for his praise of the conquering hero who is raised in the imagination and also set against an order greater than himself. In the closing lines of the poem we (and Caesar) are reminded of a power and a justice of which Caesar can only be a servant.

The underlying attitude of Marvell to Cromwell in his Horatian ode is much less easy to determine; many readers have detected conflicting attitudes and some have felt the presence of an underlying irony that has the effect of signalling hostility to Cromwell.[27] In featuring both the king and Cromwell, and in explicitly weighing up the issues of history, Marvell treats the recent English Civil War with a searching candour that Horace does not extend to the Roman. (It may be relevant to point out that the ode was not published in his lifetime.) The Roman poet does not disavow his past, and mentions his undistinguished service in the army of Brutus (II, 7), but there is no poem that juxtaposes the major figures of Rome's internal dissension in the

27. For differing interpretations of the ode see the articles by Cleanth Brooks and Douglas Bush in Carey, J. (ed.) (1969) *Andrew Marvell: A Critical Anthology*, Penguin, pp. 179–210. For Marvell's classical debts see Syfret, R.H. (1961) 'Marvell's "Horatian Ode"', *Review of English Studies* NS 12, 160–72; Coolidge, J.S. 1965, 'Marvell and Horace', *Modern Philosophy* 63, 111–20; Wilson, A.J.N. 1969, 'Andrew Marvell', *Classical Quarterly* 11, 325–41. 'Marvell's "Horatian Ode" and the Politics of Genre' in Healy, T. and Sawday, J. (eds) (1990) *Literature and the English Civil War*, Cambridge University Press. Useful discussion of the poems is contained in Wilcher, R. (ed.) (1986) *Andrew Marvell: Selected Poetry and Prose*, Methuen.

years after Julius Caesar crossed the Rubicon in 49 BC. The nearest we come to a direct representation of the recent conflict is in the Actium ode (I, 37) celebrating the fall of Cleopatra *nunc est bibendum*. Caesar the warrior pursues the Egyptian queen like a hawk or a swift hunter (so Marvell uses the figure of the falcon and calls Cromwell the English hunter). Unlike Cromwell, the Roman hunter does not catch his prey. Cleopatra proudly dies a dignified death, recognition of which has its parallel in the lines on the death of Charles:

> He nothing common did or mean
> Upon that memorable scene: ·
>   But with his keener eye
>   The axe's edge did try:
> Nor called the gods with vulgar spite
> To vindicate his helpless right,
>   But bowed his comely head
>   Down as upon a bed.
> This was that memorable hour
> Which first assured the forced power.
>
> (58–67)

Comparison with Marvell here suggests that Cleopatra is treated like any other foreign enemy, and there is an obvious omission in Horace, for he draws a discreet veil over the role of Mark Antony. Nor does Horace ever pass judgement on the constitutional issues involved in the earlier conflict in which he had fought on the Republic's side on behalf of 'ancient rights'. Perhaps this is the reason for the gentle censure accorded to Horace and Virgil by Marvell in a poem written about the same time as the Ode, *Tom May's Death*:

> Then with his laurel wand –
> The awful sign of his supreme command,
> At whose dread whisk Virgil himself does quake,
> And Horace patiently its stroke does take –
>
> (33–6)

May, a former royalist who had changed his allegiance, is here berated after his death in Marvell's poem by the spirit of the former poet laureate Ben Jonson:

Far from these blessed shades tread back again
Most servile wit and mercenary pen . . .
Go seek the novice statesman, and obtrude
On them some Roman cast similitude . . .
Foul architect that hadst not eye to see
How ill the manners of these states agree . . .
When the sword glitters o'er the judge's head,
And fear has coward churchmen silenced,
Then is the poet's time, 'tis then he draws,
And single fights forsaken virtue's cause.
He, when the wheel of empire whirleth back,
And though the world's disjointed axle crack
Sings still of ancient rights and better times,
Seeks wretched good, arraigns successful crimes.
But thou, base man, first prostituted hast
Our spotless knowledge and the studies chaste,
Apostatising from our arts and us,
To turn the chronicler to Spartacus.

(39–40; 43–4; 51–2; 63–74)

The poet's sharp scorn is reserved for Tom May who, as historian
of the rebellious Parliament, is said to have prostituted his literary
talent in the service of a cause no better than the slaves' revolt led
by the Roman Spartacus. The Augustan poets are treated more
lightly, but has Horace to bear the whip of Marvell's Jonson for a
failure of candour in his odes? As 'ancient rights' echoes the
Horatian Ode (38), so 'better times' seems to echo the
commendatory verses addressed to the Cavalier poet Lovelace in
1649:

Our times are much degenerate from those
Which your sweet muse, which your fair fortune chose,
And as complexities alter with the climes,
Our wits have drawn th' infection of our times.
That candid age no other way could tell
To be ingenious, but by speaking well.
Who best could praise, had then the greatest praise,
'Twas more esteemed to give than wear the bays:
Modest ambition studied only then
To honour not herself, but worthy men.
These virtues now are banished out of town
Our Civil Wars have lost the civic crown.

(1–12)

Horace and Virgil had not known the obviously better times of the earlier lives of Lovelace and Marvell; in their youth the Roman state after prolonged civil strife must have seemed on the verge of collapse, nor did they have any poetic life before they met their Maecenas. Though almost all other Roman writers after them looked back wistfully to the ancient rights and better times of the lost Republic, the Augustan poets, even those who had been on the opposing side in the civil struggle, were able in their early maturity to look forward hopefully to the promise of a new era of stability and civil peace. When the nature and quality of his rule became fully apparent after fifteen years Horace can represent Augustus Caesar's return from campaigns in Gaul in 14 BC as the answer to a heartfelt prayer (*quaerit patria Caesarem*) and can joyfully and unequivocally, with assurance and in festive mood, herald Augustus as the prince of peace and the guarantor of a civil liberty unknown in the days of the late Republic:

> quis Parthum paveat, quis gelidum Scythen
> quis Germania quos horrida parturit
> fetus, incolumni Caesare? quis ferae
>   bellum curet Hiberiae?
>
> 'longas o utinam, dux bone, ferias
> praestes Hesperiae!'
>   (IV, 5, 25–8; 37–8)

(Who could fear the Parthian, who the icy Scythian, who the brood that horrid Germany spawns, when Caesar is safe? Who could care about the war in wild Iberia? . . . 'Long be the holidays that you grant to Italy, O blest Caesar!')

Poets who address themselves to returning princes invariably hail the prince as the guarantor of order and herald his return as the guarantee of peace. Typical in this respect is the royalist panegyric by Abraham Cowley 'On his Majesty's Return out of Scotland' in 1641:

> Welcome, great sir, with all the joy that's due
>   To the return of peace and you.
> Two greatest blessings which this age can know;
> For that to thee, for thee to heaven we owe.
>   Others by war their conquests gain,
>   You like a god your ends obtain.

Who when rude chaos for his help did call,
Spoke but the word, and sweetly ordered all. . . .
The armour now may be hung up to sight
And only in their halls the children fright.

(1–8; 23–4)

The return of Cromwell from Ireland in 1650, however, with the
king's peace so rudely shattered is not the occasion of general
rejoicing and public holiday; nor does it herald the prospect of
peace but rather prompts a call to action and to arms. Moreover,
the primacy and indeed the propriety of the laureate's calling, so
apparently assured in Horace and Virgil, are not so apparent in the
immediate aftermath of the death of the English Caesar who gives
and receives the bays, now that Cromwell 'Caesar's head at last'
had 'through his laurels blast'

> The forward youth that would appear
> Must now forsake his Muses dear,
>   Nor in the shadows sing
>   His numbers languishing.
> 'Tis time to leave the books in dust,
> And oil th' unused armour's rust:
>   Removing from the wall
>   The corslet of the hall.

(1–8)

The forward youth cannot continue to sing like Virgil *lentus in
umbra* (*Eclogues* I, 4) 'in the shadows languishing' (many of
Marvell's previous poems had been pastorals), nor can the times
adequately be served by epic poems or heroic odes: 'Our Civil
Wars have lost the civil crown.' A great gulf divides Marvell from
the Augustans here. Such is the stress under which it is written
that the English seems almost an inversion of the Roman (a
second *parodia*?), or perhaps the English Horatian ode may be said
to find its true parallel in the candid ode that Horace might have
written if, as a forward youth, he had put pen to paper at the
moment in his life when he found the Republican loyalties for
which he fought at Philippi beginning to waver as he recognised
the necessity for accommodation to a new order of political realities.

In 1650, with the unprecedented shock of the execution of
God's anointed reverberating freshly in everyone's mind, and
with new domestic campaigns in the offing and amidst fearful
uncertainty as to the nature of the coming dispensation, Marvell

composed his Horatian ode without a Maecenas in a radically different set of personal and political circumstances from those facing the Roman poets in the second civil war or after Actium. It is little wonder that a poet of his intelligence scorned the easy imposition of a Roman cast similitude upon English history and his own circumstances. Even five years later when 'the forced power' (66) was assured and his own attitudes had clarified in 'The First anniversary of the Government under His Highness the Lord Protector', Marvell eschewed the Augustan parallel applied with soporific effect by Edmund Waller in 'A Panegyric to my Lord Protector':

> As the vexed would, to find repose, at last
> Itself into Augustus' arms did cast;
> So England now does, with like toil oppressed,
> Her weary head upon your bosom rest.

In the Horatian ode, the great advantage of the darkly cast Roman similitude for the poet's purposes lies in the Olympian perspective he is able to achieve in detaching the protagonists from the Christian world of the seventeenth century and placing them in a more timeless and secular historical Roman frame. As for the Horatian connection, any ambivalence or irony in the ode itself must extend to its title, in so far as it calls to mind the laureate odes addressed by Horace to Augustus.

However, in so far as the title refers to the form of the ode, the associations are simpler. It has been pointed out that its metre is the English substitute for the Alcaic form used by Sir Richard Fanshawe, a son of Ben, in several of his versions of Horace's odes in the 1630s.[28] The regular tightly knit stanzas are indeed something like Horace, particularly when considered in contrast to the more elaborate Pindaric ode, whether in the triadic structure that Ben Jonson gave to his Cary/Morison ode or in the irregular form made popular in English by Abraham Cowley in his *Pindaric Odes written in Imitation of the Style and Manner of the Odes of Pindar* of the 1650s. The style and manner of the Pindaric ode had already been imitated by Ben Jonson in 'An Ode to James, Earl of Desmond':

---

28.   Simeone, W. (1952) *N & Q* **197**, 316–18.

Where art thou genius? I should use
  Thy present aid; arise invention,
Wake, and put on the wings of Pindar's muse,
  To tower with my intention
  High as his mind, that doth advance
Her upright head above the reach of chance,
    Or the time's envy;
    Cinthius, I apply
My bolder numbers to thy golden lyre:
    O then inspire
Thy priest in this strange rapture; heat my brain
    With Delphic fire
So that I may sing my thoughts in some unvulgar strain.

                                                    (1–13)

The 'bolder numbers' attempting 'this strange rapture' in their
manner and their irregular form are very unlike the more compact
form of Horace and Marvell's Horatian ode.

Horace and Pindar

Comparison between Pindar and Horace that became commonplace in the second half of the seventeenth century is first
broached by Horace himself in a famous ode (IV, 2), addressed to
a fellow poet, Antonius Iulus (the son of Mark Antony and
Fulvia), with whom Horace associates the Pindaric talent that will
be necessary to sing of Augustus's military achievements and to
celebrate the long-hoped-for return of the conquering hero to
Rome (he had been away for two years from 16–14 BC restoring
order to Roman Gaul after the incursions of German tribes
invading from north of the Rhine). Here is the version of Sir
Richard Fanshawe:

Who thinks to equal Pindar, tries
With waxen wings to reach the skies,
Like him that (falling) a name gave
      To his watery grave.
As a proud stream that swollen with rain

Comes pouring down the hills amain,
So Pindar flows, and fears no drowth,
      Such his deep mouth,

Worthy the bays, whether he pour
From unexhausted springs a shower
Of lawless dithyrambs, and thunders
      In bolder numbers:

Or sings of gods and heroes (seed
Of gods) whose just swords did outweed
The Centaurs, and Chimaera stout
      Her flames put out:

Or mourns some youth, from his sad spouse
Unkindly torn, whose strength and prowess
And golden mind he lifts to the sky,
      And lets not die.

This Theban swan, when he will sing
Among the clouds, raises his wing
On a stiff gale. I like the bee
      Of Calabria

Which (toiling) sucks beloved flowers
About the thymy groves, and scours
Of fount-well Tiber, frame a terse
      But humble verse.

Thou, Antony, in higher strains
Chant Caesar, when he leads in chains
Fierce Germans, his victorious brows
      Crowned with bay boughs;

Thou whom a greater thing, or good
Heaven hath not lent the earth, nor should
Though it refined the age to the old
      Saturnian gold.[29]

In the boldness and aptness of his figurative language in likening
the mouth of Pindar to a raging torrent Horace is able to evoke
the tone and manner of the Pindaric style in the very act of
warning of the pitfalls that await anyone attempting to emulate
them, just as he fulfils his laureate role whilst seemingly declaring

29.   First printed in Fanshawe, R. (1652) *Selected Parts of Horace . . . Now newly
      put into English*. See Buxton, J. (1967) *A Tradition of Poetry*, Macmillan,
      Chapter 6, 'Sir Richard Fanshawe'. Buxton prints the first three stanzas.

himself inadequate to the task. The sublime swan and the humble bee suggest a clear contrast in scale, ambition and style. The bee is particularly appropriate for a poet who worked by industrious imitation of the Greek lyric tradition, and there is a latent contrast between the freely expressive force of natural genius in the Greeks[30] and the laborious and regular artistry of Roman imitation (similar to the contrast drawn in the Renaissance between Homer and Virgil). The figure of the bee subsequently became a Renaissance commonplace in its association with the workings of poetic imitation (see Jonson's *Discoveries*, 3068). The bee amidst the thyme, while suggesting a modest recoil from grandeur that is more typical of Horace than of the Roman culture that produced him, is itself an image of beauty and charm, that are evident too in the description of the tender calf at the end of the poem. All the elements are integrated into a complex whole that contrives to be grand yet subtle, and clear yet rich in implication. In its total effect it bears out the praise accorded by Quintilian to Horace's lyric achievement: 'Of our lyric writers Horace is almost the sole poet worth reading: for he rises at times to a lofty grandeur and is full of sprightliness and charm, while there is great variety in his figures, and his boldness in the choice of words is only equalled by his felicity' (*The Education of an Orator* X, 1, 96).

The Cowleyan Pindaric

To explore further the differences between the Horatian and the Pindaric, we need only put alongside Fanshawe's translation the Pindaric version of the same original composed by Abraham Cowley, to which he gave the title 'The Praise of Pindar':

> Pindar is imitable by none;
> The Phoenix Pindar is a vast species alone.
> Who e're but Daedalus with waxen wings could fly
> And neither sink too low, nor soar too high?
>   What could he who followed claim,
> But of vain boldness the unhappy fame,

30. Pindar himself says that the true poet is he who knows much by gift of natural genius, *phua*: *Olympian* II, 154.

And by his fall a sea to name?
Pindar's innavigable song
Like a swoll'n flood from some deep mountain pours along,
The ocean meets with such a voice
From his enlarged mouth, as drowns the ocean's noise.

So Pindar does new words and figures roll
Down his impetuous dithyrambic tide,
Which in no channel deigns t' abide,
Which neither banks nor dykes control.
Whether th' immortal gods he sings
In a no less immortal strain,
Or the great acts of god-descended kings,
Who in his numbers still survive and reign.
Each rich embroidered line
Which their triumphant brows around,
By his sacred hand is bound,
Does all their starry diadems outshine.

Whether at Pisa's race he please
To carve in polished verse the conquerors' images,
Whether the swift, the skilful, or the strong,
Be crowned in his nimble, artful, vigorous song:
Whether some brave young man's untimely fate
In words worth dying for he celebrate,
Such mournful, and such pleasing words,
As joy to his mother and his mistress grief affords
He bids him live and grow in fame,
Among the stars he sticks his name:
The grave can but the dross of him devour,
So small is death's, so great the poet's power.

Lo, how th' obsequious wind, and swelling air
The Theban swan does upwards bear
Into the walks of clouds, where he does play,
And with extended wings opens his liquid way.
Whilst, alas, my timorous Muse
Unambitious tracks pursues;
Does with weak unballast wings,
About the mossy brooks and springs;
About the trees new-blossomed heads,
About the garden's painted beds,
About the fields and flow'ry meads,

> And all inferior beauteous things
>   Like the laborious bee,
>   For little drops of honey flee,
> And there with humble sweets contents her industry.

As the title suggests, the design of Cowley's imitation, which is confined to the comparison between the two poets, is the praise of Pindar. In fact, the balance of his lines tilts radically in favour of Pindar, for, despite his modesty, Horace does not call his muse 'timorous', or say that he pursues 'unambitious tracks' flitting with 'weak unballast wings' about 'inferior beauteous things', where the position of the pun entails undue self-deprecation. It may be felt that there is a radical indecorum in the poem, since in contradiction of the opening proposition, 'Pindar is imitable by none', Cowley proceeds to Pindarise Horace, wittily converting the Roman terms of praise into the style and manner of Pindar as suggested by Horace here and reinforced by the words of Quintilian which the English poet cites in his notes to the poem: 'Of the nine lyric poets Pindar is by far the greatest, in virtue of his inspired magnificence, the beauty of his thoughts and figures, the rich exuberance of his language and matter, and his rolling flood of eloquence, characteristics which, as Horace rightly held, make him inimitable' (*The Education of an Orator* X, 1, 61).

The most strikingly Pindaric feature of those mentioned by Quintilian which differentiates 'The Praise of Pindar' from Horace is its superabundance of matter and words *rerum verborumque copia*. The magnificent manner entails quite literally magnifying, enlarging upon, amplifying and expanding. In its Pindaric reincarnation the Horatian bee goes about and about and about and about. Quintilian also refers to Pindar's *sententiae*, his figures and his stream of eloquence. Here Cowley is not greatly sententious, but where Horace simply has words, he adds figures in his description of Pindar's flood of eloquence:

> So Pindar does new words and figures roll
> Down his impetuous dithyrambic tide . . .

'The figures are unusual and bold, even to temerity, and such as I durst not have to do withal in any other kind of poetry' ('Preface to Poems'). Hyperboles and bold metaphors abound. In contrast Horace shows restraint and economy in his deployment of metaphor (to which he gives no mention at all in his *Art of Poetry*). Other rhetorical figures are prominent in 'The Praise of Pindar'. The balanced parallelism and antithesis beloved of Augustan couplet writers are pronounced in stanza three (notably in lines 3 and 4, 7 and 8 and in the sententious final couplet). The same stanza contains a bold stroke of hyperbolic wit in a conceit that is not in the least like the Greek poet (or the Roman) but can be sanctioned by the general notion of boldness loosely associated with the word Pindaric:

> Whether some brave young man's untimely fate
> In words worth dying for he celebrate.

The perils of this figurative boldness ('his enlarged mouth' and 'swelling air' teeter on the brink of absurdity) are recognised in the address to the muse that concludes 'The Resurrection', the poem that follows 'The Praise of Pindar'.

> Stop, stop, my Muse, allay thy vigorous heat,
>   Kindled at a hint so great.
> Hold thy Pindaric Pegasus closely in,
>   Which does to rage begin,
> And this steep hill would gallop up with violent course,
> 'Tis an unruly, and a hard-mouthed horse,
>   Fierce, and unbroken yet,
>   Impatient of the spur or bit.
> Now prances stately, and anon flies o'er the place,
> Disdains the servile law of any settled pace,
> Conscious and proud of his own natural force.
>   'Twill no unskilful touch endure,
> But flings writer and reader too that sits not sure.

The Pindaric Pegasus, a figurative embodiment of the unruly *furor poeticus*, delights in its own natural force and is impatient of restriction and control; especial artistry is needed if the exhilarating ride is not to end in disaster. Pegasus also suggests the poet's licence 'boldly to deviate from the common track'.[31] This entails not only lofty subject matter but also the free treatment of it sanctioned by Pindar's digressive structuring. 'This ode is truly Pindarical falling from one thing into another after his enthusiastical manner', Cowley commented in notes to 'The Resurrection'.

---

31. Pope, *An Essay on Criticism* (1709), 146–57.

But above all the freedom is metrical, as suggested by the conclusion of the ode 'Upon Liberty':

> If life should a well-ordered poem be
>   In which he only hits the white
> Who joins true profit with the best delight;
> The more heroic strain let others take
>   Mine the Pindaric way I'll make;
> The matter shall be grave, the numbers loose and free.

In its stanzaic form the Cowleyan Pindaric, in contrast to the regular triadic structure of Jonson's Cary/Morison ode or of the smaller-scale monostrophic odes of Horace himself, is marked by its irregularity. The long stanzas have different numbers of lines, the lines vary greatly in length and the rhyme schemes are also varied throughout. The classical authority for this irregularity has been thought to be Horace himself in this ode in praise of Pindar:

> seu per audaces nova dithyrambos
> verba devolvit numerisque fertur
>   lege solutis
> (10–12)

(whether he pours down new words through his bold dithyrambs and is borne along in measures free from rule.)

But the irregularity here is associated with Pindar's dithyrambs (hymns to Dionysus, none of which survives). In his note on the passage Cowley clearly appreciated this. Of the extant odes he writes in the Preface, 'we must consider that our ears are strangers to the music of his numbers, which sometimes (especially in songs and odes) almost without anything else makes an excellent poet; for though the grammarians and critics have laboured to reduce his verses into regular feet and measures . . . yet in effect they are little better than prose to our ears'. Evidently the efforts of Renaissance editors did not help Cowley to a positive appreciation of the formal properties of the Greek, but it does not seem likely that his adoption of an irregular stanzaic form is a result of either a misunderstanding or a careless reading of Horace's words, though misapplication of the Horatian passage became commonplace after him. It is more likely that, taking a hint from Horace here, he judged that he could best represent the Pindaric manner in English by means of the latitude afforded by an irregular stanza. Nor, if this was his judgement, was it a foolish one, for the rhythm and movement of the often large syntactical units of Pindar do seem looser and freer (whether or not the ear comprehends their metrical pattern) than the more regular and 'severer Muses'[32] of the more familiar poets of Rome.

Cowley's encounter with Pindar has all the marks of a sudden conversion; even though he found the metre strange, he was greatly struck by 'his way and manner of speaking; which has not been yet (that I know of) introduced into English, though it be the noblest and highest kind of writing in verse'. His imitations are an attempt to see 'how it will look in an English habit'.

Before Cowley's Pindarics, there is little evidence that Pindar had been much read or taken notice of in England. He had not been translated into English. Neither Ben Jonson's brief evocation of the Pindaric manner in 'An Ode to James, Earl of Desmond' nor his imitation of the triadic form in the Cary/Morison ode (which he did not call a Pindaric) produced any imitations amongst his followers. Shorn of its accompanying music and dance, the tripartite structure has no obvious function for English poets. Indeed, Jonson does not use the divisions for any clear purpose in the deployment of theme or argument in the Cary/Morison ode. Milton's lofty poem 'On the Morning of Christ's Nativity' has sometimes been called a Pindaric ode by modern scholars, though there is nothing in it that definitely suggests Pindaric inspiration or might call Pindar clearly to mind to readers of his century. For in the Renaissance no Greek author, let alone one as difficult as Pindar, was naturally a part of every educated person's upbringing and schooling as were Horace, Virgil and Ovid. Cowley had the best education available in the seventeenth century at Westminster school (also the *alma mater* of Jonson and Dryden) but it seems that he was surprised by Pindar at a later date when on the king's service in Jersey in the 1650s. According to his friend and biographer Thomas Sprat:

> The occasion of his falling on the Pindaric way of writing was his accidental meeting with Pindar's works in a place where he had no other books to direct him. Having considered at leisure the height of his invention and the majesty of his style, he tried immediately to

---

32. *Musas colimus severiores* 'we [the Romans] cultivate more unbending Muses [than the Greeks]' Martial IX, 11, 17.

imitate it in English. And he performed it without the danger that Horace presaged to the man who should dare to attempt it.[33]

Sprat is right to say when speaking of the imitating of Pindar that it 'may perhaps be thought rather a new sort of writing than a restoring of an ancient', for his reading of Pindar awakened Cowley to the exciting possibility of creating something new in English. The resulting *Pindaric Odes* offers a very clear programme starting with a preface[34] clarifying his mode of imitation which is fittingly free and liberal: 'I have in these two odes of Pindar taken, left out and added what I please, nor make it so much my aim to let the reader know precisely what he spoke, as what was his way and manner of speaking.' The preface contains an attack on the practice of literal translation where there is no addition of 'wit and the spirit of poetry'. 'And I would gladly know what applause our best pieces of English poetry could expect from a Frenchman or an Italian, if converted faithfully, and word for word, into French or Italian prose?' The attack turns imperceptibly from translation to 'exact imitation', where there is no addition of wit or invention: 'which being a vile and unworthy kind of servitude, is incapable of producing anything good or noble. I have seen originals both in painting and poetry much more beautiful than their natural objects; but I never saw a copy better than an original, which indeed cannot be otherwise; for men resolving in no case to shoot beyond the mark, it is a thousand to one if they shoot not short of it.' Translators 'have not sought to supply the lost excellencies of another language with new ones of their own'. In the two odes of Pindar that follow the preface he puts these liberal principles into practice, striking a note of grand enthusiasm:

> Queen of all harmonious things,
>> Dancing words and speaking strings,
>> What god, what hero wilt thou sing?
> What happy man to equal glories bring?
>> Begin, begin thy noble choice,
> And let the hills around reflect the image of thy voice.
>> ('The Second Olympic Ode of Pindar', 1–6)

33.   'An account of the Life and Writings of Mr Abraham Cowley' in Spingarn, J.E. (ed.) (1908–09) *Critical Essays of the Seventeenth Century*, 3 vols, Oxford University Press, vol. 2, p. 131.
34.   In Waller, A.R. (1905) p. 155. See also Cowley's remarks in his 'Preface to Poems', Springarn, J.E. (1908) vol. 2, p. 86.

Notes to the poems which cite the Greek and a literal Latin
version demonstrate that the project is grounded in learning and
scholarship, and enable Cowley to explain Pindar and himself to
his readers. There follows 'The Praise of Pindar' which provides
further classical authority for the style and kind of writing that it
characterises and promotes. Then come 'The Resurrection' and
'The Muse' which, Cowley tells us in his notes, developed out of
hints from Pindar. Odes follow on philosophical and religious
themes such as 'Destiny', 'Life and Fame', 'The 34 Chapter of
Isaiah' and 'The Plagues of Egypt'. On the example and authority
of Pindar a new verse form with its own characteristics of style
has been introduced into English.

Two Pindaric odes of Dryden

The vogue for the Pindaric in the second half of the seventeenth
century and beyond did not produce many poems to survive their
times. But there are two Pindarics which alone make Cowley's
efforts worth while. The first is Dryden's translation of the
twenty-ninth ode of the third book of Horace, 'paraphrased in
Pindaric verse' and published in the *Sylvae* of 1685.

> One ode which infinitely pleased me in the reading, I have attempted
> to translate in Pindaric verse; 't is that which is inscribed to the present
> Earl of Rochester . . . . 'Tis his darling in the Latin and I have taken
> some pains to make it my masterpiece in English; for which reason I
> took this kind of verse, which allows more latitude than any other.
> Everyone knows it was introduced into our language, in this age, by
> the happy genius of Mr Cowley . . . . But if I may be allowed to speak
> my mind modestly, and without injury to his sacred ashes, somewhat
> of the purity of English, somewhat of more equal thoughts, somewhat
> of sweetness in the numbers, in one word, somewhat of a finer turn
> and more lyrical verse, is yet wanting. As for the soul of it, which
> consists in the warmth and vigour of fancy, the masterly figures and
> the copiousness of imagination, he has excelled all others in this kind
> . . . . Since Pindar was the prince of lyric poets, let me have leave to
> say that, in imitating him our numbers should for the most part be
> lyrical . . . the cadency of one line must rule that of the next; and the
> sound of the former must slide gently into that which follows, without
> leaping from one extreme into another.[35]

35. 'Preface to *Sylvae*' (1685), Watson, G. (1962) vol. 2, p. 31.

Dryden here analyses the poetic task to be done (this was his first Pindaric) and describes the nature of his achievement.

> Descended of an ancient line
>   That long the Tuscan sceptre swayed,
> Make haste to meet the generous wine
>   Whose piercing is for thee delayed;
> The rosy wreath is ready made;
>   And artful hands prepare
> The fragrant Syrian oil that shall perfume thy hair.
>
>   (1–7)

No one had given the Pindaric such purity of English, such sweetness of sound and such lyrical numbers before. Yet the new lyricism which seems to have been a principal aim, to judge from Dryden's prose comments, cannot alone account for the success of the poem. It is also a consequence of what he calls 'more equal thoughts', perhaps thoughts that are better proportioned to the verse form, or more equable thoughts without the overheated striving for elevation that is so often a feature of Cowley's Pindarics, and sometimes of his own even where he is lyrical. In the following year, for example, as poet laureate he made his most ambitious attempt in this form with his 500-line *Threnodia Augustalis: A Funeral-Pindaric sacred to the Happy Memory of King Charles II*. Here is his rendering of the arrival of the Duke of York (the future James II) at the royal bedchamber:

> Arrived within the mournful room, he saw
>   A wild distraction, void of awe,
> And arbitrary grief unbounded by a law.
>   God's image, God's anointed lay
>   Without motion, pulse, or breath,
>   A senseless lump of sacred clay,
>   An image now of death:
> Amidst his sad attendants' groans and cries,
>   The lines of that adored forgiving face,
>   Distorted from their native grace;
> An iron slumber sat on his majestic eyes.
> The pious duke – forbear, audacious Muse,
> No terms thy feeble art can use
> Are able to adorn so vast a woe:
> The grief of all the rest like subject-grief did show
>   His like a sovereign did transcend;

No wife, no brother, such a grief could know,
    Nor any name, but friend.

(60–77)

Line 70 (a formula derived from Virgil) is a sublime touch in a passage where sublimity constantly teeters on the brink of absurdity, the line between the two being notoriously thin. A great talent is clearly straining at the task. But in the translation of Horace, Dryden found safe anchorage in a subject that proved deeply congenial, so that he achieved through Horace what is rare in any Pindaric ode and certainly eluded him in his laureate Pindaric, a fine decorum of content and form.

Dryden does not attempt to Pindarise Horace as Cowley had done, with some point, in 'The Praise of Pindar'; the images and expression are dignified but restrained as they are in Horace who is, after all, offering modest pleasures. And Dryden is here striving to maintain the poetic character of Horace as he describes it in his preface:

> That which distinguishes his style from all other poets is the elegance of his words and the numerousness of his verse: there is nothing so delicately turned in all the Roman language. There appears in every part of his diction, or (to speak English) in all his expressions a noble and bold purity. . . . But the most distinguishing part of all his character seems to be his briskness, his jollity and his good humour; and these I have chiefly endeavoured to copy.[36]

Horace addresses his rich friend and patron Maecenas and with good humour invites him to condescend to come down from his lofty edifice on the Esquiline:

    Thy turret that surveys from high,
  The smoke, and wealth, and noise of Rome;
    And all the busy pageantry,
    That wise men scorn and fools adore:
  Come, give thy soul a loose, and taste the pleasures of the poor

(17–21)

If this is to be taken literally, Horatian poverty can be seen as such only when contrasted to sybaritic Roman luxury. But Horatian

36.   Watson, G. (1962) vol. 2, p. 31. For extensive commentary upon this ode see Mason, H.A.(1981) 'Living in the Present: Is Dryden's "Horat Ode 29 Book 3" an Example of "creative translation"?', *Cambridge Quarterly* **10**, 91–129.

poverty is largely symbolic and has to do with acceptance of a modest lot. Horace invites Maecenas 'to give his soul a loose', to set it free from enthralment to material cares in careless relaxation. After painting a picture of the sweltering heat of a torrid Mediterrean high summer from which escape seems only too welcome, the poet imagines Maecenas burdened with the anxiety attendant upon cares of state:

> Thou what befits the new Lord Mayor,
> And what the city faction dare,
> And what the Gallic arms will do,
> And what the quiver-beaming foe,
> Art anxiously inquisitive to know.
>
> (40–4)

Dryden brings these cares home to his contemporary world, and the anaphora skilfully suggests a never-ending succession as they come one after another into his unquiet mind. Then comes the lofty Epicurean perspective that effectively puts human business and anxiety in their place:

> But God has, wisely, hid from human sight
>   The dark decrees of future fate,
>   And sown their seeds in depth of night:
> He laughs at all the giddy turns of state,
> When mortals search too soon, and fear too late.
>
> (45–9)

At a point halfway through the poem is its central injunction – *carpe diem*:

> Enjoy the present smiling hour,
> And put it out of Fortune's power.
>
> (50–1)

translating the Latin *quod adest memento/componere aequus* (32–3) 'as to what is at hand remember to settle it with equal mind'. Here is the desideratum of the Horatian *aequa mens* followed immediately by a powerful evocation of the tide of human business that always threatens to overwhelm it.

> The tide of business, like the running stream,
>   Is sometimes high and sometimes low,
>   A quiet ebb or a tempestuous flow,

> And always in extreme.
> Now with a noiseless gentle course
> It keeps within the middle bed;
> Anon it lifts its head,
> And bears down all before it with impetuous force;
> And trunks of trees come rolling down,
> Sheep and their folds together drown:
> Both house and homestead into seas are borne;
> And rocks are from their old foundations torn,
> And woods, made thin with winds, their scattered honours mourn.
>
> (52–64)

After such threatening disturbance comes the calm reassurance of the happy man at the poem's epicentre:

> Happy the man and happy he alone,
> He who can call today his own;
> He who, secure within, can say:
> 'Tomorrow do thy worst, for I have lived today.
> Be fair, or foul, or rain or shine,
> The joys I have possessed, in spite of fate, are mine.
> Not Heaven itself upon the past has power;
> But what has been, has been, and I have had my hour.'
>
> (65–72)

The emphatic rhythms and measured expressions of Dryden are both dynamic and steady, an unusual combination present in the whole poem which, as a consequence, is the most animated expression of Horatian equanimity in English. Where Milton is guarded in his response to the Epicurean relaxations he is anticipating in his sonnet to Lawrence, Dryden full-heartedly embraces the Epicurean philosophy at the lyric's core in his assurance of pleasure possessed. Given the literal meaning 'freedom from care' the adjective in 'secure within', derived from the Latin *securus* and translating the key Horatian phrase *potens sui* (42) 'in control of himself', is an inspired choice to suggest the basis of all true human happiness.

As the threat of turbulence preceded the philosophic calm at the poem's centre, so recognition of the destructive power of Fortune follows it:

> Fortune, that with malicious joy
> Does man her slave oppress,

Proud of her office to destroy,
    Is seldom pleased to bless:
    Still various and unconstant still,
But with an inclination to be ill,
    Promotes, degrades, delights in strife,
    And makes a lottery of life.
    I can enjoy her while she's kind;
    But when she dances in the wind,
    And shakes her wings, and will not stay,
    I puff the prostitute away;
The little or the much she gave is quietly resigned;
    Content with poverty, my soul I arm;
    And virtue, though in rags, will keep me warm.

                               (73–87)

Unlike the Stoic diehard who aspires to total indifference, Horace happily welcomes the gifts of Fortune but can dismiss her when she becomes fickle. Dryden wittily extends the personification whereby Fortune is the fickle female to diminish her in the witty line 'I puff the prostitute away'. If Fortune proves to be a prostitute, then the poet's dismissal of her is not unduly self-righteous. His wit is effectively disarming; most readers can aspire to this kind of virtue.

Having fully acknowledged and given full poetic force to the disturbing factors within and without that threaten human happiness, the poet earns the right to claim for himself the possibility of a detached equanimity modestly figured in the imagery and underscored by the finely modulated cadences of the close:

           What is't to me,
    Who never sail in her unfaithful sea,
        If storms arise, and clouds grow black;
        If the mast split, and threaten wreck?
    Then let the greedy merchant fear
        For his ill-gotten gain;
    And pray to gods that will not hear,
While the debating winds and billows bear
        His wealth into the main.
    For me, secure from Fortune's blows,
    (Secure of what I cannot lose,)
    In my small pinnace I can sail,
    Contemning all the blust'ring roar;

> And running with a merry gale,
> With friendly stars my safety seek,
> Within some little winding creek;
> And see the storm ashore.
>
>   (88–104)

The poet is in full possession of his subject; his poem radiates a remarkable inner calm even as it faces turbulence so that it is the perfect embodiment of its own philosophy. Horace prompted Dryden, in the midst of a hectic and sometimes turbulent literary life, to the lyrical expression of a deeply felt philosophy of equanimity; it is difficult to suppose that he would have been moved to any such expression without him. As the Latin prompted something new in him, so he has given new life to the Latin, recreating a refreshingly philosophical lyric for English readers and illustrating the workings of the classical tradition at its best.

The same equanimity and detachment are apparent in *Alexander's Feast: or The Power of Music* composed in 1697 for the celebration of the feast of St Cecilia. Again the subject proved deeply congenial and, as it is embodied in what purports to be actual history, the poem has none of the ingrown egotism that so often disfigures poetic celebrations of the power of art. The anecdote which provided the basis for the narrative was well known. Spenser's annotator E.K. records the story of Alexander:

> to whom when as Timotheus the great musician played the Phrygian melody, it is said, that he was distraught with such unwonted fury, that straight way rising from the table in great rage, he caused himself to go to war (for that music is very warlike): And immediately whenas the musician changed his stroke into the Lydian and Ionic harmony, he was so far from warring, that he sat as still, as if he had been in matters of counsel.[37]

In other tellings Alexander is actually moved, as in Dryden's poem to the conquest of Persepolis, by the musician's power. Dryden's poem is a great one because with extraordinary technical virtuosity he uses the freedom of the Pindaric form to recreate all the various modes and moods of lyric to evoke the godlike hero, to celebrate the joys of Bacchus, to infuse soft pity, to move to

---

37. In his ninth comment on 'October'.

love and finally to inspirit a warlike fury. In all its variety, the
poem provides a grand summation of all that the lyric is famed
for, and in its rhythms and harmonies creates its own musical
accompaniment, so that Pope could later speak of its 'style of
sound'.[38]

> The mighty master smiled to see
> That love was in the next degree:
> 'Twas but a kindred sound to move,
> For pity melts the mind to love.
>> Softly sweet in Lydian measures,
>> Soon he soothed his soul to pleasures.
> 'War', he sung, 'is toil and trouble;
> Honour but an empty bubble;
>> Never ending, still beginning,
> Fighting still, and still destroying:
>> If the world be worth thy winning,
> Think, O think it worth enjoying;
>> Lovely Thais sits beside thee,
>> Take the goods the gods provide thee.'
>> (93–106)

So comprehensive is the poem that wit and humour are not
wholly excluded as the great conqueror becomes the easy
plaything of the artist:

> The many rend the skies with loud applause;
> So Love was crowned, but Music won the cause.
>> The prince, unable to conceal his pain,
>>> Gazed on the fair
>>> Who caused his care,
>> And sighed and looked, sighed and looked,
>> Sighed and looked, and sighed again:
> At length, with love and wine at once oppressed,
> The vanquished visitor sunk upon her breast.
>> (107–15)

Having been a less than wholly successful Timotheus at the Court
of the Stuarts, in his old age when he had long since lost the
laureateship Dryden doubtless enjoyed the freedom the fable gave

38. In a letter to Henry Cromwell, 25 November 1710, on versification in
     Sherburn, G. (ed.) (1956) *The Correspondence of Alexander Pope*, 5 vols,
     Oxford University Press, vol. 1, p. 108.

him to subordinate the power of kings to a power that is more sublime. That power is figured in the form of the classical lyrist effecting the composition and performance of a grand choral ode:

> Timotheus, placed on high
>   Amid the tuneful choir,
>   With flying fingers touched the lyre:
> The trembling notes ascend the sky,
>   And heavenly joys inspire.
>
>   (20–4)

Dryden's performance prompted a fine poetic tribute:

> Hear how Timotheus' varied lays surprise,
> And bid alternate passions fall and rise!
> While, at each change, the son of Libyan Jove
> Now burns with glory, and then melts with love;
> Now his fierce eyes with sparkling fury glow,
> Now sighs steal out, and tears begin to flow:
> Persians and Greeks like turns of Nature found,
> And the world's victor stood subdued by sound!
> The power of music all our hearts allow,
> And what Timotheus was, is Dryden now.
>
>   (Pope: *An Essay on Criticism*, 374–83)

Chapter 4

Pastoral and Georgic

> But for all this, I do deny that the Eclogue should be the first and most ancient form of artificial poesie, being persuaded that the poet devised the eclogue long after the other dramatic poems, not of purpose to counterfeit or represent the rustical manner of loves and communication but under the veil of homely persons and in rude speeches to insinuate and glance at greater matters, and such as perchance had not been safe to have disclosed in any other sort, which may be perceived by the Eclogues of Virgil, in which are treated by figure matters of greater importance than the loves of Tityrus and Corydon. These eclogues came after [drama] to contain and inform moral discipline for the amendment of man's behaviour, as be those of Mantuan and other modern poets.
>
> (Puttenham, *The Arte of English Poesie*, 1589)[1]

Working back from his knowledge of the eclogue as used by modern poets and Virgil (with whom the word meaning 'selection' is first associated with pastoral), though he does not pronounce with confidence on its origin, Puttenham avoids the frequent Renaissance mistake of imagining that the pastoral represented the oldest kind of poetry coming from a time before the development of civilisation. He recognises its late origin, its figurative tendency and its artificial representation of rustic life. Nevertheless, the originator of the genre, the Greek poet Theocritus, would have been greatly surprised by Puttenham's moral emphasis.

Greek beginnings

The Sicilian-born Theocritus lived in the first half of the third century BC some time after the Macedonian conquests had put an

1. Smith, G.G. (1904) vol. 2, p. 40.

end to the independent city states of classical Greece. He was part of a sophisticated literary circle in Alexandria, the metropolis on the Nile delta founded by Alexander the Great which, by the time of Theocritus, was the foremost commercial and literary centre of the Greek-speaking world and its largest city. In later times his poems were called *eidyllia*, a diminutive of the Greek word *eidos* meaning form. There was an Alexandrian tendency deliberately to avoid large-scale forms. The poet Callimachus is reputedly the author of the slogan *mega biblion, mega kakon*[2] 'big book, big bore'. Theocritus's 'little forms', written mostly in hexameters, include court poems, an epithalamium, short mythological pieces and epigrams as well as poems featuring scenes and characters from ordinary life (not generally a feature of classical poetry outside comedy) amongst which are urban mimes and the bucolic poems by which he is chiefly known and which are regarded as the first pastorals.[3] Though pastoral is derived from the Latin word for shepherd, bucolic comes from the Greek for cowhand, and his rustic characters may have charge of cattle and goats as well as sheep. They speak in the Doric dialect of Greek, which artificially sets them apart from standard Greek whether literary or of the city. The pastorals, like the other poems of Theocritus, are the product of a culture in which art was no longer so rooted in the community as it had been in the classical city state, and represent a disengagement from political or social concerns in favour of a more esoteric cultivation of art for art's sake. All the poems of Theocritus are highly finished and deliberately artificial. His shepherds, for example, are not to be found engaging in the more unsavoury tasks of animal husbandry, but spend their time showing off their skills in singing competitions, and falling in and out of love. Despite this artificiality, they are lively and lusty and can trade in bantering insult, and there is a real feeling for the beauty of the Sicilian countryside melodiously conveyed in richly sensuous imagery in a way that made Theocritus the archetypical poet of the pastoral idyll. He is therefore not a peasant-poet, but a literary man who had left the country for the big city from which

2. Fragments 359.
3. The anonymous translation of 1588 *Six Idillia that is, six small or petty poems or aeglogues chosen out of the right famous Sicilian poet Theocritus*, Joseph Barnes, Oxford includes several poems that are not pastorals. The translations are very feeble.

he looks back with nostalgia to the landscape of his boyhood. His poems are not figurative in the way in which Puttenham conceives pastoral, but Idyll VII, *Thalysia*, 'harvest festival', set on the island of Cos (where Theocritus had lived between Sicily and Alexandria), features the poet himself, according to the ancient scholiast, under the name of Simichidas, so that Theocritus pointed the way towards later developments in the genre.

Virgilian pastoral

As most Renaissance readers knew of Theocritus not first hand but through commentaries where he is quoted as Virgil's source, the Greek inheritance may be appropriately illustrated by way of Virgilian imitation. Pastoral VII, 'Meliboeus', recreates what might be called the pure pastoral following the Theocritean archetype. Meliboeus reports an encounter with Daphnis who persuades him to stay and listen to a singing match between Corydon and Thyrsis. Here we find the *dramatis personae* of Theocritus retaining their Greek names (which must have had something of the romantic sound to Latin ears that they have to the modern world): Daphnis derived from *daphne* laurel, an emblem of poetry, the mythical herdsman whose death is the subject of Thyrsis's song in Idyll I; the shepherd Thyrsis recalling the *thyrsos* or wand of the Bacchic reveller and thus the Dionysiac inspiration of the poet, and the goatherd Corydon (the Greek word for lark) and Meliboeus whose name suggests 'keeper of cattle'. The simple plot provides the occasion for what is one of the main Theocritean forms, the *amoebean*, from the Greek word to answer. The opening lines set the scene for the contest and form an appropriate prelude.

> Forte sub arguta consederat ilice Daphnis,
> compulerantque greges Corydon et Thyrsis in unum,
> Thyrsis oves, Corydon distentas lacte capellas,
> ambo florentes aetatibus, Arcades ambo,
> et cantare pares et repondere parati.
> huc mihi, dum teneras defendo a frigore myrtos,
> vir gregis ipse caper deerraverat, atque ego Daphnim
> aspicio. ille ubi me contra videt, 'ocius' inquit
> 'huc ades o Meliboee; caper tibi salvus et haedi;

et, si quid cessare potes, requiesce sub umbra.
huc ipsi potum venient per prata iuvenci;
hic virides tenera praetexit harundine ripas
Mincius, eque sacra resonant examina quercu.'
quid facerem? neque ego Alcippen nec Phyllida habebam,
depulsos a lacte domi quae clauderet agnos,
et certamen erat, Corydon cum Thyrside, magnum.
posthabui tamen illorum mea seria ludo.

(1–17)[4]

(Daphnis by chance had sat beneath a whispering ilex, and Corydon and Thyrsis had driven their flocks together, Thyrsis his sheep swollen with milk, Corydon, his goats swollen with milk, both Arcadians, both in the flower of youth, and both well matched in singing and ready to reply. Hither, while I was protecting my tender myrtles from the cold, my he-goat himself the lord of the herd had strayed, and lo and behold I see Daphnis. When he in turn sees me, 'quickly', he says, 'come here Meliboeus, your he-goat and the kids are safe, and if you can stop a while, rest beneath the shade. Hither come the steers over the meadows to drink, here the Mincius borders his green banks with young reeds, and from the sacred oak resound the humming bees.' What was I to do? I didn't have an Alcippe or a Phyllis at home who might pen the new weaned lambs in the fold, and the contest, Corydon with Thyrsis, was a mighty one. I put their sport before my work.)

Though Thyrsis and Corydon are said to be *Arcades* (perhaps like Arcadians), the scene is set by the banks of the Mincius, a tributary of the River Po that flowed through Mantua, the place of Virgil's birth and youth. As Meliboeus is sheltering his myrtles from night-frost, and has newly weaned lambs at home, the time of year is likely to be late spring or early summer. The myrtle, sacred to Venus, is an emblem of beauty, and as such has always been a favourite poetic image. But this Mediterranean shrub was also useful; oil could be extracted from its berries and its wood, when mature, provided spears for soldiers and fencing for the farmer. Much of the charm of Virgilian pastoral stems from this happy interplay between the realistic and the symbolic in carefully selected detail. Daphnis, sitting beneath the rustling leaves of a holm-oak, invites Meliboeus to join him in the shade on the river

4. A useful modern edition is Coleman, R. (ed.) (1977) *Vergil: Eclogues*, Cambridge Greek and Latin Classics, Cambridge University Press.

bank. The imagery of the youthful steers coming over the meadows to drink, the green river banks fringed with tender reeds (themselves green and pliable in the spring breeze) and the hum of the bees swarming in the sacred oak (redolent of the golden age) makes this an idyllic scene, a *locus amoenus* in sight and sound. Furthermore, the allusions to the goats distended with milk and to the swarm of bees delicately suggest that this is a land flowing with milk and honey, Arcadia indeed. The mood is set in the third line: *ambo florentes aetatibus, Arcades ambo*; a youthful bloom sits equally on man and nature. The Arcadian mood is all the more enticing because of the delicate hints of contrast, in the winter now past, in present cares (Daphnis reassures Meliboeus about his erring he-goat) and in future work that awaits the farmer at home (he must pen his lambs). Despite the pressures of work, Meliboeus finds the invitation of Daphnis irresistible: *posthabui tamen illorum mea seria ludo* 'I put their sport before my work', or, as Dryden interprets the line: 'And I preferred my pleasure to my gain'. In the pastoral interlude, we see *homo ludens* at leisure and temporarily withdrawn from the world of his serious everyday concern.

The contest itself, which takes up the rest of the poem, consists of six parts in which Corydon first sings four lines on a topic, to which Thyrsis replies with an answering song of equal length with which he hopes to outdo his rival. The competition is all; the *amoebean* form is an ideal medium for the exhibition of poetic talent. The first song invokes the inspiring powers, and the second promises gifts to the gods. The third expresses the lover's yearning for his beloved:

> Nerine Galatea, thymo mihi dulcior Hyblae,
> candidior cycnis, hedera formosior alba,
> cum primum pasti repetent praesaepia tauri,
> si qua tui Corydonis habet te cura, venito.
>
> (37–40)

> (Galatea, child of Nereus, sweeter to me than the thyme of Hybla, whiter than the swans, more beautiful than pale ivy, when first the bulls return from pasture to the stalls, if you have any care for your Corydon, come!)

> Immo ego Sardoniis videar tibi amarior herbis,
> horridior rusco, proiecta vilior alga,

si mihi non haec lux toto iam longior anno est.
ite domum pasti, si quis pudor, ite iuvenci.

(41–44)

(May I seem truly more bitter to you than Sardinian herbs, rougher than gorse, and more worthless than strewn seaweed, if this day is not longer for me than a whole year. Go home my well-fed steers, if you have any shame, go home!)

The responses of Thyrsis variously echo the syntax and rhetorical arrangement of Corydon's songs. Here the correspondence of comparatives (*amarior*, *horridior* and *vilior* with *dulcior*, *candidior* and *formosior*) to express a contrast of characters and tone in which Corydon is the sweeter and Thyrsis the more sharp is neat and artful. Corydon then sings of the comforts of summer; Thyrsis replies with a song evoking the pleasures of winter.

muscosi fontes et somno mollior herba,
et quae vos rara viridis teget arbutus umbra,
solstitium pecori defendite; iam venit aestas
torrida, iam laeto turgent in palmite gemmae.

(45–8)

(Ye mossy springs, and grass softer than sleep, and the green arbute which shelters you with its chequered shade, keep the mid-summer's heat from the flock: now comes torrid summer, now the buds swell on the gladsome vine.)

hic focus et taedae pingues, hic plurimus ignis
semper et adsidua postes fuligine nigri:
his tantum Boreae curamus frigora, quantum
aut numerum lupus aut torrentia flumina ripas.

(49–52)

(Here is a hearth and pitchy pine-torches, here is a good fire burning and door-posts black with much soot, here we care for the cold winter winds only as much as the wolf heeds the size of the flock or the rushing torrents the river-bank.)

Coming first, of course, Corydon has the easier task. In his song nature provides her own solace, and the imagery is soothing and idyllic. In Thyrsis's reply refuge is sought from nature and the imagery is darker and more violent. There follow more equally matched songs celebrating the beloved by means of one of the main figures of the pastoral, the sympathy figure (akin to the pathetic fallacy). Nature smiling till the beloved departs is neatly contrasted with nature barren till the lover returns. Finally the beloved is variously compared to the beauty of trees.

At the end Corydon is declared victor. Given the character of Thyrsis's songs, it is hardly surprising; there is more of the pure pastoral about Corydon, a hint of something darker in Thyrsis. Yet if the pastoral were to be all the expression of Corydon, it would be monotonous, cloying and bland; even the beauty of the purest pastoral must be offset by some admixture of the impure. And what is it that makes the beauty of the poem? It is surely the artful contrast of the competing characters who are not crudely juxtaposed, for the songs of Thyrsis also have beauty, ingenuity and force. And what motivates the poet? Principally it is the dedication to art for art's sake; the poetry is its own end and serves no overt social or political purpose; in fact it represents an Alexandrian disengagement from the concerns of the community. Virgil, like his two singers in the pastoral, seeks to excel in the poetic art and his rivalry is with the singers of the Greek tradition, here represented by Theocritus. There is no overt extant literary source for this poem, but we may believe that Virgil began his poetic career by exercising and testing his poetic talent in competition with the Greek, translating the themes, conventions and techniques of the pastoral into Latin.

Elements of contrast inherent in even the purest pastoral are consciously exploited to give variety of effect in different ways. In 'Alexis' (Eclogue II) the harmony of the pastoral idyll is wholly disrupted by *eros*.

> Formosum pastor Corydon ardebat Alexim,
> delicias domini; nec quid speraret habebat.

(The shepherd Corydon desired the beautiful Alexis, the darling of his master; he did not have what he hoped for.)

The love-longing that features as a pretty motif in the songs of Thyrsis and Corydon in the previous poem is here the cause of a fevered frustration that sets Corydon apart from the rest of nature, resulting in a reversal of the sympathy figure:

Now the green lizard in the grove is laid,
The sheep enjoy the coolness of the shade,
And Thestylis wild thyme and garlic beats
For harvest hinds, o'erspent with toil and heats,
While in the scorching sun I trace in vain
Thy flying footsteps o'er the burning plain.
                              (Dryden, 7–12)

After singing of his own attractiveness on the grounds of his
wealth, his skill in singing and his personal appearance, Corydon
expresses his ardent wish:

o tantum libeat mecum tibi sordida rura
atque humiles habitare casas . . .
                              (29–30)

(If only you were willing to live with me in what to you are the sordid
fields and humble cottages.)

It is clear that Alexis does not share the values of the *pastor*; he is a
young man about town, so that Dryden can translate this passage:

O leave the noisy town! O come and see
Our country cots, and live content with me!
To wound the flying deer, and from their cotes
With one to drive afield the browsing goats;
To pipe and sing, and, in our country strain,
To copy or perhaps contend with Pan.
Pan taught to join with wax unequal reeds;
Pan loves the shepherds, and their flocks he feeds.
                              (Dryden, 35–42)

Alexis is not likely to be attracted to this praise of the rural life,
but Corydon continues promising gifts in an elaborate catalogue
of flowers and fruit, offering 'the sweets' of pastoral:

Come to my longing arms, my lovely care,
And take the presents which the nymphs prepare.
White lilies in full canisters they bring,
With all the glories of the purple spring.
The daughters of the flood have searched the mead
For violets pale, and cropp̀ed the poppy's head,
The short narcissus and fair daffodil,
Pansies to please the sight, and cassia sweet to smell;
And set soft hyacinths with iron blue,

To shade marsh marigolds of shining hue;
Some bound in order, others loosely strowed,
To dress thy bower, and trim thy new abode.
Myself will search on planted grounds at home
For downy peaches and the glossy plum;
And thrash the chestnuts in the neighbouring grove,
Such as my Amaryllis used to love.
The laurel and the myrtle sweets agree,
And both in nosegays shall be bound for thee.

(Dryden, 59–76)

Then comes a remarkable shift as in a moment of self-awareness he suddenly recognises the futility of it all: *rusticus es Corydon, nec munera curat Alexis* (56) 'You are a country fool, Corydon; Alexis does not care for your gifts'. In calling himself *rustic*, Corydon reveals that he too can see himself in the light of the sophisticated perspective of the townsman. In this gentle stroke of wit, Virgil, *poeta urbanus*, plays with the pastoral convention for comic and pathetic effect as Theocritus had done before him in Idyll XI, on which it is loosely based, where Homer's savage giant, the Cyclops Polyphemus, is transmogrified into a grotesquely lovelorn swain, lamenting the cruelty of his rejection by the beautiful sea-nymph Galatea. Incongruity lies at the heart of both these poems. Corydon recognises the harm he has done to himself: in pastoral language,

The boar amid my crystal streams I bring
And southern winds to blast my flow'ry spring.

(Dryden, 83–4)

Nevertheless, he shifts again, asking Alexis why he shuns him: all creatures long for something, *trahit sua quemque voluptas* (65) 'each man's pleasure draws him on'. The gently lengthening shadows of evening traditionally close the pastoral day; here the imagery serves as a contrast to the inner fire still burning in Corydon whose passion has caused him to neglect his proper pastoral concerns:

a Corydon Corydon, quae te dementia capit?

(69)

(Ah Corydon, Corydon, what madness has seized you?)

The shadows lengthen as the sun goes low.
Cool breezes now the raging heats remove:
Ah, cruel Heaven, that made no cure for love!
I wish for balmy sleep, but wish in vain;
Love has no bounds in pleasure or in pain.
What frenzy, shepherd, has thy soul possessed?
Thy vineyard lies half pruned, and half undressed.

(Dryden, 98–104)

Despite Corydon's brief determination at the end to set about useful tasks and to find another Alexis, the pastoral harmony is not restored. We are presented with the shifts and delusions of unrequited love.

Such are the limits of pure pastoral, since humankind craves variety and cannot bear much perfection, that pastoral is often on the verge of becoming something else; here this poem has much in common with a love elegy. Why not, then, write a love elegy in the first place? Or to put the question in another way, what is the advantage of giving the theme of unrequited love a pastoral setting with all the trappings of the pastoral convention? The pastoral affords us an easily and instantly apprehended image of perfection and beauty and a seductive dream of happiness to which all but the most hard-bitten are susceptible. The marring or loss of this through some discordant element has a particular poignancy. Just as we appreciate Milton's paradise not so much as an image of perfection but as an image of vulnerable perfection which is constantly juxtaposed with the imperfection of the fallen world to come which we know too well, so Virgil's pastoral paradise is not quite Eden. In the words of his shepherd Damoetas, *latet anguis in herba* (III, 93) 'a snake lurks in the grass'.

We are now in a position to adduce the earliest testimony we have as to the singular merit of Virgil's pastorals in the words of his contemporary Horace:

molle atque facetum
Vergilio adnuerunt gaudentes rure Camenae
(*Satire* I, x, 44–5)

(To Virgil the Muses rejoicing in country life have granted sweetness and charm.)

The precise meaning of the phrase *molle atque facetum* has been much debated. *Mollis*, 'soft, gentle or sweet', is the antithesis of

the severe old Roman austerity and may suggest a quality
apparent in the Arcadian element well conveyed by Dryden's
version; *facetus* (the root of 'facetious') 'witty, elegant or
charming' also suggests a sophisticated and civilised virtue
perhaps evident in the artfully dextrous handling of the pastoral
convention, as in the play on *rusticus* here.

To the sophisticated literary artist of Augustan Rome, rusticity
is in fact a negative value associated with the primitive and
agrarian past before Rome had been civilised by her own conquest
of the Greeks.

> Graecia capta ferum victorem cepit et artes
> intulit agresti Latio. . . .
>> sed in longum tamen aevum
> manserunt hodieque manent vestigia ruris.
>> (Horace, *Epistle* II, i, 'To Augustus',
>> 156–7, 159–60)

> (Captive Greece took her savage victor captive and brought the arts
> into rustic Latium. . . . but there remained for many a long year and
> still remain today traces of rusticity.)

The earliest Roman literature worthy of the name had come with
the translation of Greek tragedy and epic into Latin by the likes of
Ennius (who was half Greek himself) after the Punic wars which
brought Rome into contact with centres of Greek civilisation in
southern Italy and Sicily. But Ovid called Ennius *arte rudis* (*Tristia*
II, 424) 'artistically crude'. The Augustan poets sought a new
standard of artistic refinement and polish as they emulated their
Greek masters. In the generation before Virgil, the neoterics or
'new poets', of whom Catullus is our only surviving example,
brought a new refinement to the small-scale genres that had been
popular with the Alexandrians. Virgil, in the pastoral (a genre not
attempted by Catullus), is continuing this endeavour and breaking
new ground in the refinement of the dactylic hexameter (a
difficult metre for the Romans as Latin is naturally trochaic). The
sweetness that Horace praises in Virgil is to a great extent
metrical. Catullus achieved a new smoothness in the individual
single hexameter line,[5] but Virgil's refinement wrought the
further improvement of supple metrical variety within the line

---

5. See particularly LXII.

and smooth connection between lines in drawing out the sense, the beginnings in fact of the periodic style that he developed more fully in later work. Never before in Roman literature had there been such sweetness long drawn out.

It is something of a paradox that the only Virgilian pastoral actually to be set in Arcadia ('Meliboeus' is set near Mantua, 'Alexis' in Sicily) features the plight not of a shepherd but of a named contemporary of Virgil, the poet Gallus. In the tenth pastoral he is represented *in propria persona* as grief-stricken for the loss of Lycoris, identified as his mistress Cytheris:

> Extremum hunc, Arethusa, mihi concede laborem.
> pauca meo Gallo, sed quae legat ipsa Lycoris,
> carmina sunt dicenda: neget quis carmina Gallo?
>
> (1–3)

(Allow me this last task, Arethusa. A few verses must be sung for my Gallus, but such as Lycoris herself may read. Who can deny songs for Gallus?)

Arethusa is invoked as the river nymph of the fountain in the island of Otygia near Syracuse who inspired the pastoral poetry of Sicily. Virgil places Gallus in an Arcadian setting where, echoing Theocritus in Idyll I, he asks a famous question:

> quae nemora aut qui vos saltus habuere, puellae
> Naides, indigno cum Gallus amore peribat?
> nam neque Parnasi vobis iuga, nam neque Pindi
> ulla moram fecere, neque Aonie Aganippe.
>
> (9–12)

(What groves or glades held you, nymphs, when Gallus was dying for unrequited love? For neither the tops of Parnassus nor those of Pindus delayed you, nor did the Aonian fountain Aganippe.)

Mount Parnassus, whence rises the Castalian spring, Mount Pindus and the fountain of Aganippe on Mount Helicon are all sacred to the Muses who are here reproached for neglecting one of their devotees in contrast to the surrounding trees and hills:

> illum etiam lauri, etiam flevere myricae
> pinifer illum etiam sola sub rupe iacentem
> Maenalus et gelidi fleverunt saxa Lycaei.
>
> (13–15)

(For him even the laurels, even the tamarisks wept, even pine-clad
Maenalus and the crags of snowy Lycaeus wept for him as he lay on a
lonely crag.)

The real Arcadia is a rugged mountainous region in the Greek
Peloponnese (sufficiently remote to Virgil's readers). Given its
idyllic association, it is ironic that its snowy mountains and crags
are used in this poem to underscore the suffering and isolation of
Gallus. As Gallus is a stranger to Arcadia (this *poeta urbanus* is an
elegiac rather than a pastoral poet), he is urged not to look down
upon the gathering flock. Virgil then follows Theocritus in Idyll I
in having a visitation of gods. First comes Apollo who tells Gallus
that Lycoris has followed another amidst snows and horrid
military camps (to Gaul, the scholiast explains). Then comes
Silvanus and finally Pan with the rebuke that cruel love cares
naught for tears. Gallus then addresses the Arcadians:

> How light would lie the turf upon my breast,
> If you my sufferings in your songs expressed!
> (Dryden, 51–2)

He wishes he had been an Arcadian himself:

> Ah! that your birth and business had been mine;
> To pen the sheep, and press the swelling vine!
> Had Phyllis or Amyntas caused my pain,
> Or any nymph, or shepherd on the plain
> (Though Phyllis brown, though black Amyntas were,
> Are violets not sweet, because not fair?)
> Beneath the sallows, and the shady vine,
> My loves had mixed their pliant limbs with mine:
> Phyllis with myrtle wreaths had crowned my hair,
> And soft Amyntas sung away my care.
> (53–62)

He imagines himself with Lycoris in this Arcadian dream:

> hic gelidi fontes, hic mollia prata, Lycori,
> hic nemus, hic ipso tecum consumerer aevo.
> (42–3)

(Here are cold springs, here soft meadows, Lycoris, here woodland,
here with thee I would be consumed by time.)

But the thought of Lycoris brings him back from wishful dreaming to a contrasting reality:

> Now I to fighting fields am sent afar,
> And strive in winter camps with toils of war;
> While you, (alas that I should find it so!)
> To shun my sight, your native soil forgo,
> And climb the frozen Alps and tread th' eternal snow.
> Ye frosts and snows, her tender body spare!
> Those are not limbs for icicles to tear.
>
> (Dryden, 67–73)

From this intention to follow her, he shifts ground vowing to sing to the accompaniment of the shepherd's pipe, and he envisages for himself a pastoral life of hunting with the nymphs on the snows of Mount Maenalus (not quite the pure pastoral life of the Arcadian shepherd). But even this poetic and pastoral consolation is only momentary:

> As if with sports my suffering I could ease,
> Or by my pains the god of love appease.
> My frenzy changes; I delight no more
> On mountain tops to chase the tusky boar:
> No game but hopeless love my thoughts pursue –
> Once more, ye nymphs, and songs, and sounding woods, adieu!
> Love alters not for us his hard decrees . . .
> In hell, and earth, and seas, and heaven above,
> Love conquers all; and we must yield to love.
>
> (86–92, 98–9)

> omnia vincit amor, et nos cedamus amori
>
> (69)

After these final words of Gallus, Virgil brings the eclogue to a close with the coming of evening.

The plight of Gallus is reminiscent of that of Corydon with this difference, that where in 'Alexis' we feel the poignancy of paradise lost, here Gallus is no true Arcadian but an outsider and an alien in a pastoral paradise which he can only really imagine for himself and cannot gain, and there are even hints of discordant elements in Arcadia itself which has rugged mountains and snowy peaks as well as soft meadows, cool fountains and groves. The haunting phrase *Et in Arcadia ego* 'Even in Arcadia, there am I', purportedly

the words of Death,[6] is not actually Virgilian (indeed the phrase
is hardly metrical), but the idea could well have been prompted by
the undercurrent of melancholy in Virgil's pastoral vision that
surfaces here in this most elegiac of pastorals.

The pronounced elegiac strain contrasting with the pastoral
dream is strongly felt in the opening pastoral 'Tityrus':

> Tityre, tu patulae recubans sub tegmire fagi
> silvestrem tenui Musam meditaris avena;
> nos patriae fines et dulcia linquimus arva:
> nos patriam fugimus; tu, Tityre, lentus in umbra
> formosam resonare doces Amaryllida silvas.
>
> (1–5)

(You, Tityrus, resting beneath the cover of a spreading beech, practise
your woodland song on your slender pipe, we leave the bounds of our
country and its pleasant fields, we fly our country; you, Tityrus at ease
in the shade, teach the woods to re-echo 'fair Amaryllis'.)

So many details of these famous lines have themselves been
constantly re-echoed in subsequent literature; through Virgil
modern Europe has inherited not only a range of words and
images resonant with poetic associations but also an idyllic picture
of the poet in an Arcadian setting as the shepherd reclining
beneath the cover of a spreading beech, meditating on the sylvan
muse or practising his woodland music on his slender reed (the
oaten Pan-pipe being appropriate to the shepherd-singer as is the
golden lyre to Apollo), at leisure in the shade and free from care,
making the woods re-echo to the beautiful sound of his love-song
featuring Amaryllis (the name means 'sparkling'). Amaryllis may
be thought of as the poet's theme and inspiration, but the tribute
is to the beauty of his song caught in the liquid beauty of the
loved one's name sweetly resonating in this most melodious line
with its delicate assonance, its subtle alliteration and its smooth
and dignified rhythm gently rising to a wave-like climax in
Amarýllida that is restfully resolved in the softly sounding *silvas*
(especially if the v is pronounced w). 'You teach the woods to re-
echo fair Amaryllis' may simply be regarded as an elegant way of

6. Explained in Panovsky, E., 'Et in Arcadia Ego: Poussin and the Elegiac
   Tradition' in Klibansky, R., Paton, H.J. (eds) (1936) Philosophy and History,
   Oxford University Press.

suggesting the beauty of the poet's music echoing in the woods, but the language perhaps also suggests not only that the poet dwells in beauty and is the servant of beauty but also that, like Orpheus, he is a teacher who has a quasi-magical power to create beauty through art that can charm nature itself. But how artful of Virgil to make us see this charming idyll through the eyes of one who is about to be excluded from it, for the speaker Meliboeus is leaving the sweet fields of home for foreign parts. Once again it is the contrasting discordant element, the elegiac note, that gives the pastoral its charge.

The whole poem juxtaposes the happiness of Tityrus with the sadness of Meliboeus (who has the slightly longer part, 46 lines to 37). Tityrus, it emerges from the poem, is an elderly slave who has just recently been to Rome for the first time where he has been granted his freedom. He can live at home in peace. For him the city, *urbs Romana*, the ultimate source of his happiness, also proves to be a source of wonder:

> verum haec tantum alias inter caput extulit urbes,
> quantum lenta solent inter viberna cupressi.
>
> (24–5)

(Indeed, the city has raised her head amongst others as high as cypresses are wont to do among the pliant shrubs.)

Praise of Rome, the preoccupation of so much early Latin literature, here foreshadows Virgil's own later preoccupations, but for the time being Tityrus returns to the Mantuan pastoral life. Meliboeus, by contrast, is losing his farm to make way for another. By a fine stroke of art it is Meliboeus who transforms the stony weed-choked Mantuan reality into a pastoral idyll:

> fortunate senex, ergo tua rura manebunt,
> et tibi magna satis, quamvis lapis omnia nudus
> limosoque palus obducat pascua iunco.
>
> (46–8)

(Happy old man, so this countryside will remain yours and it is sufficient for you, even though bare stones and marsh with slimy rushes cover all your pasture.)

Your teeming ewes shall no strange meadow try,
Nor fear a rot from tainted company.
Behold! yon bordering fence of sallow trees
Is fraught with flowers, the flowers are fraught with bees:
The busy bees, with a soft murm'ring strain,
Invite to gentle sleep the lab'ring swain;
While, from the neighb'ring rock, with rural songs,
The pruner's voice the pleasing dream prolongs;
Stockdoves and turtles tell their am'rous pain,
And, from the lofty elms, of love complain

                                        (Dryden, 69–78)

Servius, the Roman grammarian of the fourth century whose commentary on Virgil survived antiquity and accompanied the text in Renaissance editions,[7] confirms what we might guess, that the context of the eclogue was the upheaval in Italy caused by the civil war that followed the assassination of Julius Caesar in 44 BC. The ancient lives of Virgil record the tradition that the family farm in Mantua was among those confiscated to allow for the resettlement of veterans from Philippi where the triumvirs Mark Antony, Lepidus and Octavian had defeated the Republicans Brutus and Cassius in 42 BC. Virgil, through his patrons, made a successful appeal to Octavian Caesar (Julius's great-nephew and heir) who, after he had defeated Antony and Cleopatra in the second civil war, later took the name Augustus in 27 BC.

o Meliboee, deus nobis haec otia fecit.
namque erit ille mihi semper deus; illius aram
saepe tener nostris ab ovilibus imbuet agnus.
ille meas errare boves, ut cernis, et ipsum
ludere quae vellem calamo permisit agresti.

                                        (6–10)

(O, Meliboeus, a god made this peace for us. For he will always be a god to me; often a young lamb from our flocks will stain his altar. He gave permission for my herds to roam, as you see, and that I should play what I wish on my country pipe.)

This has always been read as an expression of gratitude on Virgil's part to Octavian for the return of his farm. It is also a recognition

---

7. Thilo, G. (ed.) (1887) *Servii grammatici qui feruntur in Vergilii Bucolica et Georgica*, Teubner, Leipzig.

that the poet's freedom and security (*otia*) and hence his capacity to exercise his poetic talent are dependent upon stability and peace in the political order; more specifically, the lines (probably written about 40 BC), together with the praise of the godlike youth at 40–5, signal Virgil's political allegiance and his acceptance of the patronage of Caesar's heir. In this sense, the poem might be called an Augustan poem ahead of its time, foreshadowing later preoccupations in other genres. In the act of translating it to Rome Virgil has transformed this Alexandrian genre, and greatly extended its possibilities.

The happiness and gratitude of Tityrus, however, are more than balanced by the misery of Meliboeus whose complaints reflect the plight of the dispossessed and may be construed as being critical of the new regime for, unlike Tityrus, Meliboeus is clearly representative of great numbers who are envisaged as having to travel to live among the far-flung peoples of the earth including Africans and Scythians, *et penitus toto divisos orbe Britannos* (66) 'and the Britons wholly sundered from all the world', a savage fate indeed.

> But we must beg our bread in climes unknown,
> Beneath the scorching or the freezing zone; . . .
> O! must the wretched exiles ever mourn,
> Nor after length of rolling years return?
> Are we condemned by fate's unjust decree
> No more our houses and our homes to see?
> Or shall we mount again the rural throne,
> And rule the country kingdoms, once our own?
> Did we for these barbarians plant and sow?
> On these, on these, our happy field bestow?
> Good Heaven! what dire effects from civil discord flow!
> Now let me graff my pears, and prune the vine;
> The fruit is theirs, the labour only mine.
> Farewell, my pastures, my paternal stock,
> My fruitful fields, and my more fruitful flock!
> No more, my goats, shall I behold you climb
> The steepy cliffs, or crop the flow'ry thyme! . . .
> No more my sheep shall sip the morning dew;
> No more my song shall please the rural crew
> Adieu, my tuneful pipe! and all the world, adieu!
>   (Dryden, 85–6, 91–105, 110–12)

Meliboeus envisages his country kingdom *mea regna* (69) being invaded by some godless soldier *impius miles* (70) or barbarian *barbarus* (71). Tityrus courteously invites him to spend a last pastoral evening with him, and so the poem closes. Once again were are as conscious, if not more so, of paradise lost as of paradise regained.

> Sicelides Musae, paulo maiora canamus!
> non omnes arbusta iuvant humilesque myricae;
> si canimus silvas, silvae sint consule dignae.
>
> (IV, 1–3)

> (Sicilian Muses, let us sing something a little greater. Ordinary trees and the humble tamarisks do not please everyone. If we sing of trees, let the trees be worthy of a consul.)

The *paulo maiora* of this most famous eclogue, dedicated to Pollio who was consul in 40 BC, refers to both content and style and is reflected in the handling of the imagery of its opening. The trees have little of the pictorial reality usual in Virgil (who was a great lover of trees, which feature much more in his pastorals than in those of Theocritus) but are here almost wholly figurative: *arbusta*, a generic plural, suggests the familiar and the commonplace, *myricae* signifies the humbler eclogues and *silvae* grander poems in a loftier strain, as here, where Virgil takes upon himself for the first time the prophetic mantle of the *vates* who sings of what is past, passing or to come. For in this poem he prophesies the birth of a child who will restore the golden age, a mythical time of peace and innocence ruled by Saturn, father of Jupiter. With Saturn's reign Virgil associates Astraea, the virgin goddess of justice who was said to have left earth for heaven when mankind became wicked. The Sibylline books, supposed to be the utterances (*fata*, whence fate) of the famous Sibyl of Cumae (the Cumaean Sibyl later escorts Aeneas through Hades where he is given prophecies of the Roman future in the *Aeneid*), told of a new circuit of the ages after the age of iron had passed:

> ultima Cumaei venit iam carminis aetas;
> magnus ab integro saeclorum nascitur ordo.
> iam redit et Virgo, redeunt Saturnia regna;
> iam nova progenies caelo demittitur alto.
> tu modo nascenti puero, quo ferrea primum

desinet ac toto surget gens aurea mundo,
casta fave Lucina.

(4–10)

(The last age of the Cumaean prophetic song has now come. The mighty order of the ages is born anew. Now too the Virgin goddess returns and the reign of Saturn returns. Now a new race is sent down from heaven on high. You, chaste Lucina [the goddess of childbirth], favour the child at birth, under whom the iron generation first shall cease and the golden spring up all over the world.)

The child is to be born in Pollio's consulship and shall rule a world to which his father's virtues have brought peace: *pacatumque reget patriis virtutibus orbem* (17). As he grows up the world, both natural and human, will gradually become a better place: *occidet et serpens* (24) 'the serpent will perish', *pauca tamen suberunt priscae vestigia fraudis* (31) 'but traces of our old wickedness will remain'. There will still be seafaring (frequently a negative symbol of acquisitiveness in Roman literature), there will be other Argonauts led by another helmsman like Tiphys in quest of some Golden Fleece. There will be other wars and men will still practise agriculture. But when the child has reached manhood, trade and agriculture too will cease as nature will produce everything spontaneously everywhere in abundance. Virgil does not directly call the new golden race *pastores*; he does not need to be too specific about golden age occupations. It is sufficient that the evils of civilisation (commerce, war and agriculture) are gradually to be undone. For the 'Pollio', like all Virgil's eclogues, works through the juxtaposition of contrasting images. The Arcadian dream of the golden age is contrasted with the reality of the *prisca fraus*, the old wickedness that is manifest in human aggression and greed. His vision of the coming of the golden age, with all its constituent images and its contrasts with the reality which it is to replace, has been so potent a source of inspiration for poetic imitation that it may here be generously represented in the fine rendering of Dryden:

> But when heroic verse his youth shall raise,
> And form it to hereditary praise,
> Unlaboured harvests shall the fields adorn,
> And clustered grapes shall blush on every thorn;
> The knotted oaks shall showers of honey weep,

And through the matted grass the liquid gold shall creep.
Yet of old fraud some footsteps shall remain:
The merchant still shall plough the deep for gain;
Great cities shall with walls be compassed round,
And sharpened shares shall vex the fruitful ground;
Another Tiphys shall new seas explore;
Another Argo land the chiefs upon the Iberian shore;
Another Helen other wars create,
And great Achilles urge the Trojan fate.
But when to ripened manhood he shall grow,
The greedy sailor shall the seas forego;
No keel shall cut the waves for foreign ware,
For every soil shall every product bear.
The labouring hind his oxen shall disjoin;
No plough shall hurt the glebe, no pruning hook the vine . . .

(31–50)

The remainder of the poem is a joyful and dignified invocation of the child.

The identity of the child has always been and remains a puzzle. In the twilight of the Western empire, the fathers of the Early Church linked the poem to the prophecies of the Old Testament,[8] and it has often since been called the Messianic eclogue. They conjectured that Virgil had read Isaiah or that he had been led by the natural inspiration of the muse towards the truth divinely revealed in Scripture. The poem was seen in later ages as a *preparatio evangelii*, evidence of the Holy Spirit preparing the world for Christ, and of the longing of that world for renewal through the rule of a prince of peace. The timing of the eclogue put the greatest poet of Rome (and for most of the Renaissance, the greatest poet of antiquity) in a poignant and symbolic relation to the new Christian order. Even if the poem was thought to refer not to Christ but to another child who might rule in a temporal order of peace, it might be felt in a general way to be prophetic of the *pax Augusta*, the Roman peace first celebrated in the *Aeneid*, which endured for four centuries and which was a necessary cradle for the infant religion born as Roman civilisation and empire reached their maturity and the necessary conduit through

8.   See 'Vergil as prophet of Christ' in Comparetti, D. (1908) *Vergil in the Middle Ages*, trans. E.F.M. Benecke, Swan Sonneschein, London; Macmillan, New York, pp. 96–104.

which it spread throughout the world. 'And it came to pass in those days that there went out a decree from Caesar Augustus that all the world should be taxed' (Luke 2: 1) Even Caesar had his role in the grand design. The poem also signals Virgil's aspiration to greater things later to culminate in the *Aeneid* which in medieval allegory embodied in its secular form the journey of the soul through this vale of tears towards the goal of the heavenly city. The great virtue of Aeneas, *pietas*, unlike the Homeric *arete*, looks and sounds like a religious value. So through the eclogue links were made between the old pagan world and the new Christian dispensation that eventually replaced it. Even more than Socrates, because he was more familiar, Virgil became in the eyes of future time the great representative of the best in classical culture, the good pagan and prophet of Christ, informed in Tertullian's phrase by *anima naturaliter Christiana* 'an instinctively Christian soul', Dante's guide through the *Inferno*, even if he could not be admitted to Paradise.[9]

Neo-Latin pastoral: Petrarch and Mantuan

Given the symbolic and actual role played by Virgil as enlightening guide through the darkness and gloom of the post-classical world, the invocation of him by Petrarch, one of the great founding fathers of the Italian Renaissance, in his pastoral imitation the *Bucolicum Carmen*, is a moment worth pondering. In these twelve eclogues, which Petrarch called eglogues as he derived the word from *aigon*, the Greek word for goat (so that, as E.K. explains in his notes on Spenser,[10] *aeglogai* might be tales of goats or songs of goatherds), Petrarch restores to the world classical Latin purged of its medieval accretions and classical metre freed from the barbarity of rhyme. The opening poem, written in 1346–7, has the title 'Parthenias', 'the maiden', the ancient nickname given to Virgil according to Servius on account of the upright manner of his living. The poem is an encounter between two shepherds of differing points of view as Petrarch explains in a

9. See Chapter XIV, 'Dante', in Comparetti (1908) cited in the previous note.
10. In 'The general argument of the whole book' prefacing the first poem.

letter to his brother Gerhardo;[11] one, called Silvius, represents the
poet himself, the other, representing Gerhardo, who was a
Carthusian monk, has the name Monicus after the one-eyed
Cyclops, for of the two eyes given us for earthly and heavenly
things, Gerhardo sees only the heavenly. At the opening we are
introduced to the plight of Silvius:

> *Silvius.* Monice, tranquillo solus tibi conditus antro,
> et gregis et ruris potuisti spernere curas;
> ast ego dumosos colles silvasque pererro.
>
> $(1-3)^{12}$

(Monicus, hidden away alone in your quiet cave you have been able to
spurn the cares of the flocks and countryside. But I wander all over the
thicketed hills and woods.)

The quiet cave suggests the monastic vocation of Monicus in
withdrawal from the world, here represented in a startling
inversion of the pastoral norm as *curas ruris et gregis*, concerning
which Petrarch tells Gerhardo: 'Interpret the countryside and the
flocks as the city and mankind'.[13] Monicus has little sympathy
for his brother's restlessness which in his view is entirely self-
inflicted:

> *Monicas.* Silvi, quid quereris? cunctorum vera laborum
> ipse tibi causa es. quis te per devia cogit?
> quis vel inaccessum tanto sudore cacumen
> montis adire iubet, vel per deserta vagari
> muscososque situ scopulos fontesque sonantes?
>
> (6–10)

(Silvius, why are you complaining? You yourself are the cause of all
your troubles. Who is driving you over such lonely places? Who bids
you climb with such exertion to the mountain tops, over crags
moulding with moss and by sounding cataracts?)

Anyone expecting a revival of Arcadian pastoral might be
surprised by the imagery here, which is far from Arcadian.

11. Bernardo, A.S. (translator) (1982) *Francesco Petrarca: Letters on Familiar
     Matters, Rerum Familiarum Libri IX-XVI*, Johns Hopkins University Press,
     Baltimore and London, Book X, 4, pp. 69–76.
12. For text and translation see Bergin, T.G. (ed.) (1974) *Petrarch's Bucolicum
     Carmen*, Yale University Press, New Haven and London.
13. Bernardo, A.S. (1982) p. 73.

Indeed, Petrarch explains the images allegorically, saying that the wastelands represent modern studies, the crags the rich and powerful, and the cataracts men of intellect and learning.[14] Without the benefit of this thorough-going allegorical interpretation (a mode, in this extreme form, associated more with the medieval than the classical world) the imagery suggests the isolation, difficulty and drama attendant upon humanist aspirations, a far cry from the happy Tityrus singing at ease beneath the beechen bowers, *lentus in umbra*.

Silvius goes on to explain that he is driven by love. This turns out to be not the love that tormented Corydon and Gallus but love of the muse. In his youth, he explains, Parthenias had sung with him on the shores of Lake Garda; as he grew up:

> audebam, nullo duce iam per opacum
> ire nemus nec lustra feris habitata timebam.
> (16–17)

(I dared now with no guide to go through the dark forest, nor did I fear the woods as the haunt of wild beasts.)

The words here bring to mind Virgil's role as Dante's guide through the *selva oscura* of the *Inferno*[15] inhabited by the lion and the wolf. Petrarch is growing up and becoming independent:

> mutatamque novo frangebam carmine vocem
> emulus, et famae dulcedine tactus inani
> (18–19)

(In a newly broken voice I changed my song, in emulation and touched by the empty sweetness of the desire for fame.)

Then a shepherd from foreign parts ravishes his ear with his song and he compares his verses with those of Parthenias, recognising the latter's source. Fired by these two shepherd-singers (Virgil and Homer), he returns to the hill-tops (of aspiration). He is prepared to die in the service of the Muses. So far it is clear that 'Parthenias' represents Petrarch's self-dedication to poetry with its origins in his youthful love of Virgil and his admiration in particular for the heroic.

14. Bernardo, A.S. (1982) p. 74.
15. Dante, *Inferno*, Canto I: line 2 for the 'selva oscura'.

Monicus then invites Silvius to cross the stony threshold into
his cave. Silvius refuses, rejecting the silence.

> o! iterum breve si mecum traducere tempus
> contingat, sileatque fragor rerumque tumultus,
> dulcius hic quanto media sub nocte videbis
> psallere pastorem!
>
> (53–6)

(O, if only you could spend a brief time with me again, and let the
noise and tumult of the world fall silent, here in the depth of night you
will see a shepherd stringing the cithara much more sweetly.)

Silvius eventually recognises that Monicus is alluding to the
Psalmist:

> o! ego novi hominem cives, et moenia parvae
> saepe Jerosolimae memorat, nec vertitur inde;
> semper habet laerimas et pectore raucus anhelat.
> hi Romam Troiamque canunt et proelia regum
> quid dolor et quid amor possit, quidve impetus irae . . .
>
> (72–6)

(O, I recognise the fellow. He often sings of the people and city of
little Jerusalem, and is never diverted from this theme. He is always
weeping and wailing, and panting for breath hoarsely. These [Virgil
and Homer] sing of Rome and Troy and the battles of kings, telling
what grief and love can do and what the impulsions of anger . . .)

Monicus is not cowed but offers a lengthy panegyric of the
psalmist, stressing his subject matter and rebuking Silvius for
calling him *raucus*:

> vox solida est penetransque animos dulcore latenti.
>
> (104)

(His voice is true and penetrates the soul with a hidden sweetness.)

Silvius says that he will try him if fate permits but announces that
he must go, for love of the muse is pressing, *urget amor musae*
(112); he is working on a poem that will sing the praises of Scipio
(his later epic the *Africa*). Monicus has the last word:

> I sospes, variosque viae circumspice casus.
>
> (124)

(Go safely, and watch for the various hazards of the journey.)

The claims of religion and culture as embodied in the figures of
Monicus and Silvius in this dialogue are not reconciled; both
parties go their own way. The obvious synthesis whereby Silvius
announces an intention to give classical form to Christian
substance is clearly avoided. While it may be felt that the
enclosing of brother Gerhardo (and perhaps Petrarch's own
Augustinian conscience) in a Virgilian pastoral is itself a
subordination of all that Monicus stands for, the ignorance of
Silvius and his deliberate belittling of Jerusalem tell against him
and make him a slightly comic figure. Monicus, though one-eyed,
is allowed his viewpoint. The poem seems to be a playfully
balanced treatment of what was a deeply troubling question for
the Middle Ages and the Renaissance, implicit in Augustine's
repentance of his early love of Virgil which in the *Confessions*[16] he
calls vain, and posed directly by Jerome: 'what has Horace to do
with the Psalter, Virgil with the Gospels and Cicero with Paul?'[17]
In this famous letter, Jerome goes on to relate a nightmarish
experience that induces rejection of the pagan classics on the
grounds that they endanger salvation. On a journey from Rome
to Jerusalem he is taken ill and imagines himself before the seat of
judgement where he is rebuked for being a Ciceronian rather than
a Christian: 'for where your treasure is, there will your heart be
also' (Matthew 6: 21). In the 'Parthenias' we may not feel that
Petrarch is greatly anxious that he will receive a similar rebuke for
being a Virgilian, or that the salvation of his soul is seriously an
issue; nevertheless Jerome's question hovers about the poem and
lingers on, reminding us that even after the classics resurfaced in
their triumphant renaissance of the fourteenth century, they
emerged into a predominantly alien world often hostile to their
very existence. Ten centuries of Christian persecution left their
mark, and attempts to bridge the divide and to reconcile pagan
and Christian in response to the demands of the contemporary
world sometimes produced extraordinary results.

Here there are a number of ironies for a reader contemplating
the Renaissance after-life of the pastoral. Following the hint of
Theocritus in Idyll VII and the more pronounced tendency of

16. St Augustine, *Confessions* I, XIII–XIV.
17. Jerome, Letter XXII, 29ff.

Virgil accentuated in the Servian commentary, the form has become wholly allegorical. Theocritus selects details of rural life that make an idyllic picture because anything sordid or laborious is excluded, but the picture is still real in the sense that it communicates a genuine feeling for the beauty of the natural world. This remains true of Virgil's Arcadian landscape though the figurative element is more strongly felt. In Petrarch, however, the language is entirely figurative to the extent that it communicates no real feeling for the rural world but functions, through allegory, as a kind of complex code. 'Parthenias' and the poems to which it is a prelude are not in the least idyllic or Arcadian, and in subject matter they go way beyond the bounds of the classical pastoral. Here it is ironic that the humble pastoral has become the vehicle through which Petrarch expresses his fervent aspiration to complete a grand epic poem. 'Parthenias' expresses homage to and suggests continuity with Virgil, but in breaking out into a new voice (18–19) Petrarch, in the best humanist spirit, whatever we may think of the result, signals a conscious desire to put the form to new uses, and indeed he is the first to make it a vehicle for ecclesiastical satire. Virgil's Meliboeus had denounced the evils of civil discord in eclogue I, but in the guise of Pamphilus in eclogue VI we find St Peter denouncing with satirical bitterness the failings of his successor as *pastor* of the church, Pope Clement VI.[18] Monicus and Silvius make strange bedfellows indeed.

The blending of classical form with edifying Christian content that Petrarch might have made the resolution of the dilemma posed in 'Parthenias' is what made a success of the Latin eclogues of Baptista Spagnoli, 'the second Virgil' who called himself Mantuan from the place of his birth. Petrarch's eclogues were first published in 1473 and reprinted many times with an extensive commentary in the sixteenth century, but those of Mantuan first printed in 1498 far surpassed his in popularity and became a favourite school text.[19] Even those with little Latin could recall the opening line of his first eclogue.

18.   Also in Bergin, T.G. (1974).
19.   See Mustard, W.P. (1911) *The Eclogues of Baptista Mantuanus*, Johns Hopkins Press, Baltimore, and Grant, L.W. (1965) *Neo-Latin Literature and the Pastoral*, University of North Carolina Press, Chapel Hill.

Fauste precor gelida quando pecus omne sub umbra
ruminat –

And so forth. Ah, good old Mantuan! I may speak of thee as the
traveller doth of Venice

Venetia, Venetia
Chi non ti vede, non ti pretia

Old Mantuan, old Mantuan! Who understandeth thee not, loves thee
not

(Love's Labour's Lost IV, ii, 89)

The last remark, which does not quite chime with the Italian
quotation in meaning (though it follows its structure) and is not
particularly intelligent, is perhaps a joke at Holofernes' expense,
so that it may be that Shakespeare did not share his pedantic
schoolmaster's enthusiasm for this staple of the grammar-school
curriculum. Certainly, though his own pastoral world tends to
feature real shepherds it is nevertheless presented as an idyllic
contrast to the cares of government in *Henry VI* Part III (II, v,
21–41) or to the falsity of court life in the Forest of Arden in *As
You Like It*, whereas Mantuan imports into his unidyllic pastorals
all the iniquities of the world. Moreover, Mantuan's shepherds
have a hard life and undergo suffering reflected in the descriptions
of storms and winter scenes – cold pastoral indeed. As for love,
semel insanivimus omnes (I, 118) 'we have all been mad once'.
Mantuan wrote the first eight of his ten eclogues while he was still
a student; the last two he added after he became a Carmelite
monk. Four of them are directly about aspects of the religious life;
they are all moralistic and didactic, and in most of them there is a
pronounced feeling of *contemptus mundi* reflected in the sharp satire
directed against illicit love (2 and 3), the waywardness of women
(3), rich men's neglect of poets (4), the corruption of town life (6)
and ecclesiastical abuses at Rome (9). In the seventh, the tale is
told of the visitation of the Virgin to an unhappy shepherd whom
she directs towards Mount Carmel:

There after thou hast led
A happy hurtless life
   devoid of vile offence:
Then into places ever green
   and flourishing from thence

I will advance thee straight,
  a better lodge to dwell:[20]

Arcadia is not of this world. The first English pastorals, *Five Eclogues* (1513–14) by Alexander Barclay, a monk at Ely, are all Mantuanesque in conception and spirit, while two are direct reworkings. Mantuan is also the model for Barnabe Googe's *Eglogs* (1563) and for Francis Sabie's *Pan's Pipe* (1595).

English pastoral: Spenser

There have been few pastorals as variously constituted as the twelve 'Aeglogues' that make up Spenser's *Shepheardes Calendar* (1579). He seems to have been familiar with Theocritus and it has been suggested that his use of Lancastrian words is an attempt to imitate the effect of the Doric dialect used by the originator of the genre. He had more direct knowledge of classical pastoral through Virgil, whose career, moving from pastoral to georgic and to epic, made possible by the patronage of Maecenas and Augustus, represents the ideal wistfully contrasted to the lamentable neglect of poets in England:

Indeede the Romish Tityrus, I heare,
Through his Maecenas left his oaten reede
Whereon he earst had taught his flocks to feede,
And laboured lands to yield the timely eare,
And eft did sing of warres and deadly drede,
So as the heavens did quake his verse to here.

But ah Maecenas is yclad in claye,
And great Augustus long ygoe is dead:
And all the worthies liggen wrapt in leade,
That matter made for poets on to play: . . .
                    ('October', 55–64)[21]

---

20. Bush, D. (ed.) (1977) *The Eclogues of Mantuan Translated by George Turbeville* (*1567*), Scholars' Facsimiles and Reprints, Delmar, New York, pp. 70–1.
21. The text here retains Spenser's spelling but dispenses with most capitals and italics. See Smith, J.C. and De Selincourt, E. (1912) *The Poetical Works of Edmund Spenser*, Oxford University Press.

But though he occasionally uses classical figures, his main inspiration seems to come from other sources:

> The god of shepheards Tityrus is dead,
> Who taught me homely, as I can, to make.
> He, whilst he lived, was the soveraigne head
> Of shepheards all, that bene with love ytake:
> Well couth he wayle hys woes, and lightly slake
> The flames, which love within his heart had bredd,
> And tell us mery tales, to keepe us wake,
> The while our sheepe about us safely fedde.
>
> ('June', 81–8)

Spenser's annotator E.K. identifies Tityrus, whom the shepherd-poet acknowledges as his master, not with Virgil (who told no merry tales) but with Chaucer.[22] Colin Clout, representing the poet, is a name taken from the satirist Skelton and the character Piers may recall Langland, by way of *Piers Plowman*, another medieval source. Thenot and Perigot are rustic French names taken over from Marot, one of whose allegorical eclogues (written in the vernacular) introduces the idea of the changing seasons. E.K. distinguishes three kinds amongst the 'Aeglogues', the plaintive, the recreative and the moral 'which for the most part be mixed with some satirical bitterness', including 'July' and 'September', 'on the subject of dissolute shepherds and pastors';[23] this suggests the influence of Mantuan. There are ordinary English names too such as Willie and Cuddie, marking the element of rustic realism in his pastoral, and figures like Palinode perhaps representing the Catholic priesthood and Hobbinol alluding to Spenser's friend Gabriel Harvey, indicative of an allegorical tendency. The historical connection is directly made in the inclusion of the queen under her own name, Elisa, with whom Spenser associates all the sweets of pastoral in a beautiful 'recreative' lyric in 'Aprill' (37ff.).

The variety of names and sources indicates a wide thematic and generic range embracing ecclesiastical satires and religious debate, discussion of poetry, interludes, complaints of love, an elegy and panegyric of the monarch. Add to this the varied use of different metrical forms and the attempt to broaden the contemporary

22. E.K.'s comments are usually printed after each poem.
23. In 'The general argument of the whole book' preceding the first poem.

linguistic range of English poetry with the incorporation of archaic and dialect forms (which earned Spenser the celebrated rebuke from Ben Jonson that he 'writ in no language'[24]) and we can perhaps begin to see why the Elizabethans were excited by the novelty of the poetry. Indeed, most of E.K.'s introduction addressed to Gabriel Harvey is a vigorous championing of the language of the 'new poet'.[25] Virgil's eclogues and Spenser's *Shepheardes Calender* have this at least in common, that to future literary historians each work heralded a new golden age of poetry, Roman Augustan and English Elizabethan respectively.

Colin is a sad shepherd who has lost the love of his faithless Rosalind and is destined, unlike Tityrus happily teaching the woods to re-echo 'fair Amaryllis', to

> learne these woods, to wayle my woe,
> And teache the trees, their trickling teares to shedde.
>
> ('June', 95–6)

The seasonal range enables Spenser to use the sympathy figure of classical pastoral in his opening poem to express sterility, alienation and unhappy withdrawal unmitigated by any hint of a contrasting idyllic vision elsewhere:

> Thou barrein ground, whome winters wrath hath wasted,
> Art made a myrrhour, to behold my plight:
>
> ('Januarye', 19–20)

Poor Colin, the speaker here, even breaks his oaten pipe (72). Things brighten up in 'June' but Colin is still the outsider:

> O happy Hobbinoll, I blesse thy state,
> That Paradise hast found, whych Adam lost.
>
> (9–10)

He remains resolutely inconsolable even when offered by Hobbinol this enticing invitation to 'pierlesse pleasures':

> . . . to the dales resort, where shepheards ritch
> And fruictful flocks bene every where to see.
> Here no night ravens lodge more black then pitche,
> Nor elvish ghosts, nor gastly owles doe flee.

24. *Discoveries* 2238.
25. The phrase comes from the headnote of E.K.'s letter which precedes 'The general argument'.

> But frendly Faeries, met with many Graces,
> And lightfote Nymphes can chace the lingring night,
> With heydeguyes, and trimly trodden traces,
> Whilst systers nyne, which dwell on Parnasse hight,
> Doe make them musick, for their more delight:
> And Pan himself to kisse their christall faces,
> Will pype and daunce, when Phoebe shineth bright:
> Such pierlesse pleasures have we in these places.
>
> (21–32)

The mingling here of the presiding genii of classical pastoral (the nymphs, the Graces, Pan and the Muses dwelling on Parnassus) with popular and folk elements (elvish ghosts, friendly fairies and country dancing 'heydeguyes') invigorates the former and dignifies the latter. The poetic charm of the pastoral has been naturalised and translated into a new vernacular language.

The plaintive note in Spenser differs in effect and cause from the elegiac in Virgil. The cause is perhaps apparent in the debate between Piers and Palinode representing, according to E.K., the 'two forms of pastors or ministers or the Protestant and the Catholic'.[26] Palinode begins with a lively evocation of merry England in 'Maye':

> Is not thilke the mery moneth of May
> When love lads masken in fresh aray? . . .
> Sicker this morrowe, ne lenger agoe,
> I sawe a shole of shepeheardes outgoe,
> With singing, and shouting and jolly chere:
> Before them yode a lusty tabrere,
> That to the many a horne pype playd,
> Whereto they dauncen eche one with his mayd.
> To see those folkes make such iouysaunce,
> Made my heart after the pype to daunce.
> Tho to the greene wood they speeden hem all,
> To fetchen home May with their musicall:
> And home they bringen in a royall throne,
> Crowned as king: and his Queene attone
> Was Lady Flora, on whom did attend
> A fayre flocke of Faeries, and a fresh bend
> Of lovely Nymphs. (O that I were there,
> To helpen the ladyes their maybush beare)

---

26. In the 'argument' preceding 'Maye'.

Ah Piers, bene not they teeth on edge, to thinke,
How great sport they gaynen with little swinck?

(1–2, 19–36)

This seems on the surface to be referring to real merrymaking
rustics enjoying the rites of spring. But the delight Palinode takes
in May Day ceremonies (in which churchmen participated in
Elizabethan England) meets with a stern rebuke from the
Protestant Piers who uses the language of pastoral to play a very
different tune. To him the jolly shepherds are like the hireling
who neglects the flock because it is not his own, in Christ's
parable of the good shepherd, in St John's gospel (Chapter 10).

Perdie so farre am I from envie,
That their fondnesse inly I pitie.
Those faytours little regarden their charge,
While they letting their sheepe runne at large,
Passen their time, that should be sparely spent,
In lustihede and wanton meryment.
Thilke same bene shepeheards for the Devils stedde,
That playen, while their flockes be unfedde.
Well is it seene, theyr sheepe bene not their owne,
That letten them runne at random alone.
But they bene hyred for little pay
Of other, that caren as little as they,
What fallen the flocke, so they han the fleece
And get all the gayne, paying but a peece.
I muse, what account both these will make,
The one for the hire, which he doth take,
And thother for leaving his Lords taske,
When great Pan account of shepeherdes shall aske.

(37–54)

E.K. explains that great Pan 'is Christ, the very God of all
shepherds'.[27] Spenser is clearly using the language of pastoral to
juxtapose two different attitudes that seem to have more to do
with this-worldly and other-worldly perspectives than a simple
division between Catholic and Protestant. Whether or not his
apparently worldly tendencies are meant to signify a worldly
Catholicism, Palinode is certainly a spokesman for pleasure in
terms that recall the classical ideal of *otium*:

27.   In the thirteenth note to 'Maye'.

What shoulden shepheards other things tend,
Then sith their God his good does them send,
Reapen the fruite thereof, that is pleasure,
The while they here liven, at ease and leasure?

(63–6)

If we are tempted simply to regard Palinode as a representative of pagan attitudes that have been superseded by a superior Christian spirituality, we may recall the words of Christ in the parable: 'I am come that men may have life and that they may have it abundantly. I am the good shepherd: the good shepherd gives life to his people' (John 10: 10–11). But there is no mistaking the attitude of Piers, who proceeds to talk of wolves in sheep's clothing, to the words of Palinode: 'Ah, Palinodie, thou art a worldes childe' (73). In this debate, it has usually been felt that the balance is weighted in favour of Piers, yet Palinode (like Monicus in 'Parthenias') is allowed a point of view that commands respect:

Sorrowe ne neede be hastened on:
For he will come without calling anone.
While times enduren of tranquillitie,
Usen we freely our felicitie.

(152–5)

Given the judgement and perspective of Piers, however, it is hardly surprising that Spenserian pastoral is not more happily Arcadian. To Piers, with his contempt of the world, merry England, like the Bower of Bliss, is a snare and a delusion, so that the very idea of Arcadian pastoral ease is not merely ignoble but positively harmful to the soul.

Wherever it is thought the balance lies, and however this 'aeglogue' is interpreted as a whole, it is clear that it is the product of an internal debate between different (and perhaps competing) values, attitudes and perspectives that are the constituent elements of what may be called Spenser's Christian humanism. The crux of the debate is not quite the same but is analogous to that which troubled Augustine and Jerome and with which Petrarch toyed in 'Parthenias'. The pastoral form functions imaginatively here both as a crucible (a vessel that is distinctly weird in shape) in which the elements are separated out and differentiated, and as a catalyst in which they may be converted into something new. Yet it is not strictly a catalyst, for the pastoral eclogue itself is transformed in the process. William Empson's formula that pastoral is a 'process of putting the complex into the simple'[28] may seem apt, though if we recall the simple form of Theocritean pastoral it is equally clear that here the simple has become complex.

It is an irony that the pastoral idea, which is subject to rigorous scrutiny in the pastoral form of the 'Aeglogues', flourished more straightforwardly in Spenser's later epic *The Faerie Queene* (1596). Here, in the episode in which the courteous knight Calidore falls in love with the fair Pastorella (VI, x), the heroic and the pastoral are juxtaposed, and the pastoral functions as an idyllic contrast to the brutal forces that come to shatter it.

Other versions of pastoral

The Renaissance eclogue, in fact, as the description of it by Puttenham cited at the opening of this chapter suggests, often lost all connection with the classical idyll.[29] Conversely, the Arcadian ideal flourished in the other forms, notably the prose romance and romantic drama. For the former, there was a model in the prose tale of the Hellenistic writer Longus, *Daphnis and Chloe*; Sannazaro's *Arcadia* (1504) was an Italian forebear of the courteous pastoral romance of Sidney who, in *The Old Arcadia* (c. 1577), seeks to give a fictional reality to an Arcadian world which gave rise to the poetic form of the eclogue (which also features in the work). As the work developed, it broke the bounds of pastoral romance to become a full-scale prose epic incorporating features of chivalric romance with courtly love and sophisticated character analysis prefiguring the later development of the novel. The dramatic possibilities of pastoral (the Theocritean idyll has its origin in mime) were first exploited in Italy by Tasso with *Aminta* (1573) and Guarini with *Il Pastor Fido* (1585). John Fletcher's *The Faithful Shepherdess* (1608) reinterpreted these for the English stage. Ben Jonson's unfinished play *The Sad Shepherd* (1640) naturalised this tradition with a plot featuring Robin Hood and his men together with Maid Marian set in Sherwood Forest.

28. Empson, W. (1966) *Some Versions of Pastoral*, Penguin, p. 25 (first published in 1935).
29. See Heninger, S.K. (1961) 'The Renaissance Perversion of Pastoral', *Journal of the History of Ideas* **22**, 254–61.

The sweets of pastoral flourished in the lyric and the madrigal. 'The Passionate Shepherd to his Love' by Marlowe may be representative.

> Come live with me and be my love,
> And we will all the pleasures prove
> That vallies, groves, hills and fields,
> Woods, or steepy mountain yields.[30]

The gold buckles, coral clasps and amber studs that he offers as bait are clearly designed to appeal to a sophisticated taste. His enticement prompted the realistic reply of a worldly-wise nymph:

> But could youth last, and love still breed;
> Had joys no date, nor age no need;
> Then these delights my mind might move
> To live with thee and be thy love.
>   ('The Nymph's Reply', Walter Ralegh[31])

Though we never hear the voice of a classical shepherdess, it is one of the strengths of the eclogue form that, unlike the pure lyric, it could accommodate different points of view.

Milton's pastoral elegy: Marvell

The element of masquerade in pastoral (at the opening of *The Faerie Queene*, Spenser says that his Muse 'did maske . . . in lowly shepheards weeds') made it ideal for the masque itself. Milton, for example, used pastoral in different ways in *Arcades* (1633) and *Comus* (1634) before the occasion which prompted what has often been regarded as the finest reincarnation of the pastoral in English, his elegy *Lycidas* on the death of Edward King, a fellow of Milton's Cambridge college and contemporary with him there who had written verses and taken holy orders and so could be a literary reincarnation of the shepherd–singer of classical pastoral and of the Christian shepherd of the medieval and Renaissance tradition. 'In this monody the author bewails a learned friend, unfortunately drowned in his passage from Chester to the Irish

30. Orgel, S. (ed.) (1971) *Christopher Marlowe: The Complete Poems and Translations*, Penguin, p. 209.
31. In the above, p. 212.

Seas 1637. And by occasion foretells the ruin of the corrupted clergy then in their height'. Milton's headnote suggests *paulo maiora*, something greater going beyond the bounds of classical pastoral and incorporating ecclesiastical satire in the manner of Petrarch and Mantuan. *Lycidas* is remarkable not least for embracing, fusing and transcending the whole history of the genre from Theocritus onwards.[32]

The structure of *Lycidas*, many of its topics and motifs and much of its imagery and feeling are determined by its relation to classical pastoral. The address in the opening lines to the laurels, myrtles and ivy (emblems of poetic beauty and achievement) and the direct echo of Virgil's 'Gallus' ('Who would not sing for Lycidas?' (10), *neget quis carmina Gallo*? (X, 3)) signal Milton's laureate design in which the horror of King's death by drowning is countered by the sweet beauty of classical pastoral elegy which functions both as a tribute to Lycidas and as a *remedium doloris* to console the poet:

> He must not float upon his watery bier
> Unwept, and welter to the parching wind,
> Without the meed of some melodious tear.
>
> (12–14)

There follows an invocation of the inspiring powers not just of pastoral but of all poetry as Milton calls upon the Muses dwelling by the fountain of Aganippe on Mount Helicon where an altar to Jove marks the dignity and importance of the poetic function:

> Begin then, sisters of the sacred well,
> That from beneath the seat of Jove doth spring,
> Begin, and somewhat loudly sweep the string.
>
> (15–17)

This is the resounding lyre, not the pretty sound of the 'oaten flute' on which 'rural ditties' are played, as the poem will contain loftier strains than those of the humble pastoral. And in contrast to most English pastoral before him, Milton's solemn music and

---

32. For the sources of *Lycidas* the fullest account is Hanford, J.H. (1910) 'The Pastoral Elegy and Milton's *Lycidas*', *Proceedings of the Modern Language Association* **25**, 403–47. A revised version is available in Patrides, C.A. (ed.) (1961) *Milton's 'Lycidas': The Tradition and the Poem*, Holt, Rinehart & Winston, New York. See also the commentary accompanying the text in Carey, J., Fowler, A. (eds) (1968) *The Poems of John Milton*, Longman.

sonorous cadences recall those of Virgil singing *paulo maiora*. Whatever he may have owed to study of Italian for the verse form of *Lycidas*,[33] it is of course the weight and gravity of Latin that we hear in this monody as so often elsewhere in his poetry.

The specifically pastoral imagery starts as Milton looks back to his past association with the departed to evoke a time of shared experience and youthful poetic endeavour, a time now nostalgically recalled in soft and idyllic tones:

> For we were nursed upon the self-same hill,
> Fed the same flock; by fountain, shade, and rill.
>   Together both, ere the high lawns appeared
> Under the opening eye-lids of the morn
> We drove a-field, and both together heard
> What time the grey-fly winds her sultry horn,
> Battening our flocks with the fresh dews of night,
> Oft till the star that rose, at evening, bright,
> Toward heaven's descent had sloped his westering wheel.
> Meantime the rural ditties were not mute,
> Tempered to the oaten flute,
> Rough satyrs danced, and fauns with cloven heel,
> From the glad sound would not be absent long,
> And old Damoetas loved to hear our song.
>
>   (23–36)

The primary function of the imagery is to create a mood and feeling contrasting to the 'heavy change' (37) wrought by the death of Lycidas. The allegory is less easy to determine, though it is not difficult to see that the satyrs and fauns might be Milton's fellow undergraduates at Christ's College, young barbarians at play, temporarily charmed by the young poet's art.

Conventional pastoral continues with the sympathy figure as wild nature mourns for Lycidas, though Milton's use of it is restrained (when compared, for example, to Moschus in the lament for Bion),[34] and the rustic analogy to which the sympathy figure adduces realistic examples of death in nature.

---

33. See Prince, F.T. (1954) *The Italian Element in Milton's Verse*, Oxford University Press.
34. Bion's 'Lament for Adonis' and Moschus's 'Lament for Bion' are both included with Theocritus's Idylls in Edmonds, J.M. (ed.) (1912) *The Greek Bucolic Poets*, Loeb Classical Library, Heinemann, London; Harvard University Press, Cambridge, Mass.

Thee shepherd, thee the woods and desert caves,
With wild thyme and the gadding vine o'ergrown,
And all their echoes mourn. . . .
As killing as the canker to the rose,
Or taint-worm to the weanling herds that graze,
Or frost to flowers, that their gay wardrobe wear,
When first the white-thorn blows;
Such, Lycidas, thy loss to shepherd's ear.

(39–41, 45–9)

Following Theocritus and Virgil,[35] Milton reproaches the nymphs for their absence from the scene of Lycidas's death which they might have prevented; the motif is adapted to the Welsh scene with allusions to the Druidical bards and the 'wizard stream' of the Dee (55).

Where were ye nymphs when the remorseless deep
Closed o'er the head of your loved Lycidas?
For neither were ye playing on the steep,
Where your old bards, the famous Druids, lie,
Nor on the shaggy top of Mona high,
Not yet where Deva spreads her wizard stream.

(50–5)

Then, unlike his predecessors, the elegist breaks the pastoral mood and questions the convention.

Ay me, I fondly dream!
Had ye been there . . . for what could that have done?

(56–7)

The inability of the nymphs to save their devotee prompts questions about the efficacy not only of pastoral poetry in which they figure and of the consoling power of pastoral elegy, but also of poetry itself. Orpheus, so often a symbol in the Renaissance of the civilising artist (because of his ability to tame wild nature), found no salvation though he was the son of the Muse (Calliope) when he was set upon by Thracian Bacchanals who tore him apart and threw his head into the river Hebrus:

What could the muse herself that Orpheus bore,
The muse herself for her enchanting son

---

35. Theocritus, Idyll I, 66ff.; Virgil. Eclogue X, 9ff.

Whom universal nature did lament,
When by the rout that made the hideous roar,
His gory visage down the stream was sent,
Down the swift Hebrus to the Lesbian shore.

(58–63)

The poet proceeds to question with increasing bitterness the value of a laborious dedication to poetic art, using the language of pastoral but divorcing it (like Petrarch) from its usual associations, for poetry is hard work requiring discipline; conversely *otium* is an alternative life of pleasure and desire that is antithetical to the poet's calling:

Alas! What boots it with uncessant care
To tend the homely slighted shepherd's trade,
And strictly meditate the thankless muse,
Were it not better done as others use,
To sport with Amaryllis in the shade,
Or with the tangles of Neaera's hair?

(64–9)

Like Petrarch, he identifies the poet's motivation as the desire for fame, but the early death of King provokes a bitter moment of humanist doubt which is in turn quashed by the prompting of his Christian faith:

Fame is the spur that the clear spirit doth raise
(That last infirmity of noble mind)
To scorn delights, and live laborious days;
But the fair guerdon when we hope to find,
And think to burst out into sudden blaze,
Comes the blind Fury with th' abhorred shears,
And slits the thin-spun life.

(70–6)

Milton moves from worldly to other-worldly perspective by skilful deployment of a famous motif in Virgil when Phoebus Apollo as the god of poetic inspiration admonishes the poet for going beyond pastoral to contemplate writing epic:

cum canerem reges et proelia, Cynthius aurem
vellit et admonuit: 'pastorem, Tityre, pingues
pascere oportet oves, deductum dicere carmen'

(VI, 3–5)

(when I would sing of kings and battles, Cynthius Apollo plucked my
ear and warned: 'a shepherd, Tityrus, ought to feed fat sheep, but sing
a fine-spun song'.)

> But not the praise,
> Phoebus replied, and touched my trembling ears;
> Fame is no plant that grows on mortal soil,
> Nor in the glistering foil
> Set off to the world, nor in broad rumour lies
> But lives and spreads aloft by those pure eyes,
> And perfect witness of all-judging Jove;
> As he pronounces lastly on each deed,
> Of so much fame in heaven expect thy meed.

(76–84)

The identification of pagan and Christian here is infinitely more
subtle than the frequently jarring association of Apollo or Pan
with Christ (as in Petrarch's 'Parthenias' where Apollo appears in
the river Jordan to be bathed by *puer hispidus ille* 'that famous
hirsute youth', John the Baptist). In fact there is a fine decorum in
Milton's uniting of the classical and the Christian sources of his
inspiration here, for it is clear that they are not crudely equated.
The moment makes us aware that the sources of Milton's
inspiration are inevitably wider than Virgil's, even if Virgil is here
the bridge mediating between the two worlds of active humanist
endeavour and a transcendent Christian spirituality. Furthermore,
in this allusion to Virgil is a perfect illustration of Milton's
modulation of the pastoral elegy into a higher key.

After this first climax comes the second pastoral invocation of
Arethusa, the Sicilian fountain recalling the Theocritean source of
the pastoral, and of the Mincius, the modest river of the Mantuan
plain where Virgil was born who continued the genre in his
smooth-sliding verse:

> O fountain Arethuse, and thou honoured flood,
> Smooth-sliding Mincius, crowned with vocal reeds,
> That strain I heard was of a higher mood:
> But now my oat proceeds
> And listens to the herald of the sea . . .

(85–9)

The literal and figurative are finely balanced in the 'vocal reeds',
which suggests both the sound of the wind in the reeds and the

pastoral poems of Virgil echoing through the ages. How discreet is the movement from fountain to river to sea as Milton now manipulates a major pastoral motif derived from Theocritus's Idyll I and Virgil's 'Gallus', the visitation of gods, first Neptune who seeks the cause of calamity, then the grieving river of Cam (the river of Cambridge) and finally 'the pilot of the Galilean Lake' (109), St Peter, who contrasts the departed with bad shepherds remaining amongst the clergy here bitterly denounced in the manner of Mantuan.

The movement away from pure pastoral mirrors that of the opening section and is marked by a third invocation, of Alpheus, the river that was reputed to flow from Arcadia beneath the sea to emerge in the fountain of Arethusa:

> Return Alpheus, the dread voice is past,
> That shrunk thy streams; return Sicilian muse,
> And call the vales, and bid them hither cast
> Their bells, and flowrets of a thousand hues.
>
> (132–5)

The third and final movement of the poem looks for consolation and begins like the other two with the adaptation of a pastoral motif, the traditional catalogue of pastoral 'sweets', here, as in other elegies, turned into a floral tribute in which the flowers too (like the earlier woods and groves) are to mourn sympathetically for Lycidas. The soothing beauty of these poetic flowers, like the beauty of real flowers at an actual funeral, has only limited effect; the traditional consolations of pastoral elegy are not adequate to the occasion. There follow contrasting images of the reality of Lycidas's actual death at sea.

> Bid amaranthus all his beauty shed,
> And daffadillies fill their cups with tears,
> To strew the laureate hearse where Lycid lies.
> For so to interpose a little ease,
> Let our frail thoughts dally with false surmise.
> Ay me! whilst thee the shores, and sounding seas
> Wash far away, where'er thy bones are hurled . . .
>
> (149–55)

In Virgil's fifth eclogue, 'Daphnis', consolation is found in the apotheosis and translation to the stars of the mythical shepherd-singer (usually identified as Julius Caesar). The note of joy and celebration with which this pagan elegy concludes is triumphantly Christianised in the vision of Lycidas resurrected and placed in a celestial *locus amoenus* of eternal beatitude:

> Through the dear might of him that walked the waves;
> Where other groves, and other streams along,
> With nectar pure his oozy locks he laves,
> And hears the unexpressive nuptial song,
> In the blest kingdoms meek of joy and love.

(173–7)

For the third and final time Milton transcends his pastoral sources before the calm resolution of the close.

The relation between classical and Christian elements in *Lycidas* anticipates *Paradise Lost*:

> and in Ausonian land
> Men called him Mulciber; and how he fell
> From heaven, they fabled, thrown by angry Jove
> Sheer o'er the crystal battlements; from morn
> To noon he fell, from noon to dewy eve,
> A summer's day; and with the setting sun
> Dropped from the zenith like a falling star,
> On Lemnos the Aegean isle: thus they relate,
> Erring . . .

(I, 739–47)[36]

Milton translates this famous moment from the *Iliad* (I, 590ff.) recalling the grandeur of its context while adapting it to his own grand manner (in Homer it is also part of the divine comedy) in order to incorporate it into the very texture of the epic, thereby extending its poetic range, while at the same disowning it in the name of a higher truth. The consoling power of pastoral elegy is likewise a fond dream (56) and a false surmise (153). He is entirely clear-sighted about these fables, dreams and surmises in which his poetic imagination so susceptibly delighted and without which (if he had been sterner with himself) it would never have functioned so freely. In composing a formal tribute in *Lycidas*, he sought imaginative stimulus from past 'melodious tears' in order to snatch something beautiful from the jaws of death. Strewing the

36. Carey, J., Fowler, A. (1968) pp. 504–5.

laureate hearse with poetic flowers 'to interpose a little ease' is the artistic equivalent of laying a wreath. There is solace in funeral flowers and some mitigation in the dignity of ceremony. But however consoling the purest form of poetic beauty in the pastoral might be, it can never be adequate for the Christian elegist; hence the moments of transcendence in the poem that take it beyond the classical inheritance in matter, mood and style. As a result *Lycidas* is a wider-ranging poem of greater depth than any of the sources out of which it is made. Yet the artifice of the pastoral in which so many of the conventions and images have to do with art itself proved an ideal medium for the poet seeking artistic solace in the face of death. Through classical imagery is figured a variety of feelings including sweet melancholy but also ranging from bitterness through nostalgia to a sense of injustice leading to self doubt. It is doubtful whether the range of these feelings and preoccupations would have been confronted if Milton had been writing more straightforwardly in the person of a Protestant poet offering a Christian consolation. As it is, the ebb and flow of the poem's feeling and structure, as the elegist invokes, moves beyond and returns to the conventions of the genre, represent both the fluctuations of mourning that are psychologically convincing and an internal dialogue conducted by the modern Christian poet with the sources of his poetic inspiration recalled from the classical past.

As to the propriety of Milton's incorporation of Christian elements into his pastoral, questioned in the famous denigration of the poem by Dr Johnson in his 'Life of Milton',[37] Milton's early readers brought up on Mantuan and perhaps still familiar with Spenser might not have found anything jarring in the poem, particularly as its transitions are so skilfully managed and marked. In theory, Milton placed the highest value on decorum if his later words are to be believed when, writing *Of Education* in 1642, he calls poetry:

> . . . that sublime art which in Aristotle's *Poetics* in Horace and the Italian commentaries of Castelvetro, Tasso, Mazzoni, and others, teaches what the laws are of a true epic poem, what of dramatic, what of lyric, what decorum is, which is the grand masterpiece to observe.

37.   'Milton', 181 in Hill, G.B. (ed.) (1905) *Lives of the English Poets by Samuel Johnson*, 3 vols, Oxford University Press, vol. 1, p. 163.

This would make them soon perceive what despicable creatures our common rhymers and play-writers be, and show them what religious, what glorious and magnificent use might be made of poetry, both in divine and human things.[38]

Those who find indecorum in *Lycidas* might reflect how little the theoretical pronouncements of poets may have to do with their actual poetic practice. Those who find no basic impropriety in the poem might use *Lycidas* to help clarify and illustrate the meaning of Milton's prose formulation, and argue that observing decorum even for the most classically inclined of Renaissance poets did not necessarily imply a slavish adherence to the laws of genre. Milton in *Lycidas* is clearly in control of his sources (and any laws that may be deduced from them) and uses them to satisfy his own artistic demands and to suit the needs of his own particular occasion. Furthermore, the uplifting spirit in which he recommends recourse to the critical tradition precludes pedantry as he has his sights set upon the noblest ends.

Writing in the latter half of the eighteenth century when the pastoral had been done to death, Dr Johnson in his comments on *Lycidas* calls the pastoral form 'easy, vulgar and therefore disgusting'. The modern reader coming to the poem for the first time without the benefit of a classical education is more likely to find it, as used in *Lycidas*, difficult, esoteric and therefore disconcerting. Some familiarity with the conventions of genre and recognition of specific allusions are a necessary basis for appreciation of *Lycidas*. Not that the poem was in this sense recondite to its first readers. It was published in an academic collection of memorial verses by Edward King's acquaintances,[39] but any educated reader of poetry would have recognised its echoes appreciating smooth-sliding Mincius, crowned with vocal reeds.

For as Europe learned its grammar and syntax by way of the Latin language, so too did schoolchildren have their first experience of poetry through the Latin classics to which Virgil's eclogues (together with those of Mantuan) formed a frequent

38. 'Of Education' in Patterson, F.A. (ed.) (1933) *The Student's Milton*, 2nd edn, Appleton-Century-Crofts, New York, p. 729.
39. *Justa Eduardo King naufrago ab Amicis moerentibus amoris &* μνείας χαρὶν. See Carey, J., Fowler, A. (1968) p. 232.

introduction, preparatory to the more difficult tasks of lyric or the epic. The bucolic was manageable in length and simple to construe without the grammatical and syntactical complexity of the developed style of Virgil and Horace. The easy verse of Terence might also be read early in school but as an introduction not to poetry but to good conversational Latin. Through the pastoral, children had a simple introduction to poetry proper, a *gradus ad Parnassum*, in one of its major metrical forms, the dactylic hexameter which they might be expected to imitate for themselves, as envisaged by the humanist educator Vida in his *Art of Poetry*:

> But in no Iliad let the youth engage
> His tender years and inexperienced age;
> Let him by just degrees and steps proceed,
> Sing with the swains and tune the tender reed.[40]

Through study and imitation of Virgil's pastorals, many a grammar-school youth had his first acquaintance with metrical scansion and the various figures of sound and sense. This might entail the identification of specific tropes and figures, but also in a general sense the discovery that the whole language of poetry as presented by pastoral is figurative, for the intelligent student would soon appreciate that these literary shepherds were not quite like the shepherds of their everyday acquaintance, if indeed the sons of the well-to-do had any contact with smocks and crooks. Nor need there be any fear of contamination, linguistic or social, from these literary shepherds whose Latin, apart from one or two colloquialisms from comedy, is entirely pure, for Virgil does not employ any dialect equivalent of Theocritus's Doric Greek; on the contrary his shepherds speak good classical Latin and do not, like Spenser's, lapse into what E.K. calls 'rustical rudeness'.[41] The largely innocuous subject matter of pastoral could be deemed particularly suitable for children, as it was by the Tudor humanist Sir Thomas Elyot in *The Governor*: 'For what thing can be more familiar than his *Bucolics*? Nor no work so nigh approacheth to the common dalliance and manners of children, and the pretty controversies of the simple shepherds therein contained wonder-

---

40.   Vida, *De Arte Poetica* (1527), I, 459–61. See Pitt, C. (1725) *Vida's Art of Poetry Translated into English Verse* (lines 613–16).
41.   At the opening of his letter to Gabriel Harvey.

fully rejoiceth the child that heareth it well declared, as I know by my own experience.'[42] Even if schoolmasters fought shy of the bisexual element (of which they may not have been so conscious as their liberated twentieth-century successors), a time-hallowed tradition of allegorical interpretation was readily available to render it safe. When his suspicions are aroused by Hobbinol's pursuit of Colin in *Januarie*, E.K. is quickly able to sanitise them with reference to Plato. Through the pastoral the beginner would learn that art even in its purest form was not quite the same as nature and social reality, though it could never be entirely divorced from them even if it aspired to create a beautiful world far transcending these. Nevertheless, the sentiments of Sidney surely echo the experience of a world brought up on an idea of poetry embodied in Virgil: 'Nature never set forth the earth in so rich tapestry as diverse poets have done; neither with so pleasant rivers, fruitful trees, sweet-smelling flowers, nor whatsoever else may make the too much loved earth more lovely. Her world is brazen, the poets only deliver a golden.'[43]

The golden world of pastoral as an alternative to the brazen world of the human social order can often be traced in poems where formal pastoral trappings are dispensed with. *The Garden*, possibly written when Marvell was employed as tutor to Fairfax's daughter at Nunappleton House just after the turmoil of the English civil war, has no shepherds or even mowers, but the poem can be regarded as a version of the pastoral in which the idea is reconstituted, transformed and spiritualised. The classical paradise is turned into a playful vision of the Garden of Eden not only before the fall of man but also before the creation of woman, in a witty stroke that extirpates *eros*, so often the discordant element in Arcadia. Unlike Spenser and Milton, Marvell has no qualms about the pleasures of *otium* that he celebrates in his 'delicious solitude' (16). Disengagement from the world of civic, military or even poetic ambition and the retreat from passion open up the possibility of a wondrous life of sensuous satisfaction in a golden age that needs no cultivation.

42. From Book I quoted in Martindale, J. (ed.) (1985) *English Humanism: Wyatt to Cowley*, Croom Helm, p. 82.
43. *The Defence of Poesy*, 182–5 in Duncan-Jones, K. (1989) p. 217.

What wondrous life is this I lead!
Ripe apples drop about my head;
The luscious clusters of the vine
Upon my mouth do crush their wine;
The nectarine, and curious peach,
Into my hands themselves do reach;
Stumbling on melons as I pass,
Ensnared with flowers, I fall on grass.
                    (33–40)[44]

Satisfaction of the senses makes possible the liberation of higher faculties. The mind is released in creative thought, and so much at one with nature is the poet that, in a reversal of the pastoral sympathy figure where nature feels with man, his soul merges into the very essence of the trees whose beauties far exceed those of any human lover (in a neat reversal of pastoral love, the poet will carve the names of trees on the trees' barks), so that the whole poem may be regarded as an intense and witty meditation on the sylvan muse:

> Tityre, tu patulae recubans sub tegmine fagi
> silvestrem tenui musam meditaris avena.

Marvell's toying with the pastoral idea creates a beautiful green world far transcending pastoral, a sweet and witty release for the soul, into something, as Horace said of Virgil's pastorals, *molle atque facetum*.

The georgic: Hesiod

From pastoral, Virgil went on to write his *Georgics*, a substantial work on different aspects of farming (the Greek word *georgos* means 'worker of the land') treating in four books the cultivation of crops, trees, animals and bees. Because they feature rural life, links have been made between the georgic and the pastoral, though Virgil is here renewing an older form, recognising as his model (II, 176) the Greek poet Hesiod (perhaps as early or even earlier than Homer in the eighth century BC). In his *Works and Days*, written in the dactylic hexameter, the poet is found in the role of teacher addressing his brother Perses who evidently needs

44.   Donno, E.S. (ed.) (1972) *Andrew Marvell: The Complete Poems*, Penguin.

to be taken sternly to task. The rendering of Chapman published in 1618 captures the moral and didactic tone:

> Do thou, then, ever in thy memory place
> My precepts, Perses, sprung of sacred race;
> And work out what thou know'st not, that with hate
> Famine may prosecute thy full estate,
> And rich-wreathed Ceres (reverenced of all)
> Love thee as much, and make her festival
> Amidst thy granaries. Famine evermore
> Is natural consort of the idle boor.
> Whoever idly lives, both Gods and men
> Pursue with hateful and still punishing spleen.
> The slothful man is like the stingless drone,
> That all his power and disposition
> Employs to rob the labours of the bee,
> And with his sloth devour her industry.
> Do thou repose thy special pleasure, then,
> In still being conversant with temperate pain,
> That to thee still the Seasons may send home
> Their utmost store. With labour men become
> Herd-full and rich; with labour thou shalt prove
> Great both in human and the Deities' love.
> One with another, all combined in one,
> Hate with infernal horror th' idle drone.
>
> (*The Georgics of Hesiod*)[45]

Hesiod freely offers Perses the benefit of his wisdom on a variety of matters affecting the conduct of his life, but much of the poem has to do with the good works necessary for agricultural success and the identification of the most propitious times and days when they may be done. By way of introduction, the poet puts Perses into the right frame of mind with a series of gloom-laden mythological excursuses, including the tale of Pandora and an account of the degeneration of the world from the golden through the silver and bronze to the present iron age. The vision of the iron age here sets the overall mood and tone:

> Ill-lunged, ill-livered and ill-complexioned Spite
> Shall consort all the miserable plight

45. Anon. (1875) *The Works of George Chapman: Poems and Minor Translations*, with an introduction by Algernon Swinburne, Chatto & Windus (no line numbers). There is no good modern edition of this translation.

Of men then living. Justice then and Shame
Clad in pure white (as if they never came
In touch of those societies) shall fly
Up to the gods' immortal family
From broad-wayed earth: and leave griefs to men
That (desperate of amends) must bear all then.
(*The Georgics of Hesiod*)

The most extended description is of a winter storm (504–56) that wreaks havoc and causes pain to man and beast alike. Even summer is torrid. There is little time for relaxation from this hardship, and little room for a *locus amoenus* in the poetic landscape of the *Works and Days*.

Virgil's *Georgics* in Dryden's translation

Virgil used Hesiod as a base to work from and to express his own rather different philosophical outlook and temper:

The sire of gods and men with hard decrees
Forbids our plenty to be brought with ease,
And wills that mortal men, inured to toil,
Should exercise with pains, the grudging soil;
Himself invented first the shining share
And whetted human industry by care;
Himself did handicrafts and arts ordain
Nor suffered sloth to rust his active reign.
Ere this, no peasant vexed the peaceful ground,
Which only turfs and greens for altars found:
No fences parted fields, nor marks nor bounds
Distinguished acres of litigious grounds;
But all was common, and the fruitful Earth
Was free to give her unexacted birth.
Jove added venom to the viper's brood,
And swelled with raging storms the peaceful flood;
Commissioned hungry wolves t'infest the fold
And shook from oaken leaves the liquid gold; . . .
That studious need might useful arts explore,
From furrowed fields to reap the foodful store . . .
And various arts in order did succeed,
What cannot endless labour, urged by need?
(Dryden; *Georgic* I, 183ff., translating 121ff.)

tum variae venere artes. labor omnia vicit
improbus et duris urgens in rebus egestas
(*Georgic* I, 146–7)

(Then came various arts. Hard work and pressing need in hard
circumstances conquered everything.)

The vision is still hard, but we are more conscious in Virgil of the
purposes of a provident Jupiter. The loss of the golden age has
resulted in a compensating growth in human skill and inventive-
ness which is variously celebrated throughout the poem in man's
cultivation of nature. Nature retains her wild and wayward power
in the *Georgics*; for example, Virgil has a description of a storm
which may be said to outdo that of Hesiod in effect as it comes in
autumn and destroys the crops (I, 316–34). Likewise he concludes
his third book with more than 150 lines describing the causes and
effects of disease in animals culminating in a gruesome account of
the plague (III, 414–566). But beside the unruly power and
cussedness of nature is the human capacity through improving
cultivation and perfection of her potential substantially to tame
that wildness and harness her productive power. It is not difficult
to deduce from this account of the growth of arts, the classic
(Aristotelian) view of art itself. Just as the ploughman introduces
order and regularity amid the random chaos of uncultivated
nature to make her productive, so the artist through the
imposition of form (and in the case of the poet, metre) improves
nature by tapping her latent power and actualising her potential,
thus completing her purposes to express some definite end.

It is this human capacity to improve nature that is celebrated in
one of the most famous of georgic idylls in the fourth book
featuring the old man of Corycia; he has little, and the little he has
is not particularly promising, but with hard work and an instinct
for nature, his allotment flourishes.

I chanced an old Corycian swain to know,
Lord of few acres, and those barren too,
Unfit for sheep or vines, and more unfit to sow:
Yet, lab'ring well his little spot of ground,
Some scatt'ring pot-herbs here and there he found,
Which, cultivated with daily care,
And bruised with vervain, were his frugal fare.
Sometimes white lilies did their leaves afford,

With wholesome poppy flowers, to mend his homely board;
For, late returning home, he supped at ease,
And wisely deemed the wealth of monarchs less:
The little of his own, because his own, did please.
To quit his care, he gathered, first of all,
In spring the roses, apples in the fall;
And, when cold winter split the rocks in twain,
And ice the running rivers did restrain,
He stripped the bear's-foot of its leafy growth,
And, calling western winds, accused the spring of sloth.
He therefore first among the swains was found
To reap the product of his laboured ground,
And squeeze the combs with golden liquor crowned.
His limes were first in flowers; his lofty pines,
With friendly shade, secured his tender vines.
For ev'ry bloom his trees in spring afford,
An autumn apple was by tale restored.
He knew to rank his elms in even rows,
For fruit the grafted pear tree to dispose,
And tame to plums the sourness of the sloes.
With spreading planes he made a cool retreat,
To shade good fellows from the summer's heat.
        (Dryden, *Georgic* IV, 188–217, translating, 127–47)

Towards the end of the description it seems that nature is
rewarding him and responding sympathetically to his labour and
care. Agriculture, a symbol of human wickedness in pastoral, is
man's salvation in the *Georgics* and while nature provides idyllic
scenes of her own accord in pastoral, man makes his own
contribution to the *locus amoenus* of the georgic. And so the spirit
in which Virgil presents the relationship between man and nature
in the *Georgics* is quite different in effect from that of Hesiod in the
Works and Days. Sir Thomas Elyot in *The Governor* responds to its
poetic delights:

> In his *Georgics*, Lord, what pleasant variety there is; the diverse grains,
> herbs and flowers that there be described, that reading therein, it
> seemeth to a man to be in a delectable garden or paradise! What
> ploughman knoweth so much of husbandry as there is expressed?
> Who, delighting in good horses, shall not be thereto more inflamed
> reading there of the breeding, choosing and keeping of them?[46]

46.   See note 42 above.

Addison, writing an introduction to Dryden's translation of 1697, compares Virgil favourably with Hesiod:

> Virgil has drawn out the rules of tillage and planting into two books, which Hesiod has despatched in half a one but has so raised the natural rudeness and simplicity of his subject with such a significance of expression, such a pomp of verse, such variety of transitions and such a solemn air in his reflections that if we look on both poets together we see in one the plainness of a downright countryman and in the other something of a rustic majesty, like that of a Roman dictator at the plough-tail. He delivers the meanest of his precepts with a kind of grandeur, he breaks the clods and tosses the dung about with an air of gracefulness.[47]

These last remarks may have been prompted by passages in the first *Georgic*:

> But if the soil be barren, only scar
> The surface, and but lightly print the share
> When cold Arcturus rises with the sun;
> Lest wicked weeds the corn should over-run
> In wat'ry soils; or lest the barren sand
> Should suck the moisture from the thirsty land.
> Both these unhappy soils the swain forbears
> And keeps the sabbath of alternate years:
> That the spent earth may gather heart again
> And, bettered by cessation, bear the grain.
> At least where vetches, pulse, and tares have stood
> And stalks of lupins grew (a stubborn wood)
> Th' ensuing season, in return may bear
> The bearded product of the golden year.
> For flax and oats will burn the tender field
> And sleepy poppies harmful harvests yield.
> But sweet vicissitudes of rest and toil
> Make easy labour, and renew the soil.
> Yet sprinkle sordid ashes all around,
> And load with fatt'ning dung thy fallow ground.
> Thus change of seeds for meagre soils is best,
> And earth manured, not idle, though at rest. . . .
> Nor is the profit small the peasant makes
> Who smooths with harrows, or who pounds with rakes

47. 'Essay on Virgil's Georgics' in Guthkelch, A.C. (1914) *The Miscellaneous Works of Joseph Addison*, 2 vols, Bell, vol. 2, p. 9.

The crumbling clods: nor Ceres from on high
Regards his labours with a grudging eye;
Nor his, who ploughs across the furrowed grounds
And on the bank of earth inflicts new wounds:
For he with frequent exercise commands
Th' unwilling soil, and tames the stubborn lands.

    (Dryden, *Georgic* I, 100–21; 137–44, translating I, 67–83; 94–9)

If pastoral showed how pure poetry could be made by an ideal selection from nature excluding her impurities, then Virgil's post-pastoral georgic showed how the inclusion of nature's impurities need not be inimical to the poetical spirit. The *Georgics*, in fact, were often regarded, as by Addison here, as a model of what might be done with seemingly unpromising material. Nor need the raising of the natural simplicity and rudeness of a subject necessarily entail the importation of a pompous and elevated poetic diction to substitute for ordinary words. There is no mistaking the reality of things being referred to in these precepts concerning the need to rotate crops and use manure to enhance the productivity of barren soil. In the phrases 'significance of expression', 'pomp of verse' and 'rustic majesty', Addison is not confining himself to diction but summing up the total effect brought about by Virgil's metrical mastery and management of emphasis. It is the *delivery* that is grand. This grandeur is partly a consequence of the deployment of figurative language in its widest sense. This is the means by which, in Dryden's phrase, Virgil 'maintains majesty in the midst of plainness'.[48] But just as a delicate touch of the plough is prescribed for barren soil, so it is an artistic principle inherent in Virgil's georgic style that the poet/ploughman (to continue Addison's figure) must be sparing in his use of the ornaments of art when the nature of his subject matter is simple and rude.

    As both Elyot and Addison suggest, an artful variety in the larger design and in the particular parts is one of the causes of Virgil's success in the georgic that we may see reflected in the version of his translator. In the first six lines, ornament is provided by the star sign, by the animation of the weeds and by the vivid activity of the barren sand. Dryden's happy addition of the swain keeping 'the sabbath of alternate years' is the most

48. 'Preface to *Sylvae*', Watson, G. (1962) vol. 2, p. 22.

daring figure in the passage used to bring out its main point, and helped by the extension of figurative language in the 'unhappy soils' and 'the spent earth' that will 'gather heart again'. The language is then plain until the climactic periphrasis: 'the bearded product of the golden year' where the imagery is both pictorial and figurative in suggesting profitable fruitfulness, thus emphasising a major theme of the work. The rest of the passage reverts to the plain style for plain precept, and throughout Dryden has followed Virgil in using the basic vocabulary of prose. In the second passage, after the play on 'profit' (similar to that on 'product'), the language is plain until the chain of figurative verbs – 'inflicts', 'Commands' and 'tames' – which develops Virgil's *imperat arvis* (99) 'he gives orders to the fields'. Again the figurative language emphasises one of the main georgic themes, the dominion of man in the cultivation of nature. It may be said that the art of georgic consists very much in a judicious control of transitions from the plain to the figurative and its decorum in a matching of language to subject wherein the figurative is reserved expressly to highlight main themes.

Virgil's *Georgics* were not often imitated directly in the Renaissance (in the sense that they inspired poems on farming) but they were much read and the georgic style may be discerned in poems that do not have georgic themes.[49] But they did provide one of the main sources for the classical idea of the 'happy man', specifically the happy countryman, an ideal that surfaces in many poems of retirement, particularly in the seventeenth century.[50]

The happy man of Cowley's georgic

Abraham Cowley, after a dangerous and disappointing career in royal service, turned to the classics for consolation in his own retirement from the world in his last years, after the Restoration of Charles II.

---

49. See Fowler, A., 'The Beginnings of English Georgic' in Lewalski, B.K. (ed.) (1986) *Renaissance Genres*, Harvard University Press, Cambridge, Mass. and London, pp. 105–25.
50. See Rostvig, M. (1954) *The Happy Man: Studies in the Metamorphosis of a Classical Ideal*, vol. I, 1600–1700, Oslo University Press, Oslo.

Blest be the man (and blest is he) whom e're
(Placed far out of the roads of hope or fear)
A little field, and little garden feeds;
The field gives all that frugal nature needs,
The wealthy garden liberally bestows
All one can ask, when she luxurious grows.
The specious inconveniences that wait
Upon a life of business, and of state
He sees (nor does the sight disturb his rest)
By fools desired, by wicked men possessed.
Thus, thus (and this deserved great Virgil's praise)
The old Corycian yeoman passed his days . . .
So let me act, on such a private stage,
The last dull scenes of my declining age . . .

('The Country Life')[51]

Among a number of free versions of poems of moral reflection
from Horace and Martial in particular, included in essays on such
topics as liberty, solitude, obscurity, the garden, and greatness, is
a version at the end of the essay *Of Agriculture* of the closing 80
lines of Virgil's second *Georgic*.

O fortunatos nimium, sua si bona norint
agricolas!

(II, 458–9)

(O happy farmers, too happy, if they knew their blessings!)

Oh happy, (if his happiness he knows)
The country swain, on whom kind heaven bestows
At home all riches that wise Nature needs;
Whom the just earth with easy plenty feeds.
'Tis true, no morning tide of clients comes,
And fills the painted channels of his rooms,
Adorning the rich figures, as they pass,
In tap'stry wrought, or cut in living brass; . . .
Instead of these his calm and harmless life
Free from the alarms of fear, and storms of strife,
Does with substantial blessedness abound,
And the soft wings of peace cover him round:

51. One of the poems appended to his essay 'Of Agriculture' in Waller, A.R.
     (ed.) (1906) *Abraham Cowley: Essays, Plays and Sundry Verses*, Cambridge
     University Press.

Through artless grots the murmuring waters glide;
Thick trees both against heat and cold provide,
From whence the birds salute him; and his ground
With lowing herds, and bleating sheep does sound;
And all the rivers, and the forests nigh
Both food and game, and exercise supply.
Here a well hardened active youth we see
Taught the great art of cheerful poverty.
Here, in this same place alone, there still do shine
Some streaks of love, both human and divine.
From hence Astraea took her flight, and here
Still her last footsteps upon earth appear.

In Cowley's Virgil, the grim vision of Hesiod has been softened into a happy idyll recalling the golden age when Astraea still lived in a world of peace and innocence. The country, contrasted as in pastoral to the court or city, is a *locus amoenus* that provides a healthy life in which nature rewards man's labours and teaches him to be content with the satisfaction of his basic needs. The poet then expresses his highest aspiration: as priest of the Muses to see into the mystery of things and understand the processes of nature. If the destiny of the philosopher-poet is beyond his reach (an aspiration in large measure fulfilled in the *Georgics* themselves) then the next best thing is the life of rural retirement:

> let woods and rivers be
> My quiet though inglorious destiny;
> In life's cool vale let my low scene be laid;
> Cover me, gods, with Tempe's thickest shade.

In the original, Virgil proceeds to praise the philosophic poet in lines often thought to refer to Lucretius who, in his *De rerum natura*, brought the enlightenment of Epicurean philosophy to Rome:

> felix qui potuit rerum cognoscere causas,
> atque metus omnes et inexorabile fatum
> subiecit pedibus strepitumque Acherontis avari.
>
> (490–2)

(Happy the man who has been able to discern the causes of things, and has subjected beneath his feet all fears and inexorable fate and the noise of greedy Acheron.)

In his Garden, Epicurus pursued his ideal of pleasure and happiness in living a concealed life of philosophic contemplation in tranquillity and unconcern for the world. A materialist who does not believe in any survival of the 'soul', the Epicurean is freed from the superstitious fear of death (tales of Acheron). On the other hand, the man of knowledge who is impervious to the blows of fortune sounds like the self-sufficient and invincible Stoic who puts all the courage of his conviction in the validity of his own *virtus*, and this is the interpretation given to the lines by Cowley prompted doubtless by his own experience and temperament:

> Happy the man, I grant, thrice happy be
> Who can through gross effects their causes see:
> Whose courage from the depths of knowledge springs,
> Nor vainly fears inevitable things
> But does his walk of virtue calmly go
> Through all th' alarms of death and hell below.

Even if he does not know it, Virgil's countryman leads a practical working equivalent of this philosophic life in which, we may say, the harshness of the Stoic is tempered a little by the softness of the Epicurean (his countrymen have holidays in which they drink, and enjoy sport, 527–31). This blend, inclining more to the Epicurean, is apparent in other ideals of the good life, notably in Horace, another lover of the fields and woods, happy away from Rome on his Sabine farm. Here Cowley inclines to the Stoic:

> Happy! but next such conquerors, happy they
> Whose humble life lies not in fortune's way
> They unconcerned from their safe distant seat,
> Behold the rods and sceptres of the great.
> The quarrels of the mighty without fear,
> And the descent of foreign troops they hear.
> Nor can even Rome their steady course misguide,
> With all the lustre of her perishing pride.
> Them never yet did strife or avarice draw,
> Into the noisy markets of the law,
> The camps of gowned war, nor do they live
> By rules or forms that many mad men give.
> Duty for Nature's bounty they repay,
> And her sole laws religiously obey. . . .
> From such firm footing Rome grew the world's head

Such was the life that even till now does raise
The honour of poor Saturn's golden days: . . .
Before new ways of perishing were sought
Before unskilful death on anvils wrought.

So Virgil provided a philosophical underpinning for the country
life, and, as priest of the Muses, called upon his rich and
sophisticated readers of metropolitan Rome to look back to their
past and return to nature. To many seventeenth-century poets
who could make the choice, this poetic version of the happy
country life, associated with contemplation and knowledge,
whether of nature or the self, was both a consolation in times of
upheaval in the civil order and a sanction for their own
withdrawal from the world of affairs.

Augustan georgic

Virgil's idealisation of the country life, like the pastoral alternative, is partly a reaction against the complexities of the modern
urban world that has grown out of it and turned its back upon it.
It is also intimately bound up with a deep yearning for peace in
the wake of two major civil wars that had seriously disrupted the
life of the Italian countryside. The *Georgics* were published in
29 BC, two years after the battle of Actium which finally settled
the Caesarean succession. The first *Georgic* (which may have been
written earlier) closes with a fervent prayer to the gods of the
Roman state for the preservation of the youthful Caesar
(Augustus) who, it is implied, is the guarantor of the peace
necessary to uphold the rural order (the regeneration of rural Italy
became official Augustan policy):

quippe ubi fas versum atque nefas, tot bella per orbem,
tam multae scelerum facies: non ullus aratro
dignus honos, squalent abductis arva colonis,
et curvae rigidum falces conflantur in ensem.

(I, 505–8)

(for here right and wrong are inverted; there are so many wars
throughout the world and so many species of wickedness: there is no
honour worthy of the plough, the fields, their cultivators removed, go
wild, and the curved pruning hooks are forged into stiff swords.)

At the close of the fourth book, Virgil returns to the praise of
Caesar as the prince of peace who is restoring the golden age to
Italy (a more acceptable hyperbole, given the historical context
and the verdict of history, than most of the hyperbolic praise of
those who have applied the imagery to later princes):

> Thus have I sung of fields and flocks and trees
> And of the waxen work of lab'ring bees;
> While mighty Caesar, thund'ring from afar,
> Seeks on Euphrates' banks the spoils of war:
> With conquering arts asserts his country's cause,
> With arts of peace the willing people draws:
> On the glad earth the golden age renews,
> And his great father's path to heaven pursues.
> While I at Naples pass my peaceful days
> Affecting studies of less noisy praise;
> And bold, through youth, beneath the beechen shade,
> The lays of shepherds, and their loves have played.
> (Dryden, *Georgic* IV, 807–18)

> illo Vergilium me tempore dulcis alebat
> Parthenope, studiis florentem ignobilis oti,
> carmina qui lusi pastorum audaxque iuventa,
> Tityre, te patulae cecini sub tegmine fagi.
> (IV, 563–6)

> (at that time sweet Naples nourished me, Virgil, flourishing in studies
> of ignoble ease; me who amused myself with the songs of shepherds,
> and, bold in youth, sang of you, Tityrus, beneath the shady cover of a
> spreading beech.)

The poet flourishing privately in studious ease quietly juxtaposes
himself with the triumphant Caesar achieving great things in the
public sphere, by virtue of which that flourishing ease is possible.
In the Roman order of things Caesar has the glory, not Caesar's
poet; that the *otium* is ignoble is not perhaps merely the irony of
modesty. Yet in the ideal Augustan order the antithesis between
public and private worlds is not finally antagonistic. The
harmonious poise of the ending here is a triumph alike for Caesar
and his poet.

In the later *Aeneid*, by contrast, there is an antagonistic
antithesis between the inner world of private happiness and
historical impulsions from without. It is felt throughout, but

nowhere more poignantly than in primitive Italy where the rural bliss of the simple king Evander is rudely shattered by the war between the native Italians and incoming Trojans. (Spenser uses pastoral in his epic in a similar though simpler way.) This memorable episode, in which Aeneas travels up the Tiber to Evander's settlement at Pallanteum, the site of Rome that is to be, is recalled by Cowley in his essay, *Of Agriculture*:

> among the Romans we have in the first place, our truly divine Virgil, who, though by the favour of Maecenas and Augustus, he might have been one of the chief men of Rome, yet chose rather to employ much of his time in the exercise, and much of his mortal wit in the praise and instructions of a country life, who though he had written before whole books of Pastorals and Georgics could not abstain in his great and imperial poem from describing Evander, one of his best princes, as living justly after the homely manner of an ordinary countryman. He seats himself on a throne of maple, and lays him but upon a bear's skin, the kine and oxen are lowing in his courtyard, the birds under the eaves of his window call him up in the morning, and when he goes abroad, only two dogs go along with him for his guard: at last when he brings Aeneas into his royal cottage, he makes him say this memorable compliment, greater than ever yet was spoken at the Escurial, the Louvre or our Whitehall.

> haec (inquit) limina victor
> Alcides subiit, haec illum regia cepit,
> aude, hospes, contemnere opes, et te quoque dignum
> finge deo, rebusque veni non asper egenis.
>
> (VIII, 362–5)

> This humble roof, this rustic court (said he)
> Received Alcides crowned with victory.
> Scorn not (great guest) the steps where he has trod,
> But contemn wealth, and imitate a god.

Evander addresses the Trojan Aeneas as the leader of an opulent and luxurious civilisation from the east. Symbolically the moment has been regarded as representing the 'Romanisation' of Aeneas who is to embrace the more austere and simple values of agrarian Italy. For present purposes, it may be remarked that in the epic is the most thorough presentation of all the factors in human experience and psychology that thwart and contaminate the dreams of happiness entertained in Virgilian pastoral and georgic.

Chapter 5

Ovidian Genres: The Epyllion, the Love Elegy and the Heroic Epistle

> *Holofernes.* Here are only numbers ratified; but for the elegancy, facility and golden cadence of poetry, *caret.* Ovidius Naso was the man. And why indeed, 'Naso'[1] but for the smelling out the odoriferous flowers of fancy, the jerks of invention? *Imitari* is nothing: so doth the hound his master, the ape his keeper, the tired horse his master.
>
> (Love's Labour's Lost, IV, ii, 115–20)

> As the soul of Euphorbus was thought to live in Pythagoras so the sweet witty soul of Ovid lives in mellifluous and honey-tongued Shakespeare; witness his Venus and Adonis, his Lucrece, his sugared sonnets among his private friends etc.
>
> (Francis Meres, Palladis Tamia)[2]

Shakespeare's schoolmaster Holofernes, using Ovid as a touch-stone to dismiss the highly conceited love sonnet of Berowne, expresses the general enthusiasm of his times as well as the particular regard of his creator (whatever the truth about his small Latin) for this staple of the grammar-school curriculum. Ovid's facility made him the easiest of the Augustans; his subject matter, at least in the *Metamorphoses*, had immediate imaginative appeal and provided more varied stimulus for poets and painters than perhaps any other classical author in the Renaissance.

In England, Golding's translation of the *Metamorphoses* published in 1567 was a popular text frequently reprinted and known to Shakespeare. Marlowe's translations of Ovid's Elegies, traditionally attributed to his Cambridge years 1580–84 though they

---

1. Naso, the cognomen of Ovid, is also the Latin word for nose.
2. Smith, G.G. (1904) vol. 2, p. 317.

were not published until after his death, must have circulated in manuscript and are probably the catalyst that gave rise to a burst of enthusiasm for Ovidian poems beginning with Lodge's *Glaucus and Scylla* (1589) and including Marlowe's *Hero and Leander* and Shakespeare's *Venus and Adonis*, both of 1593. Though Meres mentions the sonnets in which there are Ovidian echoes particularly of the speech of Pythagoras from the fifteenth book of the *Metamorphoses* on the subject of mutability, it is the narrative poems in which the Ovidian debt is most obvious in Shakespeare's case, though there are many traces and echoes of Ovid in his plays, from early comedies like *A Midsummer Night's Dream* with its comic version of Pyramus and Thisbe right through to *The Tempest* and Prospero's great address to the spirits as he relinquishes his art which draws upon Medea's invocation:

> Ye airs and winds, ye elves of hills, of brooks, of woods alone,
> Of standing lakes, and of the night, approach ye everychone.
> Through help of whom (the crooked banks much wondring at the
>   thing)
> I have compelled streams to run clear backward to their spring.
> By charms I make the calm seas rough and make the rough seas plain
>   And cover all the sky with clouds and chase them thence again.
> By charms I raise and lay the winds, and burst the viper's jaw.
> And from the bowels of the earth both stones and trees do draw.
> Whole woods and forests I remove: I make the mountains shake
> And even the earth itself to groan and fearfully to quake.
> I call up dead men from their graves: and thee O lightsome moon
> I darken oft, though beaten brass abate thy peril soon.
> Our sorcery dims the morning fair, and darks the sun at noon.
>   (Golding, VII, 265–77)[3]

> Ye elves of hills, brooks, standing lakes, and groves;
> And ye that on the sands with printless foot
> Do chase the ebbing Neptune, and do fly him
> When he comes back; you demi-puppets that
> By moonshine do the green sour ringlets make,
> Whereof the ewe not bites; and you whose pastime
> Is to make midnight mushrooms, that rejoice

3. Quotations are taken from Nims, J.F. (ed.) (1965) *Ovid's Metamorphoses: The Arthur Golding Translation*, Macmillan, New York. For comment on the translation see 'Golding's Ovid' in Braden, G. (1978) *The Classics and English Renaissance Poetry*, Yale University Press, New Haven and London, pp. 1–55.

To hear the solemn curfew; by whose aid –
Weak masters though ye be – I have bedimmed
The noontide sun, called forth the mutinuous winds,
And 'twixt the green sea and the azured vault
Set roaring war. To the dread rattling thunder
Have I given fire, and rifted Jove's stout oak
With his own bolt; the strong-based promontory
Have I made shake, and by the spurs plucked up
The pine and cedar. Graves at my command
Have waked their sleepers, op'd, and let 'em forth
By my so potent art.

(V, i, 33–50)

Although Ovid is praised by Holofernes as Shakespeare himself was praised by Milton as 'fancy's child', a poet of instinctive natural genius who makes us feel that *imitari* is nothing, Prospero's speech on the nature of his art shows only too well that even for the master of invention *imitari* is something. The potency of Shakespeare's art makes Golding's seem rough, but his translation is the medium through which Ovid's material comes to be given new form in one of the myriad metamorphoses undergone by its various elements in the poet's rich after-life in the Middle Ages and the Renaissance.

The organisation of this chapter reflects the chronological sequence of Ovidian influence in English, beginning with the early formative translations of Golding and Marlowe, before discussing related Ovidian poems, which are treated in roughly the order of their composition, beginning with the Elizabethans and concluding in the Restoration.

The *Metamorphoses*

As a poetic handbook of mythology, the *Metamorphoses* is one of the world's great source-books which has had a general influence that has been deeply assimilated. It also specifically gave rise to the Elizabethan minor epic or epyllion. The use of the Greek word *epyllion* (a diminutive of *epos*, epic) to describe a brief narrative featuring heroic personages in hexameter verse appears to be modern. It is a shorthand term more convenient than 'short mythological hexameter narrative'. The form it describes is

Hellenistic in origin; its deployment and popularity are part of the Alexandrian reaction against the grand in form and conception. An early epyllion is Theocritus's Idyll XIII featuring the story of Heracles and Hylas, emphasising the affection of the former for the latter and portraying the muscular Heracles in a softer and more tender light. One of the most famous of epyllia (no longer surviving) was the *Hecale* of Callimachus featuring Theseus and his victory over the bull of Marathon. Callimachus emphasised not the heroic victory but the heroic poverty of Hecale who gave the hero hospitality on his way to Marathon. The scene of the rustic meal occurs in Ovid in the story in which Baucis and Philemon unwittingly entertain the gods in disguise (VIII, 602ff.). These two epyllia are typical in the psychological interest (especially in relation to *eros*) and in the dwelling upon picturesque details of description. Not only is the narrative shorter than epic but the heroic element is also diminished in the epyllion. Callimachus, despite his aversion to large books, composed a 7,000-line narrative poem in elegiac couplets on causes, the *Aetia*, which seems to have featured a number of aetiological legends connected with Greek history, customs and rites and which is the kind of poem that inspired Ovid's work on the Roman calendar, the *Fasti*. Callimachus has some mythological tales in the *Aetia*, but the idea of coupling a succession of short mythological narratives into a longer poem united by the theme of metamorphosis seems to have been Ovid's own.

The scope and design of Ovid's *Metamorphoses* are apparent in the opening lines:

> Of bodies changed to various forms I sing:
> Ye gods, from whom these miracles did spring,
> Inspire my numbers with celestial heat;
> Till I my long laborious work complete,
> And add perpetual tenor to my rhymes,
> Deduced from nature's birth to Caesar's times.
>
> (Dryden)[4]

Altogether there are about 150 stories and about 200 metamorphoses, starting with the transformation of chaos into the world

---

4. Dryden's translations from Ovid's *Metamorphoses* can be found in vols 2 and 4 of Kinsley, J. (ed.) (1958) *The Poems of John Dryden*, 4 vols, Oxford University Press. See also note 8 below.

created by *deus* or *natura* and ending with the transformation of Julius Caesar into a comet.

Although it has been called an epic (and the poem certainly has scale), the *Metamorphoses* differs from the great classical epics the *Iliad*, the *Odyssey* and the *Aeneid* in its multi-faceted and fabulous theme and in its linear construction. The fabulous element in the normative classical epics is usually confined to episodes in past narratives and is not part of the main plot in which the free agency of the protagónists is emphasised. The distance of Ovid from the traditional ethos of the heroic poem may be suggested in the adverse criticism frequently attracted by the single metamorphosis in Virgil's *Aeneid* whereby the Trojan ships are changed into sea-nymphs (IX, 80ff.), on the grounds that it violates nature. And far from beginning *in medias res* at some critical point in a single great action, Ovid's *perpetuum carmen* (I, 4) begins at the beginning. In its multiplicity of stories and characters the poem lacks the concentrated unity of classical epic. Even though some stories are enclosed within others, they flow easily from one to another with little interrelation so that it is possible with the help of an index or table of contents to dip into the work at any point. It has probably been more often read in this way than as a continuous narrative and has functioned particularly in the Renaissance as a poetic handbook of classical, that is largely Greek, myth.

The connection with the Roman present is not, as it is in the *Aeneid*, central to the design and meaning of the whole work. It occurs first in the penultimate book where, after the Trojan narrative, Aeneas lands in Italy. Virgil's Trojan hero is not accorded an emphatic role in Ovid as the narrative of his adventures is persistently interrupted with other mythological tales. The inclusion of Julius Caesar, the only Roman historical figure in the poem, occurs in the final book and is a convenient way of rounding it off. Even here the poet reserves his last words to claim his own immortality. Unlike Virgil and Horace, therefore, Ovid is not concerned with what might be called Roman values.

In some respects Ovid in the *Metamorphoses* may be said to be nearer to Homer than to Virgil, for while Virgil makes Homer's gods into dignified figures who are concerned with the grand issues of human history, Ovid depicts them in the more detached serio-comic fully anthropomorphic form in which we find them in the *Iliad* where divine motives and divine behaviour are usually entirely self-centred and only too human. In the opening book of the *Iliad*, for example, Zeus is both dignified and all-powerful when he assents to the plea of Thetis that the Trojans be granted success so that the Greeks will rue their treatment of her son Achilles. The grand description of his assenting nod that shakes Olympus (I, 528–30) is said to have inspired the famous statue of Olympian Zeus sculptured by Pheidias that was one of the seven wonders of the ancient world. On the other hand, soon afterwards we see him henpecked by Hera (who is suspicious of his relations with Thetis) to the extent that he loses his temper and threatens to throw her off Olympus. Their son Hephaestus has to intervene to cool things down. This dichotomy is if anything accentuated in Ovid where Jupiter is solemn and magisterial when he organises the flood because the world has grown too wicked, but seen in a quite different light as the philandering male later in the book when he pursues the beautiful maiden Io. Homer does not show Zeus behaving badly in this way, though we are aware of his reputation, but in Ovid we see him engaged in a prolonged cat and mouse game to outwit and deceive his wife Juno.

He first creates the cover of a cloud so that his pursuit of the nymph will not be seen. After his prolonged absence during which he accomplishes the object of his designs, Juno becomes suspicious and descends to investigate, whereupon, to cover up his wicked deed, he turns poor Io into a cow. Still suspicious, Juno admires the beauty of the heifer and cleverly solicits Jupiter to present it to her as a gift. She then delivers her present to Argus to watch over with his hundred eyes. Not to be thwarted, Jupiter enlists the aid of Mercury who lulls Argus to sleep by telling him the tale of Pan and Syrinx. At the end of the story, all one hundred eyes are shut, whereupon Mercury cuts off his head. His eyes Juno scatters on the tail of her peacock. Before Jupiter can turn Io back into a nymph, Juno sends a gadfly to torment her. In her flight, she swims the Ionian sea which takes its name from her. Eventually there is a settlement. Juno consents to the release of Io on the condition that Jupiter will have nothing further to do with her. Here is the comedy of Olympus and an even more grotesque incongruity between the upper and lower natures of Jupiter than we find in Homer. But there is not only comedy but also cruelty and torment in the treatment of Io who, quite apart from having to yield to Jupiter, retains her human consciousness as she is forced to eat grass and chew the cud like any other ruminant before being driven over land and sea by a gadfly. There are several moments in Ovid's narrative where comedy yields to pathos in her own reactions to her plight and those of her distraught father. Characteristically Ovidian is the combination of the grotesque, the comic, the cruel and the pathetic.

When Jupiter takes the form of a bull to court Europa, Ovid intervenes in the narrative to remark that majesty and love do not go well together, humorously highlighting the dichotomy but leaving the reader to draw any moral about the relation between the human and animal:

> Between the state of majesty and love is set such odds,
> As that they cannot dwell in one. The sire and king of gods
> Whose hand is armed with triple fire, who only with his frown
> Makes sea and land and heaven to quake, doth lay his sceptre down
> With all the grave and stately port belonging thereunto:
> And putting on the shape of bull (as other cattle do)
> Goes lowing gently up and down among them in the field
> The fairest beast to look upon that ever man beheld.
>
> (Golding, II, 1057–64, translating 847–51)

There follows (what Golding's last line well promises) an engaging description of the animal's great beauty and gentleness designed to attract the fair maiden and to mitigate the bestial in its romantic glamour.

In these stories Jupiter is quite immoral but elsewhere Juno herself is no better, proving quite malicious in her treatment of Tiresias in a short tale which shows us the rules of transformation:

> They say that Jove disposed to mirth as he and Juno sat
> A-drinking nectar after meat in sport and pleasant rate,
> Did fall a-jesting with his wife, and said: 'A greater pleasure
> In Venus games ye women have than men beyond all measure'.
> She answered no. To try the truth, they both of them agree
> The wise Tiresias in this case indifferent judge to be,
> Who both the man and woman's joys by trial understood.
> For finding once two mighty snakes engendring in a wood
> He strake them overthwart the backs, by means whereof behold
> (As strange a thing to be of truth as ever yet was told)
> He being made a woman straight, seven winter lived so.
> The eight he finding them again did say unto them tho:

'And if to strike ye have such power as for to turn their shape
That are the givers of the stripe, before you hence escape,
One stripe now will I lend you more'. He strake them as beforne
And straight returned his former shape in which he first was born.
Tiresias therefore being ta'en to judge this jesting strife,
Gave sentence on the side of Jove. The which the queen his wife
Did take a great deal more to heart than needed, and in spite
To wreak her teene upon her judge, bereft him of his sight.
But Jove (for to gods it is unleefull to undo
The things which other of the gods by any means have do)
Did give him sight in things to come for loss of sight of eye,
And so his grievous punishment with honour did supply.

(Golding, III, 399–422, translating 318–38)

As most of the transformations are made by the gods, it follows
that they will be randomly made. Some are punishments, some
rewards, some justly earned, some viciously inflicted; there is no
overall pattern. In this world, the poet does not seek to justify the
ways of gods to men, nor on the other hand is he an agonising or
questioning spirit seeking to make sense of it all. The stories speak
for themselves and are their own justification.

If Ovid's gods behave badly, then his heroes are not necessarily
any better. A hero can technically be described as any offspring of
the union between a god and a mortal. Heroes tend, therefore, to
excel ordinary mortals in beauty and strength, and to be capable
of superhuman feats. But excellence has its costs and Ovid does
not necessarily celebrate heroic achievement. The heroes are often
seen in the same ironic light as his gods. In the contention
between the jealous Ajax and the politic Ulysses over the arms of
Achilles (XIII), eloquence wins the day over heroic courage, as a
result of which the defeated Ajax commits suicide. In Homer, the
heroes exhibit the impulses of common humanity, but we are
invited to judge their behaviour by the high standards of Homeric
civilisation. When Achilles dishonours the corpse of Hector, he
earns the disapproval of men and gods alike; such excessive
behaviour is frowned upon. But in Ovid's mythical world, there
is no background standard equivalent to Homer's heroic code, the
only laws being those of nature. There are few examples of
admirable virtue in the *Metamorphoses*. Hercules, for example, a
redoubtable physical and moral hero, elsewhere is famous for his

choice of virtue over pleasure and for his twelve labours in cleansing the earth of assorted pests and monsters. Ovid does not mention the choice, and barely alludes to his labours. We see him instead as we see him in the tragic poets as a figure who torments others and is tormented himself. He is not therefore presented as a civilising force.

None of the traditional civilisers is so regarded in Ovid. Prometheus, who gave men fire, is hardly mentioned. Even more surprisingly in view of Ovid's self-confident dedication to his own art, the artist is not a hero in the poem either. The most famous myth featuring the artist is that of the sculptor Pygmalion who is deluded into falling in love with the beauty of his own creation, the victim of his own illusions (X). Orpheus, the very type of the civilising artist, who is also associated with advances in religion, can move nature and charm the dead, but he is chiefly a tragic figure whose magic is impotent against the fury of the Thracian Bacchanals who tear him to pieces and throw his head into the river Hebrus (X). (His impotence is alluded to by Milton in *Lycidas* (58–63).) Dark forces overcome the light.

Nor does Ovid tell his stories to express any progressive philosophy. One myth that has been interpreted as expressing the triumph of civilisation over barbarism is the battle between the Centaurs, creatures who are half horse and half human, and the Lapiths, who have a fully human form. There is a representation of the battle on the frieze of the Parthenon on the Athenian acropolis sculpted in Periclean Athens under the direction of Pheidias. The Lapith triumph is traditionally interpreted as the triumph of spirit over flesh, reason and intellect over the animal passions or culture over nature. The battle begins, in Ovid's version (XII, 210) when one of the Centaurs under the influence of too much wine tries to rape the bride at a Lapith wedding to which the Centaurs have been invited. The battle that ensues is a bloody and gory affair from which the Lapiths do not emerge with especial credit. Ovid adds a tender story in which a female Centaur commits suicide after her Centaur lover has expired in her arms having been killed by a Lapith arrow. The narrative hardly allows the story to represent the victory of culture over nature – rather the reverse. In fact the radiant clarity of the myths as Ovid narrates them expresses the darker side of the human psyche; in Freudian terms, the id without interference from the

superego, erotic compulsions and aggressive drives that are not
controlled, refined or sublimated in the course of the poem but
simply pursued as Apollo pursues Daphne until rendered
inoperative by death or metamorphosis. Ovid starts with creation
and comes down to his own times in the final book with a long
philosophic speech of Pythagoras and the transformation of Julius
Caesar. But the movement from myth to history and philosophy
does not entail a belief in progress. Perhaps there is a growth in
consciousness in that in some of the later stories characters are
more aware of their own actions and those of others. There is
great tenderness and reciprocal affection in the story of Ceyx and
Alcyone in book XI, for example, in marked contrast to the one-
sided passion of Apollo for Daphne in the opening book, and the
argument between Ajax and Ulysses over Achilles' arms in book
XIII, even if it puts these characters in a questionable light, shows
a more developed consciousness than the story in which Perseus
chops off Medusa's head in book IV. But essentially nature
changes only to remain the same.

This is an important part of the philosophy in the long speech
delivered by Pythagoras on the nature of transformation and
change in the final book. Ovid's philosopher in his detached and
general perspective communicates a calm and dignified acceptance
of the dynamic processes of mutable nature.

And since, like Tiphys, parting from the shore,
In ample seas I sail, and depths untried before,
This let me further add, that Nature knows
No steadfast station, but or ebbs or flows:
Ever in motion; she destroys her old,
And casts new figures in another mould.
Ev'n times are in perpetual flux, and run,
Like rivers, from their fountain, rolling on;
For time, no more than streams, is at a stay:
The flying hour is ever on her way;
And, as the fountain still supplies her store,
(The wave behind impels the wave before,)
Thus in successive course the minutes run,
And urge their predecessor minutes on,
Still moving, ever new: for former things
Are set aside, like abdicated kings;

And every moment alters what is done,
And innovates some act till then unknown.
(Dryden, 'Of the Pythagorean Philosophy',
260–77, translating XV, 176–85)

The Ovidian passage is ultimately the source of Shakespeare's imagery in one of his best known sonnets:

Like as the waves make towards the pebbled shore
So do our minutes hasten to their end;
Each changing place with that which goes before,
In sequent toil all forwards do contend.
(Sonnet 60, 1–4)

Contemplating mutability from the standpoint of the human individual, Shakespeare is always melancholy in the sonnets. In Ovid, nature may destroy her old but she also creates new figures in another mould. As story flows into story in the *Metamorphoses* there is the impression created of a poetic world of great and varied activity and endless radiant energy. Ovid's art is a celebration of this activity and energy.

While Ovid has no overt didactic design in the whole or the parts, the stories do not in fact appear as they might in a dictionary of mythology as neutral versions of traditional material. Let us take, for example, one of the most well known, the first extended tale featuring Apollo's hot pursuit of the reluctant Daphne and her subsequent metamorphosis into a tree, the laurel tree which from that moment becomes sacred to Apollo. Daphne is the Greek word for laurel so that there is an aetiological element, apparent too in the transformation of Argus's eyes and the journey of Io over the Ionian sea. Ovid's interest in causes, however, goes deeper than this and is more human.

The story follows Apollo's conquest of the Python, a gigantic and monstrous snake that had been a terror to newly created man. Like Prometheus and Hercules elsewhere, Apollo is here cast in the role of heroic cleanser of the earth and friend to man. Ovid, however, does not dwell upon this conquest which is narrated in a mere six lines, and it is Apollo not the poet who celebrates the deed as he comes upon Cupid flexing his bow and haughtily offers him this rebuke:

And what hast thou, thou wanton baby, so
With warlike weapons for to toy? It were a better sight,
To see this kind of furniture on our two shoulders bright:
Who when we list with steadfast hand both man and beast can wound,
Who t'other day with arrows keen, have nailed to the ground
The serpent Python so forswolne, whose filthy womb did hide
So many acres of the ground in which he did abide.
Content thyself, son, sorry loves to kindle with thy brand,
For these our praises to attain thou must not take in hand.

(Golding, I, 550–8, translating 456–62)

Cupid responds by dispatching two arrows, one to inflame Apollo
with desire and another to confirm Daphne, daughter of the river-
god Peneus and devotee of the chase, in her aversion to love. The
magic arrows introduce one of the great themes of the
Metamorphoses, the overriding power of *eros* over gods and mortals
– in this there is no distinction between them – and they serve to
prick the bubble of Apollo's pride as he is forced in helpless lust to
acknowledge the power of a greater god.

And as light hame when corn is reaped, or hedges burn with brands,
That passers-by when day draws near throw loosely from their hands,
So into flames the god is gone and burneth in his breast
And feeds his vain and barren love in hoping for the best.
Her hair unkembed about her neck down flaring did he see,
'O lord and were they trimmed' (quoth he) 'how seemly would she be'.
He sees her eyes as bright as fire the stars to represent,
He sees her mouth which to have seen he holds him not content.
Her lily arms' mid part and more above the elbow bare,
Her hands, her fingers and her wrists, him thought of beauty rare.
And sure he thought such other parts as garments then did hide
Excelled greatly all the rest the which he had espied.

(596–607, translating 492–502)

Daphne immediately flees his presence, whereupon Apollo plies
his suit, bidding her to consider the dignity of the person from
whom she is fleeing. He is no shepherd or country clown but the
talented son of Jove:

By me is known that was, that is, and that that shall ensue,
By me men learn to sundry tunes to frame sweet ditties true.
In shooting have I steadfast hand, but surer hand had he
That made this wound within my heart that heretofore was free.
Of physic and of surgery I found the arts for need,

The power of every herb and plant doth of my gift proceed.
Now woe is me that ne'er an herb can heal the hurt of love
And that the arts that others help their lord doth helpless prove.

(631–8, translating 517–24)

There is an amusing incongruity in his boasting of his spiritual powers as he is in hot pursuit of sexual gratification. It might be said that male vanity is being exploded here. It is one of the fundamental ironies of the story that the enlightened god of prophecy, poetry and healing cannot help himself. It is a fine stroke of wit on Ovid's part to make Apollo conscious of his own embarrassment. We remember the sacred command 'Know Thyself' inscribed on the portal of his temple at Delphi. He is learning to respect the power of *eros* but his new self knowledge does not enable him to do anything about it.

Daphne is not impressed, and off she flies.

And as she ran the meeting winds her garments backwards blew,
So that her naked skin appeared behind her as she flew,
Her goodly yellow golden hair that hanged loose and slack,
With every puff of air did wave and toss behind her back.
Her running made her seem more fair, the youthful god therefore
Could not abide to waste his words in dalliance anymore.
But as his love advised him he gan to mend his pace
And with the better foot before the fleeing nymph to chase.
And even as when the greedy grewnde doth course the silly hare
Amidst the plain and champion field without all covert bare,
Both twain of them do strain themselves and lay on footmanship,
Who may best run with all his force the tother to outstrip,
The t'one for safety of his life, the tother for his prey,
The grewnde aye pressed with open mouth to bear the hare away,
Thrusts forth his snout and girdeth out and at her loins doth snatch,
As though he would at every stride between his teeth her latch:
Again in doubt of being caught the hare aye shrinking slips
Upon the sudden from his jaws, and from between his lips:
So fared Apollo and the maid: hope made Apollo swift,
And fear did make the maiden fleet devising how to shift.

(641–60, translating 527–39)

This is an exciting narrative. The dexterity of Ovid as a story-teller is evident here too. He can vividly present a credible physical reality – Daphne's attempts to escape excite the lustful god even more as he catches glimpses of her naked body revealed by the wind – which at the same time embodies the larger psychological truth that denial, rejection and flight often serve to heighten desire. The animal simile involving the greyhound in pursuit of the hare (vigorously rendered by Golding) further dramatises the urgency of the chase, makes the emotions of the protagonists clear and effectively brings out the violence and rapacity of Apollo's pursuit.

Daphne's prayer to her divine father for release is answered in the nick of time:

> This piteous prayer scarcely said: her sinews waxed stark,
> And therewithal about her breast did grow a tender bark.
> Her hair was turned into leaves, her arms in boughs did grow,
> Her feet that were ere while so swift, now rooted were as slow.
> Her crown became the top, and thus of that she erst had been,
> Remained nothing in the world but beauty fresh and green.
> Which when that Phoebus did behold (affection did so move)
> The tree to which his love was turned he could no less but love,
> And as he softly laid his hand upon the tender plant,
> Within the bark new overgrown he felt her heart yet pant.
> And in his arms embracing fast her boughs and branches lithe,
> He proferred kisses to the trees, the tree did from him writhe.
>
> (671–82, translating 548–56)

There is a comic element in the timing of the metamorphosis, cheating the god at the last moment so that he embraces a tree. For the first time he becomes tender in his actions and feelings, though Daphne is constant in her aversion which is finely represented in the final swerve of the tree. In a stately speech Apollo declares that the laurel will be his sacred tree and its leaves will be the mark of the greatest achievement. The resolution of the tale is neatly achieved:

> The laurel to his just request did seem to condescend,
> By bowing of her new made boughs and tender branches down,
> And wagging of her seemly top, as if it were her crown.
>
> (697–700, translating 566–7)

The condescension is a nice touch on Golding's part, as is the felicity of the final simile, but the *seeming* comes from Ovid. It is apt in two ways, physically and psychologically. For the reactions of the vegetable world (Daphne is now a tree) cannot be fully humanised, and to have made Daphne's response to her fate (which was not of Ovid's devising) one of unequivocal joy would have been insensitive.

There is wit, humour and irony here, but it is not solely a comic tale at Apollo's expense. The ironies it contains have serious point and despite the humour we sympathise with Daphne and feel her fear in the chase, even though the tale is not presented particularly from her point of view. As to its overall point, Golding has this to say:

> in the tale of Daphne turned to bay,
> A mirror of virginity appear unto us may,
> Which yielding neither unto fear, nor force nor flattery,
> Doth purchase everlasting fame and immortality.
>
> (*The Epistle*, 67–70)[5]

In this long introductory epistle, he laboriously explains the moral content of the fables book by book, illustrating the principle that he puts forward in the preface, 'To the Reader':

> For this do learned persons deem of Ovid's present work:
> That in no one of all his books the which he wrote do lurk
> Mo' dark and secret mysteries, mo' counsels wise and safe,
> Mo' good ensamples, mo' reprooves of vice in youth and age,
> Mo' fine intentions to delight, mo' matters clerkly knit,
> No, nor more strange variety to show a learned wit.
>
> (185–90)

Allegorical interpretation of the myths goes back to archaic Greece when the first philosophers who began the Greek enlightenment challenged the mythical view of the world contained in the Homeric poems. Defenders of Homer had resorted to allegory to prove that under the cloak of his fables lurked the insights of later philosophy in disguise. When the products of the pagan imagination had to be accommodated to the overriding authority of the spiritual and moral norms of a prevailing Christian culture, allegorical interpretation of pagan myth itself became the norm and reached its apogee in the high Middle Ages with the *Ovide Moralisé*.[6] In one medieval interpreta-

---

5. See Nims, J.F. (1965) p. 407. The epistle and the preface to the reader follow the translation in this edition.
6. De Boer, C. (ed.) (1915–38) *Ovide Moralisé*, 5 vols, Amsterdam. See also Rees, C. (1971) 'The Metamorphosis of Daphne in Sixteenth and Seventeenth Century English Poetry', *Modern Language Review* **66**, 251–63.

tion, for example, Daphne and Apollo come to represent the
Virgin and Christ so that the god's donning of the laurel crown
becomes the deity putting on the flesh of his mother's body in an
allegory of the incarnation. Golding's allegories are not so
outlandish, but the habit of mind they reveal, despite the ridicule
of spirits like Rabelais,[7] continues into the seventeenth century
where it can be seen in the notes that Sandys wrote to his version
of 1632, and was not finally killed off until the enlightenment. Yet
it is remarkable how little (if at all) the translation itself is affected
by the attitudes contained in the introduction and preface. This
may be attributed to two interrelated reasons: first, an honest
desire on the part of the translator to be his author's faithful
interpreter, and second, his genuine delight in Ovid's 'fine
inventions' and 'strange variety' to which he allowed his
imagination to respond in spite of the moralising tradition and his
own Calvinism.

Golding's interpretation is not likely to satisfy the modern
reader, who is more likely to emphasise male vanity and rapacity
in relation to the power of *eros*. It is one of the fascinations of
myth that it tends to be polysemous, and Ovid is not an intrusive
narrator who tells his reader how to interpret his tales. He shows
rather than tells. Here, his narrative is swift, vivid, direct and
explicit. It is narrated in the eternal present with no allusions to
the past or the future that might impede the straightforward
narrative flow. There are magic arrows and a fantastic metamorphosis, but everything is explained. There is no mystery because
the chain of cause and effect is very clear, starting with Apollo's
initial insult to Cupid from which all naturally flows. Daphne
prays to her divine father for a change which he accomplishes
because he has promised to protect her chastity. Even the
transformation is vivid because we see the process taking place
before our eyes. It may not be a fully human world, but there is
no doubting its reality, and the similes connect the mythical
material with the familiar natural world. It is not difficult to see
why Ovid was a favourite of painters in the Renaissance.
Everything is clear in outline, physically realised and vividly
presented to the eye.

7. See 'The Author's Prologue to Gargantua' in Cohen, J.M. (translator) (1955)
    The Histories of Gargantua and Pantagruel by François Rabelais, Penguin, p. 38.

A story without humour where the ironies are grimmer is the myth of Actaeon the hunter who unwittingly catches sight of Diana, the goddess of chastity, as she bathes naked in her grotto in the woods. From the start Ovid makes it clear that it was pure *error* (III, 142) not *scelus*, a crime (in other versions he is spying on the goddess and is sexually aroused by the sight of her). Again the story is told with great dexterity. It opens with Actaeon returning from a successful hunt, and hot from the chase he seeks refuge from the heat of the midday sun. There follows a beautiful description of Diana's grotto, here represented in Addison's Augustan version:

> Down in a vale with pine and cypress clad,
> Refreshed with gentle winds and brown with shade,
> The chaste Diana's private haunt, there stood
> Full in the centre of the darksome wood
> A spacious grotto, all around o'er-grown
> With hoary moss, and arched with pumice stone.
> From out its rocky clefts the waters flow,
> And trickling swell into a lake below.
> Nature had ev'rywhere so played her part,
> That ev'rywhere she seemed to vie with art.
> Here the bright goddess, toiled and chafed with heat,
> Was wont to bathe her in the cool retreat.
>
> (translating 155–64)[8]

Nature, of course, always vies with art in Ovid; this kind of simple sophistication is a great part of his attraction. Into this cool chaste idyll stumbles Actaeon quite unwittingly. The outraged goddess promptly turns him into a stag; in his new form Actaeon flees only to be tracked down by his own hounds. The hunter is horribly hunted. Like Io he retains his human consciousness throughout and can hear his unwitting servants calling to their master to witness the kill. The pathos and cruelty that are felt mutedly in the fates of Io and Daphne are brought to the fore here. Though there are many pictures of pure beauty in the poem,

---

8. Published in the collaborative edition: Garth, S. (ed.) (1717) *Ovid's Metamorphoses in Fifteen Books*, Jacob Tonson, London. There is a modern facsimile reprint of a later edition of this translation. Orgel, S. (ed.) (1976) *Metamorphoses Amsterdam 1732 Ovid translated by Garth, Dryden et al*, Garland Publishing Inc., New York and London.

like that of Diana's grotto, the *Metamorphoses* offers more than pretty paganism.

The nature and depth of Ovid's imaginative appeal are beautifully illustrated in one of the most famous allusions to him in subsequent poetry, in the fourth book of *Paradise Lost* at the point where Milton is describing the Garden of Eden before the fall. Satan has entered the garden but has not yet tempted Eve. He looks round in wonder at the paradise which Milton proceeds to describe:

> Not that fair field
> Of Enna, where Proserpine gathering flowers
> Her self a fairer flower by gloomy Dis
> Was gathered, which cost Ceres all that pain
> To seek her through the world; nor that sweet grove
> Of Daphne by Orontes and the inspired
> Castalian spring might with this Paradise
> Of Eden strive.

> (IV, 268–75)

The primary allusion here is to the rape of Proserpina, the daughter of Ceres, the goddess of nature, by Pluto, god of the underworld, who presides over the kingdom of the dead. It is a moment when a paradise is abruptly shattered, with dire consequences of pain and loss:

> Not far removed from Enna's high-built wall,
> A lake there is, which men Pergusa call.
> Cayster's slowly gliding waters bear
> Far fewer singing swans than are heard there.
> Woods crown the lake and clothe it round about
> With leavy veils, which Phoebus' beams keep out.
> The trees create fresh air, th' earth various flowers:
> Where heat nor cold th' eternal spring devours.
> Whilst in this grove Proserpina disports,
> Or violets pulls, or lilies of all sorts,
> And while she strove with childish care and speed
> To fill her lap and others to exceed,
> Dis saw, affected, carried her away,
> Almost at once. Love could not brook delay.
> The sad-faced goddess cries (with fear appalled)
> To her companions, oft her mother called.
> And as she tore th' adornment of her hair,

Down fell the flowers which in her lap she bare.
And such was her sweet youth's simplicity,
That their loss also made the virgin cry.
The ravisher flies on swift wheels; his horses
Excited by name, and their full speed enforces:
Shaking for haste the rust-obscured reins
Upon their coal-black necks and shaggy manes.

(Sandys, translating V, 385–404)[9]

Superficially Milton is contrasting the Garden of Eden with the fair field of Enna. Doctrine requires that the Judaeo-Christian paradise far excels the imaginings of a mere pagan, however inspired may be the draughts that he draws from the Castalian spring, the haunt of the classical Muses. His own imagination, however, has recourse to pagan beauty and in the course of dismissing it the poet seeks to incorporate it as well as transcend it in his poem. Here it is the similarities that are really important. In the simile we see the fate of Eve predicted in the fate of Proserpina and to a lesser extent Daphne (who would have been raped but for the intervention of a fabulous metamorphosis). Milton echoes Ovid poignantly to suggest the vulnerability of innocence and beauty.

The art of Ovid in the handling of his mythical material has often been likened to Vulcan's craftsmanship in the poetic description of the gorgeous palace of the sun:

The princely palace of the sun stood gorgeous to behold
On stately pillars builded high of yellow burnished gold,
Beset with sparkling carbuncles that like to fire did shine.
The roof was framed curiously of ivory pure and fine.
The two door-leaves of silver clear a radiant light did cast:
But yet the cunning workmanship of things therein far passed
The stuff whereof the doors were made.

(Golding, II, 1–7, translating 1–5)

The Latin words rendered faithfully in Golding's last two lines – *materiam superabat opus* (5), 'the workmanship triumphed over the material' – have often been thought to be applicable to Ovid's own artistry, here and elsewhere. There follows a description of the fictitious world carved in relief by Vulcan on the doors. It is

9. See Orgel, S. (ed.) (1976) *Ovid's Metamorphoses Englished Oxford 1632 by George Sandys*, Garland Publishing, New York.

largely a seascape with a number of deities including Doris and
her daughters:

> facies non omnibus una
> non diversa tamen, qualem decet esse sororem.
>
> (13–14)

> Not one in all points fully like another could ye see,
> Not very far unlike but such as sisters ought to be.
>
> (Golding, 19–20)

Praise of the decorum achieved by the artistry of Vulcan in his
representation of the sisters reminds us, as does the whole
passage, of the most famous tribute to the classical artist given by
Homer in his description of the great shield made for Achilles,
also the work of the divine artificer Vulcan (Hephaestus, called
Mulciber by Ovid here). To decorate the shield, the god creates a
series of pictures, scenes from everyday life that have little to do
with the heroic world or the theme of the *Iliad*. Not all the
pictures are idyllic. He begins with two cities, which Homer calls
beautiful, one at peace and one at war. In the latter soldiers fight
and drag off their dead 'like real living men' (XVIII, 539). What
the poet admires is the realism of the picture and the ability of the
god to bring it all to life. It has the beauty of accurate and lively
representation. There are many touches that testify to the god's
ability to make the most of his materials (by using various metals
such as gold and tin) to ensure that vital details stand out clearly in
relief. In the figure of Vulcan, Homer is here celebrating his own
craftsmanship. Though the shield does have its function in the
overall pattern of the work, in its description the poet is
delighting in his art for its own sake, not for what it might bring
with it in the form of spiritual enlightenment or moral uplift.

In the figure of the divine blacksmith at the forge we may see
the poetic craftsman and wordsmith making the most of the
various linguistic resources available to him. Ovid's wit and
verbal dexterity can be well demonstrated in the fate of Narcissus.
Captivated by his own image in the water, he is at first
bewildered:

> I like and see, but yet I cannot find
> The liked and seen. O love, with error blind!

What grieves me more, no sea nor mountain steep,
No ways, no walls, our joys asunder keep;
Whom but a little water doth divide,
And he himself desires to be enjoyed.
As oft as I to kiss the flood decline
So oft his lips ascend to close with mine;
You'd think we touched, so small a thing doth part
Our equal loves! Come forth whate'er thou art,
Sweet boy, a simple boy beguile not so
From him that seeks thee, whither would'st thou go?

(Sandys, translating III, 446–55)

He then recognises the truth:

Ah he is I, now, now I plainly see
Nor is't my shadow that bewitcheth me
Love of myself me burns (O too too sure!)
I suffer in those flames which I procure.
Shall I be wooed or woo? What shall I crave?
Since what I covet, I already have:
Too much hath made me poor.

(Sandys)

iste ego sum: sensi, nec me mea fallit imago;
uror amore mei: flammas moveoque feroque.
quid faciam? roger anne rogem? quid deinde rogabo?
quod cupio mecum est: inopem me copia fecit.

(III, 463–6)

Dryden commented on this speech:

Would any man who is ready to die for love, describe his passion like Narcissus? Would he think of *inopem me copia fecit* and a dozen more such expressions poured on the neck of one another, and signifying all the same thing?[10]

It might be said that a conceited style well becomes a Narcissus. What is not in doubt is Ovid's own *copia*, his rhetorical abundance. An ancient critic remarked that he did not know when to leave off.[11] He is particularly fond of *turns* (in which Dryden

10. 'Preface to Fables Ancient and Modern' (1700), Watson, E. (1962) vol. 2, p. 279.
11. See Seneca the Elder, *Controversiae* 11, 2, 8–12. Much of this is translated in Russell, D.A., Winterbottom, H. (eds) (1972) *Ancient Literary Criticism*, Oxford University Press, pp. 358–9.

believed he excelled all poets), prominent in these extracts (as they are in the passage of Milton cited above) and to some extent caught, though not always with Ovidian grace and ease, in the couplet version of Sandys. In this respect, Dryden distinguishes the style of Ovid from that of Virgil.

> The turn on thoughts and words is their [the French] chief talent; but the epic poem is too stately to receive little ornaments . . . Virgil is never frequent in those turns, like Ovid, but much more sparing of them in his *Aeneis* than in his *Pastorals* or *Georgics* . . . I have used that licence in his *Aeneis* sometimes; but I own it as my fault. 'Twas given to those who understand no better. 'Tis like Ovid's
>
> semivirumque bovem, semibovemque virum
>
> The poet found it before his critics, but it was a darling sin, which he could not be persuaded to reform.[12]

Dryden cites an example of his own sins in the Virgil translation:

> When Lausus died, I was already slain.
>
> This appears pretty enough at first sight, but I am convinced for many reasons that the expression is too bold; that Virgil would not have said it, though Ovid would.[13]

These elegant turns on thoughts and words illustrated here in the *Metamorphoses*, the only one of his poems written in hexameters, are particularly characteristic of his neat and witty style in the elegiac couplet, the metre in which all his remaining poems are written.

---

12. 'Dedication of the *Aeneis*', Watson, G. (1962) vol. 2, pp. 238–9. The Ovidian line describing the Minotaur as 'the bull half man and the man half bull' occurs in the *Ars Amatoria* II, 24. Dryden here seems to be recalling the testimony of the elder Seneca in the passage cited in the previous note that Ovid knew his own faults but loved them. Seneca goes on to transmit the anecdote that when asked by his friends that they might delete three of his lines, the poet asked to be allowed to choose three lines to be retained. It transpired that both the poet and his friends chose the same three lines. For a defence of Ovid's wit and the pleasure Dryden took in translating it (however much he protested to the contrary in his prose) see Hopkins, D.W., 'Dryden and Ovid's "Wit out of Season" ' in Martindale, C. (ed.) (1988) *Ovid Renewed*, Cambridge University Press, pp. 167–90.
13. 'Preface to *Sylvae*', Watson, G. (1962) vol. 2, p. 24.

The love elegy in Marlowe's translation

The derivation of the word elegy is uncertain; scholars think it may be connected with a word for the flute that was used to accompany recitations of poems written in the elegiac metre. In antiquity the word is associated primarily with the metre and not with any one of the different kinds of poem for which it might be used. In early Greek times it is used for convivial, historical or military poems and for dedications as well as for the epitaphs and laments with which the word has come to be associated in English. Because Ovid's refinement of the form (which he inherited from previous practitioners at Rome such as Catullus, Propertius and Tibullus) defined its Augustan practice and became the norm for all future imitation, Ovid as a classical model for good elegiac practice had a practical importance second only to Virgil who had established the norm for good hexameter practice. Horace similarly established the normative Roman practice in the various lyric metres such as the sapphic, the alcaic and the asclepiad, but where the easier elegiac was used by many subsequent poets at Rome (including Martial in many of his epigrams) and in neo-Latin literature, it is remarkable that the more difficult lyric metres seem not to have been used subsequently at Rome and could be deployed by only the most advanced Latinists of the Renaissance. Furthermore, while the influence of classical lyric metres on Renaissance vernacular practice is not so apparent, the influence of classic hexameter practice upon the development of blank verse can be paralleled and may possibly be exceeded by the influence of the elegiac upon the heroic couplet.

The *Amores*, probably his earliest collection of poems, opens with a humorous description of the metrical form in which the love elegy is cast:

ārmă grăvī nŭmĕro vĭŏlĕntăquĕ bĕllă părābam
    ĕdĕrĕ, mătĕrĭa‖convĕnĭĕntĕ mŏdĭs.
par ĕrăt infĕrĭor versŭs – rīsissĕ Cŭpīdo
    dīcĭtŭr atque unum‖surrĭpŭissĕ pĕdem.

                                        (I, i, 1–4)

(I was preparing to sing of arms and violent wars in a weighty metre, with my matter suited to my measure. The following verse was equal to the former – Cupid is said to have laughed and to have stolen one foot.)

The poet berates the interfering god and protests:

cūm bĕnĕ surrexit vērsu nŏvă pagĭnă primo,
  attĕnŭat nervos||proxĭmŭs illĕ mĕos;
nec mĭhĭ matĕrĭa est nŭmĕris lĕvĭorĭbŭs aptă,
  aut pŭĕr aut longas||comptă pŭellă cŏmas.

(I, i, 17–20)

(My new page with the first verse [the hexameter] rose well, the next [the pentameter] took away my strength; nor do I have material suitable for lighter numbers, either a boy or a girl with long and well-groomed hair.)

Cupid then obligingly transfixes him with an arrow so that he becomes a suitable subject for the form (as yet he still has no object for his aroused passion).

sex mĭhŭ surgăt ŏpus nŭmĕris, in quinquĕ rĕsi dăt;
  ferrĕă cumvestris||bellă vălĕ tĕ mŏdis!
cingĕrĕ litŏrĕa flaventĭă tempŏră myrto,
  Musă, pĕr undenos||emŏdŭlan dă pĕdes!

(I, i, 27–30)

(May my work rise in six numbers [feet] and fall back again in five. Iron wars with your measures, farewell. Surround my golden temples with your myrtle that loves the shore, O Muse, that must be measured out in elevens!)

The hexameter is not subject to any new restrictions when it is the first line in a couplet. That is to say, the final two feet must be a dactyl and spondee (or trochee) respectively, but there may be any mixture of dactyls and spondees in the first four. The lightness of touch required by Ovid's sense of the form in the love elegy is a consequence of the preponderance of dactyls over spondees where there is a choice in the first four. In only two of the six quoted hexameters is the number of dactylic and spondaic feet equal; in two, the ratio is three to one, and in two, four to nil. Flexibility remains in the use of the caesura which usually, as in all cases here, comes in the third foot (strong) but may also come in the second and fourth (weak). Pauses of sense, of course, do not necessarily coincide with the metrical caesura; in no case here is there any such obvious coincidence. In the pentameter, the metrical pattern of the second half of the line is invariable; no spondees or elisions are allowed and there is a clear medial break between the two halves. Again this is a metrical break but not necessarily a break in sense. This is the basic pattern for the form established by the Greeks and taken over, like all their metres, by the Romans. But in adopting the Greek metre, Roman elegists gradually adapted it. In Latin elegiacs, the couplets (as here) are usually closed in that, while enjambement between the hexameter and pentameter is common (as in the opening couplet), the syntax and sense are rarely carried over from couplet to couplet. This was not the case to the same extent in the form as used by the Greeks. Also, Ovid, following a practice partially introduced by Propertius, makes the final word of the pentameter (in all but a handful of cases) invariably a dissyllable, whereas in Greek elegy there was no syllabic restriction here. This has the effect of sharply attenuating the rhythm of the pentameter into a predictably falling cadence. Organised in this way, the classical elegiac couplet, particularly in its Roman form, has an inbuilt rocking see-saw motion. The different rhythms of the hexameter and the pentameter effect the major rise and fall of the form artfully reflected in the third of the quoted couplets (lines 17 and 18). The rising rhythm of the hexameter is accentuated in line 17 by the positioning of the two dactylic dissyllables *bene* and *nova* encircling the spondaic weight of *surrexit versu*. The rhythmical attenuation and fall of the pentameter in line 18 is accentuated by the weight of the sense and rhythm in the verb, noun and spondee of *attenuat nervos*, all coming in the first half of the line. In the two halves of the pentameter, too, is a subsidiary bilateral rocking movement on either side of the medial axis. The metre is cleverly described and exemplified in the following couplet of Coleridge:

In the hexameter rises the fountain's silvery column
  In the pentameter aye falling melody back.

In the lines quoted there is great metrical variety, with enjambement between the hexameter and pentameter in the opening pair. Only in one line (27) is there a strong pause in sense at the caesura (and this is not the medial strong caesura but the weaker caesura of the fourth foot). The flexible word order of Latin in which nouns and adjectives can be separated at the beginning and end of lines makes possible a cohesive fluency well illustrated in the final couplet. But it is not difficult to see that this metrical and rhythmical arrangement will encourage a distinctive rhetorical patterning in which line is played off against line, as in 17–18 and 27–8 and where half-lines can also be emphatically contrasted in a chiastic arrangement, as in the following example.

pars adaperta fuit, pars altera clausa fenestrae;
  quale fere silvae lumen habere solent,
qualia sublucent fugiente crepuscula Phoebo,
  aut ubi nox abiit, nec tamen orta dies.
(I, 5, 3–6)

(part of my window was open, the other part was closed; such light as woods are wont to have, or the faint glow of twilight when the sun is setting, or when night has gone and the day is not yet here.)

In the first and final lines there is a strong pause at the medial caesura and on either side a deliberate antithesis between open and shut and night and day. With the antithesis comes a natural syntactical balance and parallelism. The intervening lines have a quite different rhythm and movement; they are 'full resounding' with no intermediate pause and although the first couplet is end stopped, the sense clearly continues over into the next so that overall fluency is maintained by this variety, for too many lines like 1 and 4 in proximity would create a predictable rocking-horse monotony. The challenge of the Roman elegiac consists in precisely this achievement of metrical variety within a highly disciplined regularity. The development of the metre was prompted by and itself promoted the virtuoso's delight in verbal artistry.

The rhyming decasyllabic couplet is used by Chaucer, but his couplets are not predominantly closed nor do they follow the classical elegiac couplet in their characteristic rhetorical arrangement. The first couplets to exhibit these characteristics are eleven poems by Nicolas Grimald included in Tottel's Miscellany of 1557. Eight of these are translations of Latin elegiac verse from Ovid, Martial and neo-Latin poets.[14] However, the first couplets of quality that made the Ovidian form fashionable were Marlowe's translations of Ovid's *Amores*, probably completed in the 1580s. These translations exhibited the exciting possibilities of the couplet form in a genre that provided a witty and erotic alternative to the Petrarchan sonnet. We may believe that the poems made their impact by virtue of this happy decorum of content and form, for the sophisticated and witty verbal play admirably expresses the libertine playfulness of their subject. Here is Marlowe's translation of one of the Romans' most familiar playboy fantasies:

In summer's heat, and mid-time of the day,
To rest my limbs upon a bed I lay;
One window shut, the other open stood,
Which gave such light as twinkles in a wood,
Like twilight glimpse at setting of the sun,
Or night being past, and yet not day begun.
Such light to shamefast maidens must be shown,
Where they may sport and seem to be unknown.
Then came Corinna in a long loose gown.
Her white neck hid with tresses hanging down,
Resembling fair Semiramis going to bed,
Or Lais of a thousand wooers sped.
I snatched her gown; being thin, the harm was small,
Yet strived she to be covered therewithal,
And striving thus as one that would be cast,
Betrayed herself, and yielded at the last.
Stark naked as she stood before mine eye,
Not one wen in her body could I spy.

14.   See Shannon, G.P. (1930) 'Nicolas Grimald's Heroic Couplet and the Latin Elegiac Distich', *Proceedings of the Modern Language Association* **45**, 532–42; Wallerstein, R. (1935) 'The Development of the Rhetoric and Metre of the Heroic Couplet', *Proceedings of the Modern Language Association* **50**, 186–93 and Piper, W.B. (1969) *The Heroic Couplet*, Press of Case Western Reserve University, Cleveland, Ohio.

What arms and shoulders did I touch and see,
How apt her breasts were to be pressed by me!
How smooth a belly under her waist saw I,
How large a leg, and what a lusty thigh!
To leave the rest, all liked me passing well;
I clinged her naked body, down she fell.
Judge you the rest: being tired she bade me kiss;
Jove send me more such afternoons as this.

(I, 5)[15]

It may be felt that Marlowe has wilted a little at the climax where in Ovid's penultimate line, *lassi requievimus ambo* (25) 'wearied we lay quiet', it is clear that the repose is post-coital (this is not so clear in the translation), but apart from this blemish the translator renders not only the matter but also the Ovidian manner with great dexterity. It may be doubted whether anyone had written couplets in English before with such neat parallelism, such elegant precision, such terse definition and such witty and teasing verbal play.

Ovid was well aware that his matter and manner would not please everyone; he was particularly concerned about severity of judgement from the opposite sex:

Hoc quoque composui Paelignis natus aquosis,
    ille ego nequitiae Naso poeta meae.
hoc quoque iussit amor – procul hinc, procul este, severae!
    non estis teneris apta theatra modis.

(II, 1, 1–4)

(This too I have composed, born among the humid Paeligni, I that Naso, the poet of my own wantonness. This too love commanded – far hence, far hence be severe ladies. You are not a fit audience for my tender strains.)

There seems to be a witty adaptation of a religious formula here: *procul hinc este profani* 'be hence ye profane'. The poet knew that his profanity would not please severe women and he was right.

---

15. Orgel, S. (ed.) (1971) *Christopher Marlowe: The Complete Poems and Translations*, Penguin. For comment see Jacobsen, E. (1958) *Translation, a Traditional Craft. An Introductory Sketch with a Study of Marlowe's Elegies*, Classica et Medievalia Dissertations VI, Gyldendalske Boghandel Nordisk Fotlag, Copenhagen, and Gill, R., 'Snakes Leape by Verse' in Morris, B. (1968) *Mermaid Critical Commentaries: Christopher Marlowe*, Benn.

Let maids whom hot desire to husbands lead
And rude boys touched with unknown love, me read;
That some youth hurt as I am with Love's bow
His own flame's best acquainted signs may know,
And long admiring say 'By what means learned
Hath this same poet my sad chance discerned?'
(Marlowe, II, 1, 5–10)

Ovid's word *sponsus*, 'one who has promised', is rather more open to possibilities than Marlowe's 'husbands', and the love that he celebrates in the *Amores* is 'illicit' in the sense that it is extra-marital. The beloved (not always named as Corinna) is a mistress, not a would-be wife, and in some poems it is apparent that she belongs to another *vir* (which might be her husband or simply her 'man'). In I, 4 the poet advises his girlfriend what arts and what secret love signs she might use at a banquet she will be attending with him and her *vir*. In I, 6 the lover addresses the janitor who keeps his girl under lock and key. In II, 19 the poet berates a rival for not taking more care of his *puella*, who becomes a wife in Marlowe's version:

Fool, if to keep thy wife thou hast no need,
Keep her for me, my more desire to breed;
We scorn things lawful, stol'n sweets we affect,
Cruel is he that loves whom none protect.
(1–4)

Later the poet remarks sententiously that anyone who can make love to the wife of a fool can steal sands from the deserted shore (45–6). This time the word *uxor* is used. The sophisticated society of metropolitan Rome doubtless afforded well-to-do men the opportunities to maintain a variety of relationships with women, from marriage to the use of a prostitute with much that lay in between. In I, 10 the poet castigates his girl because she has asked for money:

The mare asks not the horse, the cow the bull,
Nor the mild ewe gifts from the ram doth pull;
Only a woman gets spoils from a man,
Farms out herself on nights for what she can . . .
Why should I lose and thou gain by the pleasure
Which man and woman reap in equal measure?
(27–30; 35–6)

If Corinna or the *puella* of the poems is to be imagined as a real person, then perhaps she is a high-class lady of pleasure with whom the lover aspires to a relationship of happy equality.

After he had fallen foul of Augustus who had not liked his *Ars Amatoria* ('The Art of Love') and had banished him for some unknown *error* to the shores of the Black Sea, 'honest Ovid' 'among the Goths'[16] in later life protested to the emperor that he had been misjudged:

> haec tibi me invisum lascivia fecit, ob artes,
>   quas ratus es vetitos sollicitare toros.
>
>   (*Tristia* II, 345–6)

(This wantonness has made me hateful to you for the arts which you thought disturbed unions that ought not to be attacked.)

Lascivia, whence comes lasciviousness, can also have the lighter meaning of playfulness. He begins with a defence of the *Ars* but goes on to include his *juvenilia* as fictitious play:

> crede mihi, distant mores a carmine nostri –
>   vita verecunda est, Musa iocosa mea –
> magnaque pars mendax operum est et ficta meorum:
>   plus sibi permisit compositore suo.
> nee liber indicum est animi, sed honesta voluptas;
>   plurima mulcendis auribus apta feret.
>
>   (*Tristia* II, 353–8)

(Believe me, my moral character differs from my verse. My life is chaste, my muse is playful. The great part of my works is unreal and fictitious; it has allowed itself more licence than its author in life. Nor is a book an index of the mind that created it, but the cause of honourable pleasure. It will contain many things suited to charm the ear.)

Modern scholars have come round to the view that Corinna, who is but vaguely described even if she is a strong erotic presence, is indeed a fiction. The line distinguishing between the poet's life and the muse is a famous one. Herrick used it as the epigraph to his *Hesperides* with the translation 'Jocund his muse was, but his life was chaste'.

---

16. *As You Like It* III, iii, 5–6.

The playful jocularity of Ovid is indeed the key to his distinctive contribution to the love elegy. It has been suggested that his persona in the *Amores* parodies that of the older Roman elegist Propertius.[17] Ezra Pound alerted the world to the wit of Propertius,[18] but wit can work in a variety of ways and no one has ever described Propertius's muse as jocund.

The essential playfulness is apparent in the programmatic poems introducing the three books. In the first, the presiding genius of the love elegy, Cupid, appears as a laughing and mocking god. In the second, the poet imagines himself being interrupted in the composition of a *Gigantomachia* by the need to write verses to his beloved who has shut her door on him. The thunderbolts with which Jove defeated the giants have to be laid aside.

> blanditias elegosque levis, mea tela resumpsi;
> mollierunt duras lenia verba fores.
>
> (II, 1, 21–2)

(I have taken up the light and bantering elegy, my weapons, again; its gentle words have softened the hardest doors.)

In this fiction, the elegist woos the beloved by writing verses and pinning them upon her door as the sonneteer envisages courtship by way of his sonnets. In the opening of the third book, upbraided by Roman Tragedy, Elegy, who wants the poet for herself, characterises herself as a sophisticated go-between who makes love an exciting game:

> Light am I, and with me, my care, light love,
> Not stronger am I than the thing I move.
> Venus without me would be rustical;
> This goddess' company doth to me befall.
> What gate thy stately words cannot unlock
> My flatt'ring speeches soon wide open knock. . . .
> By me Corinna learns, cozening her guard,
> To get the door with little noise unbarred;

17. Du Quesney, I.M. le M., 'The *Amores*' in Binns, J.W. (1974) *Ovid*, Routledge & Kegan Paul.
18. In his reworkings of Propertius in *Homage to Sextus Propertius*. See Sullivan, J.P. (1964) *Ezra Pound and Sextus Propertius*, University of Texas, Austin (includes the text).

And slipped from bed, clothed in a loose nightgown,
To move her feet unheard in setting down.
(Marlowe, III, 1, 41–6, 49–52)

Ovid's lover celebrates *eros* with a frank, confident and sometimes boastful zeal:

Yea, let my foes sleep in an empty bed,
And in the midst their bodies largely spread.
But may soft love rouse my drowsy eyes,
And from my mistress' bosom let me rise.
Let one wench cloy me with sweet love's delight,
If one can do't, if not, two every night.
Though I am slender, I have store of pith,
Nor want I strength, but weight, to press her with.
Pleasure adds fuel to my lustful fire,
I pay them home with what they most desire.
Oft have I spent the night in wantonness,
And in the morn been lively ne'er the less.
He's happy who love's mutual skirmish slays,
And to the gods for that death Ovid prays.
Let soldiers chase their enemies amain,
And with their blood eternal honour gain;
Let merchants seek wealth with perjured lips,
Bring wracked, carouse the sea tired by their ships;
But when I die, would I might droop with doing,
And in the midst thereof, set my soul going,
That at my funerals some may weeping cry,
'Even as he led his life, so did he die.'
(Marlowe, II, 10, 17–38)

In an impudent and provocative inversion of the commonplace notion that love mollifies and enervates, he argues that it is the great motivator that animates and energises:

Doubtful is war and love: the vanquished rise,
And who thou never think'st should fall, down lies.
Therefore whoe'er love slothfulness doth call,
Let him surcease: love tries wit best of all. . . .
Myself was dull and faint, to sloth inclined,
Pleasure and ease had mollified my mind;
A fair maid's care expelled this sluggishness,
And to her tents willed me myself address.
Since mayst thou see me watch and might-wars move:
He that will not grow slothful, let him love.
(Marlowe, I, 9, 29–32, 41–6)

The life of love and the private world are exalted over that of the soldier and the public world, just as elegy is exalted over epic, or at least clearly distinct from it. Ovid calls his elegiacs *imbelles* (III, 15, 19) 'weak' and unfit for epic in a self-deprecating sense, but also 'unwarlike' in a more positive meaning. In III, 8 he expresses disgust that his mistress is enjoying the embraces of one who as a soldier has shed blood.

Despite the evident jocularity of the poet, the erotic life has its complexities and problems. Though he swears undying loyalty, he is indifferently responsive to dark, brown and fair (II, 4)[19] and himself strays elsewhere. In II, 7, addressed to Corinna, he strongly defends himself against the charge that he has been making love to her maid. In a comic juxtaposition, the next poem addressed to the maid revels in this deception and asks for further favours. Though he exults in the possession of Corinna (II, 12), she is not always available and proves unfaithful. In a poem not without humour but not wholly humorous our usually robust and effective lover discourses on the baffling mysteries and humiliating effects of impotence:

> Either she was foul, or her attire was bad,
> Or she was not the wench I wished t'have had.
> Idly I lay with her, as if I loved not,
> And like a burden grieved the bed that moved not.
> Though both of us performed our true intent,
> Yet could I not cast anchor where I meant.
> She on my neck her ivory arms did throw,
> Her arms far whiter than the Scythian snow,
> And eagerly she kissed me with her tongue,
> And under mine her wanton thigh she flung.
> Yea, and she soothed me up, and called me 'Sir',
> And used all speech that might provoke and stir.
> Yet like as if cold hemlock I had drunk,
> It mocked me, hung down the head and sunk.
> Like a dull cipher or rude block I lay,
> Or shade or body was I, who can say?
> What will my age do, age I cannot shun,
> When in my prime my force is spent and done?

19.   This is the source of Donne's poem 'The Indifferent'.

I blush, that being youthful, hot and lusty,
I prove neither youth nor man, but old and rusty.
(Marlowe, III, 7, in Marlowe's numbering 1–20)

In II, 14 he rebukes Corinna for procuring an abortion. The
subject provides an occasion for the exercise of his forensic wit
when the poet argues that had Venus aborted Aeneas, Rome
would have been deprived of the Caesars who are descended from
him, a pleasantry hardly calculated to endear him to Augustus.
Little sensitivity is shown to Corinna here, but he does, however,
express considerable guilt in I, 7 that he has injured her in a
physical attack.

The Ovidian love elegy is marked by two interrelated formal
features emulated by subsequent practitioners of the genre. They
are the witty deployment of argument and the use of conceits.
The first may be illustrated in I, 13 in which the poet addresses the
dawn and bids her not to hasten. The dawn is personified as
Aurora the goddess who has an aged husband Tithonus and a
young love Cephalus. The personification enables the poet to
denounce her as a tyrant and a spoilsport. In the first half of the
poem she is made responsible for all the ills the new day brings:

Poor travellers, though tired, rise at thy sight,
And soldiers make them ready to the fight.
The painful hind by thee to field is sent,
Slow oxen early in the yoke are pent.
Thou cozen'st boys of sleep, and dost betray them
To pedants that with cruel lashes pay them.
Thou mak'st the surety to the lawyer run,
That with one word hath nigh himself undone.
The lawyer and the client hate thy view,
Both whom thou raisest up to toil anew.
By thy means women of their rest are barred,
Thou set'st their labouring hands to spin and card.
All I could bear; but that the wench should rise
Who can endure, save him with whom none lies?
(Marlowe, I, 13, 13–26)

In the second half the poet makes use of mythological allusions,
which always serve to advance an argument in the elegies and are
never purely decorative, to attribute her early rising to sexual
frustration:

Would Tithon might but talk of thee awhile,
Not one in heaven should be more base and vile.
Thou leav'st his bed because he's faint through age,
And early mount'st thy hateful carriage:
But held'st thou in thine arms some Cephalus,
Then would'st thou cry 'Stay night, and run not thus.'

(35–40)

The personification allows a witty displacement and projection of his own feelings of despondency and frustration. The ingenuity is relatively simple when compared with that of Donne in 'The Sun Rising' where the sun is similarly personified and denounced. Nevertheless, in Ovid as in Donne there is a strong argumentative line that is designed to appeal to the intellect; the feelings of despondency and frustration are distanced, filtered through and therefore controlled by a playful and sophisticated intelligence.

The delight in witty argumentation which can permeate whole poems such as this is complemented by the ingenious use of far-fetched conceits. Ovid's conceits are only far-fetched in the sense that they are taken a long way in their application not in the sense that applies to metaphysical wit as defined by Dr Johnson,[20] where heterogeneous elements are yoked unexpectedly together, as in the celebrated deployment of the pair of compasses in Donne's 'Valediction Forbidding Mourning'. A favourite Ovidian conceit that is quite commonplace and comes with the imagery surrounding Cupid with his bow and arrows is contained in the opening phrase of I, 9 – *militat omnis amans* 'every lover is a soldier'; here it is extended throughout the whole poem, which depends for its effect upon the poet's ability to vary and sustain the analogy. Within the analogy is also an implied contrast: the life of the lover is superior to that of the soldier. The figure is ingeniously applied.

The delight in witty argument allied to the use of conceits has the effect of making Ovid's tone often difficult to gauge. Like Donne and for similar reasons, he is so often at the interface between humour and seriousness, and many serious-minded readers have become impatient with his cleverness. Nevertheless, his sophisticated wit and his verbal dexterity in the elegantly

20. 'Cowley' in Hill, G.B. (ed.) (1905) *Lives of the English Poets by Samuel Johnson*, 3 vols, Oxford University Press, vol. 1, p. 20.

refined couplets exerted a powerful influence on Renaissance love
poetry and the development of the heroic couplet in English.

The licentiousness of the *Amores*, however seriously or playfully
it is taken, can certainly be related to an underlying philosophy of
poetry. In elegy III, 12, for example, the poet playfully complains
that his poetry has made Corinna common property:

> The bawd I play, lovers to her I guide:
> Her gate by my hands is set open wide.
> (III, 11, in Marlowe's numbering 11–12)

He goes on to doubt whether poetry is good for much; certainly it
has been harmful to him:

> When Thebes, when Troy, when Caesar should be writ,
> Alone Corinna moves my wanton wit.
>   (15–16)

He wishes the muse had looked the other way when he had begun
(so that Corinna would not have become famous). Yet usually no
one credits what poets witness; after all, poets have created the
monsters and marvels of mythology: Scylla, Pegasus, Cerberus:

> The east winds in Ulysses' bags we shut,
> And blabbing Tantalus in mid-waters put.
> Niobe flint, Callist we make a bear
> Bird-changed Progne doth her Itys tear;
> Jove turns himself into a swan, or gold,
> Or his bull's horns Europa's hand doth hold. . . .
> Poet's large power is boundless and immense,
> Nor have their words true history's pretence.
> And my wench ought to have seemed falsely praised.
> Now your credulity harm to me hath raised.
>   (29–34, 41–4)

Given Ovid's later exile and the subsequent criticism of the
Amores, his playful rebuke of his audience for their credulity
acquires a strange anticipatory resonance. The rebuke, of course,
is not to be taken at face value. On the one hand, nobody believes
in the literal truth of the old mythological tales which he was later
to make the subject of his *Metamorphoses*; on the other hand,
everybody acknowledges the potency of their imaginative appeal,
such is *fecunda licentia vatum* (41). He is here celebrating the power
of art, in particular of his own art, but also indirectly aligning

himself with the old quasi-magical *fecunda licentia* allowed to poets from the beginning. Ovid, of course, is a great champion of poetic licence, unlike Horace whose *Art of Poetry* opens with the famous picture of the poetic monster which is designed to suggest the limits to be placed upon that licence. The Horatian warning is primarily against artistic indecorum and as such the Augustan artist in Ovid would have had no quarrel with it, but it is nevertheless the case that Ovid, though no less rigorous an artist, chose to exercise his talents with a greater freedom than his fellow Augustans.

The heroic epistle

Mention must be made here of Ovid's *Heroides*, twenty-one verse letters in elegiac couplets written by famous fictional women, except one written by Paris to Helen and another written by Leander to Hero, to which Helen and Hero reply and have the last word. The *Heroides* have much in common with the *Amores*, for Ovid is still witty and rhetorical, but he is not quite so jocular as he presents the unfortunate situations of his fictional women. He has been much praised for his sympathetic presentation of his heroines, who are characteristically forlorn and deserted and have much to complain about in the treatment meted to them by fate or by their lovers or by both. Their benign content – they lack the lasciviousness of the *Amores* – made them popular school texts and through them many pupils must have had their first experience of the comparatively easy delights of the Latin elegiac.[21]

The Elizabethan erotic epyllion: Marlowe, Chapman, Shakespeare

Marlowe's *Hero and Leander* (1592) was not the first, though it has been considered the finest, example of the Elizabethan erotic epyllion, a genre that has always been described as Ovidian in inspiration and effect. His immediate source is the Greek narrative

21.   The first translation is Turbeville, G. (1567) *The Heroycall Epistles of Pub Ovidius Naso, in Englishe verse*, H. Denham.

poem on the subject by Musaeus dating from the fifth century AD, to which may be added the letters between the two lovers in Ovid's *Heroides* (XVIII and XIX). What is immediately striking, however, is how wholeheartedly Marlowe has entered into the spirit of the pagan mythological world of romantic glamour and sensuous appeal that he so often evokes in the imagery of his plays, most memorably in Faustus's lines on Helen of Troy:

> Was this the face that launched a thousand ships
> And burnt the topless towers of Ilium?[22]

The vivid description of Venus's temple distills the essence of this radiant world:

> The walls were of discoloured jasper stone,
> Wherein was Proteus carved, and o'erhead
> A lively vine of green sea agate spread;
> Where by one hand light headed Bacchus hung.
> And with the other wine from grapes outwrung.
> Of crystal shining fair the pavement was;
> The town of Sestos called it Venus' glass.
> There might you see the gods in sundry shapes,
> Committing heady riots, incest, rapes:
> For know that underneath this radiant floor
> Was Danae's statue in a brazen tower,
> Jove slyly stealing from his sister's bed,
> To dally with Idalian Ganymede,
> Or for his love Europa bellowing loud,
> Or tumbling with the Rainbow in a cloud;
> Blood-quaffing Mars, heaving the iron net
> Which limping Vulcan and his Cyclops set:
> Love kindling fire, to burn such towns as Troy;
> Sylvanus weeping for the lovely boy
> That now is turned into a cypress tree,
> Under whose shade the wood-gods love to be.
>   (I, 136–56)[23]

The presiding genii in love's temple are Proteus, a trickster god of changing shapes and disguise, and Bacchus, the jolly god of intoxicating pleasure who is light-headed and freely enjoying

---

22. *The Tragical History of Doctor Faustus*, Act V, i, 97–8 in Steane, J.B. (ed.) (1969) *Christopher Marlowe: The Complete Plays*, Penguin, p. 330.
23. Quotations from Orgel, S. (1971) see note 15 above.

himself rather like the poet in the poem. The temple is a marvel to behold; there is cunning workmanship in the way in which it emerges that the various statues are underneath the crystal floor so that they are reflected in Venus's glass. The description recalls Ovid's temple of the sun in which the workmanship of the god outshone his materials, *materiam superabat opus* (II, 5). With due decorum the 'heady riots, incest, rapes' reflect the intoxicating power of love in myriad forms. Here we have the polymorphously perverse, love wholly unrestrained and unconfined but not necessarily the gentle and romantic love of a sentimental golden age. The first statue evokes its brazen power, nowhere better illustrated than in the amorous descent of Jove upon the imprisoned Danae in a shower of golden rain. We then see him deceiving his wife (whom Marlowe provocatively but rightly calls his sister) for gentle homoerotic dalliance with Ganymede, or ebulliently bellowing aloud for Europa, or taking a tumble with Iris (the Rainbow). The witty way in which Marlowe's words fit the mythological images and also have sexual reference is thoroughly Ovidian. The triumph of Venus over Mars is the ultimate expression of love's power turned to comedy by Marlowe, following Ovid and ultimately Homer in the *Odyssey* where Venus's unlikely husband the lame blacksmith captures the adulterous pair *in flagrante delicto* so that from heaving in the toils of love they find themselves heaving in the tangle of Vulcan's nets. From the comic bravura of his couplet on Mars, Marlowe proceeds to the destructive effect of love in the allusion to the Trojan story that gives instant credibility to love's burning power and to a claim that otherwise might seem hyperbolic, just as in Faustus's question it serves as a backcloth to evoke absolute beauty. Classical mythology provides a reservoir of imagery that is instantly accessible (given a little learning) and puts before us archetypes that are often beautiful in themselves and always beautiful representationally because of the sharp clarity of their imagined forms. After the indiscriminate power of love and from the hint of danger comes the pathos of an unhappy ending. In Ovid it is Apollo who weeps for Cyparissus, the beautiful youth who inadvertently killed his stag and thereafter pined in grief. In substituting Sylvanus, god of the woods, for Apollo, Marlowe increases the pathos of the story which acquires greater cohesion as the wood god weeps sympathetically with and for the funereal

cypress. The pleasure the woods-spirits take in the shade of the
cypress mitigates the effect of the metamorphosis and its cause in
the Ovidian manner. The images in love's temple revel in the
Protean polymorphism of Greek mythology; in quick succession
the poet paints a series of vivid vignettes, giving them continuity
with the repetition of the present participle which decorously
helps to express the eternal energy captured in the stories. The
images are decorative but not merely so; not only do they express
love's power but they run the whole gamut of love's progress in
the story from light-headed intoxication to heady riot to
destructive effect to unhappy ending with a hint of death. In the
fate of Cyparissus may be foreshadowed the tragic conclusion that
Marlowe could undoubtedly have handled had he completed his
tale.

In some respects Marlowe's creative emulation of the Ovidian
takes him beyond the Roman, notably in his extravagant
description of Hero's clothes at the poem's opening which is
almost a parody of classical realism:

> Her veil was artificial flowers and leaves,
> Whose workmanship both man and beast deceives.
> Many would praise the sweet smell as she passed,
> When 'twas the odour which her breath forth cast;
> And there for honey bees have sought in vain,
> And beat from thence, have lighted there again.
>
> (19–24)

That Hero should be 'Venus' nun' (I, 45), though a witty
adaptation of a phrase in Musaeus where she is said to be Venus's
priestess, is a sharper irony than is possible in Ovid. Generally
speaking, the comic ironies are more marked and more long-
drawn-out in Marlowe as, for example, in Leander's ignorance of
the climactic 'amorous rites' (II, 64) contrasting with his earlier
knowingness when he takes the part of a 'bold sharp sophister' (I,
97). In the *Metamorphoses*, where the tales are shorter and have
more dramatic action, an independent narrative presence is rarely
established. Marlowe, like the poet in the *Amores*, takes delight in
both teasing the reader and distancing himself from his subject
matter throughout, notably in his extended opening description of
Leander's physical beauty where he intrudes to remark:

>   but my rude pen
>   Can hardly blazon forth the loves of men,
>   Much less of powerful gods.
>
>   (I, 69–71)

The witty play on 'loves of men' which partially disguises Marlowe's meaning in the contrast with gods highlights the narrator's consciousness that his story is causing him, or allowing him, to venture into territory that is usually forbidden. Some of the most affecting lines of the poem concern Neptune's unreciprocated courtship of Leander which is handled with a mixture of light comedy and tender pathos that is characteristically Ovidian. It has always been an attraction of pagan myth that it facilitates a freedom of imaginative play uninhibited by the Christian moral censor. Since Shakespeare does to some extent blazon forth the love of men in his sonnets, it is not entirely true to say that mythological stories provided the only outlet for the surfacing of such unconventionality, but the peculiar circumstances surrounding the publication and withdrawal of the sonnets and the subsequent embarrassment they have caused perhaps suggest the obvious advantages afforded by the disguise of myth.

In these various respects Marlowe is a disciple going beyond his master. He is a disciple too in his style and rhetorical panache, in his delight in witty argumentation and the use of conceits and in his neat turns on thoughts and words accomplished in couplets that have a fluency and variety that he had only fitfully achieved in the crisp, sententious and epigrammatic style to which he had aspired in his translation of the *Amores*:

>   It lies not in our power to love or hate,
>   For will in us is overruled by fate.
>   When two are stripped, long ere the course begin
>   We wish that one should lose, the other win;
>   And one especially do we affect
>   Of two gold ingots like in each respect.
>   The reason no man knows: let it suffice,
>   What we behold is censured by our eyes.
>   Where both deliberate, the love is slight;
>   Who ever loved, that loved not at first sight?
>   (I, 167–76)

The continuation of the poem by Chapman published in 1598 is in an altogether different vein:

More harsh (at least more hard) more grave and high
Our subject runs, and our stern muse must fly;
Love's edge is taken off, and that light flame,
Those thoughts, joys, longings, that before became
High unexperienced blood, and maids' sharp plights,
Must now grow staid, and censure the delights,
That being enjoyed ask judgement;

                              (III, 3–9)[24]

Had Marlowe completed the story, his 'light flame' must have undergone a change to accommodate the tragic conclusion in which Leander drowns and Hero commits suicide. But Marlowe could never have become *staid*, nor is it conceivable that he would have introduced so clear a note of censure or judged the lovers in the manner of Chapman, who finds in their fate poetic justice and a clear-cut moral lesson. Hero has broken her vow; Leander has been incontinent in his desire; the untimely consummation of their love violates 'all states-ordering Ceremony'. Ceremony, who keeps in check Barbarism and Avarice (III, 138), is conceived as a goddess who leads Religion and whose shadows are Devotion, Order, State and Reverence (112–23). The ceremony that has been neglected is of course marriage, to the praise of which Chapman devoted 400 lines in the tale within the tale of the solemn wedding of Hymen and Eucharis.

Chapman's version is not without its Ovidian traits. When Hero tries to persuade herself that she has not really broken her vow, her conceited rhetoric might remind us of Marlowe:

That is a good deed that prevents a bad;
Had I not yielded, slain myself I had.
Hero Leander is, Leander Hero:
Such virtue Love hath to make one of two.
If then Leander did my maidenhood get,
Leander being myself I still retain it.
We break chaste vows when we live loosely ever;
But bound as we are, we live loosely never.

                              (III, 355–62)

But the comparison is to Chapman's disadvantage. The strained inversions, uncertain rhymes and lack of fluent rhythmical variety show that he could not (in 1598) write closed couplets with

<hr>

24. Chapman's continuation is also included in Orgel, S. (1971).

Marlowe's élan, and here the conceited rhetoric does not so much communicate the author's delight in his subject as show that Hero is deceiving herself. Much more successful is the periodic narrative style which Chapman can use on occasions to sensuous effect.

> Her plenteous hair in curled billows swims
> On her bright shoulder; her harmonious limbs
> Sustained no more but a most subtle veil
> That hung upon them, as it durst not assail
> Their different concord; for the weakest air
> Could raise it swelling from her beauties fair;
> Nor did it cover, but adumbrate only
> Her most heart-piercing parts, that a blest eye
> Might see (as it did shadow) fearfully
> All that all-love-deserving paradise.
>
> (IV, 25–34)

The playful description of the embroidery on what Chapman calls the 'conceited scarf' (76) which Hero had made to wear in Venus's temple would surely have pleased Ovid himself:

> There (since the first breath that begun the wrack
> Of her free quiet from Leander's lips)
> She wrought a sea in one flame full of ships;
> But that one ship where all her wealth did pass
> (Like simple merchants' goods) Leander was;
> For in that sea she naked figured him;
> Her diving needle taught him how to swim
> And to each thread did such resemblance give,
> For joy to be so like him it did live.
>
> (IV, 47–55)

But in none of the genres in which he worked could Ovid have been attracted to Chapman's moral argument. Marriage is the great bugbear of the elegiac life. In the *Heroides*, the letters written by the lovers when they are kept apart by bad weather which prevents Leander from swimming the Hellespont are full of foreboding but neither party feels any of the guilt that is prominent in Chapman. Had Ovid told the tale in the *Metamorphoses* their doom would surely have been brought about, as it is in Musaeus, by the ill chance of wind and wave. In the mythical world, characters do not obey the commandments of civilisation.

It was one of the attractions of the epyllion to the Elizabethans that it offered a holiday from morality and was a subversive genre that broke the rules. Chapman is exceptional in eschewing the freedom it offered and putting it firmly back into the framework of a traditional hierarchy of moral values.

In the year in which Marlowe wrote *Hero and Leander*, at a time when an outbreak of the plague had caused the theatres to be closed, Shakespeare turned to narrative with *Venus and Adonis* which he dedicated to the Earl of Southampton with an Ovidian motto that might suggest that the young poet desired to appeal to the taste of the rich and the famous in this newly fashionable genre

> vilia miretur vulgus: mihi flavus Apollo
> pocula Castalia plena ministrat aqua.
> (*Amores* I, 15, 35–6)

> Let base-conceited wits admire vile things
> Fair Phoebus lead me to the Muses' springs.
> (Marlowe)

> Kneel hinds to trash: we let bright Phoebus swell,
> With cups full flowing from the Muses' well.
> (Jonson)

The story of Venus and Adonis is a decorative feature of Hero's gown in Marlowe's *Hero and Leander*:

> Her wide sleeves green, and bordered with a grove
> Where Venus in her naked glory strove
> To please the careless and disdainful eyes
> Of proud Adonis that before her lies.
> (I, 11–14)

Ovid's version of the tale is comparatively short (some 70 lines if the tale within the tale which Venus tells to Adonis to warn him of the dangers of the hunt is discounted) and is presented from Venus's point of view. She accompanies Adonis in his hunting, which is his main delight. Though he does not reject her and is not, like Marlowe's Adonis, proud, it is not clear that her love is reciprocated, nor does it appear to have been consummated. The expansion and development are therefore Shakespearian. The larger dramatic antithesis (only latent in Ovid) whereby Venus's love is unreciprocated by the youthful Adonis, who would rather be off hunting with his friends, is the central donnée which occasions many Ovidian serio-comic ironic antitheses in the linguistic format of the poem:

> Poor queen of love in thine own law forlorn,
> To love a cheek that smiles at thee in scorn!
>
> (251–2)

> She's love, she loves, and yet she is not loved.
>
> (610)[25]

The fable of the erotic epyllion allows a free treatment of the transforming power of *eros* with all its anticipatory pleasures and experiential pains. There are similarities with the sonnets – the praise and courting of a superlative male beauty who is exhorted to breed (163ff.) and a disquisition on differences between love and lust (793ff.) – but the narrator, unlike the sonneteer, is detached and can enjoy the absurdities as well as representing the pains of his subject, so that Shakespeare is in ebullient mood as he represents a love affair observed and felt from the outside.

As Venus is the main character, *eros* does not mask itself as *agape*, even though she uses neo-Platonic arguments as she praises Adonis (433–50); it is her senses that are set on fire:

> But O what a banquet wert thou to the taste,
> Being nurse and feeder of the other four!
>
> (445–6)

Naturally she is a powerful proponent of venereal pleasures; nevertheless, despite her panting, sweating and aggressive wooing, all of which have excited adverse comment, what she offers is beautiful, joyous and heavenly:

> Bid me discourse, I will enchant thine ear,
> Or like a fairy trip upon the green,
> Or like a nymph with long dishevelled hair
> Dance on the sands, and yet no footing seen.

25.   The most useful edition of the poem with introductory material and a very full commentary is: Roe, J. (ed.) (1992) *The Poems*, The New Cambridge Shakespeare, Cambridge University Press.

Love is a spirit all compact of fire,
Not gross to sink, but light and will aspire.
(145–50)

Shakespeare, unlike Marston in *Pygmalion's Image* (1598), does not use the epyllion as an occasion and cover for salaciousness. Nor on the other hand does he denigrate her power; on the contrary, the poem in its copious natural imagery appeals strongly to all the senses and wonderfully celebrates the power of *eros* in the natural world in the long narrative describing the reaction of Adonis's horse to the breeding jennet that chances by (259–318):

What recketh he his rider's angry stir,
His flattering 'Holla' or his 'Stand, I say'?
What cares he now for curb or pricking spur,
For rich caparisons or trappings gay?
  He sees his love, and nothing else he sees,
  Nothing else with his proud sight agrees.

Look when a painter would surpass the life
In limming out a well-proportioned steed,
His art with nature's workmanship at strife,
As if the dead the living should exceed –
  So did this horse excel a common one,
  In shape, in courage, colour, pace and bone.
(283–94)

The description of his perfect beauty follows his arousal and precedes the devoutly wished consummation that is to come (only in the equine sphere). Beauty is here linked to *eros* and to the life force itself. The simile expresses the aspirations of the painter to exceed nature in his art as the classical artist aspires to the ideal in his depiction of the human form. The poetic challenge to the artist seeking to express the excellence of the imagined forms that populate the mythological world is to create images of beauty that sufficiently retain the natural elements which they perfect. Shakespeare meets this challenge in his depiction of the horse, which is the perfection of the essentially equine. Adonis is irritated with his unruly palfrey but Venus is able to draw on Ovidian moral:

How like a jade he stood tied to the tree,
Servilely mastered with a leathern rein;

But when he saw his love, his youth's fair fee,
He held such petty bondage in disdain,
 Throwing the base thong from his bending crest,
 Enfranchising his mouth, his back, his breast.

(391–6)

Love brings to its adherents a new freedom, confidence and power. However undignified and comic are the postures struck by the goddess, she remains a goddess and love is never bestial in a pejorative sense. The real beast of the piece is the boar.

For all her power, the goddess is unable to command a reciprocating response, and at a point midway through the poem Adonis announces his intention to go hunting the following day. This occasions a comic moment when Venus in her anxiety embraces him so forcefully that he falls on top of her:

Now is she in the very lists of love,
Her champion mounted for the hot encounter.
All is imaginary she doth prove;
He will not manage her, although he mount her:
 That worse than Tantalus' is her annoy,
 To clip Elysium and to lack her joy.

(595–600)

Unlike Marlowe, Shakespeare has not filled his poem with other mythological references, but the allusion to Tantalus, whose eternal punishment was to be faced with food and drink just out of reach, finely captures her frustration. Thereafter the comic element is subdued as Venus, solicitous for Adonis's safety, attempts to dissuade him from the hunt. Her foreboding causes dark thoughts. In a complicated argument she comes to see the fatality of beauty; in fashioning Adonis nature has played a trick:

And therefore hath she [Cynthia] bribed the destinies
To cross the curious workmanship of nature,
To mingle beauty with infirmities,
And pure perfection with impure defeature,
 Making it subject to the tyranny
 Of mad mischances and much misery:

(733–8)

Like the pastoral convention, the mythological world offers images of pure perfection which makes the contrast with 'impure defeature' (disfigurement) all the more poignant and more obviously striking than such contrasts might seem in the everyday world.

After the comedy and pathos attendant upon the frustration of love's raging but impotent desire, the poem ends in sorrow and tender pathos when beauty is finally destroyed by the beast.

> For he being dead, with him is beauty slain,
> And beauty dead, black chaos comes again.
>
> (1019–20)

The lament for beauty's death itself occasions poetic beauty.

> Alas, poor world, what treasure hast thou lost?
> What face remains alive that's worth the viewing?
> Whose tongue is music now? What canst thou boast
> Of things long since, or anything ensuing?
>   The flowers are sweet, their colours fresh and trim,
>   But true sweet beauty lived and died with him.
>
> (1075–80)

The erotic epyllion, like the pastoral, opens up a beautiful world with a strange imaginative appeal but unlike the pastoral offers a sophisticated exploration of sexual passion in all its comic and serious aspects. It affords the poet opportunities for eloquent verbal display and sensuous description, and challenges him to endow his beautiful forms with a lively psychological realism. The form was in vogue for only a short time. Its temporary demise was attributed to the powerful influence of Donne by his admirer Thomas Carew, in well-known lines of his elegy written in 1633:

> But thou art gone, and thy strict laws will be
> Too hard for libertines in poetry;
> They will repeal the goodly exiled train
> Of gods and goddesses, which in thy just reign
> Were banished nobler poems; now, with these,
> The silenced tales o' th' Metamorphoses
> Shall stuff their lines, and fill their windy page.[26]
>
> (61–7)

Although mythological narratives are indeed a rarity in the seventeenth century, the *Metamorphoses* continued to be popular.

---

26.   Dunlap, J. (1949) *The Poems of Thomas Carew*, Oxford University Press.

Sandys completed his translation in 1632. The best version, an Augustan composite put together by Samuel Garth in 1717, involved leading talents like Dryden, Congreve and Addison.[27]

The heroic epistle in English: Drayton and Donne

In *England's Heroical Epistles* (1597), four pairs of fictional letters between notable figures in English history, Michael Drayton revitalised the Ovidian form and found a poetic medium in which he channelled and expressed his historical interests more success-fully than in any other. The characters confine themselves to their immediate circumstances but, as if to acknowledge a debt to the Latin, in the opening letter in which Rosamond addresses her lover Henry II from the labyrinth in Woodstock where she was living in hiding from the jealous eyes of Queen Elinor, the poet puts his forlorn heroine in a setting and situation that deliberately call Ovid to mind.

> Here in the garden, wrought by curious hands,
> Naked Diana in the fountain stands,
> With all her nymphs got round about to hide her,
> As when Actaeon had by chance espied her:
> This sacred image I no sooner viewed,
> But as that metamorphosed man, pursued
> By his own hounds; so, by my thoughts am I
> Which chase me still, which way soe'er I fly.
>   ('Rosamond to Henry', 139–46)[28]

She also recalls a casket sent to her by Henry before she had yielded to him and is able to see her own plight reflected in the mythical scene that decorates it:

> And in this casket (ill I see it now)
> That Jove's love Io, turned into a cow;
> Yet was she kept with Argus' hundred eyes:
> So wakeful still be Juno's jealousies;
> By this I well might have fore-warned been,
> T'have cleared myself to thy suspecting queen
> Who with more hundred eyes attendeth me,

---

27. See note 8 above.
28. Buxton, J. (ed.) (1953) *Poems of Michael Drayton*, 2 vols, The Muses Library, Routledge & Kegan Paul, vol. 2, p. 447.

Than had poor Argus single eyes to see.
In this thou rightly imitateth Jove,
Into a beast thou hast transformed thy love;
Nay, worser far (beyond their beastly kind)
A monster both in body and in mind.

(163–74)

Her complaint elicits from Henry, campaigning in France, a sympathetic response in a letter in which he seeks to find consolation for the cares of kingship in the love of Rosamond. The epistles seek to reveal and unravel tensions between the public and private worlds of the authors rather than present them in a heroic light. The protagonists, though famous, are no more 'heroical' than Ovid's fictional writers, who may belong to a world of great deeds but who are seen in a more private light.

The most remarkable English heroic epistle is 'Sapho to Philaenis', printed as Donne's in 1633, though its authorship has been questioned.[29] The title, the epistolary form and the situation of its famous heroine, bereft and appealing to her lover, all recall the heroical epistles of Ovid. Within the Ovidian *corpus* is a letter from Sappho to a male lover Phaon (XV, the authorship of which has also been questioned) at the end of which Sappho announces her intention to throw herself into the sea if Phaon does not return. The English poem differs from the Latin in being addressed to a woman so that with due decorum it becomes a poem of frankly lesbian passion. In the Latin, Sappho's lesbianism scarcely features, though it was so famous that there is a brief mention of it at the beginning of the letter: 'my eyes joy not in Atthis as once they did, nor in the other hundred maids I have loved', *non sine crimine* (19) 'not without reproach'. The use of *crimen*, a criminal charge, implies social disapproval if not self-blame and the phrase in which it occurs may be regarded as a concession to conservative Roman feeling. There are no such concessions in the English poem where the story of her suicide

---

29. Helen Gardner, for example, prints it among the Dubia in her edition, questioning Donne's authorship largely on internal grounds: 'I find it difficult to imagine him wishing to assume the love-sickness of Lesbian Sappho . . . I am unable to recognise in the poem any characteristics of Donne's style' (p. xlvi), Gardner, H. (ed.) (1965) *John Donne: The Elegies and the Songs and Sonnets*, Oxford University Press. For comment on the poem see Holstun, J. (1987) ' 'Will you rent our ancient love asunder?': Lesbian Elegy in Donne, Marvell and Milton', *Journal of English Literary History* **54**, 835–67.

brought upon by a failed heterosexual passion has been discounted:

> Such was my Phao awhile, but shall be never
>   As thou wast, art, and, oh, mayst thou be ever.
>
> (25–6)

The man is relegated to the past; Philaenis (there is a record of a poetess of this name who lived some time after Sappho) takes centre stage, with Sappho becoming a powerful embodiment and proponent of Sapphic love.

This suggests a further subtle difference from the Latin. The Roman Sappho explains that she can no longer write lyric poems, which require a carefree mind; she can write only elegiac poems, for elegy is the mode of complaint. The English poem is not really a complaint in the thorough-going way that is typical of the letters of Ovid's forlorn heroines. Philaenis has gone and Sappho is indeed alone:

> Only thine image, in my heart, doth sit,
>   But that is wax, and fires environ it.
> My fires have driven, thine have drawn it hence;
>   And I am robbed of picture, heart and sense.
>
> (9–12)

But the implication here is that though Philaenis has felt similar fires and the love has been reciprocated, the intensity of Sappho's passion has frightened her into withdrawal. Sappho does not so much complain that she has been deserted like her Roman counterpart as encourage Philaenis to have the courage of her natural inclinations and instincts.

At any rate the poem is a sensitive presentation of Sappho's passion, what she calls her 'loving madness' (57), in the course of which the poet allows her to put forward a witty but dignified persuasion to love on the basis that its consummation is not only devoutly to be wished but also greatly to be enjoyed to the mutual benefit and health of both partners. Unlike Myrrha facing her incestuous passion (X, 324–31), Sappho is not torn in two directions or afflicted with guilt; she is frank, open and self-accepting. But like those of Myrrha, her arguments flout convention and appeal to nature:

Thy body is a natural paradise,
  In whose self, unmanured, all pleasure lies,
Nor needs perfection; why shouldst thou then
  Admit the tillage of a harsh rough man?
                    (35–8)

This of course is not the conventional paradise of the Garden of
Eden with its blissfully unconscious heterosexual pair, but wild
uncultivated nature before it has known the plough, the nature of
the classical golden age when love was free. The poet wittily
defends the dignity and beauty of the female body as a perfect
entity that is complete in itself and contains within itself all that is
necessary for its own pleasure. At the same time a mutual sharing
of pleasure is what Sappho desires and what she offers Philaenis.
She imagines her lover choosing a girlish boy but points out that
he is but an empty substitute who will not remain girlish for long:

Plays some soft boy with thee, oh there wants yet
  A mutual feeling which should sweeten it.
His chin, a thorny hairy unevenness
  Doth threaten, and some daily change possess.
                    (31–4)

The Roman Sappho had referred to her lesbian passion with the
word *crimen* as a subject for reproach. The English Sappho, in a
neat reversal, refers to men's love as a sin, and a messy one with
untold consequences:

Men leave behind them that which their sin shows,
  And are as thieves traced, which rob when it snows.
But of our dalliance no more signs there are
  Than fishes leave in streams or birds in air,
And between us all sweetness may be had;
  All, all that Nature yields, or Art can add.
                    (39–44)

This is indeed sweetly imagined and sweetly expressed. There is
wit and humour in the poem but it is not coarse and never
directed at women. The humour is at the expense of men, with
blind men (17), silly man (19), and there is a man in 'unmanured'
(36), a decorous stroke of wit in view of the associations of
manure with unsavoury odours and fertilisation.

Since what the poem celebrates is the mutual feeling in the
physical as well as the emotional sense that for Sappho and
Philaenis can be sympathetically provided only by a member of

the same sex, the poem offers not libertine titillation but a serious
plea for sexual tolerance and freedom:

> My two lips, eyes, thighs, differ from thy two,
>> But so, as thine from one another do;
> And, oh, no more; the likeness being such,
>> Why should they not alike in all parts touch?
> Hand to strange hand, lip to lip none denies;
>> Why should they breast to breast, or thighs to thighs?

(45–50)

The praise of likeness takes us into unusual and delicate territory:

> Likeness begets such strange self flattery,
>> That touching myself, all seems done to thee.
> Myself I embrace, and mine own hands I kiss,
>> And amorously thank myself for this,
> Me in my glass I call thee; but alas,
>> When I would kiss, tears dim mine eyes, and glass.

(51–6)

Her self-love, delicately presented, is not merely narcissistic as she
fuses her own self imaged in the mirror with that of her beloved.
This fusion of images prepares us for the conclusion of the poem
in which Sappho begs her lover to cure her of her loving madness
by returning. It is taken for granted by Sappho that the cure for
her condition is not sublimation or denial but union. Implicitly
the cure will work for them both, sustaining them in the illusion
that they can stave off the ageing process and the decay that comes
with it. The prayer that Philaenis will always be a beauty to
inspire envy and love is a kind of benediction and itself an act of
love confirming the sweetness of the lesbian vision contained in
the poem as a whole. This sweetness is brought out in the suavity
of language, the neatness of expression and metrical fluency. A
notable and decorous exception to the latter is the 'thorny hairy
unevenness' of the boy's chin, which sticks out rather promin-
ently as a consequence. All the parallelism, antithesis and balance
aptly underscore the thematic content as well as emulating the
dexterity of Ovid in his *Heroides*. The Ovidian form, rein-
vigorated with fresh content and presented in the Ovidian manner
(light, conceited and revelling in elegant turns and witty
argument), has made possible an exploration and expression of
feelings that would surely have remained unexpressed and perhaps
been unimagined without it.

English love elegies: Donne, Carew, Rochester

> An elegy? No, muse; it asks a strain
> Too loose and cap'ring for thy stricter vein.
> Thy thoughts did never melt in amorous fire
> Like glass, blown up, and fashioned by desire. . . .
> Then, leave these lighter numbers, to light brains,
> In whom the flame of every beauty reigns,
> Such, as in lust's wild forest love to range,
> Only pursuing constancy, in change.
>
> ('Proludium', 1–4, 7–10)

This neat antithetical style Jonson did in fact employ on occasions in the love elegy, but the resulting poems are not of the loose and capering kind. Ovid appears as a character in *The Poetaster* where his banishment by Augustus for daring to imitate the gods in a masquerade at a banquet is one of the central actions of the drama. Horace protests that it is but harmless play, but to no avail. Despite his words, there is little resistance to his fate. Jonson's imagination is primarily engaged with the stricter Augustans Virgil, and above all 'thine own' Horace, who are the ideal figures working in more dignified genres which they put to the service of the *civitas* and upholding the cause of poetry against the poetaster Crispinus, alias Marston, the author of a very loose and capering epyllion *Pygmalion's Image*.

For Donne, on the other hand, Ovid is probably the closest of all his poetic affinities, certainly among classical poets. His elegies have a clear generic relation to those of Ovid.[30]

> Come, Madam, come, all rest my powers defy,
> Until I labour, I in labour lie.
>
> ('To His Mistress Going to Bed', 1–2)[31]

The provocative directness of address, the frank and enticing sensuality, the witty word play, the neatness of the rhetorical organisation, all recall Ovid. His couplets may be enjambed but a majority are end-stopped and, as befits the decorum of the genre, they are smoother, neater and more consciously artful than the rough and craggy lines of his earlier satires (also in couplets). He

---

30. See Gill, R., '*Musa Iocosa Mea*: Thoughts on the Elegies' in Smith, A.J. (ed.) (1972) *John Donne: Essays in Celebration*, Methuen, pp. 42–72.
31. Smith, A.J. (ed.) (1971) *John Donne: The Complete English Poems*, Penguin.

shares with Ovid a delight in the use of conceits and in the deployment of witty argumentation, even if this delight takes him extravagantly in different directions. Common to all these poems, as to the *Amores*, is what Donne calls in his elegy 'On His Mistress' 'my words' masculine persuasive force' (4).

Commentators have identified specific allusions to Ovid in a number of the elegies. 'Jealousy', for instance, draws on the Ovidian elegy in which the poet advises his mistress how they are to pay court to one another in the presence of her husband with nods and winks and various secret signs. 'Love's War' takes up the theme of *Militat omnis amans* (I, 9) 'every lover is a soldier'. 'The Perfume' has been described as a translation into Elizabethan terms of the tone and spirit of the Ovidian elegy with the 'grim eight-foot-high iron-bound serving-man' (31) being a Donnish equivalent of Ovid's porter or guardian of the gate, an obstacle to be circumvented by the lovers.[32] There are a number of such parallels but clearly Donne's elegies are not imitations of Ovid in any close meaning of the term. What we have is a generic relation in the course of which the love elegy undergoes a transformation as it is carried over through the wit of Donne into the English Renaissance. 'Change' is an elegy which recasts Ovidian elements from the *Metamorphoses* into the more playful form of the love elegy. The argument used to support the proposition that inconstancy is the natural condition of women recalls that of Myrrha defending her incestuous passion (X, 324–31) with an appeal to nature:

> Foxes and goats, all beasts change when they please,
> Shall women, more hot, wily, wild than these,
> Be bound to one man, and did Nature then
> Idly make them apter to endure than men?
>
> (Dryden, 11–14)

The concluding assertion that 'change is the nursery (11–14) of music, joy, life and eternity' brings to mind the great speech of Pythagoras at the end of the *Metamorphoses* with its dynamic account of nature's flux. The celebration of nakedness in 'On His Mistress Going to Bed', 'Full nakedness all joys are due to thee', brings to the surface an attitude implicit in the *Amores* though not

---

32. See Leishman, J.B. (1951) *The Monarch of Wit*, Hutchinson University Library, pp. 52ff.

actually found in Ovid. The philosophy underlying the libertinism of the love elegy is argued for by Donne with a confidence
and provocative daring that go beyond his master.

Though not formally called an elegy, Thomas Carew's 'A
Rapture' has all the characteristics of the genre.

> I will enjoy thee now, my Celia, come,
> And fly with me to love's Elysium.
>
> (1–2)

The poet's Elysium is a brilliantly imagined fantasy world of
perfect erotic freedom:

> there the hated name
> Of husband, wife, lust, modest, chaste, or shame
> Are vain and empty words, whose very sound
> Was never heard in the Elysian ground.
> All things are lawful there that may delight
> Nature or unrestrained appetite.
> Like and enjoy, to will and act is one;
> We only sin when love's rites are not done.
>
> (107–14)

Those who on earth have not done love's rites are to pay for their
sins in an erotic after-life of eternal pleasure, and there follows an
impudently witty list of the chaste, the modest, the virginal and
the Petrarchan who are duly punished for their sins of denial. The
first figure subject to witty reversal is Lucrece, chastest of Roman
matrons, who committed suicide to atone for the disgrace she felt
at her rape by Tarquin. She is to be found reading Aretino, the
Italian pornographer, to provoke her attacker to new efforts.
Then we find Penelope, the faithful wife of Odysseus, forgetting
her lord and preferring the 'amorous sport of gamesome nights'
(129) with the suitors. Next Carew undoes the Ovidian
metamorphosis of Daphne, who now yields willingly to the god
of poetry and prophecy. Their consummated love inspires her to
ecstatic poetic heights worthy of the bays:

> Daphne hath broke her bark, and that swift foot
> Which th' angry gods had fastened with a root
> To the fixed earth, doth now unfettered run
> To meet th' embraces of the youthful sun.
> She hangs upon him like his Delphic lyre,
> Her kisses blow the old and breathe new fire;

Full of her god, she sings inspired lays,
Sweet odes of love, such as deserve the bays
Which she herself was.   (131–9)

The final picture in this erotic Elysium suggesting the ultimate triumph of the love elegy over the vestiges of Renaissance Petrarchanism is of Laura comforting Petrarch who is lying in her arms finding relief from his torment at last.

Next her, Laura lies
In Petrarch's learned arms, drying those eyes
That did in such sweet smooth-paced numbers flow,
As made the world enamoured of his woe.   (139–42)

'A Rapture' is a libertine fantasy of playful wish-fulfilment. Later in the century poets express an earthier affinity with Ovid[33] who, in Rochester's fine version of *Amores* II, 9, comes to speak in the accents and express the creed of the Restoration rake:

But the old soldier has his resting place
And the good battered horse is turned to grass.
The harassed whore, who lived a wretch to please,
Has leave to be a bawd and take her ease.
For me, then, who have freely spent my blood,
Love, in thy service, and so boldly stood
In Celia's trenches, were't not wisely done
E'en to retire, and live at peace at home?
No! Might I gain a godhead to disclaim
My glorious title to my endless flame,
Divinity with scorn I would forswear,
Such sweet dear tempting devils women are.
Whene'er those flames grow faint, I quickly find
A fierce black storm pour down upon my mind.
Headlong I'm hurled, like horsemen who in vain
Their fury-foaming coursers would restrain.
As ships, just when the harbour they attain
By sudden blasts are snatched to sea again,
So Love's fantastic storms reduce my heart
Half rescued, and the god resumes his dart.
                                        (19–38)[34]

33. See Love, H., 'The Art of Adaptation: Some Restoration Treatments of Ovid' in Coleman, A., Hammond, A. (eds) (1981) *Poetry and Drama 1570–1700: Essays in Honour of Harold F. Brooks*, Methuen, pp. 136–55.
34. Vieth, D.M. (ed.) (1968) *The Complete Poems of John Wilmot Earl of Rochester*, Yale University Press, New Haven and London.

In 'The Disabled Debauchee' Rochester's wit takes the love/war conceit about as far as it can go in comparing himself, as days of impotence approach, to a superannuated admiral too old for the fight. Reliving old battles:

> I'll tell of whores attacked, their lords at home,
>   Bawds quarters beaten up, and fortress won:
> Windows demolished, watches overcome
>   And handsome ills by my contrivance done.
>
> (33–6)

The theme of 'The Imperfect Enjoyment' echoes that of *Amores* III, 7 (cited earlier in Marlowe's version), except that the impotence it laments is preceded by premature ejaculation. He can perform with a common jade but not with the current superior flame:

> Trembling, confused, despairing, limber, dry
> A wishing, weak, unmoving lump I lie.
> This dart of love, whose piercing point, oft tried
> With virgin blood, ten thousand maids has dyed;
> Which nature still directed with such art
> That it through every cunt reached every heart –
> Stiffly resolved, 'twould carelessly invade
> Woman or man, nor aught its fury stayed:
> Where'er it pierced, a cunt it found or made –
> Now languid lies in this unhappy hour,
> Shrunk up and sapless like a withered flower. . . .
>
> And may ten thousand abler pricks agree
> To do the wronged Corinna right for me.
>
> (35–45, 71–2)

On the one hand, the extremity of Restoration libertinism in both idea and expression in a poem such as this, or in the even more obsessive and shocking case of 'A Ramble in St James's Park' (in which the figure denounced is also called Corinna), makes Ovid seem comparatively tame. Light Ovidian playfulness has been interpenetrated by something slightly disconcerting, desperate and manic. Libertines in poetry have far exceeded the classical model. On the other hand, Ovid's limitation keeps him within more acceptable human and more pleasing aesthetic bounds. The Roman poet allows his readers an imaginative release that is rarely if ever soiling or coarsening in its effect.

Chapter 6

Satire

Hence with these fiddlers whose oil buttered lines
Are panders into lusts and food to sins!
Their whimpering sonnets, puling elegies,
Slander the Muses, make the world despise
Admired poesie, mar resolution's ruff
And melt true valour with lewd ballad stuff. . . .
The Satyre only and Epigrammatist
(Concise Epigram and sharp Satyrist)
Keep diet from this surfeit of excess
Temp'ring themselves from such licentiousness.

(Guilpen)

Satire is indeed all our own; in this the first to win great praise was Lucilius . . . his learning is remarkable, and so too his freedom of speech (*libertas*) whence comes his sharpness (*acerbitas*) and abundant wit. Horace is terser and purer and if I am not over-partial, pre-eminent. Persius too, though he wrote only one book, has deserved his considerable reputation. There are also notable men of our time[1] who will be named by posterity.

(Quintilian, The Education of an Orator X, 1, 93–4)

The classical satirists

Satire in a non-generic sense dates from the earliest times. The sixth-century Greek poet Archilochus, whose work survives only in fragments, wrote invectives in iambics. Their potency is reflected in the anecdote reporting that some of his victims hanged

---

1. This was often understood in the Renaissance to refer to Juvenal, who was a younger contemporary of Quintilian.

themselves. *At non effugies meos iambos,*[2] 'but you shall not escape my iambics' writes Catullus ominously. There are several invectives written in iambics in Horace's epodes, including one cursing the poet Maevius for no apparent reason (*Epode* X). Motiveless or malignant cursing is not quite satire, though such poetic invectives might often contain satire. In classical Greece, old comedy has satire of individuals, middle comedy satire of types. In the Hellenistic period, adherents of philosophical schools, especially the Cynics and the Stoics, wrote evangelical prose diatribes to popularise their views which might contain invectives against other sects or denunciations of the pursuit of wealth or worldly power. The Diatribes of the Stoic Epictetus dating from the first century AD, which influenced the emperor Marcus Aurelius, are in this tradition. At Rome, Quintilian himself goes on to refer to a kind of satire even older than Lucilius mixing prose and verse of which Terentius Varro is the chief exponent (X, 1, 95). But what is called formal verse satire was not written by the Greeks, and Lucilius (whose work survives only in fragments) is hailed as its *inventor* by Horace (*Satire* I, 10, 48).

It is in critical response to Lucilius that Horace defines his own ideal of Augustan satire:

> Eupolis atque Cratinus Aristophanesque poetae,
> atque alii quorum comoedia prisca virorum est,
> si quis erat dignus describi quod malus ac fur,
> quod moechus foret aut sicarius aut alioqui
> famosus, multa cum libertate notabant,
> hinc omnis pendet Lucilius, hosce secutus
> mutatis tantum pedibus numerisque; facetus,
> emunctae naris, durus componere versus:
> nam fuit hoc vitiosus: in hora saepe ducentos,
> ut magnum, versus dictabat stans pede in uno:
> cum flueret lutulentus, erat quod tollere velles:
> garrulus atque piger scribendi ferre laborem,
> scribendi recte:
>
> (I, 4, 1–13)

(Eupolis, Cratinus and Aristophanes, true poets, and other writers of old comedy, if anyone deserved to be described as a knave and a thief, or an adulterer or murderer or as infamous in any other way, usually

2. One of the fragments usually printed after the poems in editions of Catullus.

marked him out with great freedom. On these Lucilius wholly hangs; these he has followed changing only metre and versification; a man who was witty, with keen scented nostrils but harsh in the composition of his verse. Here lay his chief fault; in an hour he would dictate two hundred verses as if it were a great achievement, standing as it were on one foot. Since he flowed like a muddy stream, there was much you would wish to remove; he was garrulous and too lazy to bear the labour of writing – of writing correctly that is.)

He shares the virtues of the writers of old comedy: *sale multo / urbem defricuit* (I, 10, 3–4) 'he rubbed the city down with much salt', but he is a harsh versifier; his verses run on a halting foot *incomposito pede* (I, 10, 1). He is prolix, unclear, and a careless writer.

> quid vetat et nosmet Lucili scripta legentes
> quaerere, num illius, num rerum dura negarit
> versiculos natura magis factos et euntes
> mollius?
>
> (I, 10, 56–9)

(Reading the writings of Lucilius, what forbids us from asking whether it was his own harsh nature or the nature of his subjects that denied him verses better made and running more smoothly?)

> fuerit Lucilius, inquam
> comis et urbanus, fuerit limatior idem
> quam rudis et Graecis intacti carminis auctor
> quamque poetarum seniorum turba: sed ille
> si foret hoc nostrum fato delapsus in aevum,
> detereret sibi multa, recideret omne quod ultra
> perfectum traheretur.
>
> (I, 10, 64–70)

(Grant, I say, that Lucilius was genial and urbane; grant that he was more polished than might be expected of the author of a new kind of poem untouched by the Greeks, and more polished than the crowd of older poets: but if he had been fated to fall in our age [he was born over a hundred years before Horace], he would have retrenched everything which trailed beyond the limit of perfection.)

Horace recommends brevity ('the soul of wit'),[3] clarity and control:

---

3. According to Polonius: *Hamlet* II, i, 90.

ergo non satis est risu diducere rictum
auditoris: et est quaedam tamen hic quoque virtus:
est brevitate opus, ut currat sententia, neu se
impediat verbis lassas onerantibus aures;
et sermone opus est modo tristi, saepe iocoso,
defendente vicem modo rhetoris atque poetae
interdum urbani, parcentis viribus atque
extenuantis eas consulto. ridiculum acri
fortius et melius magnas plerumque secat res.

(I, 10, 7–15)

(Therefore it is not enough to make your hearer's mouth draw apart in laughter – though there is even some merit in this. There must be brevity that the thought may flow and not be impeded by words that burden weary ears: and there is a need for a style, now grave now gay, sustaining the part now of orator and poet, and sometimes of the wit moderating his strength and controlling it with purpose. Joking cuts through knots more effectively and better than vituperation.)

The recommendation looks beyond the superficialities of style to the artistic and moral values that the style must embody. The satire is to be varied with shifting tones; the satirist must adopt a variety of parts (not simply that of the censorious scourge) and as *vir urbanus*, an urbane man of the world, will control his attack, often preferring mockery to invective. Here in a nutshell is the Augustan preference for controlled satire and refined raillery rather than sustained invective and constant railing.

Urbanity is the keynote. His defence of satire against the charge that it arises from malicious pleasure (*laedere gaudes* 'you enjoy hurting', *Satire* I, 4, 78) makes it seem an entirely reasonable and sane extension of the habit of self-examination inculcated by his father who had taught the growing boy not by preaching any philosophical doctrine but by pointing to specific neighbouring examples of good and bad. Thanks to this training he is free from disastrous vices, though prone to lesser frailties, among which is the jotting down on paper of his thoughts about the rights and wrongs of conduct (*Satire* I, 4, 103–43). His defence is modest and self-deprecating, and, since we know of the immense pains he took (*ludentis speciem dabit et torquebitur* [the genuine poet] 'will give the appearance of playing yet be on the rack', *Epistle* II, 2, 124), not without a measure of dissimulation. In the *Art of Poetry* he recommends study of the *Socraticae chartae* (310) as the basis for good writing and his *sermones* are probably more consistently Socratic than were those of Lucilius in their use of irony and humour in the cause of self-examination and enlightenment:

> praeterea, ne sic, ut qui iocularia, ridens
> percurram: quamquam ridentem dicere verum
> quid vetat? ut pueris olim dant crustula blandi
> doctores, elementa velint ut discere prima:
> sed tamen amoto quaeramus seria ludo:
> (Sat I, 1, 24–8)

(Furthermore, not to run over the subject with too much mirth like one intent on making jokes – although what is to prevent one from telling the truth as he laughs just as coaxing teachers give sweets to children when they want to teach them the first elements? – still putting joking aside let us turn to serious things.)

Horace's moral interest can be less than Socratic (in *Satire* I, 2, for example) but generally speaking he avoids aggressive personal invective (many of the named individuals in his satires prove not to be contemporaries but names already notorious and suggesting types), claims only to attack those who deserve it, maintains a high moral tone and seldom falls below the standards required for the humorist by Aristotle in his *Nicomachean Ethics* where refined wit is a mean between the boorishness of the humourless and the joking of the scurrilous jester who will stop at nothing to exercise his wit.[4] Although he humorously refers to himself as *Epicuri de grege porcum* (*Epistle* I, 4, 16) 'a hog from Epicurus's sty', he is an eclectic with no system to impart. In his ethical stance he is tolerant and discriminating, mocking the Stoics for their dogmatic insistence upon the equality of faults though sharing with them a tendency to regard the passions, including anger, so often the satirist's friend, as folly (I, 3). If there is a consistent habit of mind underlying and embodied in the satires it is perhaps reflected in the following favourite Horatian commonplace:

> est modus in rebus, sunt certi denique fines,
> quos ultra citraque nequit consistere rectum.
> (Sat I, 1, 106–7)

4. See p. 96.

(There is a measure in all things. There are, in short, certain boundaries beyond and short of which right can find no place.)

These lines come from the opening satire addressed to his patron and friend Maecenas on two favourite themes of Cynic and Stoic popular philosophy, discontent with one's lot (*mempsimoiria*) and avarice (*aischrokerdia*). The satire causes the reader to reflect upon the true source of human happiness and is in fact something of a moral essay scarcely differing in character from the later epistles, which Horace also called *sermones* although they are not so obviously satirical. In both the satires and the epistles Horace follows Lucilius in his autobiographical candour. Indeed, generations of readers have found Horace's praise of Lucilius applicable to himself:

> ille velut fidis arcana sodalibus olim
> credebat libris, neque si male cesserat, usquam
> decurrens alio, neque si bene; quo fit, ut omnis
> votiva pateat veluti descripta tabella
> vita senis. sequor hunc . . .
>
> (*Sat* II, 1, 30–4)

> He, as his trusty friends, his books did trust
> With all his secrets; nor, in things unjust,
> Or actions lawful, ran to other men:
> So that the old man's life described, was seen
> As in a votive tablet in his lines:
> And to his steps my genius inclines;
>
> (Ben Jonson[5])

The apparent intimacy of the *sermones*, in marked contrast to the more formal Horatian odes, is in large part a consequence of the plain and familiar style in which they are written. This kind of verse Horace puts low in the generic hierarchy, disclaiming for it the status of poetry altogether:

> primum ego me illorum, dederim quibus esse poetas,
> excerpam numero: neque enim concludere versum
> dixeris esse satis; neque, si qui scribat uti nos
> sermoni propiora, putes hunc esse poetam.

5. Jonson appended his translation of Horace's *Satire* II, 1 (a defence of satire) from which this extract is taken to the version of the *Poetaster* included in his *Works* of 1616.

ingenium cui sit, cui mens divinior atque os
magna sonaturum, des nominis huius honorem.
idciro quidam Comoedia necne poema
esset quaesivere, quod acer spiritus ac vis
nec verbis nec rebus inest, nisi quod pede certo
differt sermoni, sermo merus.

(*Sat* I, 4, 39–48)

(First I will take myself from the number of those to whom I would give the name poet: for you would not say it is enough to complete a verse, nor, if anyone like me writes what is nearer to prose, would you consider him a poet. You will give the honour of this name to whoever has genius and something of a divine soul, and a tongue that can speak in the grand style. And so some have questioned whether comedy is poetry; for in neither its matter not its style has it the fire and force of inspiration, and except that it differs from the language of prose in its regular feet, is pure prose.)

He proceeds to quote a grandiloquent fragment of Ennius with the conclusion that even if the words of it were to be arranged in prose order, thus destroying its metrical effect, anyone could recognise *disiecti membra poetae* (62) 'the limbs of the dismembered poet'. Elsewhere he refers to the *musa pedestris* (*Satire* II, 6, 17), 'the prosaic muse', of satire. Addressing the emperor in the 'Epistle to Augustus', he is again all modesty and self-deprecation:

nec sermones ego mallem
repentes per humum quam res componere gestas,
terrarumque situs et flumina dicere, et arces
montibus impositas et barbara regna, tuisque
auspiciis totum confecta duella per orbem,
claustraque custodem pacis cohibentia Ianum,
et formidatam Parthis te principe Romam,
si quantum cuperem possem quoque; sed neque parvum
carmen maiestas recipit tua, nec meus audet
rem temptare pudor quam vires ferre recusent.

(*Ep* II, 1, 250–9)

(I would not prefer my conversations creeping on the ground rather than compose the story of great exploits and tell of the rivers and sights of strange lands, of citadels crowning mountain tops and foreign kingdoms, of wars ended under your auspices throughout the globe, of the bars keeping Janus in his temple as guardian of the peace and of

Rome becoming a terror to the Parthians now that you are her first
citizen; if only I had the power equal to my desire; but your greatness
does not admit of lowly strains nor does my modesty dare to attempt a
task for which I have not the strength.)

Since, however, he rises to dignified heights in his description of
what he is politely refusing to sing, we can see that the *sermo* style,
though its general tenor may be humble, can rise to unaccustomed
heights as its author varies the roles of poet and orator with that
of the plain man of the world. It is also clear that, whether
Augustus appreciated it or not, there is a fine irony in the self-
deprecation here. Nevertheless, the apparent estimate of Horace
on his own *sermo* style has often been taken at face value.

The plain style is what an interlocutor in his fifth satire
attributes to the silver-age satirist Persius:

> verba togae sequeris iunctura callidus acri
> ore teres modico, pallentes radere mores
> doctus et ingenuo culpam defigere ludo.
> (14–16)

(You follow everyday expression, skilful in clever combinations of
words with a rounded but modest style, knowing how to lash vicious
manners and to censure faults with well-mannered jesting.)

The phrasing here echoes a well-known passage in Horace's *Art of
Poetry*:

> in verbis etiam tenuis cautusque serendis
> dixeris egregie, notum si callida verbum
> reddiderit iunctura novum.
> (46–8)

(With delicacy too and caution in stringing words together you will
succeed in expressing yourself well if a clever placing makes a familiar
word new.)

In fact the Persian style differs considerably from the Horatian in
its abruptness, compression and odd choice of words. Persius does
not have the habitual ease of Horace; the difficulty of his style has
caused him to be thought of as a type of the crabbed and harsh
satirist. His poems are redolent of a stern Stoicism and tend to be
homiletic. Nevertheless, he recognises Lucilius and Horace as his

literary masters, neatly characterising them in thumbnail sketches
that have become famous:

> secuit Lucilius urbem
> te Lupe, te Muci, et genuinum fregit in illis.
> omne vafer vitium ridenti Flaccus amico
> tangit et admissus circum praecordia ludit,
> callidus excusso populum suspendere naso:
>
> (I, 114–18)

> Yet old Lucilius never feared the times,
> But lashed the city, and dissected crimes.
> Mutius and Lupus both by name he brought;
> He mouthed 'em, and betwixt his grinders caught.
> Unlike in method, with concealed design,
> Did crafty Horace his low numbers join:
> And, with sly insinuating grace,
> Laughed at his friend, and looked him in the face:
> Would raise a blush, where secret vice he found;
> And tickle, while he gently probed the wound:
> With seeming innocence the crowd beguiled;
> But made the desperate passes when he smiled.
>
> (Dryden: *The First Satire of Persius*, 223–34)[6]

He has a high moral notion of the satirist's calling, which in the
opening poem is set against the debased taste for high-flown
dramatic recitation and enervate mythological narratives prevalent
in Nero's Rome. He has high expectations of his audience, too.
Only those who appreciate the old comedy of the Greeks are
welcome as his readers, not self-important people who laugh at
the unfortunate or scoff at education and philosophy (I, 123–34).

The introductory satire of Juvenal recalls that of Persius in
making a contrast between satire and other prevalent literary
forms; jokingly, satire is to be an appropriate kind of requital:

> Still shall I hear, and never quit the score
> Stunned with hoarse Codrus' *Theseid*, o'er and o'er?
> Shall this man's elegies and t'other's play
> Unpunished murther a long summer's day? . . .
> But, since the world with writing is possessed,

6. Dryden's translations of Juvenal and Persius can be found in volume 2 of
    Kinsley, J. (ed.) (1958) *The Poetical Works of John Dryden*, 4 vols, Oxford
    University Press.

I'll versify in spite; and do my best,
To make as much waste paper as the rest.
   (Dryden: *The First Satire of Juvenal*, 1–4, 22–4)

The poet further reveals the cause of his provocation:

But why I lift aloft the Satire's rod,
And tread the path which famed Lucilius trod,
· Attend the causes which my Muse have led:
When sapless eunuchs mount the marriage-bed;
When mannish Maevia, that two-handed whore,
Astride on horseback hunts the Tuscan boar;
When all our lords are by his wealth outvied,
Whose razor on my callow beard was tried;
When I behold the spawn of conquered Nile,
Crispinus, both in birth and manners vile,
Pacing in pomp, with cloak of Tyrian dye,
Changed oft a day for needless luxury;
And finding oft occasion to be fanned,
Ambitious to produce his lady-hand;
Charged with light summer-rings his fingers sweat,
Unable to support a gem of weight –
Such fulsome objects meeting everywhere,
'Tis hard to write, but harder to forebear.
  To view so lewd a town, and to refrain,
What hoops of iron could my spleen contain!
                        (26–45)

difficile est saturam non scribere. nam quis iniquae
tam patiens urbis, tam ferreus, ut teneat se . . .
                        (30–1)

This is written unashamedly from the conservative standpoint of
old Rome when men were men and when women and members
of the lower orders like his barber knew their allotted places, and
before the city, as a result of her conquests, was awash with filthy
upstart foreigners bringing with them their depraved taste for
enervating luxuries. Juvenal's shocking satire is not inhibited by
any promptings from a progressive liberal conscience. Lack of any
such inhibition is part of its very nature.

From old Roman prejudice, the satirist then changes the target
of his attack to the more obviously vicious:

What indignation boils within my veins,
When perjured guardians, proud with impious gains,

Choke up the streets, too narrow for their trains!
Whose wards, by want betrayed, to crimes are led
Too foul to name, too fulsome to be read! . . .
    Such villainies roused Horace into wrath;
And 'tis more noble to pursue his path,
Than an old tale of Diomede to repeat,
Or lab'ring after Hercules to sweat,
Or wand'ring in the winding maze of Crete;
Or with the winged smith aloft to fly
Or flutt'ring perish with his foolish boy [Icarus].
            (67–71, 78–84, translating 45–8, 51–4)

Satire prompted by men's villainies is a nobler poetic form than
repetitious labour on mythological subjects, epic aspirations that
end in bathos: *parturient montes, nascetur ridiculus mus* (Horace, *Art
of Poetry*, 139) 'mountains will labour, to birth will come a
ridiculous mouse'. After further delineation of a world in which
the wicked triumph and prosper while *probitas laudatur et alget* (74)
'honesty is praised and left out in the cold', come the famous
words:

    si natura negat, facit indignatio versum
    qualemcumque potest, quales ego vel Cluvienus.
                        (79–80)

(If nature deny, indignation will prompt verse of whatever kind it be,
such as I can write or Cluvienus.)

The scholiast tells us that Cluvienus was a feeble scribbler of his
day, a ridiculous mouse. Dryden finely modernises the joke,
referring to the hero of his *MacFlecknoe*:

    If nature could not, anger would indite
    Such woeful stuff as I or Shadwell write.
                        (121–2)

The first line is often cited without the second, which with the
bathetic joke at its end (the four-syllable name is emphatic not
only by position but in its length which breaks the predominant
pattern of dissyllable or trisyllable endings of the hexameter line)
punctures the apparent gravity of the indignation. Nature, as we
have seen, gave Juvenal ample stores of what was necessary for his
kind of satire; righteous moral indignation is an incidental
accompaniment rather than its mainspring.

quidquid agunt homines, votum timor ira voluptas
gaudia discursus, nostri farrago libelli est.

(85–6)

(whatever mankind does, its vows, fears, anger, pleasure joys and coming and going, is the mixture that makes up this little book.)

What humankind desires, and what they shun,
Rage, passions, pleasures, impotence of will,
Shall this satirical collection fill.

(130–2)

The substance of the *farrago* suggests a variety of human concerns though the question immediately following, *et quando uberior vitiorum copia* (87) 'and when has there been a richer crop of vices?', makes it clear that in the satire all will be distorted. The wishes will be vain, the pleasures lewd, the joys depraved and the comings and goings aimless or self-serving. There is a further slight tension of opposites here: on the one hand, the suggestion that the poet is simply dealing with the general human condition, on the other the notion that the present age is particularly vicious. *Omne in praecipiti vitium stetit* (149) 'all vice is at its acme'.

No age can go beyond us; future times
Can add no farther to the present crimes.
Our sons but the same things can wish and do;
Vice is at a stand, and at the highest flow.
Then, Satire, spread thy sails; take all the winds can blow.

(220–4, translating 147–50)

Juvenal then imagines an interlocutor asking whether he has the talent equal to the task, *ingenium par materiae* (150). So effective is Juvenal's *ingenium* that his vision (together with that of the historian Tacitus) has been responsible for the creation of what has been called the imperial legend wherein Rome in the first century festers in superlative depravity to the point where it teeters on the brink of total ruin. The interlocutor then asks:

unde illa priorum
scribendi quodcumque animo flagrante liberet
simplicitas?

(151–3)

(where is that simplicity of our forebears to write whatever the burning soul pleased?)

> From whence can be derived so large a vein,
> Bold truths to speak, and spoken to maintain,
> When godlike freedom is so far bereft
> The noble mind, that scarce the name is left.
>
> (227–30)

For it is hardly safe in present times to name names. Shall the guilty then go free? Yes, it is safer to write epic which offends no one (epic is again represented as the softer choice that does not confront reality like satire):

> ense velut stricto quotiens Lucilius ardens
> infremuit, rubet auditor cui frigida mens est
> criminibus, tacita sudant praecordia culpa.
> inde ira et lacrimae.
>
> (165–8)

> But when Lucilius brandishes his pen,
> And flashes in the face of guilty men,
> A cold sweat stands in drops on ev'ry part;
> And rage succeeds to tears, revenge to smart.
>
> (251–4)

Lucilius rather than Horace is the touchstone for Juvenal here because he enjoyed the freedom of the old Republic and used that freedom politically to assail contemporary men of power. Here is the Juvenalian ideal dramatically represented in the figurative language of the raging satirist with drawn sword fearlessly assailing the guilty. The times do not allow him the freedom of this ideal so he ends with the anti-climactic avowal:

> Since none the living villains dare implead
> Arraign them in the persons of the dead.
>
> (257–8)

Though critical of Lucilius as an artist, Horace had cited the precedent of the bold and fearless freedom of Lucilian satire when he defended his own against the charge that it was *nimis acer* 'too sharp', going *ultra legem* 'beyond the law' (of genre and state):

quid, cum est Lucilius ausus
primus in hunc operis componere carmina morem,
detrahere et pellem, nitidus qua quisque per ora
cederet, introrsum turpis, num Laelius aut qui
duxit ab oppressa meritum Carthagine nomen
ingenio offensi aut laeso doluere Metello
famosisque Lupo cooperto versibus? atqui
primores populi arripuit populumque tributim,
scilicet uni aequus virtuti atque eius amicis.
quin ubi se a vulgo et scaena in secreta remorant
virtus Scipiadae et mitis sapientia Laeli,
nugari cum illo et discincti ludere, donec
decoqueretur holus soliti. quidquid sum ego, quamvis
infra Lucili censum ingeniumque, tamen me
cum magnis vixisse invita fatebitur usque
invidia,

(Sat II, 1, 62–77)

How, sir, Lucilius that did first engage
In writing satires, and that lashed the age,
And stripped our foplings of their lion's skin,
In which they looked so gay, all foul within:
Did Laelius, or did Scipio hate his Muse?
Or storm, when he Metellus did abuse?
The great ones and the crowd did discommend,
And valued virtue only and her friend?
No, no; they treated him and thought him good,
And when removed from business and the crowd,
Would keep him company, would laugh and jest,
And sport until their little meat was dressed.
Whate'er I am, although I must submit
To wise Lucilius in estate and wit,
Yet I with great ones live, this all confess,
And envy, though unwilling, grants no less.

(Creech, 87–102)[7]

The defence, given by the poet in dialogue with a lawyer
Trebatius, associates Horace with a freedom he never in fact fully
exercised. Unlike his predecessor, he kept to safer social themes
without the political dimension and with little apparent rebellious-
ness. The 'Epistle to Augustus' has the complementary arguments

7. Creech, T.H. (1684) The Odes, Satyrs and Epistles of Horace: Done into English,
Jacob Tonson; printed in Appendix A of Butt, J. (ed.) (1966) Alexander Pope:
Imitations of Horace, Methuen.

that poetry civilises the community and that the community's
laws keep poetry within decent bounds (*Epistle* II, 1, 139–55).[8]
This is very much a moderate Augustan balancing in which
Horace was doubtless content to engage with all due discretion.
Unlike Juvenal, who resents his inability to flay contemporary
figures of power, Horace is characteristically silent about the
limits placed upon him. If the times did not allow him Lucilius's
freedom of expression, he nevertheless did enjoy through the
patronage of Maecenas the company of the great and the good.
The times in which Juvenal wrote were even more unpropitious
for freedom of expression, and his own position considerably less
favourable than that of Horace. The date and circumstances
surrounding the publication of his satires are not known; from
internal evidence scholars tend to the view that they were
variously published in the comparatively peaceable reigns of
Trajan and Hadrian following Domitian's reign of terror that
ended in AD 86. In the fourth satire Juvenal inveighs against
Domitian, and in the seventh his major themes have to do with
the lack of reward and difficulties attendant upon the literary life.
(Without his physical comforts Virgil could never have written
the *Aeneid* (69–72).) While Horace writes from the standpoint of
one who is in broad sympathy with the ruling order with whose
members he is on intimate terms, and as one who has a circle of
literary friends sharing similar values, Juvenal writes as an isolated
and alienated outsider, malcontented upon every front.

With Juvenalian aggression comes a very different style from
the *sermo* of the urbane Horace:

> fingimus haec altum satura sumente cothurnum
> scilicet, et finem egressi legemque priorum
> grande Sophocleo carmen bacchamur hiatu,
> montibus ignotum Rutulis caeloque Latino?
> nos utinam vani. sed clamat Pontia 'feci,
> confiteor, puerisque meis aconita paravi . . .
> (VI, 634–9)

(We are inventing this, you think, with satire taking the high heels of
tragedy? And going beyond the limits and laws of those who have

<hr/>

8. Compare also the account of the regulation of Old Comedy in the *Art of
    Poetry*, 281–4.

gone before we are ranting grandly in Sophoclean strains unknown to the Italian hills and the Latin sky? Would that we were vain! But Pontia cries 'I did it, I confess, I prepared aconite for my children.'

> You think this feigned; the satire in a rage
> Struts in the buskins of the tragic stage,
> Forgets its business is to laugh and bite;
> And will of deaths and dire revenges write.
> Would it were all fable that you read;
> But Drymon's wife pleads guilty to the deed.
> (*The Sixth Satire of Juvenal*, 828–33)

Juvenal is fully conscious of going beyond established satirical practice, beyond what Horace in his *Art of Poetry* calls the law of genre *lex operis* (135). Dryden interprets the innovation more in terms of subject matter but it might equally well refer to style, to the declamatory grandeur that distinguishes him from Horace and Persius. In subject matter and style Juvenal establishes his own decorum for the genre.

Definitions and classifications of ancient and Renaissance commentators

Renaissance perceptions of classical genres were often coloured by the accounts of them to be found in the grammatical tradition. The discussion of satire and in particular of the term *satura* by Diomedes from the fourth century AD was influential in giving rise to a mistaken view of its origins and character.

> Satire means a poem among the Romans (such as written by Lucilius, Horace and Persius) which, as things are now, is abusive and composed after the destructive fashion of old comedy to criticise the faults of men (*maledicum et ad carpenda hominum vitia . . . compositum*). But formerly a poem which consisted of various short poems (such as written by Pacuvius and Ennius) was also called satire. Moreover, it was either named satire after the *satyrs* (because ridiculous and shameful things, the kind of things vaunted and done by satyrs, were likewise related in this poem), or named *satura* after the platter (*lanx*) heaped with many and various first-fruits which among the ancients used to be paid to the gods for sacrifice and which from its abundance and very

saturation was called *satura* . . . or else after a kind of sausage (*farcimen*) with many ingredients which Varro says was usually named *satura* . . . others, however, think it was called after the law known as *satura* which could embrace many measures at once under a single roll-call, because (mark the parallel) many short poems are at once embraced in the poem known as *satura*.[9]

From this account it is possible to see why Juvenal called his *libellus* a *farrago*. Of the various derivations here the one which caught the imagination was the association of the Latin word *satura* with satyrs. It was further associated with the satyr-play from which, according to Aristotle, tragedy emerged (*Poetics* IV, 17). In Horace's *Art of Poetry*, the dramatist in presenting a satyr-play is *asper* 'rough' or 'harsh' as he turns all to jesting (220–2) with, in Jonson's phrase, his 'rough rude satyrs' (321). All these associations gave rise to the widespread notion that the essential satirist, whatever the individual character of its practitioners, was rough, rude and vehement. It was not until 1605 that Isaac Casaubon used his classical learning to explode the notion that satire was associated with satyrs, early tragedy and the satyr-play.[10] Nevertheless, the association with tragedy turns up later in Milton's criticism of Hall's 'toothless' satires:

> For a satire is, as it were, born out of a tragedy, so ought to resemble his parentage, to strike high, and adventure dangerously at the most eminent vices among the greatest persons, and not creep into every blind taphouse that fears a constable more than a satire.[11]

The association of satire with the satyr is involved in Scaliger's description of the form in his *Poetics* (1561). He divides the *genus saturae* into two *species* according to subject matter and persons – grave and important or slight – and method either savage or mocking. As to the general character of the two kinds:

> one is gentler and nearer to conversation (*sermoni propior*), like the Horatian, the other preferred by Persius and Juvenal, more spirited. The latter have their blades exposed; the former (like Horace) in the

9. *Diomedis Artis Grammaticae Libri III*, 'De Poematibus' in Keil, H. (ed.) (1858) *Grammatici Latini*, Teubner, Leipzig, vol. I, p. 485.
10. See Casaubon, I. (1605) *De satyrica grecorum poesi et romanorum satira*, A. & H. Drouart, Paris.
11. 'Apology for Smectymnus' in Patterson, F.A. (ed.) (1933) *The Student's Milton*, 2nd edn, Appleton-Century-Crofts, New York, pp. 558–9.

manner of satyrs carry their thyrsus covered with ivy with which they strike the imprudent. Concealed by the ivy, the point wounds the unwary. . . . It is a free kind of poem, similar to the nature of the satyr; holding all things of no consequence, it makes instant sallies. . . . Juvenal is fiery, attacks openly and goes for the jugular (*jugulat*). Persius is insulting. Horace mocks. And so the former called their works satires, the latter was content with the title of *sermones*.

Although in one place he berates Juvenal for his obscenity, virtually saying that he is not fit reading for an honest man, in another he gives him the palm. 'Juvenal is frank (*candidus*) and easily the prince of satirists. For his verses are by a long way better than Horace's; his *sententiae* are sharper, his phrasing more open.'[12]

The latter phrase suggests that even for a great Latinist like Scaliger Horace sometimes could be less than absolutely clear. His judgement of Juvenal, on the other hand, whatever later Elizabethan vernacular writers made of him, vindicates him as a sharp, clear writer of polished verse, vehement certainly, but not at all rough or obscure. Scaliger singles out for especial praise a feature of style that Juvenal shares with other silver Latin writers like Seneca and Tacitus, that is, his penchant for the pithy ringing phrase. He has supplied the world with many memorable tags such as *panem et circenses* (X, 81) 'bread and circuses', *mens sana in corpore sano* (X, 356) 'a healthy mind in a healthy body', *sed quis custodiet ipsos/custodes?* (VI, 347–8) 'but who will guard the guardians?', and many moral aphorisms or *sententiae*:

> nil habet infelix paupertas durius in se,
> quam quod ridiculos homines facit.
> (III, 152–3)

(ill-starred poverty has nothing harder in it than this, that it makes men ridiculous.)

and the following known to Chaucer:

> cantabit vacuus coram latrone viator
> (X, 22)

---

12. *Poetics*, Lib I, Cap XII, Lib III, Cap XCVIII.

Juvenal seith of poverte, myrily,
'The poure man, when he goth by the weye,
Bifore the theves he may synge and playe.'
(*The Wife of Bath's Tale*, 1192–4)

English Renaissance humanists like Puttenham describing satire looked back not only to the classics but to the native medieval tradition.

> There was yet another kind of poet who intended to tax the common abuses and vice of the people in rough and bitter speeches, and their invectives were called Satyrs and themselves Satyricques: such were Lucilius, Juvenal and Persius among the Latins, and with us he that wrote the book called Piers Plowman.[13]

In modern classification, Langland's satire usually comes under the general heading of complaint.[14] While classical satire deals specifically with the particulars of life and is a flexible mode which may be a vehicle for autobiographical candour or personal animus and may use a variety of personae and have shifting tones, complaint is more generalised, impersonal and abstract; it is often allegorical and tends to be homiletic in tone and more straightforwardly moral in design. The complainant, unlike the sophisticated and witty *vir urbanus* of classical satire, is often the bitter spokesman of the common man. In the sixteenth century the two modes are not entirely distinct; it is not until the seventeenth that satire entirely divests itself of the characteristics of complaint.

English beginnings: Wyatt

In the period when Renaissance humanism made its first major impact upon English literature, the courtier and diplomat Sir Thomas Wyatt wrote three satires in the 1530s subsequently printed in Tottel's *Songs and Sonnets* (1557) in *terza rima*, addressed to his friends, two to John Poyntz and a third to Sir Francis Brian.

13. *The Arte of English Poesy*, 'Of Poets and Poesy', Chapter XI in Smith, G.G. (1904) vol. 2, p. 27.
14. See Peter, J. (1956) *Complaint and Satire in Early English Literature*, Oxford University Press, and Selden, R. 1978, *English Verse Satire 1590–1705*, Allen & Unwin.

The first is a reworking of a recent Italian poem by Alamanni; the second includes a fable featuring a town and a country mouse, and the third, offering the addressee ironic advice on ways to enrich himself, has been compared to one of Horace's most trenchant satires on legacy-hunting (II, 5). It may be that Wyatt's knowledge of classical satire was mostly indirect and secondary, but through the mediating influence of the Italian he came to write a kind of moral and satirical verse epistle that is born of and prompts self-examination in the Socratic tradition of the Horatian *sermo*. This tradition emphasising interior virtue and right spirit proved deeply congenial to the reformist in Erasmus, Thomas More and Wyatt, and in many of Wyatt's lines it is difficult to separate what might be called the Protestant from the Horatian:

> Each kind of life hath with him his disease.
> Live in delight even as thy lust would

> And thou shalt find, when lust doth most thee please,
> It irketh straight, and by itself doth fade.
> A small thing it is that may thy mind appease.

> None of ye all there is that is so mad
> To seek for grapes on brambles or on briers,
> Nor none (I trow) that hath his wit so bad

> To set his hay for conies over rivers,
> Nor ye set not a drag-net for an hare.
> And yet the thing that most your heart desires

> Ye do mistake with more travail and care.
> Make plain thy heart that it be not knotted
> With hope or dread, and see thy will be bare

> From all affects, whom vice hath ever spotted.
> Thy self content with that is thee assigned,
> And use that well that is to thee allotted.

> Then seek no more out of thy self to find
> The thing that thou hast sought so long before,
> For thou shalt feel it sitting in thy mind.

> Mad if thee list to continue thy sore,
>> Let present pass, and gape on time to come
>> And deep thyself in travail more and more.
>>> ('To John Poyntz' (II), 80–102)[15]

At the conclusion of the first satire dispraising courtly life, Wyatt's withdrawal may remind us not only of Horace on his Sabine farm but also of Juvenal's friend withdrawing from Rome at the end of the famous third satire and urging the poet to invite him for a visit if he too leaves Rome for the country. Rome comes to resound wittily with a double significance both religious and secular:

> Nor I am not where Christ is given in prey
>> For money, poison, and treason at Rome,
>> A common practice used night and day.

> But here I am in Kent and Christendom,
>> Among the Muses where I read and rhyme,
>> Where, if thou list, my John Poyntz, for to come,

> Thou shalt be judge how I do spend my time.

Wyatt's family seat was in Kent, but commentators tell us that the phrase 'in Kent and Christendom' was proverbial, Kent having remained pagan for a time after the rest of England had become Christian. From this witty stroke we can take the serious point that the wellsprings that nourished Wyatt in his choice of life were in equal measure classical and Christian in an urbane Erasmian blend.

Elizabethan innovation: Hall

The Elizabethan satirists were conscious of charting new territory. Thomas Lodge may be regarded as a pioneer. *A Fig for Momus* (1595), alongside eclogues and epistles, contains a number of satires 'because I would write in that form wherein no man might challenge me with servile imitation (wherewith heretofore I have

---

15. Mason, H.A. (1985) *Sir Thomas Wyatt: A Literary Portrait*, Bristol Classical Press. Includes a modernised text with introduction and extensive commentary.

been unjustly taxed)'. His fifth satire might call to mind Juvenal's tenth on the vanity of human wishes:

> In every from Gades to Ganges flood
> Too few they be that think upon their good:
> Too few that by discretion can discern
> What profit rightly doth themselves concern.
>
> (1–4)[16]

Apart from the infelicity of the first line, the relaxed, plain and discursive style here (in marked contrast to the more florid style of Lodge elsewhere) is more in the manner of Horace. The poems, in fact, have little satirical bite and are chiefly remarkable for their neat and balanced couplets which are predominantly end-stopped and in their characteristic patterning anticipate those of Jonson and the sons of Ben:

> There lives no man so settled in content
> That hath not daily whereof to repent,
> Nor can reformed wit so justly deem
> But that it leaves true goods, for such as seem; .
> Briefly, the greatest gifts whereof we boast
> Are those which do attempt and tire us most.
> Peace brings in pleasure, pleasure breeds excess,
> Excess procureth want, want works distress:
> Distress contempt, contempt is not repaired
> Till timeless death determine, hope despaired.
>
> (15–24)

Given the moderation of Lodge, the claim of Joseph Hall in the prologue to his *Virgidemiarum Six Books* ('six books of bundles of rods') is not unreasonable:

> I first adventure, follow me who list,
> And be the second English satyrist. . . .
> Go, daring Muse, on with thy thankless task
> And do the ugly face of Vice unmask.
>
> (3–4, 19–20)[17]

16. *The Complete Works of Thomas Lodge*, 4 vols, Johnson Reprint Corporation (1966), vol. 3.
17. Davenport, A. (ed.) (1969) *The Poems of Joseph Hall*, Liverpool University Press. The following edition has a modernised text and includes the remarks of Thomas Warton: Singer, W.S. (ed.) (1824) *Satires by Joseph Hall*, Triphook. The old spelling of satyrist which continued till late in the seventeenth century is retained in this chapter.

From internal evidence it is clear that Donne had written his satires before Hall (perhaps as early as 1593) but they were not printed until later. Hall could claim to be the first formal satirist to wield the literary rod in print.

The first three books, 'Of toothless satyres: poetical, academical and moral', were published in 1597 to be followed in the next year by 'The three last books: Of biting satyres'. They started a fashion continued in, among others, *The Scourge of Villainy* (Marston, 1598), *Micro Cynicon, Six Snarling Satyres* (Middleton, 1599) and *The Whipping of the Satyre* (W.I., 1601). These fearsome titles in which their authors advertise an intention to be biting, scourging, snarling and whipping suggest that the body of poetry to which they are a prelude will be altogether painful. But Hall's muse, herself subject to a disciplined programme of classical influence, is much less cankered than the rest. In fact his couplets are an improvement on those of Lodge and often exhibit a polish and control worthy of the later Augustans. Alexander Pope thought highly of him.[18]

In the prefatory poem 'His defiance of Envy', satire is reckoned to be a humble genre with its own distinct character:

> The ruder satyre should go ragg'd and bare
>   And show his rougher and his hairy hide,
>   Though mine be smooth, and decked in careless pride.

If 'mine' refers to satire, then perhaps these lines suggest that Hall was struggling against the idea that satires, like satyrs, should be rough and rude. If on the other hand the antecedent of 'mine' is taken to be hide, then Hall is aware that he must adopt a style that to some extent goes against his natural grain. In either meaning there is an element of antagonism between the rough and the smooth here that can be seen in the collection when taken as a whole. In the prologue that follows, the address to the 'daring muse' heralds the prospect of something grander than the *sermones* dictated by the *musa pedestris* invoked by Horace:

> And if thou canst not thine high flight remit,
>   So as it mought a lowly satyre fit,

18.   'Pope' in Hill, G.B. (ed.) (1905) *Lives of the English Poets by Samuel Johnson*, 3 vols, Oxford University Press, vol. 3, p. 251.

Let lowly satyres rise aloft to thee:
Truth be thy speed, and truth thy patron be.

(21–4)

On the other hand, the opening poem not only contrasts the satirist's integrity, in the manner of Persius and Juvenal, against those who prostitute their muse in prevalent contemporary forms (in this case comprising romance, the Petrarchan sonnet, and courtly panegyric), but also recognises lack of the necessary talent to succeed in the higher and sweeter genres of epic, pastoral and drama:

Trumpet, and reeds, and socks, and buskins fine,
I them bequeath, whose statues wand'ring twine
Of yew, mixed with bays, circlen around,
Their living temples likewise laurel-bound.
Rather had I, albe in careless rhymes,
Check the mis-ordered world, and lawless times.
Nor need I crave the Muse's midwifery,
To bring to light so worthless poetry:

(19–26)

The highly self-conscious and ambivalent attitude of the satirist to the poetic status of his satires in relation to other genres is very much a reflection of the Horatian tradition. Horatian too is the standpoint from which Hall proceeds in the poems of the first book to criticise the excesses of contemporary Elizabethan literature, particularly in relation to the indecorum of the popular stage where tragedy and comedy are indiscriminately mixed, and to the extravagance of romance (where Hall's target is Ariosto recently translated by Harrington rather than Spenser whom he twice praises):[19]

Painters and poets hold your ancient right:
Write what you will, and write not what you might:
Their limits be their list, their reason will.
But if some painter in presuming skill
Should paint the stars in centre of the earth
Could ye forbear some smiles, and taunting mirth?

(I, 4, 15–20)

19. *Satire* I, 1, 30; I, 4, 21ff.

There is a clear echo here of the previous passage at the opening of
Horace's *Art of Poetry*:

> But equal power to painter, and to poet,
> Of daring all, hath still been given; we know it:
> And both do crave, and give again, this leave.
> Yet, not as therefore wild and tame should cleave
> Together: not that we should serpents see
> With doves; or lambs, with tigers coupled be.
>
> (Jonson, 11–16, translating 9–13)

The good sense of Hall's classical tendency is exemplified in his
attack on Richard Stanyhurst's translation of Virgil into English
hexameters (1582):

> Another scorns the homespun thread of rhymes
> Matched with the lofty feet of elder times:
> Give me the numbered verse that Virgil sung,
> And Virgil's self shall speak the English tongue:
> 'Manhood and garboils shall he chant' with changed feet,
> And head-strong dactyls making music meet.
>
> (I, 6, 1–6)

The allusion to Stanyhurst's translation of the opening line of the
Aeneid in Hall's line 5 justifies the heavy irony of 'music meet'.
The indecorum of the translator's diction is justly a cause of
amusing satire:[20]

> If Jove speak English in a thund'ring cloud,
> 'Thwick thwack and riff raff' roars he out aloud.
> Fie on the forged mint that did create
> New coin of words never articulate.
>
> (15–18)

He attacks the indecorum of mingling the sacred and the profane –
'Now good St Peter weeps pure Helicon' (I, 8, 5) – the
unworthiness and the unreality of contemporary love poetry (I, 7)
and the obscenity of much popular literature – 'Now is Parnassus
turned to the stews' (I, 2, 17). The targets are not randomly
chosen. His own satires point the way towards a healthier, plainer
and more austere literary culture that will be more socially

---

20. The words in quotation marks were actually used by Stanyhurst: see
     Davenport, A. (1969) p. 169.

responsible and embody the highest moral and artistic standards, a
blend of the Christian and classical.

In addition to this considered criticism of other contemporary
forms, the *Virgidemiae* contain much comment on his own satire
and its relation to the classical tradition. In the prologue to the
third book, Hall counters criticism that he is too smooth, too clear
and not bold enough in following the ancient example:

> Some say my satyres over-loosely flow,[21]
> Nor hide their gall enough from open show:
> Nor, riddle-like, obscuring their intent;
> But pack-staff plain, utt'ring what thing they meant:
> Contrary to the Roman ancients,
> Whose words were short, and darksome was their sense.
> Who reads one line of their harsh poesies,
> Thrice must he take his wind, and breathe him thrice:
> My Muse would follow them that have foregone,
> But cannot with an English pinion;
> For look how far the ancient comedy
> Passed former satyres in her liberty:
> So far must mine yield unto them of old;
> 'Tis better to be bad, than be too bold.

At the end of the toothless satires he promises to make amends:

> Thus have I writ, in smoother cedar tree
> So gentle satyres, penned so easily.
> Henceforth I write in crabbed oak tree rind,
> Search they that mean the secret meaning find.
> Hold out ye guilty and ye galled hides,
> And meet my far-fetched stripes with waiting sides.

In the division of the satires into the toothless and the biting, he is
thought to be following Scaliger's classification of the *genus saturae*
into two species.[22] There is a discernible change of emphasis in

21. Hall's first line echoes the opening of Horace's defence of satire in II, 1, 1–3.

> sunt quibus in satyra videar nimis acer et ultra
> legem tendere opus; sine nervis altera, quicquid
> composui, pars esse putat . . .

> (There are some to whom I seem too bold in my satire and to be stretching
> the work beyond lawful bounds; the other part thinks whatever I have
> composed to be nerveless.)

22. See above p. 324.

the second volume, which is considerably longer than the first. Yet despite the alarming promises of the conclusion to the toothless satires, Hall is to be found defending himself in 'A Postscript to the Reader', appended to the biting satires, from very much the same criticisms with which he began:

> It is not for everyone to relish a true and natural satyre, being of itself, besides the nature and inbred bitterness and tartness of particulars, both hard of conceit and harsh of style, and therefore cannot but be unpleasing both to the unskilful and over-musical ear; the one being affected with only a shallow and easy matter, the other with a smooth and current disposition: so that I will foresee in the timely publication of these my concealed satyres, I am set upon the rack of many merciless and peremptory censures. . . . One thinks it misbeseeming the author because a poem; another unlawful in itself because a satyre; a third harmful for the sharpness; and a fourth unsatyrelike for the mildness: the learned, too perspicuous, being named with Juvenal, Persius and the other ancient satyres; the unlearned, savourless, because too obscure . . . I see two obvious cavills to be answered. One concerning the matter; than which I confess none can be more open to danger . . . . The other concerning the manner, wherein perhaps too much stooping to the low reach of the vulgar, I shall be thought not to have any whit kindly raught my ancient predecessors whom in the want of more late and familiar precedents, I am constrained thus far off to imitate.

He goes on to say that English is inferior to Latin as a medium for satire because of the fettering of rhyme, that the 'daintiness' of the times is a hindrance to the attacking satirist, and further declares, 'let me be plain with the hope of profit rather than purposely obscure only for a bare name's sake' (that of the 'true' satirist perhaps?). In this most interesting discussion (which repays study in full) the besieged satirist, anticipating a multiplicity of reader-antagonisms, is only too well aware of the uncongeniality of the form in which he is experimenting. He seems to be wrestling with a notion of harsh and dark satire supposedly derived from the ancients which is not altogether congenial to himself. We can sense, too, that Hall as a pioneer finds the classical tradition, which is central both to his own conception of the form and to the general debate about it among his contemporaries with which he is engaging, to be both a blessing and a burden.

That Hall's idea of ancient satire was not idiosyncratic may be confirmed by the words of John Marston in the preface to *The*

Scourge of Villainy, where he shows commendable good sense (at variance with his poetic practice) in first accounting for and then dismissing what his contemporaries felt to be the obscurity of ancient satire by which they judged the modern:

> Know I hate to affect too much obscurity and harshness because they profit no sense. To note vices, so that no man understand them, is as fond as the French execution in a picture. Yet there are some (too many) that think nothing good that is so courteous, as to come within their reach: terming all satyres bastard which are not palpable dark and so rough writ, that the hearing of them read, would set a man's teeth on edge. . . . Persius is crabby because ancient and his jerks (being particularly given to private customs of his time) dusky. Juvenal (upon the like occasion) seems to our judgement gloomy. Yet both of them go a good seemly pace, not stumbling shuffling. Chaucer is hard to our understandings: who knows not the reason? How much more those old satyres which express themselves in terms that breathed not long in their days. But had we then lived, the understanding of them had been nothing hard.[23]

The decorum of speech which Marston then admits for satire embraces roughness and plainness where the latter means not so much Horace's *musa pedestris* as lack of obscurity. The reader is to understand the satirist's target:

> I will not deny there is a seemly decorum to be observed, and a peculiar speech for a satyre's lips, which I can willinglier conceive than dare to prescribe; yet let me have the substance rough not the shadow. I cannot, nay I will not delude your sight with mists; yet I dare defend my plainness against the verjuice face of the crabb'st satyrist that ever stuttered.

The notion that ancient satire was harsh and obscure derives principally from Juvenal and Persius. Persius was thought to have concealed his meaning in criticising Nero because it was not safe to do otherwise, and despite his protestations to the contrary Juvenal's denunciations were also sometimes considered to have had contemporary application. Their darkness was seen to be a product of the dark times in which they lived but also a tribute to their artistry. The darkness of Persius is compounded by a condensed and elliptical style and a love of abstract learning that

23. Davenport, A. (ed.) (1961) *The Poems of John Marston*, Liverpool University Press, pp. 100–1.

earned him a rebuke from Scaliger,[24] and indeed for these reasons, he has always been a difficult author. Dryden, for instance, records that Persius caused him more trouble to translate than Juvenal and goes on to explain why:

> Then, as his verse is scabrous and hobbling and his words not everywhere well chosen, the purity of Latin being more corrupted than in the time . . . of Horace who writ when the language was in the height of its perfection, so his diction is hard, his figures are generally too bold and daring, and his tropes particularly his metaphors insufferably strained.[25]

In his own version these hard metaphors and forced expressions are sacrificed for the sake of Dryden's habitual clarity. Yet Hall calls Horace 'dark' too, associating him with the later practitioners of the genre. Given the nature of formal satire, this is not altogether surprising. For it seldom has an easily discernible structure (the extended fable of the town and country mouse in Horace, II, 6 is the only one of its kind), and transitions in the argument and from one theme to another may seem abrupt. This abruptness was cultivated in the *sermo* to dramatise and mimic the actual processes of the mind whether in conversation with itself or another, and also to represent an aesthetic ideal. *Est brevitate opus* 'there is a need for brevity', Horace had prescribed for the satirist in I, 10, 9. *Brevis esse laboro, obscurus fio* 'I labour to be brief, I become obscure' he had warned in the *Art of Poetry* (26). Subtle shifts of tone and the use of irony are often particularly difficult to pick up in a foreign text. Editors did not always agree about the allocation of dialogue, and where a modern text might mark an internal monologue with inverted commas, Renaissance editions rarely offered such help. For all these reasons (in addition to those given by Marston) the satires of Horace, even in a heavily annotated text, are difficult and have never been an elementary school text like Virgil's pastorals or the plays of Terence. Nor for all his reputation for Augustan ease and polish was Horace necessarily felt to be an exception to the rule that satire was 'rough'. He is sometimes deliberately rough in rhythm and vocabulary for special effect; and to anyone whose standard is the

---

24. *Poetics*, Lib III, Cap XCVIII.
25. 'A Discourse Concerning Satire' in Watson, G. (1962) vol. 2, p. 118.

Latin hexameter as used by Virgil in his pastorals, georgics or epic, Horace's practice in the *sermo* can be very different. To give one example, he will end the line with a monosyllable which may be a conjunction or a preposition, sometimes creating a strong pause in the middle of the final foot and thereby entirely breaking the natural hexameter rhythm, something Virgil and Ovid never do.

Nevertheless, it was chiefly from the later satirists that the Elizabethans drew their notion of the darkly attacking satirist. At the end of his postscript, Hall tells his readers that the opening satire of the fourth book (the first of the biting satires) is a deliberate imitation of what he felt to be Juvenal's predominant poetical character:

> I think my first satyre doth somewhat resemble the sour and crabbed face of Juvenal's, which I endeavouring in that, did determinately omit in the rest, for these forenamed causes, so that I might have somewhat to stop the mouth of every accuser.

> Who dares upbraid these open rhymes of mine
> With blindfold Aquines, or dark Venusine?
> Or rough-hewn Teretismes, writ in th'antique vein
> Like an old Satyre, and new Flaccian?
> Which who reads thrice, and rubs his rugged brow,
> And deep intendeth every doubtful row,
> Scoring the margent with his blazing stars,
> And hundreth crooked interlinears . . .
> Should all in a rage the curse-beat page out-rive
> And in each dust-heap bury me alive.
> (IV, 1, 1–8, 11–12)

The opening lines are calculated to provoke precisely the response that Hall here finds attendant upon the reading of Juvenal, who came from Aquinum, Horace, who came from Venusia, and J.C. Scaliger, who wrote satires on the classical model (used as a source by Hall) called *Teretismata*, like modern followers of Quintus Horatius Flaccus, or perhaps more likely (since Horace has been mentioned already) of Aulus Persius Flaccus, a Flaccian. The allusions are deliberately dark and 'rough-hewn Teretismes' is rough stuff indeed. Yet whether we take 'open rhymes' to refer to the softer and smoother toothless satires of the previous books, or, not without irony, to refer to this poem itself, Hall is actually inviting a contrast between his own transparency and the dark and difficult tradition. This opening satire, he tells us, is a particular endeavour, not repeated again, to represent to the world what the Elizabethans understood to be Juvenal's 'sour and crabbed face'.

Though the facial expression may change in the rest of the biting satires, Juvenal remains the guiding classical inspiration:

> Pardon ye glowing ears; needs will it out
> Though brazen walls compassed my tongue about,
> As thick as wealthy Scrobio's quick set rows
> In the wide common that he did enclose.
> Pull out mine eyes, if I shall see no vice
> Or let me see it with detesting eyes.
> Renowned Aquine, now I follow thee,
> Far as I may for fear of jeopardy;
> And to thy hand yield up the ivy mace,
> From crabbed Persius and more smooth Horace . . .
> Yet name I not Mutius or Tigelline,
> Though they deserve a keener style than mine;
> Nor mean to ransack up the quiet grave;
> Nor burn dead bones, as he example gave:
> I tax the living; let dead ashes rest
> Whose faults are dead, and nailed in their chest.
> Who can refrain that's guiltless of their crime
> Whiles yet he lives in such a cruel time?
> (V, 1, 1–10, 15–22)

This is the equivalent in the *Virgidemiae* of the opening satire of Juvenal in which the indignant satirist declares *difficile est non saturam scribere* (30). There is a specific allusion to the passage at the end where Juvenal quotes the question of Lucilius then goes on to say that it is not safe to name the living:

> 'cuius non audeo dicere nomen?
> quid refert, dictis ignoscat Mucius an non?'
> pone Tigellinum: taeda lucebis in illa . . .
> (153–5)

('what man is there that I dare not name? What does it matter whether Mucius forgive my words, or not?' But just describe Tigellinus, and you will burn like a torch . . .)

Like Juvenal and for similar reasons, he does not name names, preferring instead to use type names like Scrobio, here from *scrobis* a ditch, and occasionally an initial, as in N— whereby the target is darkly concealed. Nevertheless, he does tax the living in the sense that many of his targets are not only just typical or drawn from the past but also topical and have to do, as in line 4, with iniquities attendant upon the recent enclosure of land, or with the abuse of tenants by unscrupulous landlords which features largely in this particular satire. He is as bold as the times allow.

But like Juvenal he recognises that ideally satire should have a forceful freedom and power denied to the present writer, though ironically and perhaps inconsistently he hails ancient satire as the embodiment of the ideal to which he aspires:

> The Satyre should be like the porcupine,
> 'That shoots sharp quills out in each angry line,
> And wounds the blushing cheek, and fiery eye,
> Of him that hears and readeth guiltily.
> Ye antique Satyres, how I bless your days
> That brooked your bolder style, their own dispraise,
> And well near wish, yet joy my wish is vain
> I had been then, or they were now again! . . .
> But from the ashes of my quiet style
> Hence forth may rise some raging rough Lucile,
> That may with Aeschylus both find and leese
> The snaky tresses of the Eumenides:
>   (V, 3, 1–8, 13–16)

Once again there is a familiar antithesis between Hall's 'quiet style' and the 'raging rough Lucile'. Apart from the pressures of the times, Hall was perhaps too much of a Horatian ever to have committed himself fully to this ideal. Even in the biting satires, there are intimations of a quiet and reflective spirit antithetical to that of the raging satirist. The sixth satire of his fourth book on the theme of discontentment with one's lot (*mempsimoiria*) recalls both the opening satire of Horace and Juvenal's celebrated tenth on the vanity of human wishes, but the quiet note on which it ends is in the spirit of Horace, inclining *inter silvas Academi quaerere verum* (*Epistle* II, 1, 45) 'to seek the truth in the groves of Academe'.

> 'Mongst all these stirs of discontented strife,
> Oh let me lead an Academic life,
> To know much, and to think we nothing know;
> Nothing to have, yet think we have enough,
> In skill to want, and wanting seek for more,

In weal or want, nor wish for greater store;
Envy, ye monarchs, with your proud excess
At our low sail, and our high happiness.

(IV, 6, 82–9)

Hall's academic ideal may possibly be one of cloistered virtue but it is certainly not an easy withdrawal, looking back, as it does, to the tradition of scepticism and asceticism that held sway in the Greek Academy of the third century BC (known principally through what remains of Cicero's dialogue the *Academica*). However, his prayer for 'some raging rough Lucile' was swiftly answered; they came thick and fast with the result that in the year following the publication of the biting satires came the bishops' ban on satire, prompted, no doubt, by the fear that it encouraged sedition. The *Virgidemiae* were on the initial list of proscribed texts but were subsequently reprieved. The episcopal edict may have dampened the rising enthusiasm for formal satire but the satirical spirit found a new outlet in the drama. Juvenal's name continued to exert a powerful fascination. The words of Ingenioso in the second part of *The Return from Parnassus* (c. 1601) are often quoted:

> *Difficile est Saturam non scribere, nam quis iniquae*
> *Tam patiens urbis, tam ferreus ut teneat se?*
> Ay, Juvenal, thy jerking hand is good,
> Not gently laying on, but fetching blood:
> So, surgeon-like, thou dost with cutting heal,
> Where nought but lanching can the wound avail . . .[26]

Hall is no servile imitator of Juvenal but uses his model for his own satiric programme. The old poet himself becomes a source of humour in the anti–Catholic satire of IV, 7.

> Who says these Romish pageants been too high
> To be the scorn of sportful poesy? . . .
> When once I think if carping Aquine's spright
> To see now Rome, were licensed to the light,
> How his enraged ghost would stamp and stare,
> That Caesar's throne is turned to Peter's chair.

(1–2, 9–12)

---

26. As, for example, in Selden, R. (1978) *English Verse Satire 1590–1765*, Allen & Unwin, p. 51.

The picture of the Roman's angry ghost stamping and staring is itself a sportive frame for belittling Juvenalian scorn emphatically rendered in the metamorphosis of the dignified throne into a mere chair. The stroke of deflationary wit is delivered with a pointedness almost worthy of the master.

A number of specific parallels have been noted by scholars, for many of Juvenal's topics could easily be translated into Elizabethan England which with its semi-feudal social structure was significantly nearer to Rome than the modern world. Treating the theme of the decay of hospitality in the great house, Hall found a parallel in Juvenal's fifth satire on the humiliations inflicted by the *patronus* Virro on his *cliens* Trebius. Hall takes over the names and a number of the humiliations. Juvenal is here represented in the version by George Chapman, published in 1629:

> And yet, for all this, what may be the cheer?
> To such vile wine thy throat is made the sink
> As greasy wool would not endure to drink . . .
> For Virro's self, the wine he drinks was born
> When consuls (Phoebus-like) appeared unshorn;
> A grape that long since in the wars was pressed
> By our confederate Marsians, and the rest;
> Of which no drop his longing friend can get,
> Though blown in fume up with a cardiac fit. . . .
> Virro himself in solemn bowls is served
> Of amber and disparent beryl kerved . . .
> But thy bowl stands an infinite beneath
> And bears the Beneventane cobbler's name
> Whose gallon drunk-off must thy blood enflame.[27]
>   (translating V, 24–5, 30–2, 37–9, 46–8)

> What though he quaff pure amber in his bowl
> Of March-brewed wheat, yet slakes thy thirsting soul
> With palish oat, frothing in Boston clay
> Or in a shallow cruse, nor must that stay
> Within thy reach, for fear of thy crazed brain
> But call and crave and have thy cruse again:
> Else how should even tale be registered

27. Anon (1875) *The Works of Chapman: Minor Poems and Translations*, Chatto & Windus, pp. 263–4. Chapman's translation is discussed by Kupersmith, W. (1986) *Roman Satirists in Seventeenth Century England*, University of Nebraska Press, Lincoln and London, pp. 50ff.

Of all thy draughts, on the chalked barrel's head?
And if he list revive his heartless grain [constitution]
With some French grape, or pure Canarian,
When pleasing Bordeaux falls unto his lot,
Some sourish Rochelle cuts thy thirsting throat.

(V, 2, 117–28)

The details have been duly Englished, though in theme and method there are marked similarities between the two passages. The dignity and smoothness of Virro is reflected in the rhythm and language of the lines allotted to him. The contrasting rougher treatment accorded to Trebius is reflected not only in the images but to some extent also in the rhythms and rhetorical arrangement. In Chapman, the spluttering awkwardness of the ninth line is surely designed to be deliberately deflationary after the high-flown pitch and the fluency of the previous five. In Hall, the smooth dignity of the opening (to some extent repeated in the penultimate) line contrasts sharply with the cutting and stinging (anti-)climax of the final line achieved by a well-judged witty hyperbole. Such dramatic shifting of pitch from high to low is particularly a feature of Juvenal's declamatory style and often responsible for its stinging effect. Hall, as his first imitator in English, and Chapman translating him are attuned to this feature of the Roman satirist's style which they seek to emulate in the management of their couplets.

Hall's satire, therefore, is consciously indebted to his classical predecessors with whom he is in constant dialogue. Elements of the whole tradition, from the satiric ideal represented in Lucilius to the actual practice of Horace, Persius and Juvenal as mediated through Renaissance commentators like Scaliger, are all variously compounded to make up the *Virgidemiae*, with the most potent element in their poetical formation coming from Juvenal.

Jonson and Horace

The Horatian *sermo* is similarly the most potent classical element in much of Jonson's verse. Jonson often was and always could have been a satirist in the Elizabethan mould of Asper in *Everyman out of his Humour*:

Well, I will scourge those apes
And to these courteous eyes oppose a mirror
As large as in the stage whereon we act;
Where they shall see the time's deformity
Anatomised in every nerve and sinew
With constant courage and contempt of fear.

However, when thrown on the defensive it was through the mouthpiece of a fictional Horace that he asserted his artistic integrity in the comical satire of the *Poetaster* (1601). To the edition of the play in his *Works* of 1616 he appended to the third act a translation of the defence of satire Horace makes in dialogue with Augustus's lawyer Trebatius (II, 1) in which the moral dignity of satire against the vicious is distinguished from the scurrility of libel. It is a curious anomaly in Jonson's literary career that while as imitator of the classics he followed Horace's advice not to be a *fidus interpres* translating *verbum ex verbo*, word for word, as translator he chose to be accurate above all else, with the result that his translations tend to be wooden and stilted. It is not in his formal translations (including *The Art of Poetry* and *Epode* II, 'The Happy Man') that the ripest fruits of his affinity with Horace are to be found.

The *Poetaster* contains an adaptation of a favourite Horatian *sermo*, I, 9, the poet's encounter with the bore, a pestiferous social climber who wants to worm his way into Maecenas's circle and whom Horace cannot shake off.

Ibam forte Via Sacra, sicut meus est mos,
nescioquid meditans nugarum, totus in illis,
accurrit quidam notus mihi nomine tantum
arreptaque manu, 'quid agis, dulcissime rerum?'
(1–4)

(I happened to be walking along the Sacred Way, as is my wont, musing on some trifle or other and totally absorbed in that, when up runs a fellow known to me only by name, seizes my hand and says 'How goes it, my dearest chap?')

At the opening, rather than meditating about nothing in particular, Jonson's Horace rehearses a short lyric he has composed for Maecenas:

Swell me a bowl with lusty wine,
Till I may see the plump Lyaeus swim
　　Above the brim:
I drink as I would write,
In flowing measure filled with flame and sprite.
　　　　　　　　　　(Act III, 1, 8–12)

The bore introduces himself affecting Horatian interests:

Nay, we are new turned poet too, which is more; and a satirist too,
which is more than that: I write just in thy vein, I. I am for your odes,
or your sermons, or anything indeed; we are a gentleman besides; our
name is Rufus Laberius Crispinus; we are a pretty Stoic too.

Crispinus, the poetaster (alias Marston), is the slap-dash poet from
Horace's *Satire* I, 4. He insists on giving Horace a sample of his
verse:

Rich was thy hap, sweet dainty cap,
　　There to be placed;
Where thy smooth black, sleek white may smack,
　　And both be graced.

White is there usurped for her brow; her forehead: and then sleek, as
the parallel to smooth, that went before. A kind of paranomasie, or
agnomination:

　　　　　　　　　　(85–91)

The contrast between the poet and poetaster integrates the
Horatian original into the wider concerns of Jonson's play.
In the original, Horace is the victim of his own civility and
good manners: Juvenal, we may reflect, would have given the
bore short shrift. Much of the good humour of the piece arises
from Horace's telling of the story against himself. This element is
necessarily lost in a dramatic presentation, and Horace's inner
torment has to come by way of asides. These prove to be so
numerous and testy as to strain credulity. Jonson's Horace seems
too irritable to be tolerant of such a fool. We miss, too, the
relaxed and condensed style of the *sermo*. Most of the scene is in
prose, except for certain pronouncements of Horace. For Jonson
the nub of the scene is the rejection of Crispinus's assumption that
he can advance his own interests in the salon of Maecenas by
undermining the great patron's relations with other poets:

non isto vivimus illic
quo tu rere modo; domus hac nec purior ulla est
nec magis aliena malis; nil mi officit, inquam,
ditior hic aut est quia doctior; est locus uni
cuique suus.

(48–52)

(We don't live there on such terms as you think. No house is purer or
more free from such intrigues as that. And it doesn't hurt me, I tell
you, that this man is richer or that more learned than I am. Each has
his own place.)

Here is Jonson's expansion:

Sir, your silkness
Clearly mistakes Maecenas and his house,
To think there breathes a spirit beneath his roof,
Subject unto those poor affections
Of undermining envy and detraction,
Moods only proper to base grovelling minds.
That place is not in Rome, I dare affirm,
More pure or free from such low common evils.
There's no man grieved, that this is thought more rich
Or that more learned; each man hath his place,
And to his merit his reward of grace,
Which, with a mutual love, they all embrace.

(248–59)

This perhaps is more in the manner of Asper: Jonson's comical
satire is more tormented and less genial than that of Horace. It
might seem from this that Jonson's affinity with Horace did not
naturally arise from similar poetic tempers but was acquired
through shared cultural perspectives.

Satire I, 9 has also been thought to have given Donne ideas
which he used in his first and fourth satires, in both of which is
featured an encounter with a troublesome companion. But
whereas Crispinus is simply an irritating fool of no consequence
in whom Horace has no interest, Donne seems curiously taken
with the 'fondling motley humorist' of his first. In the fourth, the
courtier has formidable talents and knowledge:

he can win widows, and pay scores
Make men speak treason, cozen subtlest whores,
Out-flatter favourites or out-lie either
Jovius or Surius or both together. . . .
He like a privileged spy whom nothing can
Discredit, libels now 'gainst each great man.
He names the price for every office paid.

                    (45–8, 119–21)[28]

He is altogether more sinister and dangerous than Crispinus so
that the poet, far from being bored or irritated, comes to feel
anxious and is contaminated by his presence:

                    for hearing him, I found
That as burnt venomed lechers do grow sound
By giving others their sores, I might grow
Guilty, he be free.

                    (133–6)

Horace, as the friend of Maecenas, writes from the assured
standpoint of the insider; Donne is the alienated outsider
oppressed by the corruption of the court which he denounces in
the remaining hundred lines of the satire. His classical affinities as
a satirist lie with Juvenal and Persius from whom it has been said
he derived the idea that satire should be harsh in its verse-form
and replete with dark conceits.

The genial comedy of Horace's poem comes out well in the
later version by Thomas Sprat. As Horace is getting desperate, up
comes a friend, Abraham Cowley in Sprat's modernisation:

While he did thus run on, who should we meet
But my friend C[owley] passing cross the street.
C[owley] straight found what kind of man he was,
Nor to see through him, need he his glass;
So when the usual compliments were passed,
I trod on's toes, and softly him embraced;
I winked and shrugged, and many signs I gave,
Which silently did his assistance crave:
But my unmerciful malicious friend
Seemed not to understand what I intend,

---

28.   Smith, A.J. (ed.) (1971) *John Donne: The Complete English Poems*, Penguin.

Enjoyed my misery, and smiled to see
What thin small plots I made to be set free.[29]

He finally escapes (as in Jonson) when Crispinus is detained in connection with a lawsuit.

To return to Jonson, the *Poetaster*, in its representation of the ideal role of art in the *civitas* and in its aspiration to classical purity of expression against the crudities of the ill-disciplined Marston and the popular stage, marks Jonson out as a Horatian disciple with a clear Augustan vision both of the artistic standards to which Elizabethan literature should aspire and of the uses to which poetry should be put. This vision he made manifest in his poetry and fostered in the work of his poetic sons.

Jonson's Augustanism was well thought out and systematic. It can be seen as a major influence upon his dramatic practice. Like Hall, he reacted against prevailing Elizabethan taste in other genres such as the Ovidian epyllion and love elegy, romance and the Petrarchan sonnet, but from the start he was surer than Hall about the character of his new alternative, and as a disciple of Horace he had no time for the idea that satire should be metrically harsh, full of dark allusions and generally obscure. In administering purifying pills to Crispinus/Marston, Horace/Jonson signals his desire for consistency of artistic refinement and polish that we find only intermittently in Hall. Artistic refinement is not, of course, incompatible with satirical bite. When, in the final scene of the *Poetaster*, Horace is falsely accused by Lupus (a wolf in his Latin name) of libelling Caesar, Virgil pronounces (after Lupus has been taken away to be whipped):

'Tis not the wholesome sharp morality,
Or modest anger of a satiric spirit,
That hurts or wounds the body of the state;
But the sinister application
Of the malicious ignorant, and base
Interpreter.

(V, 3, 137–42)

Caesar compliantly agrees. Caesar had earlier experienced for himself the sharper side of Horace's tongue when, before Virgil entered, he had asked Horace for his opinion of his poetry:

29. Cited in Kupersmith, W. (1986) pp. 91–2.

Caesar. . . . Horace, what say'st thou, that art the poorest,
   And likeliest to envy, or detract?
Horace. Caesar speaks after common men in this,
   To make a difference of me for my poorness;
   As if the filth of poverty sunk as deep
   Into a knowing spirit, as the bane
   Of riches doth into an ignorant soul. . . .
   But knowledge is the nectar that keeps sweet
   A perfect soul, even in this grave of sin;
   And for my soul, it is as free as Caesar's
   For what I know is due I'll give to all. . . .
Caesar. Thanks, Horace for thy free and wholesome sharpness.

                                        (V, 1, 77–83, 88–91, 94)

History is rewritten here to represent the idealism of Jonson's imagining.

In the real world, Jonson's circumstances were far removed from the happy ideal of Horace in the *Poetaster*, secure in his patronage and at the centre of a group of artists whose work had an honoured and influential place in the community at large. Though he fell foul of the authorities on numerous occasions, nevertheless he did not often take upon himself the persona of the isolated and alienated outsider. On the contrary, he writes like Horace, and unlike Juvenal and Persius, from the standpoint of one who is integrated into the social world, and uses his poetic talent judiciously to define and defend the best in contemporary civilisation. This is the context in which his satire functions. Its predominant style is that of 'A Speech according to Horace', where speech is Jonson's rendering of the Horatian *sermo*. The poem contains no allusions to Horace, though Jonson's editors cite parallels from the patriotic odes of the third book lamenting national degeneracy.[30] Its subject matter is entirely contemporary and concerns the growing indifference of the aristocracy to military service which is now left to amateurs such as the Artillery Company, whom the poet exhorts patriotically:

Go on, increase in virtue and in fame
   And keep the glory of the English name
Up among nations.

                                        (49–51)

---

30. See Donaldson, I. (ed.) (1975) *Ben Jonson: Poems*, Oxford University Press, p. 201.

As for the 'grandlings' who will not let their sons be trained by their social inferiors, their scorn is grandly imagined and the hollowness of their values loftily mocked:

> What need we know
> More than to praise a dog, or horse, or speak
>   The hawking language; or our day to break
> With citizens? Let clowns and tradesmen breed
>   Their sons to study arts, the laws, the creed;
> We will believe, like men of our own rank
>   In so much land a year, or such a bank
> That turns us so much moneys, at which rate
>   Our ancestors imposed on prince and state.
> Let poor nobility be virtuous.
>
> (70–9)

The only training of these 'carcases of honour' (99) is in fashionable etiquette. In its balance of praise and blame, its clear-sighted moral purpose and its essentially plain and unfanciful yet polished style that maintains a conversational decorum and is varied with the use of irony, this is indeed an English version of the Horatian *sermo*.

A poem more obviously classical in its theme is 'Inviting a Friend to Supper'. The direct contrast between the luxury and formality of the grand aristocratic dinner and the informal plain meal with conversation and poetry among friends is treated in Juvenal's eleventh satire, but like all Juvenal's *topoi* it was an old one. A *locus classicus*, particularly as it is associated with rural retreat on the Sabine farm, is the introductory section to one of Horace's most loved poems, *Satire* II, 6 (which contains the fable of the town and country mice). Here is the version by Sir John Beaumont, a son of Ben:

>   when shall my sight
> Again be happy in beholding thee
> My country farm? or when shall I be free
> To read in books what ancient writers speak;
> To rest in sleep, which others may not break,
> To taste (in hours secure from courtly strife)
> The soft oblivion of a careful life? . . .
> O suppers of the gods! O nights divine!
> When I before our Lar might feast with mine,
> And feed my prating slaves with tasted meat,

As ev'ry one should have desire to eat.
The frolick guest not bound with heavy laws,
The liquor from unequal measures draws:
Some being strong delight in larger draughts
Some call for lesser cups to clear their thoughts.
Of others' house and lands no speeches grow
Nor whether Lepos danceth well or no.
We talk of things which to our selves pertain,
Which not to know would be a sinful stain.
Are men by riches or by virtue blest?
Of friendship's ends is use or right the best?
Of good what is the nature, what excells?
(86–92, 97–111, translating 60–2, 65–76)[31]

This is hardly satire, though the contrast with less desirable
dinners of rigid formality, obligatory drinking and unworthy
conversation is clearly made. The eating and drinking are to
satisfy natural needs rather than social form, and the uplifting
conversation at this Socratic meal is to be of the self-examining
kind. It is a Roman version of plain living and high thinking for
which the easy, familiar and plain style of the *sermo* is the perfect
medium.

There are no particular echoes of Horace in Jonson's poem,
which is indebted to three good-humoured epigrams of Martial
inviting friends to modest suppers.

It is the fair acceptance, sir, creates
The entertainment perfect, not the cates.
(7–8)

Jonson's opening develops the sentiment of Martial's *vinum tu
facies bonum bibendo* (V, 78, 16) 'you will make the wine good by
drinking'. The host in the Roman epigram offers social ease and
natural behaviour. There will be no lewd dancers, no reading
from a bulky volume, but the entertainment of some lively pipe-
playing. The ending comes as a surprise with an ambiguous
reference to prior female company. The long list of plain fare
common to all three epigrams of Martial is happily anglicised by
Jonson. 'I'll tell you of more, and lie, so that you will come' (17)
is taken from XI, 52, 13, *mentiar ut venias* 'I shall lie so you will
come', and 'I'll profess no verses to repeat' (24) looks like *nil*

31. Cited in Kupersmith, W. (1986) p. 27.

recitabo tibi (16) 'I will recite nothing to you' (another lie?) from the same poem. The host here makes this promise: 'even though you read your "Giants" through again'. This sounds as if it might be stretching friendship too far. In the third epigram the host, like Jonson here, offers good-quality wine after describing his meal, ending with sentiments closely echoed by Jonson:

> accedent sine felle ioci nec mane timenda
>   libertas, et nil quod tacuisse velis:
> de prasino conviva meus venetoque loquatur
>   nec faciunt quemquam pocula nostra reum.
>
> (X, 48, 21–4)

(There shall be jests without gall, and a freedom not to be dreaded next morning and no word you might wish unsaid. Let my guest talk of rival factions in the circus; my cups do not make a man guilty of crime.)

> Nor shall our cups make any guilty men,
>   But at our parting we will be as when
> We innocently met. No simple word
>   That shall be uttered at our mirthful board
> Shall make us sad next morning, or affright
>   The liberty that we will enjoy tonight.
>
> (37–42)

Jonson's poem is a great deal more than the sum of its classical parts. To begin with, in none of Martial's epigrams is there to be real meat for the intellect (the 'Giants' hardly counts), whereas not only the reading of a classic but also free criticism of that reading is central to Jonson's classical feast:

> Howso'er, my man
> Shall read a piece of Virgil, Tacitus,
>   Livy, or of some better book to us,
> Of which we'll speak our minds, amidst our meat;
>
> (20–3)

The reading taken with the food is at the centre of the poem (exactly halfway through); its placing is decorous and has symbolic force. After the meat of the feast comes the wine of classic vintage:

> But that which most doth take my muse and me
> Is a pure cup of rich Canary wine
> Which is at the Mermaid's now, but shall be mine;
> Of which had Horace or Anacreon tasted
> Their lives, as do their lines, till now had lasted.
>
> (28–32)

Horace and Anacreon are invoked here as genial celebrants of the joys of wine which in their lyric feasts becomes a metaphor for the intense enjoyment of the living moment, nowhere better encapsulated than in their poetry itself. In the *Poetaster* Horace's lyric moment had been a song to Bacchus. Jonson's wine, therefore, must be a real enticement, not something of inferior quality which the guest is to make good in his own imagination. The rich evocation of the delight of the wine to come seems to subordinate even classic poetry to the living moment. Art is but a part of the abundant life. Yet the antithesis between their lasting lines and their long-lost lives is also a celebration of the transcendent power of their poetry and an oblique reminder of its imperative message, *carpe diem*, in the face of life's brevity. And so there is much more in Jonson's poem than in the three epigrams of Martial. It is not merely that it is longer than the longest of the three (32 lines) but that it has a depth and seriousness beneath the gaiety, wit and humour that it shares with Martial. The three Roman epigrams are all poems that are more or less confined to social manners; Martial offers his guests plain fare, the freedom of informal good fellowship and harmless pleasure. Jonson unassumingly and without the least strain offers a feast of reason culminating in the flow of soul that altogether constitutes a much more enticing and worthier ideal. In his poem we are conscious, as we are not in Martial's, of an intellectual challenge and idealism striving against the background awareness of the passage of time, which all brings to mind the lyrical Horace who is consciously invoked and the Horace of the *sermo* particularly as it is employed in the *Epistles*, despite the obvious debt to Martial and the inclusion of the poem in the *Epigrams* of 1616.

Jonson's poems may be said to illustrate and vindicate the Renaissance doctrine of imitation; as imitator he is able 'to convert the substance or riches of another poet to his own use . . .. Not to imitate servilely, as Horace saith, and catch at vices, for virtue; but to draw forth out of the best and choicest flowers with the bee and turn it all into honey, work it into one relish and savour,

make our imitation sweet' (*Discoveries*, 3056ff.). The classic advice
of Horace he rendered as follows:

> Yet common matter thou thine own mayst make
> If thou the vile broad-trodden ring forsake;
> For being a poet, thou mayst feign, create
> Not care, as thou wouldst faithfully translate
> To render word for word, nor with thy sleight
> Of imitation, leap into a strait,
> From whence thy modesty, or poem's law
> Forbids thee forth again thy foot to draw.
>   (*The Art of Poetry*, 187–94, translating 131–5)

The pitfalls attendant upon faithful translation here are successfully avoided in 'Inviting a Friend to Supper'. Nor is it necessary
to know where precisely the bee has been in order to relish the
resulting honey, though the uncovering of trace elements may
assist in the appreciation of the subtleties of its distinctive savour,
and connoisseurs of honey doubtless enjoy exercising their palates
in fine discrimination of its provenance.

The inclusion of the poem in the *Epigrams* reveals much about
his attitude to the decorum of genre. For the poem is not in an
obvious sense an epigram as either the Elizabethan or the modern
world understands the term. Although it resembles the three
Roman epigrams alluded to earlier, its style, though plain like that
of Martial, is not as curt and pointed as the Roman or as Jonson
himself can be in more obviously epigrammatic poems. The
handling of rhyme, enjambement and the position of the caesura
is flexible and free (Beaumont's couplets by contrast are stiffer and
much more epigrammatic), creating an epistolary style that is
relaxed, informal and varied in movement, something much more
like the Horatian *sermo* than the epigrams of Martial. The poem
succeeds because it has its own decorum of style and content
rather than because it fulfils some ideal notional requirement of
the classical epigram.

In the *Epigrams*, Jonson was consciously departing from
contemporary practice:

> To my Book
>
> It will be looked for, book, when some but see
>   Thy title *Epigrams*, and named of me,
> Thou shouldst be bold, licentious, full of gall,

Wormwood and sulphur, sharp and toothed withal;
Become a petulant thing, hurl ink and wit
As madmen stones, not caring whom they hit.

(1–6)

To my mere English Censurer

To thee my way in epigram seems new
When both it is the old way and the true.

(1–2)

His authority for 'the old way' was not so much Martial as the epigrams of the Greek anthology which had recently come to light and had just been edited in the first decade of the seventeenth century.[32] They include, alongside pungent satirical pieces (the favourite Elizabethan form), love poems, elegies and panegyric. In their wide range Jonson's epigrams follow the Greek tradition. As an imitator of the classics, Jonson works in the spirit of Horace's recommendation and is not inhibited by 'poem's law' (*The Art of Poetry*, 193) *lex operis* sometimes glossed as *lex generis*, the law of genre. None of his contemporaries gave as much consideration to the decorum of genre as it had operated in the ancient world, and in every form that he undertook, he changed native practice as a consequence. A classical perspective freed him from the tyranny of the fashionable in both satire and epigram. The inclusion of 'Inviting a Friend to Supper' among the *Epigrams* illustrates, too, the essential freedom of his classical practice at its best.

Cowley's country mouse

As satire gradually became one of the dominant literary modes of the seventeenth century, interest in the classical satirists grew and is manifested in many translations, paraphrases and imitations. Among the classical consolations composed by Abraham Cowley from the obscurity of his retreat from the world, first at Barn Elms near Putney then at Chertsey after the Restoration, is a delightful paraphrase of Horace's fable of the town and country mice from *Satire* II, 6. In the original it follows praise of the

32. See Atkins, J.W.E. (1947) *English Literary Criticism: The Renascence*, Methuen, p. 281.

country and an account of the vexations of the poet's life in town amidst which he exclaims *o rus, quando te aspiciam* (60) 'O countryside, when shall I see you?', leading to thoughts of a typical meal with its accompanying *sermo* (71), perhaps on the *summum bonum*. Or perhaps his neighbours will rattle off an old wives' tale like the following:

> olim
> rusticus urbanum murem mus paupere fertur
> accepisse cavo, veterem vetus hospes amicum.
> (79–81)

(Once upon a time – so the tale goes, a country mouse welcomed a city mouse in his poor hole, host and guest old friends both.)

The condensed and witty juxtaposition here of country and town, the rustic and the urbane, and the animal and the human neatly contains the essence of the tale's attraction. A pioneer of a free way of handling an original, Cowley, whose version is more than twice the length of Horace, expands this opening greatly and makes the mice strangers to each other, enabling a sharper contrast:

> At the large foot of a fair hollow tree,
> Close to ploughed ground, seated commodiously,
> His ancient and hereditary house,
> There dwelt a good substantial country-mouse:
> Frugal and grave, and careful of the main,
> Yet, one, who once did nobly entertain
> A city mouse well coated, sleek and gay;
> A mouse of high degree, which lost his way,
> Wantonly walking forth to take the air,
> And arrived early, and belighted there,
> For a day's lodging.
> (1–11)[33]

The country mouse, if he knew it, seems to be related in literary terms to Horace's happy man, translated at the same time by Cowley:

---

33. Appended to his essay 'Of Agriculture' in Waller, A.R. (ed.) (1906) *Abraham Cowley: Essays, Plays and Sundry Verses*, Cambridge University Press.

> Happy the man whom bounteous gods allow
> With his own hands paternal grounds to plough.

The town mouse, the villain of the piece, is a slippery customer, one who has lost his way in life. The rustic meal affords a plentiful supply of what is the rodents' natural fare, a point amusingly made in the climactic line of the triplet (Cowley's addition):

> Fitches and beans, peason, and oats and wheat
> And a large chestnut, the delicious meat
> Which Jove himself, were he a mouse, would eat.
> (15–17)

Bidding his guest eat, the country mouse alludes to the sermon on the mount:

> Freely (said he) fall on and never spare
> The bounteous gods will for tomorrow care.
> (22–3)

The town mouse is noticeably developed from Horatian hints. He is a condescending fellow whose 'Epicurean mind' (26) has turned its back on nature in favour of the man-made 'cakes and pies of London' (29), unnatural fare for a mouse. He offers his country host an eloquent vision of pleasure (Cowley's addition) which is all the more seductive because it is dressed up with the garnish of a Renaissance ideal (knowing men and manners). He then expresses a philosophy of pleasure derived from phrases in the original that bring to mind the lyric Horace of the *carpe diem* poems and the *beatus ille* epode:

> Why should a soul so virtuous and so great
> Lose it self thus in an obscure retreat?
> Let savage beasts lodge in a country den,
> You should see towns, and manners know, and men:
> And taste the generous luxury of the court,
> Where all the mice of quality resort;
> Where thousand beauteous shes about you move,
> And by high fare are pliant made to love.
> We all e're long must render up our breath,
> No care or hole can shelter us from death.
>   Since life is so uncertain, and so short,
> Let's spend it all in feasting and in sport.

Come, worthy sir, come with me, and partake,
All the great things that mortals happy make.

(34-47)

carpe viam . . .
dum licet, in rebus iucundis vive beatus;
vive memor, quam sis aevi brevis.

(93, 96-7)

(Seize the way . . . while you may, live happily in pleasant
circumstances, live mindful of how brief your time is.)

A contrast might be suggested here with Horace's truly Socratic
injunction translated by Cowley in 'The Dangers of Procrastina-
tion':

Begin, be bold, and venture to be wise;
He who defers this work from day to day,
Does on a river's bank expecting stay;
Till the whole stream, which stopped him, should go on,
That runs, and as it runs, forever will run on.[34]

                    sapere aude,
incipe, vivendi qui recte prorogat horam
rusticus expectat dum labitur amnis, at ille
labitur, et labetur in omne volubilis aevum.

(Epistle I, 2, 40-3)

At the halfway point, the rhetorical question added by Cowley
confirms the role of the town mouse as persuasive tempter.
Though we smile at its portentousness in an animal fable, the
question still has moral force:

Alas what virtue hath sufficient arms
T'oppose bright honour, and soft pleasure's charms?
What wisdom can their magic force repel?
It draws the reverend hermit from his cell.

(48-51)

---

34. Dr Johnson praised this last line as 'one example of representative
    versification, which perhaps no English line can equal', 'Cowley' in Hill,
    G.B. (ed.) (1905) Lives of the English Poets by Samuel Johnson, 3 vols, Oxford
    University Press, vol. 1, p. 62.

In his essay 'Of Liberty', honour and pleasure are again the delusive snares that must be rejected when Cowley meditates upon Horace's line *quisnam igitur liber? sapiens sibi qui imperiosus* (*Satire* II, 7, 83) 'who then is free? the wise man who commands himself'.

> Who governs his own course with steady hand,
> Who does himself with sovereign power command;
> Whom neither death, nor poverty does fright,
> Who stands not awkwardly in his own light
> Against the truth: who can when pleasures knock
> Loud at the door, keep firm the bolt and lock.
> Who can though honour at his gate should stay
> In all her masking clothes, send her away
> And cry, begone, I have no mind to play.

The tone then changes when, from the hint of a higher style of slightly mocking solemnity in Horace, Cowley moves fully into the mock-heroic mode; in the plain style of the animal fable, the incongruity of mythology is made more comic by Cowley's delicate yoking together of celestial beings with unwonted domestic modesty:

> It was the time, when witty poets tell,
> That Phoebus into Thetis' bosom fell:
> She blushed at first, and then put out the light,
> And drew the modest curtains of the night.
> Plainly, the truth to tell, the sun was set.
>
> (52–6)

After the gourmet meal, the country mouse finds to his cost that it is not only the country that is home to 'savage beasts':

> Lo, in the midst of a well freighted pie,
> They both at last glutted and wanton lie.
> When see the sad reverse of prosperous fate,
> And what fierce storms on mortal glories wait.
> With hideous noise, down the rude servants come,
> Six dogs before run barking into th' room;
> The wretched gluttons fly with wild affright
> And hate the fulness which retards their flight.
>
> (82–9)

Cowley intensifies both the humour and the moral by the felicitous additions of the pie as the final repository of their wantonness, the rhetorical exclamation on the power of fate and the retarding effect of the full stomachs. The country mouse sees the error of his ways and wishes to return to nature, but it is less sure in Cowley than in Horace whether he survives to escape. The old wives' tale proves to be a *sermo* on the *summum bonum* after all. The success of Cowley's delightful paraphrase intensifying in equal proportions both the humour and the moral emphasis of the original and thereby maintaining the Horatian balance *ridentem dicere verum* in telling the truth with a smile may make us wish that he had spent more time modestly with Horace than ambitiously with Pindar.

Imitations by Rochester and Oldham

Cowley together with John Denham had openly practised free treatment of the classics wherein the English version is consciously enlivened by additional invention and wit from the translator. Their successors went a stage further in writing formal imitations. John Oldham in his advertisement to *Some New Pieces* (1681) explains that in his version of the *Art of Poetry* he has put Horace 'into a more modern dress, than hitherto he has appeared in, that is, by making him speak, as if he were living, and writing now. I therefore resolved to alter the scene from Rome to London, and to make use of English names of men, places, and customs, where the parallel would decently permit, which I conceived would give a kind of new air to the poem, and render it more agreeable to the relish of the present age.'[35] In this he may have been inspired by Rochester whose earlier poem 'An Allusion to Horace, the Tenth Satire of the First Book' is the first thorough-going imitation in English.[36] 'It is a kind of middle composition between translation and original design,' wrote Dr

35. Brooks, H.F. (ed.) (1987) *The Poems of John Oldham*, Oxford University Press, p. 87, lines 23ff.
36. Vieth, D.M. (ed.) (1968) *The Complete Poems of John Wilmot Earl of Rochester*, Yale University Press, New Haven and London. The poem is also included in Springarn, J.E. (1908) vol. 2, p. 282ff. See also Brooks, H.F. (1949) 'The Imitation in English Poetry Especially in Formal Satire Before the Age of Pope', *Review of English Studies* **25**, 124–40.

Johnson,[37] 'which pleases when the thoughts are unexpectedly applicable and the parallels lucky.' Dryden as Lucilius to Rochester as Horace may seem an unexpected, inapplicable and impertinent parallel until we recall the date of the poem's composition, 1675, when Dryden was as yet principally a writer of plays whose merit, as Rochester justly observes, he overestimated and in which he had often been content to pander to the taste of an undiscriminating audience. The critic's judicious advice may well have given the playwright pause for thought:

> To write what may securely stand the test
> Of being well read over thrice at least,
> Compare each phrase, examine every line,
> Weigh every word, and every thought refine.
> Scorn all applause the vile rout can bestow,
> And be content to please those few who know.
> Canst thou be such a vain, mistaken thing,
> To wish thy works might make a playhouse ring
> With the unthinking laughter and poor praise
> Of fops and ladies, factious for thy plays?
> Then send a cunning friend to learn thy doom
> From the shrewd judges of the drawing room.
>
> (98–109)

Not all the parallels in Rochester's allusion are managed with the artful dexterity that Pope later brought to the imitation of Horace, but in assuming the mantle of the poet-critic Rochester was faced with the challenge of disciplining his powers to the rigorous demands of the original, and insofar as he was successful he raised the level of critical debate among his contemporaries by bringing to bear a classical perspective upon Restoration practice. 'An Allusion' is the only poem on a literary topic of those by and attributed to Rochester[38] that amounts to anything more than wild and salacious lampooning.

The development of the formal imitation in the period of the Restoration, whatever the uses to which individual poets put it in their particular poems, springs from a deep-seated aspiration

---

37. 'Pope' in Hill, G.B. (ed.) (1905) *Lives of the English Poets by Samuel Johnson*, 3 vols, Oxford University Press, vol. 3, p. 176.

38. See, for example, the poems attributed to Rochester in Lord, G. de F. (ed.) (1963) *Poems on Affairs of State*, vol. 1, 1660–1678, Yale University Press, New Haven and London.

stimulated perhaps by rival French success to realign contemporary culture on classical lines and thereby to raise its standards;
the classics are to serve the cause of civilisation in the present.
This is only too apparent in Oldham's imitation of Horace's *Art of
Poetry*. To cite one instance, the substitution of Ben Jonson for the
unknown Roman Quintilius brings the lesson of the original fully
home to English readers:

> Had you consulted learned Ben of old,
> He would your faults impartially have told;
> 'This verse correction wants' (he would have said)
> 'And so does this': if you replied, you had
> To little purpose several trials made;
> He presently would bid you strike a dash
> On all, and put in better in the place:
> But if he found you once a stubborn sot,
> That would not be corrected in a fault;
> He would no more his pains and counsel spend
> On an abandoned fool that scorned to mend,
> But bid you in the devil's name go on,
> And hug you dear impertinence alone.
>
> (745–57)

Only a poet who championed Horace's view of art and felt its
contemporary value could dedicate himself to an imitation of the
Art of Poetry. The imitation perhaps signals a change of direction
and emphasis in Oldham's short career, for the pose that he strikes
in the prologue to his *Satyrs upon the Jesuits* (1678) at the outset is
far from Horatian and outdoes that of Juvenal who had never
actually abjured art in his famous opening satire which Oldham's
lines clearly recall:

> 'Tis pointed satyr and the sharps of wit
> For such a prize are th' only weapons fit:
> Nor needs there art or genius here to use,
> Where indignation can create a muse:
> Should parts and nature fail, yet very spite
> Would make the arrant'st Wild or Withers write.
>
> (26–31)

The scorn directed at the spiteful Puritan satirists Robert Wild and
George Wither leads us to expect that Oldham's nobler indignation will produce poetry whose art is less rough than theirs.

Nevertheless, in these early satires we can frequently hear in Dryden's memorable phrase from his elegy 'To the Memory of Mr Oldham' 'the harsh cadence of a rugged line'.

In the later preface, Oldham hoped he had hit 'the easy and familiar way of writing which is peculiar to Horace in his epistles, and was his proper talent above any of mankind'. He took the lessons of Horace to heart in his imitations of the *Art of Poetry* and *Satire* I, 9 (on the impertinent bore) which are written in a quieter and smoother vein to meet the requirements of the Horatian *sermo*. The familiarity of the fop's conversation happily registers the life of the age:

> He all the while baits me with tedious chat,
> Speaks much about the drought, and how the rate
> Of hay is raised, and what it now goes at:
> Tells me of a new comet at the Hague,
> Portending God knows what, a dearth or plague:
> Names every wench, that passes through the park,
> How much she is allowed, and who the spark
> That keeps her: points, who lately got a clap,
> And who at the Groom-Porters had ill hap
> Three nights ago in play with such a lord:
>
> (26–35)

When in the next year he returned to Juvenal with imitations of his third and thirteenth, the satire that resulted was not of the wildly indignant kind that had scourged the Jesuits but was something altogether more sober and disciplined, reflecting Oldham's absorption of the Augustan Horace. This is not to suggest that he was any the less successful in the imitations of Juvenal. On the contrary, to give one example, the Roman's vivid imagining of the physical stresses of metropolitan living felt with particular acuteness by the urban poor – for whom the city unlike Eliot's depressing and derelict *Waste Land* is only too real – and represented in his third satire by his plain-speaking character Umbricius prompted many energetic and finely realised evocations of contemporary London:

> If you walk out in bus'ness ne'er so great,
> Ten thousand stops you must expect to meet:
> Thick crowds in every place you must charge through,

And storm your passage, wheresoe're you go:
While tides of followers behind you throng,
And, pressing on your heels, shove you along:
One with a board, or rafter hits your head,
Another with his elbow bores your side;
Some tread upon your corns, perhaps in sport,
Meanwhile your legs are cased all o'er with dirt.
Here you the march of a slow funeral wait,
Advancing to the Church with solemn state:
There a sedan and lackeys stop your way,
That bears some punk of honour to the play:
Now you some mighty piece of timber meet,
Which tott'ring threatens ruin to the street:
Next a huge Portland stone, for building Paul's
It self almost a rock, on carriage rolls:
Which, if it fall, would cause a massacre,
And serve at once to murder and inter.

                                                    (375–94)

The succession of vividly particularised images represents the
hazards and discomforts one after another as they might be
experienced by one walking in the push and shove of the city
throng, beginning with comparatively minor trips to the heels and
potentially more damaging bumps to the head and continuing
with threats from elbows and to the toes. The stops and checks
are increasingly portentous, with the solemnity of the funeral and
death juxtaposed with the mock solemnity of the rake's progress
to pleasure. After the would-be high and mighty comes the
mighty piece of timber and finally over four lines the grand
climax of the Portland stone with construction wittily threatening
destruction. The closing image teeters on the brink of hyperbole
but represents a credible actuality while bringing to a head the
sense of insecurity and danger that is increasingly felt on this
journey through the city. All is precisely imagined and clearly
conveyed; the passage has its own decorum and is not written up
to accord with a factitious notion of Juvenalian satire. The
encounter with Juvenal has provided an imaginative stimulus for
the poet to paint his own pictures in his own way. The same
encounter produced a very different result in Dr Johnson's *London*
of the next century. In the imitation the poet is freed from the
compulsion to 'reproduce' the original closely in either content or
style. It can be freely appropriated to create a rival poem where

the only real debt, but a debt without which it could never have come to be, is the imaginative stimulus itself.

Dryden's translation of Juvenal

For the closer relation that we expect in a translation we can turn now to Dryden's Juvenal (1692), the best English version in his or any age.

> A noble author would not be pursued too close by a translator. We lose his spirit when we think to take his body. The grosser part remains with us, but the soul is flown away in some noble expression or some delicate turn of words or thought.
>
> (*Discourse concerning the original and progress of satire*)[39]

In accordance with this cardinal precept, Dryden, who translated *Satires* I, III, VI and XVI, and his fellow translators who did the rest, while not modernising in the way of an imitator, allow themselves considerable latitude in omitting many of the more recondite names and allusions which previous literal translators had retained and needed to explain in voluminous notes that filled more than twice as many pages as their actual translations.

> This must be said for our translation, that, if we give not the whole sense of Juvenal, yet we give the most considerable part of it; we give it in general so clearly, that few notes are sufficient to make us intelligible. We make our author at least appear in a poetic dress. We have actually made him more sounding and more elegant than he was before in English and have endeavoured to make him speak that kind of English which he would have spoken if he had lived in England, and had written to this age.[40]

Dryden's practice in translation differs from Oldham's in his imitation, though the foregoing principle in the final sentence is not dissimilar. The primary objective is to create a contemporary poem of comparable stature to the original classic.

Dryden's genius expressed itself with a greater variety of success through translation than that of any other English poet.

---

39. From 'A Discourse Concerning Satire' (1693) prefixed to the translations of Juvenal and Persius: Watson, G. (1962) vol. 2, p. 153.
40. Watson, G. (1962) vol. 2, p. 154.

His versions of Virgil, Lucretius, Horace, Ovid and Homer are unsurpassed. If we ask why Juvenal proved so congenial in the early 1690s, perhaps part of the answer may be suggested by the obviously personal turn given by the translator to the reasoning of Umbricius departing from Rome in *Satire* III.

> Since noble arts in Rome have no support
> And ragged virtue not a friend at court,
> No profit rises from th' ungrateful stage,
> My poverty increasing with my age,
> 'Tis time to give my just disdain a vent,
> And, cursing, leave so base a government.
>
> (39–44, translating 21–6)

Having lost the laureateship and all that went with it in the revolution of 1688, Dryden was alienated from the government of England as Milton had been after the restoration of the Stuarts in 1660. But this is only a partial answer, for Dryden's poetic temper could have found kinship with Juvenal's irrespective of personal circumstances. Although in the *Discourse* he describes his portrait of 'Zimri' in *Absalom and Achitophel* as Horatian by virtue of its 'fineness of raillery',[41] the major literary source is Juvenal's picture of the *Graeculus esuriens* (III, 78) 'the hungry Greekling' who can turn himself into anything in the cause of his social advancement:

> Quick-witted, brazed-faced, with fluent tongues
> Patient of labours, and dissembling wrongs.
> Riddle me this, and guess him if you can,
> Who bears a nation in a single man?
> A cook, a conjurer, a rhetorician,
> A painter, a pedant, a geometrician,
> A dancer on the ropes, and a physician.
> All things the hungry Greek exactly knows:
> And bid him go to Heaven, to Heaven he goes.
>
> (1692: III, 133–41)

> In the first rank of these did Zimri stand
> A man so various, that he seemed to be
> Not one, but all mankind's epitome.
> Stiff in opinions, always in the wrong:

41.   Watson, G. (1962) vol. 2, p. 137.

Was everything by starts, and nothing long:
But, in the course of one revolving moon,
Was chemist, fiddler, statesman and buffoon:
Then all for women, painting, rhyming, drinking;
Besides ten thousand freaks that died in thinking.

(1681: 544–52)

In many respects his previous satirical success suggests the potential affinity with Juvenal that he confesses with conviction in the preliminary *Discourse*. Here he rehearses at length the comparison between Juvenal and Horace that had been made by scholars and critics from Scaliger to Dacier. He shifts his ground as he applies different criteria to the two poets but while he seems to find the Horatian kind to be the more desirable ideal (in an earlier preface he had given the preference to Horace 'if to laugh and to rally is to be preferred to railing and declaiming')[42] his greater actual enjoyment of Juvenal is clear:

> But after all I must confess that the delight which Horace gives me is but languishing . . .. Where he barely grins himself . . . he cannot provoke me to any laughter. His urbanity, that is his good manners, are to be commended, but his wit is faint; and his salt, if I may dare to say so, almost insipid. Juvenal is of a more vigorous and masculine wit; he gives me as much pleasure as I can bear; he fully satisfies my expectation; he treats his subject home: his spleen is raised and he raises mine: I have the pleasure of concernment in all his says . . .. Add to this, that his thoughts are as just as those of Horace, and much more elevated. His expressions are sonorous and more noble; his verse more numerous and his words are suitable to his thoughts, sublime and lofty. . . . When there is anything deficient in numbers and sound, the reader is uneasy and unsatisfied . . . and this being the manifest defect of Horace, 'tis no wonder that finding it supplied in Juvenal we are more delighted with him. And, besides this, the sauce of Juvenal is more poignant to create in us an appetite of reading him. The meat of Horace is more nourishing; but the cookery of Juvenal more exquisite: so that, granting Horace to be the more general philosopher, we cannot deny that Juvenal was the greater poet, I mean in satire.[43]

It is to be expected, of course, that Dryden will be a powerful advocate of the poet he has just translated, but in singling out particularly Juvenal's persistently sharp wit, his elevation, and the

---

42. 'Preface to *Sylvae*', Watson, G. (1962) vol. 2, p. 31.
43. Watson, G. (1962) vol. 2, pp. 129–30.

excellence of his versification, Dryden is admiring in the Roman what he had already made his own in the different kinds of heroic satire represented by *Absalom and Achitophel* (1681) and *MacFlecknoe* (1682).

Later in the *Discourse* he praises Boileau's *Le Lutrin* (1674) and Virgil's *Fourth Georgic* in similar terms, concluding:

> This I think . . . to be the most beautiful and the most noble kind of satire. Here is the majesty of the heroic, finely mixed with the venom of the other; and raising the delight which otherwise would be flat and vulgar, by the sublimity of the expression . . . had I time, I could enlarge on the beautiful turns of words and thoughts, which are as requisite in this, as in heroic poetry of which this satire is undoubtedly a species.[44]

This predilection for the heroic, which is expressed in so many facets of Dryden's career as playwright and poet laureate, in his later years finds new expression in translation where he repays to Virgil and Juvenal the debt which he had incurred from the classics in his original compositions. In the *Discourse* here, he cites lines from Virgil which in his later translation have the combination of wit, elevation and metrical polish that he admired in Juvenal's sharp satire expressed in a highly delicate form anticipating the touch of Pope in *The Rape of the Lock*:

> The gifts of heaven my following song pursues
> Aerial honey and ambrosial dews.
> Maecenas, read this other part that sings
> Embattled squadrons, and advent'rous kings:
> A mighty pomp, though made of little things.
> Their arms, their arts, their manners, I disclose
> And how they war, and whence the people rose:
> Slight is the subject, but the praise not small
> If Heaven assist and Phoebus hear my call.
>
> (*The Fourth Book of the Georgics*, 1–9)

The Juvenal translation, though in a different vein, has all the metrical refinement that Dryden learnt from English predecessors like Denham and Waller and from Virgil himself. Contemplating what advancing age might have given John Oldham if he had lived, Dryden had earlier written:

44. Watson, G. (1962) vol. 2, p. 149.

It might (what nature never gives the young)
Have taught the numbers of thy native tongue.
But satire needs not those, and wit will shine
Through the harsh cadence of a rugged line.
('To the Memory of Mr Oldham', 13–16)

His own satire exhibits the highest artistry and makes a final and
complete break with the tradition that satire should be metrically
harsh, rough in tone and riddlingly obscure.

This may be illustrated by comparing Dryden's translation with
a passage in Hall's *Virgidemiae* IV, 1, which, as commentators
point out, takes its cue from a famous Juvenalian original. For full
appreciation of its various transformations in Hall and Dryden,
here is the Latin followed by the literal version of Sir Robert
Stapylton published in 1660:

> dormire virum cum senserat uxor,
> ausa Palatino tegetem praeferre cubili,
> sumere nocturnos meretrix Augusta cucullos,
> linquebat comite ancilla non amplius una:
> et nigrum flavo crinem abscondente galero,
> intravit calidum veteri centone lupanar,
> et cellam vacuam, atque suam: tunc nuda papillis
> constitit auratis, titulum mentita Lyciscae,
> ostenditque tuum, generose Britannice, ventrem.
> excepit blanda intrantes, atque aera poposcit:
> mox lenone suas iam dimittente puellas,
> tristis abit; sed quod potuit, tamen ultima cellam
> clausit, adhuc ardens rigidae tentigine vulvae,
> et lassata viris, nondum satiata recessit:
> obscurisque genis turpis, fumoque lucernae,
> foeda lupanaris tulit ad pulvinar odorem.
> (VI, 116–32)

See the gods' rival Claudius Caesar's shame
Whose daring wife, when sleep had drowsed his head,
Preferred a mat before his royal bed.
Th' imperial strumpet with one maid, stole out
In her night-hoods, and having put about
Her black hair a red periwig, she got
Into the stews, where th' old rug still was hot,
In a sparc room, kept for her, there gold-chained
Bare-breasted stood, her name Lycisca fained,
High-born Britannicus, thy womb displayed;
Smiled upon all that came, her bargain made;

And when the wenches were dismissed, she last
('Twas all she could) surely the door made fast,
And many thirsted-for encounters tried,
Departed tired with men, not satisfied.
And found with candle-smoke, her cheeks smeared o'er
The brothel-steam to Caesar's pillow bore.

Stapylton in feeble verse has been faithful to most of Juvenal's detail but has balked at the frank physicality (decorous in context) of *adhuc ardens rigidae tentigine vulvae* (139) 'still burning with lecherousness (literally, the tension of being stretched) in her rigid *vulva*', translated in dictionaries as womb which cannot, however, be quite right here. A fine stroke of wit that does not come through in translation is the choice of the epithet *generose* (high-born or noble) for Britannicus whose paternity as Messalina's son was doubtful – he could have been sired by a gladiator – but whose indubitable nobility as a successful general was in marked contrast to the corruption of his mother and most of the rest of the imperial family into which she had married. Much of the moral charge against Messalina is delivered in this witty sally. Here is Dryden's version:

The good old sluggard but began to snore,
When from his side up rose th' imperial whore:
She who preferred the pleasures of the night
To pomps, that are but impotent delight;
Strode from the palace, with an eager pace,
To cope with a more masculine embrace;
Muffled she marched, like Juno in a cloud,
Of all her train but one poor wench allowed;
One whom in secret service she could trust,
The rival and companion of her lust.
To the known brothel-house she takes her way,
And for a nasty room gives double pay,
That room in which the rankest harlot lay.
Prepared for fight expectingly she lies,
With heaving breasts, and with desiring eyes:
Still as one drops, another takes his place,
And baffled still succeeds to like disgrace.
At length, when friendly darkness is expired,
And every strumpet from her cell retired,
She lags behind, and ling'ring at the gate,
With a repining sigh submits to fate:

All filth without, and all a fire within
Tired with the toil, unsated with the sin.
Old Caesar's bed the modest matron seeks;
The steam of lamps still hanging on her cheeks
In ropy smut: thus foul and thus bedight
She brings him back the product of the night.

(The Sixth Satire of Juvenal, 163–89)

Dryden is quite free with the detail. For clarity's sake, he has
omitted the names; perhaps he felt that Lycisca (apparently a well-
known strumpet of the day) might be a distraction; he may also
have felt that his readers might not remember the significance of
Britannicus. On the other hand, with the importation of Juno he
adds an easily recognisable mythological parallel that, like
Juvenal's epithet *generose*, is witty by virtue of a double application
for it is congruous with its suggestions of formidable power but
also incongruous for Messalina's mission is a little less than
majestic. The snoring of Claudius, the hint of his impotence, and
the contrast between the passive delights of imperial ceremonial
(perhaps not delights at all) and the active pleasures of the night
are all Dryden's additions. In Juvenal Messalina is merely
accompanied by a single maid whereas in Dryden the maid takes
part and is trustworthy in this 'secret service' (a witty play) by
virtue of her complicity. The deliberate choice of the nastiest
room is Dryden's addition. In Juvenal she graciously welcomes
the men (*blanda* is a nice touch) and takes their money, part of her
enjoyment being the act of prostitution itself. Dryden omits this
concentrating entirely upon the aggressive sexuality. The humour
in the perplexity of the succession of men who fail to satisfy her is
the translator's addition. He dwells upon her lingering and
develops Juvenal's *tristis*. Her comic metamorphosis into the
modest matron is also an addition. Dryden's final line amplifies
and perhaps extends Juvenal's, tempting the reader to supplement
the end product from the resources of his or her imagination.
Dryden's method of translation is libertine; his engagement with
the original stimulates new creation and the end product is a
radical transformation which bears witness, above all, to the
manifest pleasure he took from the original.

Here is Hall's imitation:

The close adultress, where her name is red,
Comes crawling from her husband's lukewarm bed,
Her carrion skin bedaubed with odours sweet,
Groping the postern with her bared feet.
Now play the satyr, whoso list for me
Valentine self, or some as chaste as he.
In vain she wisheth long Alcmena's night,
Cursing the hasty dawning of the light;
And with her cruel Lady-star uprose
She seeks her third roost on her silent toes,
Besmeared all with loathsome smoke of lust,
Like Acheron's steams, or smouldring sulphur dust.
Yet all day sits she simpering in her mew
Like some chaste dame, or shrined saint in show;
Whiles he lies wallowing with a westy head
And palish carcase, on his brothel bed,
Till his salt bowels boil with poisonous fire:
Right Hercules with his second Dejanire.

(IV, 1, 144-61)

Coming from Dryden, what we miss in Hall apart from the
general clarity and ease of delivery is the narrative element so well
organised and fluent in both Dryden and Juvenal but less
developed in Hall and interrupted by the curiously distracting
injunction to 'play the satyr' (Valentine possibly refers to Nashe).
Hall, too, makes considerable demands upon the reader. Despite
the commentator's reference to the prostitute's habit of writing
her name on a tablet of wood over her cell (derived from a
scholiast's comment on Lycisca)[45] the clause in the opening line
seems obscure. Hall assumes that his readers are familiar with the
story of Alcmena whom Zeus in disguise as her husband had
deceived into an adulterous night of love that he extended by
divine will to thirty-six hours. Easier is the witty reference to
Venus as Lady-star rising in the morning. The most perplexing
detail comes in the next line. What is the meaning of the 'third
roost'? Given that she is returning surreptitiously in the morning,
the phrase cannot refer to her third amour of the night.
Presumably as she started out from her husband's bed, went to
her lover's and is now returning to her husband, her final
destination could be said to be her third port of call. Like 'carrion'
and 'mew' (a place where falcons are kept), 'roost' brings birds to

45. See Davenport, A. (1969) p. 199 (his note on line 144).

mind, creatures who settle in one place for the night, so that it may be that the phrase is chosen to suggest the unnaturalness of her hopping about. It remains something of a riddle. The rest is rather easier. The physical smoke of Juvenal's lamps becomes a figurative expression of moral disgust for damnable lust. Where Dryden made a comic point in transforming Messalina into a modest matron, Hall gives us a sharp moral antithesis pointing up the adulteress's hypocrisy. The real sting comes at the end where we are forced to contemplate the repugnant and abominable consequences of this adultery. We may wonder why the husband is lying in a confused state on his brothel bed ('westy' is an obsolete dialect word meaning dizzy, first recorded in this line in the *OED*). Has he been adulterous too? He has what his contemporaries would immediately have recognised as the symptoms of venereal disease. All is dextrously revealed in the witty sting that is concentrated in the mythological parallel in the final line. There is more than one version of the story of Hercules and Deianeira but the most apposite for the context here is the one that Sophocles makes the foundation for his play *The Women of Trachis* in which Deianeira unwittingly gives to Hercules the shirt of Nessus which she believes to be a love potion but which is in fact a poisonous gift that causes her husband's flesh to be slowly consumed by fire. There is no mistaking the appalling consequences of this adultery or the product that she brings back to her husband.

It hardly needs to be said that Hall has made very different use of the Juvenalian original from Dryden. He is the lashing satirist and scourge of villainy who does not allow us to escape the moral and physical consequences of marital deceit and hypocrisy. The pictures exist to make the moral point and the best lines are those that carry the moral censure in the second half of the passage, reaching a climax in the punching sarcasm of the final line. Conversely, the moral censor in Dryden, though present in the unsated *sin*, is muted; the free play of his inhibited wit makes the Juvenalian Messalina a vehicle for the expression of what Pope called his 'energy divine'.[46]

---

46. 'The First Epistle of the Second Book of Horace Imitated' ['To Augustus'], 269. For further comment on this extract on Dryden's Juvenal and on Dryden's translations generally see Hopkins, D. (1986) *John Dryden*, Cambridge University Press, especially pp. 149–57.

In Hall's satire, in which he claimed to be imitating what he describes as 'the sour and crabbed face of Juvenal', there is no doubting the tartness of the wit; it does not amuse and delight like that of Dryden. If we take crabbed to mean obscure in sense, then it is a vexed question as to how far the satire is deliberately so; if we take it to mean rough in language, it is certainly not so. The syntax and diction (apart from one dialect word) are straightforward; the rhythms in these predominantly closed couplets are by contemporary standards smooth. We may conclude, assuming a learned readership, that whatever his critical convictions, poetically he is relatively uncrabbed. It is remarkable that Juvenal presented such a different face to Dryden, for whatever the liberties he takes in transforming the original, his delight in Juvenal's matter and manner clearly springs from the character informing the face.

Though typical in its grand extravagance, this Juvenalian portrait is untypical in that Messalina is not so obviously set up to become victim to the belittling scorn of Juvenal's deflationary wit as, for instance, is the case with Hannibal

> Go, climb the rugged Alps, ambitious fool
> To please the boys and be a theme at school.
> (*The Tenth Satire of Juvenal*, 271–2, translating 166–7)

and Sejanus, the favourite of Tiberius whose fall from grace is reflected in the treatment meted out to his statue:

> Sejanus, almost first of Roman names,
> The great Sejanus crackles in the flames:
> Formed in the forge, the pliant brass is laid
> On anvils; and of head and limbs are made
> Pans, cans and pisspots, a whole kitchen trade.
> (*The Tenth Satire of Juvenal*, 93–7, translating 62–4)

The theme of the tenth satire 'The Vanity of Human Wishes' provides many opportunities for Juvenal's wit to exercise itself in the puncturing of the grand and the elevated. In general, his kind of satire expresses itself in dramatic hyperboles matched by equally dramatic descents into bathos:

Meanwhile his lordship lolls within at ease,
Pamp'ring his paunch with foreign rarities;
Both sea and land are ransacked for the feast,
And his own gut the sole invited guest.
Such plate, such tables, dishes dressed so well,
That whole estates are swallowed at a meal.
Even parasites are banished from his board:
(At once a sordid and luxurious lord:)
Prodigious throat, for which whole boars are dressed
(A creature formed to furnish out a feast.)
But present punishment pursues his maw,
When, surfeited and swelled, the peacock raw
He bears into the bath; whence want of breath
Repletions, apoplex, intestate death.
His fate makes table talk, divulged with scorn,
And he, a jest, into his grave is borne.
　　(*The First Satire of Juvenal*, 204–19, translating 135–46)

In the fate of the gluttonous lord, both profligate and mean, rarely can Roman extravagance have been so scornfully mocked. First the gluttony is grandly envisaged in a succession of hyperboles. In Dryden's fourth line the low word 'gut', so appropriate in context, reverberates in the stately rhythm of a full resounding line, comically acting against 'guest' to reveal his lordship's meanness and thereby reducing his appetite to its basest absurdity. For many poets, the comic rapidity and poetic justice of his demise brought upon by indigestion of an extravagant delicacy would have been the full extent of the bathos, but Juvenal goes a stage further in belittling his lord with the ultimate indignity that makes him become mere table talk. It is difficult not to feel that the evident delight taken by Dryden in recreating the original fully answers the fertility of Juvenal's witty invention in the first instance.

Epilogue

From the actual practice of those poets like Jonson, Cowley, Milton and Dryden who measured themselves against classical predecessors and constantly sought to emulate their achievement in the various kinds and genres in which they worked, it is apparent that the Renaissance impulse at its best was always concerned with ways in which the classics might be used to aid fresh creative endeavour in the present. These poets desired through their commerce with the ancients both to extend their own poetic range and to raise the standards of contemporary cultural endeavour and achievement. They were not concerned to flood the market with reproduction antiques. What may seem an obvious point is worth emphasis because the doctrine of literary imitation which was central to critical theory and poetic practice in the Renaissance is so often unsympathetically represented, not only after it had ceased to be so central in the Romantic period and beyond, but even during the Renaissance and even by those poets who most consciously lived by it and recommended it to their contemporaries.

One of the best-known accounts of literary imitation, to which reference has already been made, is Jonson's in his *Discoveries*:

> The third requisite in our poet, or maker, is imitation, to be able to convert the substance, or riches of another poet, to his own use. To make choice of one excellent man above the rest, and so to follow him, as the copy may be mistaken for the principal. Not, as a creature that swallows, what it takes in, crude, raw or undigested; but, that feeds with an appetite and hath a stomach to concoct, divide and turn all into nourishment. Not, to imitate servilely, as Horace saith, and catch at vices, for virtue: but to draw forth out of the best and choicest flowers, with the bee, and turn all into honey, work it into one relish and

savour: make our imitation sweet: observe how the best writers have imitated and follow them. How Virgil and Statius have imitated Homer; how Horace, Archilochus . . ..

(3056–73)

The first two requisites are *ingenium* 'the goodness of natural wit' and *exercitatio* 'practice'; and there is a fourth, *lectio* 'the exactness of study and multiplicity of reading which maketh a full man'. Finally 'to nature, exercise, imitation and study, art must be added to make all these perfect' (3086).

Jonson is here enunciating basic principles for the proper formation of the incipient poet. Coming after *exercitatio* the injunction to choose one excellent author above the rest may well be connected in his mind with the school practice of Latin verse composition that involved very specific imitation (in Latin) of classical authors like Virgil and Ovid. Recasting modern thoughts and feelings into a classical mould has been standard grammar school practice until recent times. Yet Jonson's injunction seems a narrow one in its restriction to one author, and its end, 'as the copy may be mistaken for the principal', generates all the wrong connotations of meaning at least for the modern world, suggesting as it does (quite contrary to Jonson's beliefs as manifested in his own practice) that the poetry aspired to can at best be an imitation classic or a good fake. Given these associations, there are perhaps insuperable difficulties with the idea of literary imitation, however expressed.[1] Despite the liveliness of his figurative language insisting that the original must be inwardly digested, and despite the felicity of the simile of the bee, Jonson fails ultimately to make the process of imitation sound creative, as it undoubtedly was in poems such as his own 'Inviting a Friend to Supper'.[2]

The central ancient authority on the subject of poetic imitation is Horace in his *Art of Poetry*. Plato and Aristotle use the word *mimesis* which is sometimes translated as imitation but always in a context where literature is being related to life. The doctrine of literary imitation first appears in Alexandrian times, but it is at

1. See the conclusion of the editors in their 'epilogue' in West, D., Woodman, T. (eds) (1979) *Creative Imitation and Latin Literature*, Cambridge University Press, p. 200.
2. See above pp. 349–53.

Rome that it acquires a central importance, reflecting the actual practice of a Roman culture built upon Greek foundations from the beginning.[3] No reader of Horace can fail to feel the weight of the Greek tradition bearing down very strongly. His *Art of Poetry* has been regarded, particularly in the Romantic era and beyond, as a conservative document and sometimes as the repository of a dry-as-dust classicism. Yet in its time it was a powerful manifesto for the new literature of the Augustan age, for the modern poetry of Virgil and Varius (and implicitly of Horace himself) in reaction against the conservative Roman taste that deplored innovation and continued to venerate old father Ennius as the second Homer.[4] In general the whole thrust of the poem is a plea to the Romans to raise the level of their national literature by emulating the high artistic standards embodied in the Greek classics. This is the point of the injunction to turn over the Greeks by day and by night. He is not necessarily wishing into being Roman *Iliads* and *Oedipuses* but hoping to inspire poets to aspire to works of comparable artistic excellence. Hence he refers to himself as a whetstone – *ergo fungar vice cotis* (304) 'I shall play the part of a whetstone' – who will sharpen awareness in others. In this spirit it is unthinking Roman conservatism that he is attacking when he asks the question

> Why is he honoured with a poet's name,
> Who neither knows, nor would observe a rule?
> And chooses to be ignorant and proud
> Rather than own his ignorance and learn?
>> (Roscommon, translating 86–8;
>> for the text, see the epigraph)

He is not advocating adherence to the rules in the spirit of a classical pedant but using his poetic authority to teach his ignorant countrymen (by way of the young Pisos to whom the epistle is addressed) some elementary truths about the poetic art which was never cultivated and valued at Rome as it had been in classical Greece and of which he is a present master.

3. See Russell, D.A., '*De Imitatione*' in West, D., Woodman, T. (1979) pp. 1–16.
4. For Horace as literary critic, see Brink, C.O. (1963) *Horace on Poetry* I, *Prolegomena to the Literary Epistles*: (1971) 11, *The Ars Poetica*: (1982) 111, *The Letters to Augustus and Florus*, Cambridge University Press, and Rudd, N. (ed.) 1989, *Horace Epistles Book II and Epistle to the Pisones* ('*Ars Poetica*'), Cambridge Greek and Latin Classics, Cambridge University Press.

He is adamant in his advocacy of a more regular artistry and so puts an emphasis on the traditional rules of art derived from Greek practice, but just as he admits gradual innovation and change in poetic language which in the general cultural flux cannot be a static entity (46–72), so it is implied that the poetic forms that language serves may also gradually evolve. Only theoretical formulists like Scaliger believed in the fixity of poetic species and preached the perfectibility of genres. Horace did not cause intelligent practising poets to stumble over this.

As vernacular poets stood in relation to ancient culture rather as Horace had stood in relation to the Greeks, one of the passages most often cited from *The Art of Poetry* contains the liberal Horatian rule about imitation, used as an epigraph to this book and cited here again in the version of Ben Jonson who is momentarily more creative in this passage than in most of the rest of his translation:

> Yet common matter thou thine own mayst make,
> If thou the vile broad-trodden ring forsake.
> For, being a poet, thou mayst feign, create,
> Nor care, as thou wouldst faithfully translate,
> To render word for word: nor with thy sleight
> Of imitation, leap into a strait
> From whence thy modesty, or poem's law
> Forbids thee forth again thy foot to draw.
>
> (187–94, translating 131–5)

This is the passage alluded to in *Discoveries* when Jonson remarks, 'Not, to imitate servilely, as Horace saith, to catch at vices, for virtue' (i.e. not to imitate a poet's vices as well as his virtues because you feel it virtuous to follow your original in all things). The formulation of Horace puts the common stock of the cultural tradition (which is not solely subject matter) in the public domain, *publica materies*, and warns against the pitfalls that will ensnare a *fidus interpres* who feels inhibited by *pudor*, modesty or a sense of his own inadequacy, or the *lex operis*, the law of genre. The Horatian rule is very clear, as Jonson's verse translation appreciates, and allows more creative freedom to the imitating poet than Jonson's prose formulation, confining the poet as it does to one original to be followed till 'the copy be mistaken for the principal'. Jonson's own practice is nearer to Horace than his own prescription since as a comic poet he ranges widely over the ancient inheritance and as a lyric poet he converts to his own use the substance of Catullus, Horace and Martial, but, *pace* Jonson, there is no mistaking him for any of these (even for his own Horace when he dons the laureate wreath) any more than Horace might be mistaken for Archilochus (if we had more of the Greek) or Virgil and Statius for Homer. Horace makes liberal allowance for creative freedom in the imitating poet[5] and therefore encourages it in others more deliberately than, for example, his disciple Boileau, 'the lawgiver of Parnassus'. The insistence upon imitative freedom where the poet is exhorted not to be inhibited by generic rules counterbalances the conservative tendency to assert their validity. In Horace's theory and practice these two tendencies are held in a creative tension that balances respect for tradition with recognition of the need for innovation.

The fostering of an independent native Roman culture and of the high artistic standards which can make it a successful reality is ultimately Horace's design in *Art of Poetry*:

> Our writers have attempted every way,
> And they deserve our praise, whose daring Muse,
> Disdained to be beholden to the Greeks,
> And found fit subjects for her verse at home:
> Nor should we be less famous for our wit,
> Than for the force of our victorious arms;
> But that time and care that are required
> To overlook and file and polish well
> Fright poets from that necessary toil.
> (Roscommon, translating 285–91;
> for the text, see the epigraph)

In his imitation of this passage, Oldham uses Horace, the voice of the classical tradition, to proclaim praise for bold vernacular innovation:

5. The Horatian passage, though it did not so inspire Jonson, is often cited too by translators to justify departures from verbal accuracy (*nec verbum verbo curabis reddere fidus interpres*, 133, 'you will not care to render word for word like a faithful interpreter') and is to be found in the prefaces of such pioneers of creative translation as Denham and Cowley and their successors Oldham and Dryden.

Our authors in each kind their praise may claim,
Who leave no paths untrod that lead to fame:
And well they merit it, who scorned to be
So much the vassals of antiquity;
As those, who know no better than to cloy
With the old musty tales of Thebes and Troy:
But boldly the dull beaten track forsook,
And subjects from our country-story took.

(446–53)

In Englishing Horace, Oldham is converting the Roman's substance to his own use and praising others who in the various kinds have done likewise. There could be no clearer illustration of the best impulse of Renaissance humanism that sought not to reproduce and copy antique forms but to incorporate them into the civilisation of the present. The development of the formal imitation in the late Renaissance in France and England is the logical extension of the earlier desire to seek cultural renewal in a classical revival wherein new life is grafted on to old forms which themselves become freshly transformed in the process.

Brief Outline of the Graeco-Roman World

Early Greek culture

Nineteenth-century archaeology has established that the island of Crete was the earliest centre of civilisation in the Mediterranean. The remains of Cnossos show that the Bronze Age civilisation called Minoan (from Minos, the mythical lawgiver of Crete) was highly developed and lasted from roughly 3000 to 1000 BC. In mainland Greece, a Bronze Age civilisation centred upon royal palaces such as those excavated at Mycenae, Tiryns and Pylos developed somewhat later and lasted from about 1580 to 1120. This civilisation is called Mycenaean after what seems to have been its most powerful centre, Mycenae. In Homer, Agamemnon, leader of the Greek expedition to Troy and the most powerful of the Greek princes, comes from Mycenae which Homer calls 'rich in gold', 'broad-streeted' and 'well-built'. In the catalogue of ships in book two of the *Iliad*, the largest number come from Mycenae and Pylos. The great house of the *Odyssey* bears a resemblance to Mycenaean palaces excavated on the main sites. The region in which the palace of Odysseus was located (on the western seaboard) is thought to have been on the edge of Mycenaean civilisation. A script known as linear B on clay tablets found at Mycenae, Pylos and Cnossos establishes strong links between Minoan and Mycenaean civilisations, and the decipherment of the script in the 1950s established that their common language was an archaic form of Greek.

Excavations at Hissarlik in Asia Minor, thought by the pioneering German archaeologist Heinrich Schliemann to be the site of Troy, have revealed nine settlements, the sixth having substantial fortifications and monumental walls. The seventh of these settlements was destroyed in a great fire in the mid thirteenth century, so that archaeological evidence seems to support the possibility of an historical Trojan War of which the Homeric account is the poetic memory. Soon after this possible date for the fall of Troy, Mycenaean power began to decline until in about 1120 Mycenae and Tiryns and with them the Mycenaean culture of the Bronze Age were destroyed by the Dorians, invading from the west. The Dorians were themselves Greek-speaking and possibly lived on the fringe of the Mycenaean empire. They initiated what is often called the Dark Ages (principally because so little is known about this period), lasting from 1100 to 800 or 750. The Bronze Age gave way to the new Age of Iron. Refugees from the dispersal on mainland Greece created by the Dorian invasion now began to colonise the eastern seaboard of the Aegean Sea including Ionia in Asia Minor. The Homeric poems are generally considered to have been composed in Ionia (largely on linguistic grounds); they may therefore preserve the memory of the Mycenaean mother culture transmitted by those who had colonised Asia Minor. Various dates have been suggested for the Homeric poems, by the Greeks themselves and by modern scholars. It is now frequently suggested that the poems emanate from the end of the Dark Ages in the period 800 to 750.

The archaic and classical periods

The archaic period marks the time when the political geography of the Greek world became reasonably fixed with the development of the characteristic political unit of the city state or the *polis* from about 750 BC to the time of the Persian Wars beginning in 490. In about 700 came Hesiod, born in Boeotia in northern Greece. His *Theogony* gives a systematic account of the gods and their genealogy, and his didactic poem the *Works and Days* transmits much early Greek agricultural lore. Like Homer, he writes in the dactylic hexameter and is traditionally linked with him as one of the early fathers of Greek poetry. Early Greek lyric (surviving only in fragments) flourished in the century after Hesiod, with Sappho and Alcaeus coming towards the end (c. 620). Soon afterwards, the first Ionian philosophers began their speculative enquiries into the nature of the physical universe, challenging the mythical view of the world in the poems of Homer and Hesiod. At this time Athens was an insignificant state with no special cultural achievements, but in the second half of the sixth century BC came significant political change and cultural development. Aristocratic power was challenged with popular support by Peisistratus, who established single rule (tyranny) in 545 that he passed on to his son. Peisistratus reorganised the state festival, the Panathenaea, and later sources record that texts of Homer were brought to Athens so that rhapsodes could recite Homer in proper order at the festival. During the rule of Peisistratus the state Dionysia was established, with the beginnings of tragedy associated with Thespis. Athens also became a leading centre for the production of pottery where old techniques were perfected and new ones initiated. In this period, therefore, the foundations were laid for the future cultural and commercial pre-eminence of Athens. Nevertheless, the expulsion of the tyrants in 510 was regarded by the Athenians as a milestone in their history. In other city states aristocracy had also been replaced by tyranny but Athens was unique in what followed, for whereas tyranny was generally replaced by oligarchy, in Athens came the reforms of Cleisthenes in 508 that laid the foundations of their later radical democracy. Despite their fiercely guarded autonomy, the Greek city states did eventually form a common alliance in the face of the invading Persians. The army of Darius was defeated by the Athenians at Marathon in 490, and the forces of his son Xerxes were defeated by the Greek fleet under Athenian generalship at Salamis in 480 and by the Greek army under Spartan leadership at Plataea in 479. These events are the climax of the narrative of Herodotus (c. 490–c. 425) whose history, written in the 450s, was the first systematic attempt of its kind. The new self-confidence generated by victory in the Persian Wars resulted in a burst of creative energy at the beginning of what has subsequently been called the classical period of Greek culture in the fifth and fourth centuries BC.

For reasons of security in the face of the continuing Persian threat, Athens took the initiative in forming a league of maritime states to which members agreed to contribute ships or money on an annual basis. What began as a voluntary association gradually became the Athenian empire as Athens did not allow states to secede, transferred the treasury from Delos to Athens and interfered with the constitutions of member states, supporting democrats against oligarchs. Athens acquired an empire abroad based upon her naval supremacy, and consolidated her democratic institutions at home with further reforms in 462. For the next thirty years Pericles was the most influential figure in the Athenian state, where he dominated the assembly by virtue of his oratory and was elected to be one of the ten generals for the last fifteen years of his life until he died in 429. He proposed the rebuilding of the Greek temples destroyed by the Persians. The Parthenon was completed in 432. At this time Athens became the cultural centre of the Greek world and the host to visiting intellectuals and artists in all fields. This is the high watermark of Athenian culture. Aeschylus (524–456) produced his *Oresteia* in 458; Sophocles (496–406) and Euripides (c. 480–406) were coming into their prime. There were great achievements in architecture, sculpture and vase painting. The Greek enlightenment, that may be said to have begun with the speculations of the Ionian philosophers a century earlier, continued apace with the teachings of the sophist movement and the philosophic mission of Socrates (469–399). It is reported that Pericles summed up the Athenian ideal in the following terms: *philokaloumen gar met' euteleias kai philosophoumen aneu malakias* (Thucydides II, 40) 'we are indeed lovers of beauty with restraint and lovers of wisdom without losing our strength', and confidently asserted that in her institutions and culture Athens was 'the school of Hellas' (II, 41).

Athenian power and pre-eminence brought conflict with Sparta which resulted in the Peloponnesian War fought in various stages over nearly thirty years from 431 to 404 when, after a series of blunders, Athens was finally defeated. This conflict is the subject of the greatest ancient historian, Thucydides (c. 460–c. 400), and is the context of most of the extant plays of Aristophanes (c. 448–c. 380) and of the later work of Sophocles and Euripides. Sparta took over the empire but soon lost it. Athens attempted a second league but never regained her former pre-eminence. In the cultural sphere, the greatest achievements in the fourth century are in philosophy with first Plato (c. 427–348) and then his pupil Aristotle (384–322), and in oratory where the greatest names are those of Isocrates (436–338), famous for his educational writings which became influential at Rome, and Demosthenes (383–322) who, in his *Philippics*, sought to rouse the Athenians to what he correctly divined to be the ambitions of King Philip of Macedon. The ascendancy of Macedon, which had never developed on the lines of the Greek city states but was a scattered tribal federation ruled by an autocratic monarchy, beginning with the defeat of the Greeks at Chaeronea in 332 and confirmed at the battle of Crannon in 322 after which Athens was occupied by a Macedonian garrison and lost her democracy, traditionally marks the end of the classical era and the beginning of a new, less creative phase of Greek civilisation usually called the Hellenistic.

The Hellenistic period

Athens remained a cultural centre; Zeno (c. 333–262), founder of the Stoic school, taught at Athens, as did Epicurus (341–271). New Comedy flourished with Menander (342–c. 292). But the centre of gravity of the Greek world soon shifted to Alexandria, founded on the Nile delta in 331 by Philip's son Alexander the Great (356–323) in the course of the brief career in which he conquered the whole of the Near East. Inhabited by Greeks, Egyptians and Jews, this cosmopolitan city rapidly became a great commercial and cultural capital and was the largest city in the world by the end of the third century. Alexandrian literature is less rooted in the life of the community than the literature of the classical *polis*, and its practitioners, who were characteristically from a scholarly elite, started the practice of imitating classical models while developing new smaller-scale forms that might be vehicles for esoteric learning or express the concerns of the individual with a new realism. Similarly, much sculpture in this period tends to a greater realism and individuality, in marked contrast to the more abstract idealism of the classical period. Alexandria had the most famous library of the ancient world, and to its scholars like Aristarchus (c. 215–c. 143) we owe the preservation of what we now call the Greek classical canon in good textual order.

The rise of Rome

At almost the same time as the Athenians expelled their tyrants (510), Roman tradition records the expulsion of the Tarquin kings by Lucius Junius Brutus who became Rome's first consul in 509. The struggle between the patricians and plebeians (apparent in Shakespeare's *Coriolanus* which relates to historical events of the late 490s) echoes similar struggles in the Greek city states, but, though the Roman constitution like that of the Spartans was mixed, power remained firmly within the control of a senatorial oligarchy of the rich and privileged from whose number the chief magistrates, the two consuls, were chosen to rule with equal powers on an annual basis.

In early times the Romans were an agricultural community, land-based in their occupations and military organisation. The disciplined power of the legion was their great strength; they did not develop a navy or the commercial interests to take them overseas and extend their horizons. The art of public speaking was prized in their republican constitution, and their highly developed legal system was the product of intellectual skills of a practical kind, but speculative thinking or imaginative literature did not come easily to the Romans. The first serious attempts at a national literature were made when conquest brought them into direct contact with the Greek colonies on the coast of southern Italy in what is called Magna Graecia.

Roman ascendancy in Italy dates from the capture in 271 of Tarentum, a rich Greek city on the coast of Calabria in the south. One of those captured was a Greek named Andronicus who was taken to Rome as the slave of the noble family of Livii. As a reward for teaching his master's son, Andronicus was given his freedom, and he took his patron's name. He stayed at Rome and continued to teach, mastering Latin in the process. Greek children started their schooling by reading Homer. As there was no Roman equivalent, Andronicus translated Homer's *Odyssey* into Latin. Homer, who had educated the Greeks, now began to educate the Romans and 200 years later the Latin *Odyssey* of Livius Andronicus was still being used as a schoolbook. Andronicus went on to translate Greek plays and his translations were adapted for staging, being the first of their kind to be performed at Rome. The career of Livius Andronicus, a Greek slave who became half-Latin and went on to educate Roman children and become the first Latin author, is prophetic of the whole course of subsequent cultural relations between the Romans and the Greeks. In a literal sense, the Romans were educated by the Greeks. Their sons continued to be tutored for the most part by bilingual tutors of Greek origin. But in introducing the masterpieces of Greek epic and tragedy to Rome, Andronicus started the process by which in a deeper sense Greece educated Rome.

As a Mediterranean power, Rome soon became involved in a long struggle with Carthage whose power extended from north Africa and southern Spain to parts of Sicily. In the second Punic War (218–202), after nearly succumbing to a Carthaginian invasion of Italy led by Hannibal, the Romans decisively defeated their adversaries at the battle of Zama in 202. Quintus Ennius (239–169), who was born in Calabria and was half Greek by origin, had served in the campaign and wrote an epic in Latin celebrating the history of Rome from the beginning to the triumphal assertion of Roman power over Carthage. For this he adopted the dactylic hexameter used by Homer, abandoning the native Saturnian metre. The Greek, and specifically Homeric, inspiration is apparent in the vision at the opening of the poem in which the spirit of Homer tells Ennius that he is Homer's reincarnation. With Ennius, who also translated and adapted Greek drama for the Roman stage, the dominance of Greek forms is complete. The native Saturnian was never again used for serious literature. Although most early plays were probably adaptations from the Greek, there is some evidence too for historical drama; nor was Ennius alone in writing epic with contemporary national themes. Many later Romans like Cicero venerated their earliest writers in epic, tragedy and comedy. The only texts extant from this period are the plays of Plautus (250–184), reworkings of Greek New Comedy of the previous century.

Rome became more directly involved with Greece as she was drawn into war with Philip V of Macedon who was defeated at the battle of Cynoscephalae in 197. Alexander's empire had been divided on his death into various kingdoms which now gradually came under direct Roman control. With the conquest of Greece, leading Romans such as Scipio Aemilianus developed an enthusiasm for Greek literature, philosophy and art. The philhellenism of the Romans in this period is similar to that of the Renaissance Italian humanists of the fourteenth and fifteenth centuries except that in absorbing the Greeks into their empire the Romans really did learn from them, whereas their Italian successors, divided by history and tradition from their Greek Byzantine contemporaries in the east, proved in the end reluctant to go beyond the bounds of their own Latin inheritance in their exploration of the classical past. Lucilius (c. 180–102), the inventor of formal satire, and the comic playwright Terence (c. 190–159) are associated with the philhellenic circle of Scipio, and there is the anecdote that Terence was drowned at sea returning from Greece with manuscripts of a number of Menander's plays hitherto unknown at Rome. There was, however, some resistance to the assimilation of Greek culture. In 161, Marcus Porcius Cato, the censor, succeeded in securing the banishment of all Greek philosophers and rhetoricians from Rome on the grounds that Greek influence was undermining the solidity of the traditional Roman character. Nevertheless, this was only a temporary halt to the gradual metamorphosis of the Roman into the Graeco-Roman. Even Cato took up Greek in his old age.

The late Republic

The acquisition of a larger empire than the world had ever seen brought with it immense problems of government and administration. The last century of the Roman Republic is marked by a series of internal disorders and by the inability of the civil power to control the military. In addition to numerous foreign wars, there was an Italian revolt in 90 BC that lasted for three years, the dictatorship of Sulla who marched on Rome in 82, a slaves' revolt led by Spartacus in 73–71 and the conspiracy of Catiline in 63, foiled by Cicero who was consul at the time. Ben Jonson's play *Catiline* dramatises the events of this year. Shortly afterwards came the first triumvirate of Pompey, Crassus and Julius Caesar in 60, an unconstitutional arrangement whereby the three most powerful men of the time divided the government of the Roman world between them. After the death of Crassus in 53, relations between the two remaining triumvirs deteriorated until Caesar declared war on Pompey and the Senate by crossing the Rubicon (a small river marking the boundary of his proconsular power) and invading Italy with his legions from Gaul in 49. He defeated Pompey at Pharsalus in 48, after which Pompey was murdered in Egypt. Caesar then made himself dictator for life. What followed is dramatised by Shakespeare in *Julius Caesar* and *Antony and*

Cleopatra. The assassination of Caesar in 44 in the name of the Republic by Brutus and Cassius led to the establishment of the second triumvirate in 43 of Mark Antony, Lepidus and Octavianus Caesar, Julius Caesar's great-nephew and heir. Proscriptions followed in which many of their political opponents perished, including Mark Antony's most famous antagonist, Cicero. Other leading Republicans led by Brutus and Cassius were defeated at Philippi in 42.

The major literary figure of the late Republic is Cicero (106–43). He is the greatest of Roman orators and master of Latin prose, writing in a lucid, balanced, sonorous and periodic style that in its various applications has been a model for subsequent orators, philosophers, historians and theologians in both Latin and the vernacular. He expounded in his letters and speeches a political philosophy of liberal republicanism which he put into practice not only as consul against Catiline but also in opposing the unconstitutional activities of Julius Caesar and then Mark Antony in his *Philippics.* A cultivated philhellene, in his moral and philosophical works he mediates much of the Greek tradition in a practical way. To future time, he has seemed the embodiment of his own ideal of the patriotic and philosophic orator. In poetry, Lucretius (c. 98–55) renews the philosophy of Epicurus in his hexameter poem *De rerum natura.* Catullus (c. 84–c. 54) is the only surviving member of a group of poets called by Cicero the neoterics or new poets who reacted against the grand public and rhetorical Roman tradition, turning away from large-scale genres in favour of the short poem on private subjects or personal concerns that had been popular in the Alexandrian age. They cultivated a new artistic refinement of form and expression.

The Augustan age and the empire

The battle of Philippi in 42 may be said to have brought to an end the prolonged death throes of the Roman Republic, but it took another major upheaval before the new dispensation emerged. Mark Antony undertook the task of restoring order in the east, while Octavian controlled Italy and the western provinces. Lepidus, the least powerful of the three, was given Africa until deprived of his command by Octavian in 35. Rivalry between the remaining triumvirs resulted in the defeat of Antony and Cleopatra by Octavian at the battle of Actium in 31. Egypt became a Roman province, Octavian celebrated a Roman triumph for the defeat of Cleopatra, and the temple of Janus, open in time of war, closed in time of peace, was formally closed in 29 for only the third time in Roman history, a symbolic act which was to inaugurate a new age of peace. Octavian, like Julius Caesar before him, was the sole master of the Roman world. In 27 he formally renounced the unconstitutional powers he had held as triumvir and took the additional name of Augustus. He had all the powers held by Julius Caesar – in particular, the armed forces all swore allegiance to him as Imperator, commander-in-chief – but, aiming by all means to reconcile the Romans to his rule, he disguised his powers under traditional republican forms. Indeed, he claimed to have restored the Republic. The old republican liberty, however, had long been a thing of the past. He was hailed as first citizen, Princeps, from which his rule, which lasted to his death in AD 14, is often referred to as the principate. The main object of his foreign policy was to consolidate inherited gains and to secure existing frontiers rather than to acquire more territory. In domestic affairs, Augustus made changes that had a strongly traditional appeal. As he had 'restored' the Republic, so he set about restoring the ancient religion, rebuilding a great number of temples in and around the city of Rome. This rebuilding was part of a general restoration whereby Augustus, who had 'found Rome brick, left it marble'. In moral legislation to encourage family life and curb excessive private wealth, Augustus also appealed to traditional Roman ways (the *mores maiorum*), invoking the ancestral spirit in all he did.

Augustus had devoted his enormous personal wealth to public works, and his munificence raised magnificent monuments to Roman imperial grandeur. The literary arts were fostered through the patronage of his friend Maecenas. Some of the arts, notably oratory, suffered with the loss of freedom but, under imperial patronage, poetry flourished. The foremost Augustans, Virgil (70–19) and Horace (65–8), heralded the transformation of the Roman state, identified themselves with the new order and gave expression to the new mood of self-confidence generated by the Augustan peace. They reasserted the public role of the poet while retaining the aspiration of the neoterics towards artistic refinement and perfection of form. Their poetry, together with that of their younger contemporary Ovid (43 BC–AD 17), represents a peak of achievement in the culture of the Augustan age.

Augustus had no son and was eventually succeeded in AD 14 by his stepson Tiberius whom he had made his heir. A semblance of republican tradition was kept up in that the principate was never strictly hereditary, and the new emperor was nominally invested with his powers by the senate and people in the way in which the magistracies had traditionally been elected and confirmed. The immediate successors of Augustus maintained his constitutional arrangements but ruled without his political flair and personal authority. Ben Jonson's play *Sejanus* is a portrait of political tyranny in the reign of Tiberius. Much of the surviving literature of the imperial period is permeated with a wistful yearning for the lost republican liberty and the virtue that supposedly upheld it. The *Pharsalia*, the epic poem of Lucan (39–65) on the civil war between Caesar and Pompey, is anti-Caesarean and markedly republican in sympathy. He and Seneca (4 BC–AD 65), the Stoic philosopher and tragedian, fell foul of Nero and were required to commit suicide for complicity in the conspiracy of Piso in 65. The satirist Persius (34–62) is not, like Horace, integrated into his social and political world but writes as a detached outsider. The most vivid portraits of the world of the first century are painted in dark and gloomy colours by the historian Tacitus (c. 56–c. 117) and the satirist Juvenal (fl. 110). Both had survived the rule of Domitian (81–96) whose last seven years have traditionally been described as a reign of terror. Ironically their work seems to have been written in the tranquil period that followed in the reigns of Nerva (96–98) and Trajan (98–117) who, together with Hadrian (117–38), Antonius Pius (138–61) and Marcus Aurelius (161–80), constitute a succession of five good emperors. The age of the Antonines (138–80) was regarded by Edward Gibbon in his *Decline and Fall of the Roman Empire* as the most felicitous in human history. It is remarkable that after it there is very little classical literature.

In the reign of Constantine (306–37) Christianity became the official religion of the empire. Rome's first Christian emperor founded Constantinople on the site of Byzantium in 324 and made it his official residence in 330. The empire divided into Greek east and Latin west in 395. The eastern empire remained intact until the Moslems sacked Constantinople in 1453, but in the fifth century the western empire gradually fell into the hands of invading Vandals, Visigoths and Huns until the deposition of Rome's last emperor, Romulus Augustulus, by the German Odoacer whose proclamation as king of Italy in 476 marks the end of the western empire.

Rome continued to be the centre of Latin Christendom and the seat of the papacy, but cultural life and the necessary prerequisite of it, systematic educational provision, were severely disrupted in succeeding centuries. Early Christian intellectuals were often hostile to pagan literature; nevertheless the piecemeal survival of the Latin classics was largely a consequence of the habit of scribal copying in the monastic library and scriptorium. With the coronation of the Frankish king Charlemagne by Pope Leo III at Rome in 800 came a revival of the Roman *imperium* and an attempt to revive learning in schools attached to both monasteries and cathedrals which might ensure a decent standard of literacy. The Carolingian Renaissance was a momentous period in the transmission of classical culture; a new script was promoted and there was extensive copying of texts. Many of our oldest Latin manuscripts are from this period. Under his successors, Charlemagne's empire gradually fell apart. The emergence of the Holy Roman empire in the late tenth century entailed fruitful contact between Germany and Italy and an educational revival in Germany in the eleventh century. The high Middle Ages (1100–1300) saw the development of the first universities and scholastic education in which the classics played some part, though rigorously subordinated to theology. The emancipation of the classics and the cultivation of an interest in them for their own sake came in the fourteenth century with the early humanists of the Italian Renaissance. Most of the Latin classics that we now possess had been rediscovered, collected and disseminated by the end of the fifteenth century. The Italians travelled abroad in search of Greek texts too, and with the fall of Constantinople in 1453 many Greek scholars fled to Italy bringing with them precious manuscripts. The years that followed the invention of printing in the latter part of the fifteenth century saw the gradual publication of the whole of the classical inheritance as we now know it, first in Italy and then north of the Alps.

Chronological Chart

This is confined for the most part to literary figures and works given significant mention in this book. For a fuller version, see the table at the conclusion of Howatson, M.C. (ed.) 1989, *The Oxford Companion to Classical Literature*, New Edition, OUP. The abbreviation fl. for *floruit* (he/she/it flourished) represents a scholarly estimate where little is known for certain.

History and events	Literary figures and works
THE GREEK WORLD	
BC	
BRONZE AGE	
c. 3000–1000 Minoan civilisation	
c. 1400 Destruction of Cnossos	
c. 1580–1120 Mycenaean civilisation	
c. 1250 Destruction of Troy	
IRON AGE–DARK AGE	
c. 1100 Dorian invasions Colonisation of Asia Minor	
c. 776 The first Olympiad	
	c. 750 Homer

ARCHAIC PERIOD

c. 700 Hesiod
c. 650 Archilochus fl.
c. 610 Sappho Alcaeus fl.
c. 600 Thales of Miletus fl.
first Ionian philosopher

545–510 Tyranny of
Peisistratus at Athens
Reorganisation of the
Panathenaea
Institution of State Dionysia
510 Expulsion of tyrants
508 Democratic reforms of
Cleisthenes

c. 533 Thespis
525–456 Aeschylus
518–c. 446 Pindar

CLASSICAL PERIOD

490–479 Persian Wars
490 Battle of Marathon

480 Battle of Salamis
479 Battle of Plataea
478 Delian League formed

462 Democratic reforms of
Ephialtes and Pericles

432 Parthenon completed
431–404 Peloponnesian War

c. 496–406 Sophocles
c. 490–425 Herodotus
c. 485–406 Euripides

472 Aeschylus: *Persians*

c. 460–399 Thucydides
458 Aeschylus: *Oresteia*
c. 454 Herodotus: *Histories*
c. 445–c. 385 Aristophanes
441 Sophocles: *Antigone*
436–338 Isocrates

431 Euripides: *Medea*
430 Sophocles: *Oedipus the
King*

429 Death of Pericles
      (b. c. 495)

427–347 Plato
424 Aristophanes: *Knights*
415 Euripides: *Trojan Women*
411 Aristophanes: *Lysistrata*

404 Defeat of Athens

405 Euripides: *Bacchae*
c. 400 Thucydides: *History of
      the Peloponnesian War*

399 Trial of Socrates (b. 469)

c. 392 Aristophanes: *Women in
      the Assembly*
385 Plato founds the Academy
384–322 Aristotle
384–322 Demosthenes
c. 380 Plato: *Republic,
      Symposium*

377–355 Second Athenian
      League

351 Demosthenes: *First
      Philippic*
342–c. 292 Menander
341–271 Epicurus

338 Philip of Macedon defeats
      the Greeks at Chaeronea
336–323 Career of Alexander
      the Great

335 Aristotle founds the
      Lyceum *Nicomachean
      Ethics, Poetics*
c. 333–262 Zeno, the Stoic

331 Foundation of Alexandria
322 Battle of Crannon
      End of democracy at Athens

HELLENISTIC PERIOD

316 Menander: *Dyscolos*
310–240 Callimachus
307 Epicurus founds school at
      Athens

History and events	Literary figures and works
	300 Zeno of Citium founds Stoic school at Athens
197 The Romans defeat Philip V of Macedon at Cynoscephalae	
	180 Aristarchus heads Alexandrian library
146 The Romans destroy Corinth; Greece becomes a Roman protectorate	

AD

ROMAN PERIOD

	First century *On the Sublime* attributed to the rhetorician Longinus
	c. 46–c. 120 Plutarch: *Parallel Lives*
	c. 115–c. 180 Lucian: *Dialogues* (prose satire)

History and events	**Literary figures and works**

THE ROMAN WORLD

BC

Eighth-century Foundation of Rome, according to legend, by Romulus and Remus	
510 Expulsion of Tarquin kings	

REPUBLICAN ROME

509 L. Junius Brutus, first consul	
271 Romans capture Tarentum and dominate Italy	c. 270–240 Livius Andronicus fl. Introduces epic and drama to Rome
264–202 Carthaginian Wars	250–184 Plautus

239–169 Ennius

217 Hannibal in Italy
202 Defeat of Carthaginians at
     Zama
197 Defeat of Philip V of
     Macedon at Cynoscephalae

190–159 Terence
c. 180–102 Lucilius

161 Cato the censor procures
     the expulsion of Greeks
     from Rome
146 Sack of Corinth; Greece
     becomes a Roman pro-
     tectorate
     Destruction of Carthage

106–43 Cicero
98–c. 55 Lucretius

90–88 Social War; revolt of
       Italian allies

c. 84–54 Catullus

82–80 Dictatorship of Sulla
73–71 Slaves' revolt led by
       Spartacus

70–19 Virgil
65–8 Horace

63 Catilinarian conspiracy
    foiled by Cicero as consul
60 First triumvirate of
    Pompey, Crassus and
    Julius Caesar (100–44)
58–49 Caesar conquers Gaul
55–54 Caesar invades Britain

63 Cicero: *Orations against
    Catiline*

c. 50–c. 16 Propertius

49 Caesar crosses Rubicon
48 Battle of Pharsalus: murder
    of Pompey
47–44 Dictatorship of Caesar
44 Murder of Caesar
43 Second triumvirate of Mark
    Antony, Lepidus and

43 Cicero: *Philippics*

Octavian (63 BC–AD 14)
Proscriptions: murder of
Cicero

                   43 BC–AD 17 Ovid

42 Republican forces defeated
at Philippi; deaths of
Brutus and Cassius

END OF THE REPUBLIC AND TRANSITION TO IMPERIAL PERIOD

                   37 Virgil: *Eclogues*
                   35 Horace: *Satires* Book I

31 Octavian defeats Antony
and Cleopatra at Actium

                   30 Horace: *Satires* Book II
                   29 Virgil: *Georgics*
                       Propertius *Elegies* I

27 Octavian takes the name
Augustus
Pax Augusta   23 Horace: *Odes* I–III
                   20 Ovid: *Amores*, first edition
                   c. 20 Horace: *Epistles* Book I
                   19 Virgil dies; *Aeneid*
                       unfinished
                   15 Horace: *Epistles* Book II
                   13 Horace: *Odes* IV
                   8 Maecenas dies
                   c. 1 Ovid: *The Art of Love*

AD

                   c. 2 Ovid: *Metamorphoses*
                   8 Ovid banished
                   c. 9 Ovid: *Tristia*

14 Death of Augustus
14–37 Tiberius emperor
31 Downfall of Sejanus,
former favourite and
henchman of Tiberius
37–41 Caligula emperor

41–54 Claudius emperor
43 Invasion of Britain
54–68 Nero emperor

56–c. 117 Tacitus
62 Persius dies (b. 34): *Satires*
65 Conspiracy of Piso

65 Suicides of Lucan (b. 39),
author of *Pharsalia*,
Seneca, the tragedian
(b. 4 BC), and Petronius,
author of *Satyricon*, 'a
picaresque novel'

69 Year of four emperors:
Galba, Otho, Vitellius and
Vespasian (69–79)
79–81 Titus emperor
79 Eruption of Vesuvius;
destruction of
Herculaneum and Pompeii
81–96 Domitian emperor

86–98 Martial: *Epigrams*
c. 95 Quintilian: *Education of an
Orator*
96–98 Nerva emperor
98–117 Trajan emperor

98 Tacitus: *Agricola* (Roman
governor of Britain)
100–117 Juvenal: *Satires*
c. 106 Tacitus: *Histories*

c. 116 Tacitus: *Annals*
117–38 Hadrian emperor

119–22 Suetonius: *Lives*
138–61 Antoninus Pius
emperor
161–80 Marcus Aurelius
emperor

174–80 Marcus Aurelius:
Meditations
240 Plotinus fl.; Neoplatonism

306–37 Constantine emperor
324 Constantinople founded
330 Constantinople becomes
capital of the empire

350 Donatus fl.: grammarian,
commentator on Terence
386–400 Jerome translates
Bible into Latin: the
Vulgate

395 Division of empire into
east and west

399 Augustine of Hippo:
Confessions

410 Alaric the Visigoth sacks
Rome

413–25 Augustine: *City of God*
420 Servius fl.: grammarian,
commentator on Virgil
430 Macrobius fl.: *Saturnalia*
(includes comparison of
Homer and Virgil)

439 Vandals conquer Roman
Africa
452 Attila the Hun invades
Italy
476 Rome's last emperor
Romulus Augustulus
deposed by the German
Odoacer, who is pro-
claimed king of Italy.
End of the western empire.

Short Bibliography

I   Works of general reference

Brown, H. 1935, 'The Classical Tradition in English Literature: A Bibliography', *Harvard Studies and Notes in Philology and Literature* **18**, 7–46.

Carlsen, H. 1985, *A Bibliography to the Classical Tradition in English Literature*, University of Copenhagen Press, Copenhagen.

Kallendorf, C. 1982, *Latin Influences on English Literature from the Middle Ages to the Eighteenth Century: An Annotated Bibliography of Scholarship 1945–1979*, Garland Publishing, New York and London.

Gillespie, S. 1992, 'A Checklist of Restoration English Translations and Adaptations of Classical Greek and Latin Poetry 1660–1700', *Translation and Literature*, Edinburgh University Press, **I**, 52–68.

Hammond, N.G.L., Scullard, H.H. (eds) 1970, *The Oxford Classical Dictionary: Second Edition*, Oxford University Press.

Howatson, M.C. (ed.) 1989, *The Oxford Companion to Classical Literature*, Oxford University Press.

Lathrop, H.B. 1967, *Translations from the Classics into English from Caxton to Chapman 1477–1620*, Octagon Books, New York (first published by Wisconsin University Press, 1932).

II   Works on aspects of classical culture

Atkins, J.W.H. 1934, *Literary Criticism in Antiquity*, Cambridge University Press.

Cochrane, C.N. 1940, *Christianity and Classical Culture: A Study of Thought and Action from Augustus to Augustine*, Oxford University Press.

Kenney, E.J., Clausen, W.V. (eds) 1982, *The Cambridge History of Classical Literature II, Latin Literature*, Cambridge University Press.

Kenney, E.J., Easterling, P.E. (eds) 1985, *The Cambridge History of Classical Literature I, Greek Literature*, Cambridge University Press.

Rose, H.J. 1928, *A Handbook of Classical Mythology*, Methuen.

Rose, H.J. 1959, *Outlines of Classical Literature for Students of English*, Methuen.

Russell, D.A. and Winterbottom, M. 1972, *Ancient Literary Criticism: The Principal Texts in New Translations*, Oxford University Press.

Wardman, A. 1976, *Rome's Debt to Greece*, Book Club Associates.

West, D., Woodman, T. (eds) 1979, *Creative Imitation and Latin Literature*, Cambridge University Press.

III   The classical tradition: general works

Atkins, J.W.H. 1943, *English Literary Criticism: The Medieval Phase*, Cambridge University Press; 1947, *English Literary Criticism: The Renascence*, Methuen.

Baldwin, T.W. 1944, *William Shakspere's Smalle Latine and Lesse Greeke*, 2 vols, University of Illinois Press, Urbana.

Bolgar, R.R. 1954, *The Classical Heritage and its Beneficiaries*, Cambridge University Press.

Braden, G. 1978, *The Classics and English Renaissance Literature: Three Case Studies*, Yale Studies in English **187**, Yale University Press, New Haven and London.

Clarke, M.L. 1959, *Classical Education in Britain 1500–1900*, Cambridge University Press.

Erskine-Hill, H. 1983, *The Augustan Idea in English Literature*, Edward Arnold.

Finley, M.I. (ed.) 1981, *The Legacy of Greece: A New Appraisal*, Oxford University Press.

Fowler, A. 1982, *Kinds of Literature: An Introduction to the Theory of Genres and Modes*, Oxford University Press.

Gilbert, A.H. (ed.) 1962, *Literary Criticism: Plato to Dryden*, Wayne State University Press, Detroit.

Gillespie, S. 1988, *The Poets on the Classics: An Anthology of English Poets' Writings on the Classical Poets and Dramatists from Chaucer to the Present*, Routledge.

Highet, G. 1949, *The Classical Tradition: Greek and Roman Influences on Western Literature*, Oxford University Press.

Jenkyns, R. (ed.) 1992, *The Legacy of Rome: A New Appraisal*, Oxford University Press.

Kenney, E.J. 1974, *The Classical Text: Aspects of Editing in the Age of the Printed Book*, University of California Press, Berkeley.

Lewalski, B.K. 1986, *Renaissance Genres: Essays on Theory, History and Interpretation*, Harvard Studies in English **14**, Harvard University Press, Cambridge, Mass.

Lord, G. de F. 1987, *Classical Presences in Seventeenth Century English Poetry*, Yale University Press, New Haven.

Martindale, J. (ed.) 1985, *English Humanism: Wyatt to Cowley*, Croom Helm.

Mason, H.A. 1956, *Poetry and Humanism in the Early Tudor Period*, Routledge & Kegan Paul.

Ogilvie, R.M. 1964, *Latin and Greek: A History of the Influence of the Classics on English Life from 1600 to 1918*, Routledge & Kegan Paul.

Pfieffer, R. 1976, *History of Classical Scholarship from 1300 to 1850*, Oxford University Press.

Race, W.H. 1987, *Classical Genres and English Poetry*, Routledge.

Reynolds, L.D. and Wilson, N.G. 1974, *Scribes and Scholars: A Guide to the Transmission of Texts*, 2nd edn, Oxford University Press.

Rivers, I. 1979, *Classical and Christian Ideas in English Renaissance Poetry: A Student's Guide*, Allen & Unwin.

Sandys, J.E. 1908, *A History of Classical Scholarship*, 3 vols, Oxford University Press.

Smith, G.G. (ed.) 1904, *Elizabethan Critical Essays*, 2 vols, Oxford University Press.

Spingarn, J.E. (ed.) 1908, *Critical Essays of the Seventeenth Century*, 3 vols, Oxford University Press.

Thomson, J.A.K. 1948, *The Classical Background of English Literature*; 1951, *Classical Influences on English Poetry*, Allen & Unwin.

Watson, G. (ed.) 1962, *John Dryden: Of Dramatic Poesy and Other Critical Essays*, 2 vols, Everyman's Library, J.M. Dent.

Weinberg, B. 1961, *A History of Literary Criticism in the Italian Renaissance*, University of Chicago Press, Chicago.

Weiss, P. 1969, *The Renaissance Discovery of Classical Antiquity*, Basil Blackwell.

Wind, E. 1958, *Pagan Mysteries in the Renaissance*, Faber & Faber.

IV   The classical tradition: arrangement by genre

(1) Epic

Comparetti, D. 1908, *Vergil in the Middle Ages*, trans. E.F.M. Benecke, Swan Sonneschein, London; Macmillan, New York.

Lord, G. de F. 1956, *Homeric Renaissance: The Odyssey of George Chapman*, Chatto & Windus.

Martindale, C. 1986, *John Milton and the Transformation of Ancient Epic*, Croom Helm.

Martindale, C. (ed.) 1984, *Virgil and his Influence: Bimillennial Studies*, Bristol Classical Press.

Sowerby, R. 1992, 'Chapman's Discovery of Homer', *Translation and Literature*, Edinburgh University Press, I, 26–52.

Tillyard, E.M.W. 1954, *The English Epic and its Background*, Oxford University Press.

(2) Drama

Baldwin, T.W. 1947, *William Shakspere's Five-Act Structure*, University of Illinois Press, Urbana.

Braden, G. 1985, *Renaissance Tragedy and the Senecan Tradition: Anger's Privilege*, Yale University Press, Newhaven.

Brower, R.A. 1971, *Hero and Saint: Shakespeare and the Graeco-Roman Heroic Tradition*, Oxford University Press.

Duckworth, G.E. 1952, *The Nature of Roman Comedy*, Princeton University Press, Princeton.

Herington, C.J. 1966, 'Senecan Tragedy', *Arion* 5, 422–71.

Herrick, M.T. 1964, *Comic Theory in the Sixteenth Century*, University of Illinois Press, Urbana.

Mason, H.A. 1985, *The Tragic Plane*, Oxford University Press.

(3) Lyric
Johnson, W.R. 1982, *The Idea of Lyric: Lyric Modes in Ancient and Modern Poetry*, University of California Press, Berkeley.
Martindale, C., Hopkins, D. (eds) 1993, *Horace Made New: Horatian Influences on British Writing from the Renaissance to the Twentieth Century*, Cambridge University Press.
Maddison, C. 1960, *Apollo and the Nine: A History of the Ode*, Routledge & Kegan Paul.
Mason, H.A. 1981, 'Living in the Present: Is Dryden's "Horat Ode 29 Book 3" an Example of "creative translation"?' *Cambridge Quarterly* **10**, 91–129.
Rostvig, M.S. 1954, *The Happy Man: Studies in the Metamorphosis of a Classical Ideal*, vol. 1, 1600–1700, Oslo Studies in English, no. 2, University of Oslo, Oslo.
Shafer, R. 1966, *The English Ode to 1660*, Holt Rinehart & Winston, New York.

(4) Pastoral and georgic
Cooper, H.1977, *Pastoral: Medieval into Renaissance*, D.S. Brewer: Rowman & Littlefield, Ipswich.
Cullen, P. 1970, *Spenser, Marvell and Renaissance Pastoral*, Harvard University Press, Cambridge, Mass.
Greg, W.W. 1906, *Pastoral Poetry and Pastoral Drama*, Sidgwick & Jackson.
Heninger, S.K. 1961, 'The Renaissance Perversion of Pastoral', *Journal of the History of Ideas* **22**, 254–61.
Patrides, C.A. (ed.) 1961, *Milton's 'Lycidas': The Tradition and the Poem*, Holt Rinehart & Winston, New York.
Wilkinson, L.P. 1969, *The Georgics of Virgil*, Cambridge University Press.

(5) Ovidian genres
Binns, J.W. 1973, *Ovid*, Greek and Latin Studies: Classical Literature and its Influence, Routledge & Kegan Paul.
Bush, D. 1932, *Mythology and the Renaissance Tradition in English Poetry*, University of Minnesota Press, Minneapolis and London.
Donno, E.S. (ed.) 1963, *Elizabethan Minor Epics*, Routledge & Kegan Paul.

Martindale, C. 1988, *Ovid Renewed: Ovidian Influences on Literature and Art from the Middle Ages to the Twentieth Century*, Cambridge University Press.

Segal, C.P. 1971, 'Ovid's *Metamorphoses*: Greek Myth in Augustan Rome', *Studies in Philology* **68**, 372–80.

(6)   Satire

Fiske, G.C. 1920, *Lucilius and Horace: A Study in the Classical Theory of Imitation*, University of Wisconsin Press, Madison.

Hammond, P. 1983, *John Oldham and the Renewal of Classical Culture*, Cambridge University Press.

Kupersmith, W. 1986, *Roman Satirists in Seventeenth-Century England*, University of Nebraska Press, Lincoln and London.

Martindale, C., Hopkins, D. (eds) 1993, *Horace Made New*. Cambridge University Press.

Mason, H.A., 'Is Juvenal a Classic?' in Sullivan, J.P. (ed.) 1963, *Critical Essays on Roman Literature: Satire*, Routledge & Kegan Paul.

Selden, R. 1978, *English Verse Satire 1590–1765*, Allen & Unwin.

Index

Addison, Joseph,
  on Virgil's *Georgics*, 241–2
  translates Ovid, 266, 298
Aeschylus, 58, 60, 61–5, 339, 384
  Oresteia compared with Seneca, 61–5
  Orestes' dilemma, 79
Alamanni, Luigi, 327
Alcaeus, 45, 132–4, 146, 382
  Horace on, 133
  Quintilian on, 133
Alexander the Great, 10, 98, 141, 186, 190, 385
Alexandrianism, 139, 140, 141, 142, 190, 195, 199, 206, 253, 376, 385, 389
allegory, 9, 26, 31, 210, 212, 215, 218, 264–5, 326
Anacreon,
  Anacreontea, 155–6
  envisaged by Herrick, 156
  hailed by Jonson, 146, 352
Arcadia, 192, 193, 200–3, 215, 222, 223
Archilochus, 45, 308, 376, 379
Aretino, Pietro, 305
Ariosto, Ludovico, 331
Aristarchus, 8, 385
Aristophanes, 89, 91–4, 126, 127, 128, 129, 309, 384
  Knights, 92–4
  role of comic poet, 94
Aristotle, 5, 7, 10, 15–16, 44, 70, 82, 90, 232, 384
  catharsis, 67, 70, 28, 136
  on comedy, 90, 95–6
  on humour, 96, 312
  identified with Roman tradition, 117–18

  on musical modes, 135–6
  origins of comedy, 90
  origins of tragedy and satyr play, 61, 324
  on tragedy, 7, 16, 66–7, 80
  unities in, 117–18
  on unity in Homer, 23–5
Ascham, Roger, 38–40
Augustan age and values, 33, 41–2, 54, 56, 61, 88, 128, 150, 152, 167–9, 198–9, 209, 219, 247–8, 322, 336, 347, 377, 389–91
Augustine of Hippo, 109, 214, 222
Augustus Caesar, 10, 33, 35, 36, 37, 42, 54, 56, 149, 163, 164–70, 205–6, 210, 217, 247–8, 279, 285, 303, 314–15, 343, 389–91

Baldwin, T.W., 1, 89 n.18, 118 n.46
Barclay, Alexander, 217
Beaumont, Sir John, 349–50, 353
Bernard, Richard, 121
Bible, 157, 209, 210, 214, 221–2
Bloom, Harold, 4
Boileau, Nicholas Despréaux, 367, 379

Caesar, Julius, 33, 37, 99, 140, 163, 205, 231, 254, 259, 388–9
  on Terence, 110, 119
Callimachus, 142, 190, 253
Campion, Thomas, 138, 150
Carew, Thomas, 297
  'A Rapture', 305–6
carpe diem, 150, 156–7, 184, 352, 356
Casaubon, Isaac, 324
Cato, Marcus, Porcus, the censor, 43, 49, 388